COMPARA

MW00577055

Social Movements and Networks

COMPARATIVE POLITICS

Comparative Politics is a series for students and teachers of political science that deals with contemporary issues in comparative government and politics. As Comparative European Politics it has produced a series of high quality books since its foundation in 1990, but now takes on a new form and new title for the new millennium—Comparative Politics. As the process of globalisation proceeds, and as Europe becomes ever more enmeshed in world trends and events, so it is necessary to broaden the scope of the series.
The General Editors are Max Kaase, Vice President and Dean of Humanities and Social Sciences, International University, Bremen, and Kenneth Newton, Professor of Government at Essex University. The series is published in association with the European Consortium for Political Research.

OTHER TITLES IN THIS SERIES

Mixed-Member Electoral Systems
Edited by Matthew Soberg Shugart and Martin P. Watternberg

Parties without Partisans: Political Change in Advanced Industrial Democracies
Edited by Russell J. Dalton and Martin P. Watternberg

Political Institutions: Democracy and Social Change
Josep H. Colomer

Divided Government in Comparative Perspective
Robert Elgie

Political Parties
Richard Gunther, José Ramón Montero, and Juan J. Linz

Social Movements and Networks

Relational Approaches to Collective Action

edited by

MARIO DIANI AND DOUG McADAM

OXFORD
UNIVERSITY PRESS

OXFORD

UNIVERSITY PRESS

Great Clarendon Street, Oxford OX2 6DP
Oxford University Press is a department of the University of Oxford.
It furthers the University's objective of excellence in research, scholarship,
and education by publishing worldwide in

Oxford New York

Auckland Bangkok Buenos Aires Cape Town Chennai
Dar es Salaam Delhi Hong Kong Istanbul Karachi Kolkata
Kuala Lumpur Madrid Melbourne Mexico City Mumbai Nairobi
São Paulo Shanghai Taipei Tokyo Toronto

Oxford is a registered trade mark of Oxford University Press
in the UK and in certain other countries

Published in the United States
by Oxford University Press Inc., New York

British Library Cataloguing in Publication Data

Data available

Library of Congress Cataloging in Publication Data
Social movements and networks: relational approaches to collective action / edited by
Mario Diani and Doug McAdam.
p. cm.—(Comparative politics)
Selected papers presented at a June 24–26, 2000 meeting of American and European
scholars at Ross Priory on the banks of Loch Lomond.
Includes bibliographical references and index.
1. Social movements—Congresses. 2. Social networks—Congresses. 3. Collective behavior—
Congresses. I. Diani, Mario, 1957– II. McAdam, Doug. III. Series.
IV. Comparative politics. (Oxford, England)
HM881 .S629 2002   303.48′4—dc21   2002070200

ISBN 0–19–925177–0 (hbk.)
ISBN 0–19–925178–9 (pbk.)

3 5 7 9 10 8 6 4

Typeset by Newgen Imaging Systems (P) Ltd., Chennai, India
Printed in Great Britain
on acid-free paper by
Biddles Ltd, King's Lynn, Norfolk

For
Roger V. Gould and Alberto Melucci
Colleagues and friends

In memoriam

Preface

On 24–26 June 2000, a group of American and European scholars met at Ross Priory, on the bonnie banks of Loch Lomond, to discuss the contribution of social network perspectives to the study of social movements, collective action, and contentious politics. They consisted mainly of sociologists and political scientists, from a wide range of theoretical and methodological positions. While most participants were sympathetic to formal quantitative styles of network analysis, some were not, but shared nonetheless a broader interest in attempts to account for collective action dynamics from a relational point of view. Likewise, some did not have any specific interest in social movements, but had huge expertise in network analysis, and were happy to share their perspective of methodological insiders, but thematic outsiders, with the other participants.

This somewhat unusual mix of people resulted in an extremely lively and exciting conference. This book makes some of its main outcomes available to a broader audience. It shows how we can improve our understanding of collective action dynamics by looking at the structure of social relations linking actual and/or prospective participants in a social movement to each other and to their opponents. Drawing upon a wealth of examples spread across time and space, our authors assess the contribution of social network approaches to the analysis of contentious protest and grassroots activism, and hopefully set a research agenda for the years to come.

Others will judge the success of the intellectual enterprise. As a meeting, however, it was undoubtedly a great success. Therefore, our thanks go at the same time to those who made the meeting possible, and to those who tried hard to improve its ultimate intellectual product. Financial support came from several sources. These include the British Academy, which generously awarded Mario Diani a Conference Grant (grant BCG:29995), the New Professors' Fund and the Department of Government of the University of Strathclyde, and the Democracy and Participation Programme of the Economic and Social Research Council. The conference actually marked the start of a specific research project funded in the context of that Programme, 'Networks of Civic Organizations in Britain', led by Mario Diani with Isobel Lindsay (University of Strathclyde) and Satnam Virdee (University of Glasgow), and with the collaboration of Murray Stewart and Derrick Purdue of the University of West of England, Bristol (contract L215 25 2006). Money alone would have achieved little, though, had it not been for the outstanding assistance that came from the staff at Ross Priory, who combined friendliness with efficiency.

Apart from the contributors to this book, papers by Mustafa Emirbayer, Roberto Franzosi, Mimi Sheller, and David Tindall were also presented. Commentaries on the presentations came from Donatella della Porta, Brian Doherty, Christopher Rootes, John Scott, Sidney Tarrow, Satnam Virdee, and Alan Warde. We are sincerely grateful to them all for their insights and collegiality. Although he could not attend the meeting, Charles Tilly was a source of inspiration and encouragement during the preparation of the conference, and we are delighted to be able to include his and Lesley Wood's chapter in this book.

The Director of the Democracy and Participation Programme, Paul Whiteley, deserves a very special mention. Not only did he provide extra funds from the central budget, but he also made an outstanding contribution to the meeting both on the academic and on the social side. The opportunity to exchange views with colleagues who did not specialize in social movements was one of the great bonuses of the conference, and Paul fully played his part in this regard.

We are also grateful to the Politics editors at Oxford University Press, Dominic Byatt and Amanda Watkins, and to the anonymous reviewers who commented on the proposal and on early drafts. We are particularly indebted to Ken Newton and Max Kaase, for their intellectual openness and their decision to include our book in the Comparative Politics series. While the comparative value of the empirical materials presented in the book is limited, that of the theoretical enterprise is not. We subscribe to Giovanni Sartori's—and indeed many others'—long-established claim that any serious comparison rests on a careful specification of the basic concepts and parameters. Regarding networks, in particular, no comparative progress can be made if we do not engage in a systematic assessment of different uses of network concepts in current social movement research. That is what our book tries to do. We hope to be able to lay the foundations for a genuinely comparative analysis of movement networks.

Our last thought goes to two outstanding colleagues and friends who prematurely lost their lives when this book was at its final stages. Roger Gould, who was at Ross Priory and whose contribution appears as Chapter 10 of this volume, passed away on 29 April 2002, only a few days after *Social Movements and Networks* received its final green light from the publisher's reviewers. He was preceded by a few months by leading social movement theorist Alberto Melucci, who died on 12 September 2001. Although he was not involved in the conference, and would not strictly qualify as a 'social network analyst', Alberto's work on the role of informal networks in mobilization and identity-building processes shaped the thinking of most of us. As for Roger, even readers unfamiliar with his seminal work on networks in the Paris Commune will quickly be persuaded by his outstanding chapter of the magnitude of his role as a network scholar, and of the magnitude of our loss. We dedicate our collective action to their memory.

MD
DMcA

Trento
Stanford
May 2003

Contents

III. Networking the Political Process

IV. Theories of Networks, Movements, and Collective Action

List of Figures

List of Tables

List of Abbreviations

BDC	Berlin Document Centre
CA	Conjoint Action
HICLUS	Hierarchial Cluster
ISA	Integrative Structural Analysis
LIPU	Italian League for the Protection of Birds
KIK	Klub Inteligencji Katolickiej
KOM	Komandosy
KOR	Komitet Obrony Robotników
KPN	Konfederacja Polski Niepodległej
LAC	League for the Abolition of Hunting
LDP	Liberal Democratic Party
MOS	Material Opportunity Structure
MP	Member of Parliament
NAC	National Action Committee
NCW	National Council of Women
NS	National Socialism
NSDAP	National Socialist Party in Germany
UNE	National Student Union
NIMBY	Not In My Back Yard
NUN	Nurt Niepodległościowy
PRL	Polish People's Republic
POS	Political Opportunity Structure
PZPR	Polska Zjednoczona Partia Robotnicza
PPN	Polskie Porozumienie Niepodległościowe
PSN	Polskie Stronnictwo Narodowe
QCA	Qualitative Comparative Analysis
RUC	Ruch
ROP	Ruch Obrony Praw Człowieka i Obywatela
RWD	Ruch Wolnych Demokratów
SMO	Social Movement Organizations
SRI	Solidarność Rolnych Indiwidualnych
SKS	Students' Solidarity Committee
TAT	Taternik
TKN	Towarzystwo Kursów Naukowych
TGP	Tygodnik Powszechny
WEZ	Więż

WZZ	Wolne Związki Zawodowe
WEL	Women's Electoral Lobby
WWF	World Wildlife Fund
ZNK	Znak

Contributors

Chris Ansell is Associate Professor of Political Science at the University of California, Berkeley. His book *Schism and Solidarity in Social Movements* has been published by Cambridge University Press in 2001.

Helmut Anheier is Director of the Centre for Civil Society at the London School of Economics. His publications include *The Emerging Nonprofit Sector* (Manchester University Press, 1996, with L. Salamon) and articles in *American Journal of Sociology* and other leading outlets.

Jeffrey Broadbent is Associate Professor of Sociology at the University of Minnesota, Minneapolis. He is the author of *Environmental Politics in Japan: Networks of Power and Protest* (Cambridge University Press, 1998) and *Comparing Policy Networks* (Cambridge University Press, 1996, with D. Knoke, F. Pappi, and Y. Tsujinaka).

Mario Diani is Professor of Sociology at the University of Trento, Italy, Visiting Research Professor at the University of Strathclyde in Glasgow, and the European Editor of *Mobilization*. His publications include *Social Movements* (Blackwell, 1999, with D. della Porta) and *Green Networks* (Edinburgh University Press, 1995).

Roger V. Gould (1963–2002) was Professor of Sociology at Yale University. Previously at the University of Chicago, that he joined in 1990, he edited the *American Journal of Sociology* from 1997–2000. Apart from numerous articles in leading journals, his publications include *Insurgent Identities* (University of Chicago Press, 1995) and a book-length study of social conflict dynamics which he just managed to complete before his untimely death in April 2002.

Doug McAdam is Professor of Sociology at Stanford University, and Director of the Center for Advanced Study in the Behavioral Sciences. The author of award-winning study of American civil rights activists *Freedom Summer* (Oxford University Press, 1988), recently he co-authored *Dynamics of Contention* (Cambridge University Press, 2001, with S. Tarrow and C. Tilly).

Ann Mische is Assistant Professor of Sociology at Rutgers University. Her work has appeared in *American Journal of Sociology* and other leading outlets.

Daniel J. Myers is Associate Professor of Sociology in the Department of Sociology of the University of Notre Dame. His work has appeared in *American Journal of Sociology, American Sociological Review*, and other leading outlets.

Pamela E. Oliver is Professor of Sociology at the University of Wisconsin, Madison. She is the author of *The Critical Mass in Collective Action* (Cambridge University Press, 1993, with G. Marwell) and several articles in leading journals.

Maryjane Osa is Visiting Assistant Professor of Sociology at Northwestern University, Evanston. Her book *Solidarity and Contention: The Networks of Polish Opposition, 1954–81* was published by University of Minnesota Press in 2003.

Florence Passy is Assistant Professor of Political Science at the University of Lausanne, Switzerland. She is the author of *L'action altruiste* (Droz, 1998) and *Histoires de mobilisation politique en Suisse: de la contestation à l'integration* (Harmattan 1997, with M. Giugni).

Charles Tilly is Buttenwieser Professor of Social Science at Columbia University. His most recent book is *Stories, Identities, and Political Change* (Rowman and Littlefield, 2002).

Lesley J. Wood is a doctoral candidate in sociology at Columbia University, and the author of book chapters on collective action and the anti-globalization movement.

1

Introduction: Social Movements, Contentious Actions, and Social Networks: 'From Metaphor to Substance'?

Mario Diani

It is difficult to grasp the nature of social movements.[1] They cannot be reduced to specific insurrections or revolts, but rather resemble strings of more or less connected events, scattered across time and space; they cannot be identified with any specific organization either, rather, they consist of groups and organizations, with various levels of formalization, linked in patterns of interaction which run from the fairly centralized to the totally decentralized, from the cooperative to the explicitly hostile. Persons promoting and/or supporting their actions do so not as atomized individuals, possibly with similar values or social traits, but as actors linked to each other through complex webs of exchanges, either direct or mediated. Social movements are in other words, complex and highly heterogeneous network structures.

Since the 1970s, analysts of social movements and collective action have tried hard to make sense of these structures and their dynamics. That collective action is significantly shaped by social ties between prospective participants is not a recent[2] discovery (e.g. Pinard 1968; Booth and Babchuk 1969; Oberschall 1973; Pickvance 1975; Tilly 1978; Snow *et al.* 1980); nor is the view of social movements as networks linking a multiplicity of actors (e.g. Gerlach and Hine 1970; Curtis and Zurcher 1973). More recently however, interest in the relationship between social movements and social networks has grown both in the range of the topics addressed and the depth of the research results. Although not all relational approaches to social movements qualify as 'network analysis', the claim that social network analysis at large has moved 'from metaphor to substance' (Wellman 1988) also applies to social network approaches to the study of collective action.

I am grateful to Jeff Broadbent, Doug McAdam and Charles Tilly for commenting on a draft version of this chapter.

This book charts recent developments in this line of inquiry. As yet, the most massive set of contributions has dealt with the processes of individual recruitment. Embeddedness in specific relational contexts has been found to be conducive to various forms of collective engagement (Oliver 1984; Kriesi 1988; Opp 1989; Fernandez and McAdam 1988, 1989; Knoke and Wisely 1990; McAdam and Fernandez 1990; McPherson *et al.* 1992; McAdam and Paulsen 1993; McPherson and Rotolo 1996; Kitts 2000; Tindall 2000; Passy 2001*b*; Diani, forthcoming). Other studies have focused on the overall structure of networks in specific communities and their impact on the development of collective action, assessed both in terms of formal models (Gould 1993*b*; Marwell and Oliver 1993; Macy 1993; Oberschall and Kim 1996; Heckathorn 1996; Kim and Bearman 1997; Oliver and Marwell 2001) and in reference to specific empirical evidence (Gould 1991, 1993*a*, 1995; Barkey and van Rossem 1997). Explorations of the networks-mobilization link in social movements have also prompted broader reflections on the relationship between structure and agency and relational approaches to social theory (Emirbayer and Goodwin 1994; Emirbayer 1997; Emirbayer and Mische 1998; Emirbayer and Sheller 1999).

The structure of social movements has also attracted increasing attention. Studies in this area have focused on interorganizational exchanges, whether in the form of coalition-building (Rucht 1989; Diani 1990, 1995; Philips 1991; Hathaway and Meyer 1994; Sawer and Groves 1994; Ansell 1997, 2001) or overlapping memberships (Rosenthal *et al.* 1985, 1997; Schmitt-Beck 1989; Diani 1995; Carroll and Ratner 1996; Ray *et al.* 2001). Others have focused on networking activities in social movement communities, whether 'real' or 'virtual' (Melucci 1984; Taylor and Whittier 1992; Whittier 1995; Polletta 1999*a,b*; Pickerill 2000; Hampton and Wellman 2001). The intersection of individuals, organizations, and protest events over time has also been explored (Bearman and Everett 1993; Mische 1998; Franzosi 1999; Mische and Pattison 2000; Osa 2001). Network analysis has also facilitated the analysis of the role of advocacy groups, public interest groups, and social movement organizations in policy networks (Laumann and Knoke 1987; Broadbent 1998).

The very expansion of network studies of social movements renders an assessment of the applicability and usefulness of the concept an urgent and useful enterprise. The first reason for doing so is that empirical evidence is not universally supportive to the thesis of a link between networks and collective action. Several studies actually found a modest relationship between the two (Luker 1984; Mullins 1987; Jasper and Poulsen 1993). This has led some critics to reduce networks to a mere resource aside others (Jasper 1997). The pervasiveness of network effects has also prompted claims that the concept had been stretched too far and thus made tautological (Piven and Cloward 1992). The simple acknowledgement of a relationship between the social networks of some kind and the development of collective action (whether in the form of personal ties linking prospective participants to current activists, or of dense counter-cultural networks affecting rates of mobilization in specific areas) is no longer sufficient. Instead, it is important to specify 'how networks matter', in relation to both individual participation (e.g. What is their relative contribution vis-à-vis individual attributes such as education or profession, broader political opportunities, or emotional dynamics? What types of networks do affect what type of participation?) as well as in relation to interorganizational dynamics (e.g. what does the shape of interorganizational links tell us about the main orientations of specific movements?).

Although the need for such specification has long been recognized (e.g. Snow *et al.* 1980), attempts in that direction have clearly taken momentum in the 1990s (Marwell and Oliver 1993; McAdam and Paulsen 1993; Diani 1995; Gould 1995; Ohlemacher 1996; Kitts 2000, to mention only a few). This book charts recent developments in this particular line of inquiry and illustrates the centrality of these concerns to social movement research. There is also another ambition though, namely to provide a ground for intellectual exchange across disciplines and specific research communities. Besides asking 'What do networks mean' and 'How do networks matter', the book also addresses—albeit more indirectly— the question of 'to whom (in the social science research community) should (social movement) networks matter'. We claim that they should matter to a much broader community than those identifying themselves as social movement researchers. There are already several instances of overlap. Important contributions to social movement analysis from a network perspective actually refer to empirical objects, which would not automatically fall in the domain of social movement analysis, such as working class action (Klandermans 1984, 1997), or participation in religious groups (Snow *et al.* 1980); other studies widely used among social movement scholars include investigations of participation dynamics in voluntary associations (Wilson 2000; Anheier 2001*a,b*; McPherson *et al.* 2001).

This book intends to contribute to the cross-disciplinary exchange with those social scientists who do not consider the concept of social movement as central to their theoretical preoccupations, yet have a strong interest in the network dimension of political action at large (e.g. scholars of collective action: Macy 1990, 1991, 1993; Heckathorn 1996; Ostrom 1998; policy networks—Laumann and Knoke 1987; Kenis and Schneider 1991; Knoke *et al.* 1996; interorganizational relations—Galaskiewicz 1985; Podolny and Page 1998; Gulati and Gargiulo 1999; Pichierri 1999; social capital—Stolle 1998; Stolle and Rochon 1998; van Deth 2000; Prakash and Selle, 2003). On a more ambitious note, looking at the network dimension may serve to dispel some of the ambiguities regarding the concept of social movement and thus clear the table of issues which keep marring the debate, such as the relationship between the movement organizations and interest groups (Jordan and Maloney 1997; Diani 2001; Leech 2001), or between protest and movements (Melucci 1996). Although this will not be the main focus of the book, it will represent one of the possible developments of our thinking on the issue.

It is not difficult to see why the concept of network has become so popular in the social sciences in recent times. Its flexibility, and in many senses its very ambiguity, enables researchers to deal with phenomena of change, which are difficult to contain within the boundaries of formal bureaucracies or nation states, or at the other pole, the individual actor (Mutti 1996). Referring to networks provides a clue to assess the social location of specific actors as well as to identify general structural patterns from a relational perspective. The interest in the linkage between network concepts and social movement analysis may be located in at least three different intellectual contexts. The first one consists of the renewed interest in the meso-level of social analysis and the relation between structure and agency. Attention to the 'micro-macro link' (Alexander *et al.* 1987) has fostered the study of the patterns of social organization (including social networks), which mediate between the individual actors and macro social processes. The relation between the constraining character of social structure and the actors' capacity to affect it by adapting and modifying rules, meanings, and patterns of interaction has been addressed from several perspectives, from exchange theory (Coleman 1990; Cook and Whitmeyer 1992) to action theory (Bourdieu 1977; Giddens 1984; Sewell 1992), from neo-institutionalism (DiMaggio and Powell 1991) to explicit attempts to reformulate theories of an agency from a relational, network perspective (White 1992; Emirbayer 1997). In some cases, advocates of the integration of structure and agency have argued their cases by drawing explicitly from social movement research (Emirbayer and Goodwin 1994; Livesay 2002).

The second important trend has to do with the resurgence of interest in 'social mechanisms' (Hedström and Swedberg 1998) as a corrective to invariant explanations and the search for law-like formulations.[3] Rather than reorienting social movement research, so far the attention to mechanisms has made more explicit what was already a relevant orientation within it, namely, the tendency to focus on specific dynamics relevant to the spread of social movement activity: among them, recruitment, framing, tactical adaptation of action repertoires, and of course networking. Attention to mechanisms has also brought about a plea for greater dialogue between the social movement community and cognate fields. This has mainly taken the form of the search for mechanisms which could account for a wide range of political processes, most of which had been overlooked so far by mainstream social movement research, such as democratization (Tilly 2001; McAdam *et al.* 2001). On the other hand, moving towards mechanisms has further strengthened the tendency to use the concept of social movement in purely denotative terms, that Touraine (1981) or Melucci (1996, but originally 1982) had long exposed. 'Social movement' is in this perspective, merely the word to identify the set of phenomena ('episodes', in McAdam *et al.*'s (2001) words) within which the dynamics of substantive interest of researchers could take place.

The third important process has been the consolidation of social network analysis as a distinct field in social science. To a large extent it is still controversial whether it should be regarded as a simple set of research techniques, a distinct perspective on society, or a scientific paradigm proper (Wellman 1988). Indeed, the analysis of social networks in the broader sense may also be conducted through approaches other than those usually associated with network analysis, including qualitative techniques (Wellman and Berkowitz 1988), as Jeffrey Broadbent's chapter in this book exemplifies. Nor do structural approaches need necessarily to focus on networks—either 'concrete' or symbolic—between specific actors. According to an authoritative line of thinking, while network analysis focuses on individual actors and data, structural analysis looks at the patterns of exchanges between predefined groups which is very difficult to modify.[4]

Whatever the case, network analysis as it is best known developed with reference to a 'realist' view of social structure as networks which linked together concrete actors through specific ties, identifiable and measurable through reliable empirical instruments ('regularities in the patterns of relations among concrete entities': White *et al.* 1976). This view represented an alternative to both views of social structure as macro forces largely independent from the control of the specific actors associated with them (the working class, the capital class, the nation ...), and views of structure as aggregates of the individual actors sharing determinate specific traits (as in the political behaviour, survey-based tradition of research, where 'class factors' are frequently reduced to individual occupation).

Gradually, a different vision of network analysis has also emerged, which does not emphasize empiricism and concreteness, and highlights instead the inextricable link between social networks and culture. Following largely Harrison White's (1992) seminal contributions, social ties have been treated as consisting of processes of meaning attribution. In contrast to other versions of network analysis, which treat ties either as a precondition of culture or ideology (e.g. Erickson 1982) or as a product of a particular version of 'homophily' as shared cultural traits (e.g. McPherson *et al.* 2001; for an application to social movements, Diani 1995). Here a linkage exists only to the extent that a shared discourse enables two or more actors to recognize their interdependence and qualify its terms: 'a social network is a network of meanings' (White 1992: 67). This perspective prompts a reflection on the relationship between the social networks and the cognitive maps through which actors make sense of and categorize their social environment and locate themselves within broader webs of ties and interactions. Proponents of the cultural approach to social networks have engaged in sustained dialogue with sociological neo-institutionalists (DiMaggio and Powell 1991), encouraging developments in several specific areas, from organizations (Carley 1999) to markets (White 1988, 2002), from the study of the legal system (Breiger 2000) to literary analysis and the sociology of the arts (Mohr 2000). We have also seen ambitious attempts to develop a relational perspective on sociology with a special focus on the notion of agency (Emirbayer 1997; Emirbayer and Mische 1998).

THE CONCEPT OF NETWORK IN SOCIAL MOVEMENT ANALYSIS

Social movements have been defined in a variety of ways. For some, they are the actors of central conflicts in society, embodying fundamental oppositions regarding the direction of the historical process (Touraine 1981). For others, they represent a peculiar type of collective action, characterized by identity, solidarity, and the attempt to break limits of compatibility of a given system (Melucci 1996). For still others they are little more than expressions of preferences, that movement organizations are supposed to mobilize and turn into real action (McCarthy and Zald 1977, even though they have changed their view of movements and got closer to Tilly's; see also Zald 2000). The most popular view at the moment is probably one focusing on sustained interactions between challengers and power holders (Tilly 1994).

Trying to associate networks to a particular conception of movements would make little sense at this stage. For all their differences, the definitions mentioned above all accommodate network mechanisms within their broader frameworks (Diani 1992a,b). Moreover, we would risk overlooking the contribution that a network perspective can offer to our understanding of the multiplicity of levels of experience, usually found in processes of collective action and grassroots mobilization. It is, therefore, wiser to start by recognizing that a network perspective may illuminate different dynamics, which are essential to our empirical understanding of movements, and leave attempts to reconcile them in a unitary view of movements for a later stage (provided an integration should be needed at all, as many people in the field, including most contributors to this volume, seem to doubt).

A cautious approach also makes it more explicit that the empirical phenomena studied by 'social movement scholars' from a network perspective do not necessarily fall under a specific domain with clear-cut boundaries. For example, the chapters in this book which deal with the role of individual networks in collective action, do so by looking at organizations that need not be defined SMOs, and that one could refer to as 'public interest groups' (Passy's environmental and peace organizations) or 'revolutionary party' (Anheier's German National Socialist Party). Likewise, the study of networks between citizens' organizations (see the chapters by Diani, Ansell, and Osa in this book) has been studied by people who would not regard themselves as social movement scholars (e.g. Knoke and Wood 1981).

In order to follow some order in the presentation of the most relevant contributions of the social network perspective to social movement analysis in its inclusive version, it is worth referring to the conventional view of networks as sets of nodes, linked by some form of relationship, and delimited by some specific criteria. Although this framework is most frequently adopted by those close to the empiricist tradition rather than to the cultural one, it still leaves room for epistemological debates on what should represent a node, a tie, or a boundary, and in this particular sense it is fully compatible with the latter.

Nodes may consist of individuals, organizations, and eventually—if more rarely—other entities such as neighbourhoods (e.g. Gould 1995) or states (e.g. Breiger 1990). They may also consist of events linked by persons, or as in some recent application, even of elements of speech (e.g. Bearman and Stovel 2000). Relationships may consist of either direct or indirect ties. We have direct ties when two nodes are directly linked in explicit interaction and interdependence—for example, two activists who know each other personally, or two organizations who jointly promote a rally. We have indirect ties when a relationship is assumed to exist between two nodes because they share some relevant activity or resource— for example, due to overlaps in their activists or sympathizers, or to their joint involvement in some initiatives or events. Relations may be single or multiple depending on whether two nodes are linked by one or more types of relations, and they may also differ in term of contents, emotional intensity, and strength. The definition of what constitutes a social bond is a huge problem in itself and it is disputable whether it should stretch as far as the cognitive maps shared by people, or the exposure to a similar message, or cognitive framework (Emirbayer and Goodwin 1994). Boundaries may be defined on the basis of realist or nominalist criteria (see also Diani 2002). Nominalist criteria are predetermined by the analyst; in contrast, realist criteria include in a given network only those nodes that happen to be actually related to each other by some kind of relation. The identification of nodes, of the relevant ties between them, and of the boundaries of the network represent fundamental steps in any study of network structures.[5] They will guide our discussion of what has been achieved in social movement analysis from a network perspective.

Networks of Individuals

Social movements exist inasmuch as individuals can be convinced to become personally involved in collective action and be offered the opportunities to do so on a sustained basis. It is, therefore, not surprising that substantial attention has been paid to the contribution of social networks to individual participation.[6] As Doug McAdam notes in his contribution to this volume, the notion that prior social ties operate as a basis for movement recruitment and that established social settings are the locus of movement emergence are among the most established findings in social movement research. Typically, social movement activists and sympathizers are linked through both 'private' and 'public' ties well before collective action develops. Personal friends, relatives, colleagues, and neighbours, may all affect individual decisions to become involved in a movement; so may people who share with prospective participants some kind of collective engagement, such as previous or current participation in other movement activities, political or social organizations, and public bodies. Individuals may also be linked through indirect ties, generated by their joint involvement in specific activities and/or events, yet without any face-to-face interaction. These may range from participation in the same political or social activities and/or organizations to involvement in the same subcultures or counter-cultures (e.g. the rave parties' scene in the UK in the 1990s, or the gay and lesbian counter-cultures in the USA: Taylor and

Whittier 1992; McKay 1996). One current critical area of debate is the extent
to which exposure to the same media, whether 'traditional' (including television)
or 'computer-based' may represent a social network link, and the impact of new
forms of communication on social movement communities and the broader civil
society (Rheinghold 1993; Calhoun 1998; Diani 2000c; Norris 2002: ch. 10).
Even more fundamental is whether we should regard shared cognitive and cultural
spaces as independent sources of links and therefore as the basis for specific types
of networks (Emirbayer and Goodwin 1994).

   Both direct and indirect ties may activate a number of mechanisms, which in
turn affect the chances and forms of participation. Networks may provide opportunities for action through the circulation of information about on-going activities, existing organizations, people to contact, and a reduction of the practical
costs attached to participation. They may be the source of social pressure on
prospective participants ('if you go, I will go too'), although we should neither
forget the possibility of cross-pressures (McAdam and Paulsen 1993; Kitts 2000)
nor of opposite mechanisms, whereby people participate precisely because they
expect others not to do anything (Oliver 1984). Networks may facilitate the development of cognitive skills and competences and/or provide the context for the
socialization of individuals to specific sets of values. They may also represent the
locus for the development of strong emotional feelings (Taylor and Whittier 1995;
Melucci 1996; Goodwin *et al.* 2000). It is disputable whether direct or indirect ties
should operate differently, although in general, social pressure is more likely to be
exerted through direct links while socialization to values or cognitive skills may
also originate from involvement in similar organizational settings, regardless of
strong involvement with specific individuals.[7] Whether strong or weak ties should
matter most is also a matter of debate: one would expect strong ties to matter more
in the case of high-risk activities (della Porta 1988) but weak ties may facilitate
the contacts between a movement organization and a constituency with more
moderate or at least diversified orientations, and/or the diffusion or the spread of
a movement campaign (e.g. Ohlemacher 1996).

   Most studies in this vein look at how involvement in networks affects individual
behaviour. It is much rarer that the overall configuration of networks linking individual activists is assessed in order to evaluate the potential for collective action
in a given collectivity. Albeit indirectly, Kriesi (1988) attempted to do this while
looking at the relationship between exposure to a movement counter-culture and
chances to sign a peace petition. This exercise usually clashes with the difficulty of
collecting detailed data about a whole population of individual activists (Kitts
2000) and has, therefore, been frequently addressed through simulation data.
Marwell and Oliver (1993: 101–29; see also Oliver and Marwell 2001) have been
particularly active here, addressing the impact of centralization and cliques over
chances of collective action. So have among others Macy (1990, 1991, 1993),
Gould (1993a,b), Heckathorn (1993, 1996), Oberschall and Kim (1996), and
Bearman and Kim (1997).

The impact of individual networks on individual participation has been tested with reference to different dependent variables. These have included the presence or absence of participation (McAdam 1986, 1988*a,b*; Klandermans and Oegema 1987; Kriesi 1988; Opp 1989; McAdam and Paulsen 1993); decisions to jointly participate (McAdam and Fernandez 1990); participation in specific types of activities, for example, in conservation or political ecology groups (Diani and Lodi 1988); the continuation of participation over time (McPherson and Rotolo 1996).

However, individual networks also shape other important features of collective action. They may contribute to organizational formation, sometimes through forms of block recruitment (Oberschall 1973) and other times by providing the necessary links between the founders. They may also provide the basis for factions and coalitions within organizations and for the emergence of group leadership (Gerlach and Hine 1970; Zachary 1977; Zablocki 1980; Diani and Donati 1984; Krackhardt 1992). Looking at how members of a given movement organization interact with each other can also provide insights into its participatory rather than professional nature, the degree of internal division of labour, the subcultural elements of the group, the difficult balance between individual and group identities, etc. (Melucci 1984). Individual networks also represent the backbone of broader social movement communities where interpersonal ties are often multiple and may involve joint participation in mobilization campaigns as well as the sharing of distinctive lifestyles or of broader cultural models. While social movement scholars have studied them mostly in reference to 'new' social movements (e.g. Melucci 1984 on 'movement areas' in Milan; Taylor and Whittier 1992 on lesbian subcultures; Kriesi *et al.* (1995) on gay subcultures; McKay 1996 on alternative cultures in the UK), working class communities continue to attract considerable attention from social historians and historical sociologists (Fantasia 1988; Savage 1996; Blokland 2001; Strangleman 2001). Communitarian ties operate at a minimum to strengthen the identity and solidarity among movement activists and sympathizers. At the same time, though, they provide the specific locus of social conflict in those cases where the challenge is eminently on the symbolic side and where, in other words, the definition of identities and the preservation of opportunities for the enactment of alternative lifestyles are mainly at stake. Looking at networks may tell us to what extent certain lifestyles (e.g. fair trade businesses, microbiotic food, exchanges of Vegan boxes, and LETS schemes) reflect a distinct movement subculture or simply a niche of the broader market. This will depend on actual links between people and most importantly, on their identities and representations.[8]

Networks of Organizations

Organizations form the other major node in social movement networks. It is actually very difficult to think of a movement as consisting of one organization, or at least as having one organization in a totally dominant position. When this happens, as in the instances of the Bolshevik party in Russia or the National Socialist party in Germany it is more appropriate to drop the term 'movement' altogether and concentrate instead on the concept of political organization. Movements seem indeed to consist of multiple instances of collaboration on campaigns of different intensity and scope, with both the recurring presence of some actors and the more occasional presence of others. Direct ties between movement organizations include most prominently the exchange of information and the pooling of mobilization resources (Curtis and Zurcher 1973; Rucht 1989; Diani 1995; Jones *et al.* 2001); indirect ties cover a broad range of possibilities, from shared personnel (Curtis and Zurcher 1973; Rosenthal *et al.* 1985, 1997; Diani 1995; Carroll and Ratner 1996) to joint participation in specific actions and/or events (Laumann and Knoke 1987; Knoke *et al.* 1996), from exposure to the same media, especially computer mediated ones (Bonchek 1995; Pickerill 2000; van der Aalst and Walgrave 2001) to shared linkages to third parties (whether private or public organizations).

A particular version of the interorganizational approach looks at linkages between sets of organizations rather than individual ones (e.g. Bearman and Everett (1993) examine the links between types of political organizations in America over a long time, based on their coparticipation in protest events in Washington DC). Others (McPherson *et al.* 1992) look at how shared traits of their members may have different types of organizations engaging in competitive relationships for support in the same socio-cultural space.

Sometimes, relationships between groups and organizations are recurrent to the point that for a given social movement one can think of a distinctive 'alliance structure' and 'oppositional structure' (Curtis and Zurcher 1973; Klandermans 1990); other times this does not happen and *ad hoc* shifting coalition networks prevail. Always, however, the difference between a pure coalition, driven by instrumental principles (Lemieux 1997) and a movement network is given by identity playing a key role in boundary definition. Networks undoubtedly facilitate mechanisms like the mobilization and allocation of resources across an organizational field, the negotiation of agreed goals, the production and circulation of information, all activities which are also essential to any type of coalition, broadly defined; at the same time, however, they also may—or may not—facilitate the circulation of meaning and mutual recognition. It is the definition of a shared identity which qualifies a movement network vis-à-vis a coalition network, and draws its boundaries. The ego-network of a movement organization (i.e. the set of actors with whom an organization has links) also usually includes actors that are not perceived as being part of the same movement or 'family' of cognate movements, but simple allies on specific causes. Interorganizational networks and movement boundaries do not necessarily overlap.

The instability in movement boundaries is also reflected in movements' internal structure. Movement networks usually reflect processes of segmentation; these may sometimes be attributed exclusively or mainly to principles of division of labour or the actual differentiation of issues and other times, more explicitly to ideological conflicts and fragmentation (Melucci 1984; Philips 1991; Sower and Groves 1994; Ansell 1997). Differences in network patterns also reflect dynamics of centralization. To which extent are movement networks centralized or decentralized? What are the factors which account for some SMOs occupying specific positions in the network, either because of attracting links from many sources or playing the role of an intermediary that connects otherwise noncommunicating milieus (Diani 1995 and in this book)? In all these cases, looking at networks may facilitate our understanding of the criteria, which guide organizations mobilizing in a movement in their choice of occasional and more permanent allies. Interest in these issues among movement scholars has paralleled similar developments in the sociology of organizations (Podolny and Page 1998; Gulati and Gargiulo 1999; Pichierri 1999; Kenis and Knoke 2002). Both have explored the factors behind alliance and coalition-building, addressing questions such as, what are the traits of nodes that account for individual SMOs' centrality or marginality in a network? How do preexisting ties—both organizational and between leaders (or managers/entrepreneurs in the case of firms) affect chances of new alliances to develop, or the location of specific organizations in a broader organizational field? Answers to these questions also predict influence in the larger political system and attitudes towards collaboration with external actors (see Diani's and Ansell's chapters in this book).

Networks of Collectivities and Events

There are also other types of networks, which we should consider when assessing the overall contribution of network approaches to the study of collective action. Important insights have been generated by scholars focusing on collectivities and on the impact of their relationships on grassroots mobilization. In those cases, the dependent variables are not individual behaviours/choices, nor the location of specific organizations in a broader relational setting, but the levels of collective performance that different social units can achieve. Along these lines, Gould (1991, 1995) has demonstrated how the interdependence between Parisian neighbourhoods affected levels of resistance by the National Guard battalions in the 1870 Commune insurrection; Barkey and van Rossem (1997) have shown that the location of villages in regional networks in eighteenth century Turkey shaped their capacity to promote challenges to established powers, if largely conducted individually; Hedström and his associates have illustrated how opportunities of communication between districts in Sweden—operationalized through spatial proximity—affected the development of Trade Unions and social democratic organizations in the late nineteenth and early twentieth century (Hedström 1994; Hedström *et al.* 2000).

Other potentially interesting uses of the idea of network have only begun to be explored. One can, for example, think of network applications to the protest events dynamics. Although the whole idea of protest cycle presupposes interdependence between events and so do the techniques of event history analysis increasingly used in this area of inquiry (Koopmans and Statham 1999), the tendency to treat movements as aggregates of events is also strong (see, e.g. Kriesi *et al.* 1995). The application of a network perspective could generate important insights on the process whereby events become a movement, through meaning attribution and recognition of commonalities, that is, through processes of identity construction (Melucci 1996; McAdam *et al.* 2001; Tilly 2002). Events are linked to each other through innumerable mechanisms. Organizations operate as ties by promoting and/or participating in multiple events; individual activists operate in the same way; thirdly, events may be linked through symbolic means, that is, by representations that underline continuity between what could otherwise be largely independent and disconnected events. While the creation of a symbolic link between events is a heavily contested exercise related to competition both between movement entrepreneurs to secure property of specific issues, and between movements and opponents trying to disentangle specific events from the movement's influence, the other two types of link are much more obvious. Through their action both organizations and individuals stress the continuity between events. Continuity does not equate with perfect coherence, as there may be breaks and changes in strategies, but more broadly with a sense of compatibility between different instances of the movement experience. For example, one could easily reverse Bearman and Everett's (1993) data on the presence of different actors at demonstrations on Capitol Hill, Washington DC, to look not at the relations between types of collective actors, mediated by their joint participation in protest activities, but at the linkages and continuities between the latter, mediated by different actors' involvement in them (more on this in Diani's conclusions).

ON THIS BOOK

How does our book cover the themes just outlined? We start with the most established area of investigation, looking at the impact of networks on individual participation and at the contribution of individuals to organization foundation. Florence Passy elaborates on previous contributions (Marwell and Oliver 1993; McAdam and Paulsen 1993; Gould 1995; Kim and Bearman 1997) in her search for specific network mechanisms at the individual level. She distinguishes between *socialization functions* of social networks, which create an initial disposition to participate; *structural-connection functions*, generating practical opportunities for involvement; and *decision-shaping functions*, affecting the ultimate decision to take part. She explores these dimensions by looking at members of two Swiss political organizations, WWF and the Bern Declaration, and illuminating different dynamics in the two cases (Table 1.1 below summarizes the views of networks adopted in the different empirical chapters of this book).

TABLE 1.1. *A summary of the empirical approaches presented in this book*

Chapter	Nodes	Ties	Network concepts/measures	Dependent variables
Passy	Individual activists	Private ties (kin, personal friendship, etc.) Public ties (associations, public bodies, etc.)	Ego-networks (presence/absence of ties; range)	Participation
Anheier	Individual activists Organizations	Public ties (associations, public bodies, etc.) Joint activists	Ego networks (presence/absence of ties; range)	Organization founding Structure of the right-wing network
Osa	Organizations	Joint activists		Structure of the oppositional network
Diani	Organizations	Exchanges of resources, information, etc. Shared personnel	Centrality in network consisting of overlapping memberships Centrality in interorganizational network	Centrality in the interorganizational network Regular ties to media and institutions
Ansell	Organizations	Exchanges of resources, information, etc.	Location in movement networks (structural equivalence)	Attitudes towards collaborative governance
Tilly and Wood	Social groups	Direct ties (Claims making) (Attack)	Centrality Structural equivalence	Structure of contention (alliance and oppositional fields)
Oliver and Myers	Virtual individuals in virtual collectivities	Simulation data	Density of the network Network structure (centralization)	Participation rates in different networks
Broadbent	Local communities	Links to local elites	Ties with elites	Protest success in different communities

Helmut Anheier explores the role of individuals in promoting collective action and organizational growth. His findings on single members of the Nazi party in 1920s–30s Germany (i.e. members who operated in areas where there were no chapters and therefore acted as individual political entrepreneurs), qualify some of the propositions of mass society theory regarding the mobilization of extremism (Fangen 1999). Early Nazi activists were not marginal socially isolated persons, but came from ordinary middle class backgrounds and were embedded in organizational networks: indeed, the stronger their embeddedness, the higher their chances of establishing a local chapter of NSDAP. On the other hand, all their linkages were within the extreme right subculture and totally separated from mainstream politics. This is actually consistent with the claim (Kornhauser 1959; Lipset 1960; Linz 1967) that concentric circles (i.e. densely knit clusters of ties with little outside ramifications) generate a fragmented society and are therefore an obstacle to democratic politics.[9]

The second section presents three chapters on interorganizational networks. Maryjane Osa explores changes in the informal networks of overlapping memberships between opposition organizations in Poland between the 1960s and the 1980s. When civic organizations are subject to severe constraints, as in Communist regimes, informal networks are particularly important as alternative sources of resources (Rose 2001). There, networks not only operate as micromobilization contexts, but also provide the basic infrastructure for civil society. Linking civil society and networks explicitly, Osa asks herself 'What network characteristics are likely to facilitate movement emergence? Why are some networks less vulnerable to repression than others?' Her answers are distinctive in that she explicitly brings a time dimension into her analysis, using individuals to chart the evolution of networks over time and offering an accurate reconstruction of changes in the Polish political system as well as in the role of events with a strong emotional impact, such as the Pope's 1979 visit.

Mario Diani's focus is instead on interorganizational exchanges, analysed with reference to Italian environmentalism in the 1980s. Despite the rhetoric on social movement networks being decentralized and antihierarchical, this is not necessarily the case. Diani assesses the position of different organizations within movement networks in the light of two criteria, network centrality (Freeman 1979) and brokerage (Fernandez and Gould 1994). He argues that these measures reflect two different types of movement influence based on the capacity to attract support for specific initiatives (*centrality*) and the capacity to connect sectors of a movement who hold different stances and world views (*brokerage*). He shows how these measures are differently correlated with indicators of external prominence like access to institutions and the media. He also discusses the conditions under which central and brokerage positions tend to be occupied by the same actors, as in the Italian case, or by different ones (as in the Australian women's movement: Sawer and Groves 1994).

Chris Ansell's chapter also deals with networks of environmental organizations, yet his investigtion of the environmental movement in the San Francisco Bay Area has a different focus. While Diani's perspective is largely internal to the movement, Ansell draws upon literatures on collaborative governance, social capital and communitarianism to explore the embeddedness of social movements in local communities. In principle, social movements could be regarded either as an expression of community embeddedness, strongly rooted in specific territorial spaces and the associated systems of relationships, or as attempts to build broader networks based on the identification with a specific cause, which cut across local community loyalties and relations. Ansell is interested in exploring which of the two models is more conducive to collaborative governance: 'How does embeddedness in a particular territorial community or a particular issue-oriented community affect social movement attitudes towards collaboration? How does embeddedness in a social movement subculture affect the attitudes of groups towards collaboration?'

In the third section of the book, we present three contributions which build on network concepts and/or methods to reformulate classic concepts of the political process approach like alliance and oppositional fields (Charles Tilly and Lesley Wood), protest cycles (Pam Oliver and Dan Myers), or political opportunities (Jeffrey Broadbent, with a special focus on elites-movement interactions) from a relational perspective. Tilly and Wood present an unusual application of network analysis to collective action (see also Franzosi 1999). They do not use network analysis to map links between individuals and/or organizations and explain specific behaviours; instead, they use it to chart significant changes in patterns of relationships of attack and claim-making among different social groups (including among others royalty, parliament, local and national officials, trade, and workers) in Britain between 1828 and 1834. Building block models based on the intersection of actors and events, they map networks of contention before and after the passing of the 1832 Reform Act which increased the centrality of parliament in British politics. They highlight the process by which people through collective action not only create new forms of political repertoires, but also forge relations to other actors both at the local and the national level.

If Tilly and Wood draw upon massive historical evidence, Oliver and Myers adopt simulations to explore network mechanisms in diffusion processes and protest cycles. They unpack the idea of a protest cycle and reformulate it in order to take the network dimension into account, focusing on three processes: the flow of information, the flow of influence, and the construction of joint action. They introduce some important clarifications, noting that the repeatable and reversible nature of protest requires models of diffusion, which focus on the spread of actions and not the spread of ideas across actors (while a specific information, once diffused, remains permanently with the recipient, involvement in collective action is temporary and individuals may withdraw—and usually do withdraw—at later stages). They also emphasize the difference between diffusion and cycles: 'Diffusion processes tend to generate waves or cycles of events, but not all waves of events arise from diffusion processes. Waves of protest can also arise from rhythms and from common responses to external events'. Another important factor is constituted by media logics. Even in the case of unbiased sampling newspapers may generate fictitious cycles simply through random variations in coverage. Oliver and Myers find that 'the effect of network structure varies greatly depending upon the nature of a particular network process' and thus demonstrate the need for better specification of network mechanisms in our empirical investigations.

In his chapter, Jeffrey Broadbent presents a case for a network version of the concept of political opportunity structure. He focuses on a non-Western case of mobilization, namely, environmental protest in eight communities in Japan. This enables him to draw our attention to the fact that network analyses of mobilization are actually located in specific cultural and social contexts, with distinctive network properties. Embeddedness in specific networks shapes political action much more strongly in 'thick' societies like Japan than in Western, individualistic societies; in Japan, networks operate mostly in terms of block rather than individual recruitment, and this holds for both movements and elites. In particular, vertical ties between elites and citizens strongly shape local 'political opportunities': it is the presence of 'breakaway bosses' (i.e. local leaders who take the protesters' side) to prove the strongest predictor of success for collective action. Broadbent also contributes to the comparative analysis of mobilization processes by looking at his specific case through a broader and more ambitious theoretical framework, Integrative Structurational Analysis. His model emphasizes the role of 'plastic' processes, by which he means those patterned dynamic processes which shape cultural, material, and social factors and link structural and agency levels.

The fourth and final section of the book consist of chapters by Roger Gould, Ann Mische, Doug McAdam, and Mario Diani. With different emphases, they all link network approaches to social movements and collective action to broader currents in contemporary social science and identify possible future lines of development for research in this area. Roger Gould evaluates the contribution of the relational perspective to our understanding of individual activism by contrasting it to traditional rational choice thinking. Although available evidence consistently suggests a link between network embeddedness and participation, its insights have not been used in a way conducive to accumulate knowledge. This is due to a view of theory as identification of classes of phenomena, rather than as specification of explanatory mechanisms. Opting resolutely for the latter, Gould suggests we abandon the practice of adding new factors to our list of explanatory variables and focus instead on the interactions between those variables. In particular, he exposes the limitations of rational choice reasoning by noting that future expectations are often difficult to calculate and challenging the equation of social ties with prospects of future interaction. Alternatively, he emphasizes the dynamic role of activism in transforming lives and in doing so, changing the meaning and impact of the friendship ties in which prospective activists are involved. Gould nicely illustrates how discussions of networks and collective action can illuminate our understanding of 'social conflict and cooperation in general'.

Despite coming from a fairly different perspective, Mische elaborates on this suggestion by exploring the link between analysis of discourse and forms of talk and network analysis. In dialogue with recent developments in cultural sociology (e.g. Steinberg 1998; Mohr 2000), she looks at the forms of discourse generated by movement activists in response to the multiple relations in which they are involved. She reformulates networks as 'multiple, cross-cutting sets of relations sustained by conversational dynamics within social settings'. Relations are constituted in conversational settings. While the literature on networks has focused mostly on cohesion paradigms, little attention has been paid not only to cross-pressures, but to the fact that in order to go beyond the limited, local boundaries, movement activists need to break the limits of densely knit groups and relate to much broader sets of prospective allies. Networks, therefore, are the location for the development of movement solidarities and for the transmission of messages, identities, etc. across movements at the same time. Mische identifies several conversational mechanisms that characterize the process of network construction and reproduction. She also proposes a technique, Galois lattices, to map the complexity of conjunctures of actors and events in a dynamic way.

In what a distracted reader could interpret as yet another 'epitaph to a successful (theoretical) movement', Doug McAdam assesses the limitations of the structural paradigm for the investigation of the network-participation link, and invokes a greater role for cultural analysis in the identification of recruitment and mobilization mechanisms (McAdam *et al.* 2001). He proceeds to illustrate his general point in reference to three specific 'facts' regarding the origins of protest and contention, conventionally associated with the standard structuralist argument: prior social ties as a basis for movement recruitment, established social settings as the locus of movement emergence, and the spread of movements along existing lines of interaction. For each of these cases, he identifies mechanisms which combine structural and cultural elements. Rather than rejecting the formalization and the quest for systematic patterns, to which network concepts and methods have so much contributed in recent years, he joins Mische's call for a more dynamic integration of interpretative and structuralist research strategies.

Mario Diani concludes the book with a plea to reorient social movement research along network lines. While looking at networks as a powerful precondition of collective action has proved a very fruitful exercise in its own right, one could also take the network idea further and make it the core of a distinctive research programme. Diani argues that viewing movements as a distinctive type of social networks may reorient social movement analysis and help better specifying the relation between movements and related phenomena such as coalitions, solidarity campaigns, and political organizations. He then briefly sketches the basic traits of a research programme to the analysis of network dynamics within social movements, looking first at different network patterns and then identifying some analytical principles which also draw upon existing paradigms.

NOTES

1. To refer to them, terms as vague as 'flows' (Sheller 2000) have recently been invoked.
2. Throughout this introduction, and indeed this book, 'recent' and similar words are to be understood in relative terms. It goes without saying that one could easily trace many of the 'new insights' discussed here well back in classic sociology (Simmel's work on formal sociology and Marx's historical writings on conflicts in France being just two most obvious examples).
3. Mechanisms have been defined as 'a delimited class of events that alter relations among specified elements in identical or closely similar ways over a variety of situations' (McAdam *et al.* 2001: 11).
4. Blau (1982); Blau and Schwartz (1984). Some very influential works in the field of contentious politics (e.g. Gould 1995) are actually examples of structural analysis in this sense, rather than network analysis proper.
5. See Diani (1992*b*, 2002) for a more thorough presentation of network methods in reference to social movement analysis. For introductions to social network methods see Scott (1992) and Wasserman and Faust (1995). A useful glossary of network terms may be found at the following web address http://www.nist.gov/dads/termsArea.html#graph.
6. For thorough reviews of this field of investigation see Knoke and Wisely (1990); Kitts (2000); Diani (forthcoming).
7. McAdam and Paulsen (1993) show that direct ties do not count if people are involved in broader activities compatible with the type of participation to be explained.
8. For example, Melucci's project (1984) suggested that in the environmental field, networks developed in militant contexts had helped to set up natural food trade businesses, but that these largely identified with market activities rather than with a specific cause. In that context, the boundaries between movement community and market were vague at best.
9. Diani (2000*b*) presents a different reading of concentric circles, noting that political subcultures in countries like Italy, Belgium, or the Netherlands did not necessarily weaken democracy but provided distinct, previously excluded areas of society with political organization and opportunities for legitimacy.

Part I

Individual Networks

2

Social Networks Matter. But How?

Florence Passy

Social networks do matter in the process of individual participation in social movements. Many of the African-Americans activists involved in the civil rights movement during the 1950s and later were members of Baptist churches before they devoted their time and energy to the fight against racial discrimination in American society (McAdam 1982; Morris 1984). The young students who worked on the Freedom Summer Project in 1964 enjoyed social links which greatly facilitated their commitment to that risky campaign (McAdam 1988*a,b*). Most of the women, who contributed to the emergence of the women's movements in the United States, and probably in other countries as well were socially embedded in dense networks, mainly on the radical left (e.g. Freeman 1973). Similar processes occurred in European countries. For example, social ties crucially expanded individual support for what became one of the biggest street demonstrations in Dutch history, when 550,000 peace supporters went to The Hague to protest against the deployment of NATO cruise missiles in the country (Klandermans and Oegema 1987). Interpersonal ties have also played a key role in more radical forms of protest, such as terrorism. They were crucial to the involvement of activists in Italian and German left-wing underground organizations (della Porta 1995). Social networks also enable individual participation in nondemocratic regimes when there is a window of opportunity. The Velvet Revolutions in Eastern Europe during the late 1980s mobilized supporters through existing networks, mainly churches and intellectual circles (e.g. Opp and Gern 1993). Finally, the crucial role of social networks in processes of individual participation is apparent not only in contemporary mobilizations like those just mentioned but also in other historical contexts as well. For example, Gould's (1995) study of the Paris Commune shows that organizational linkages among residential areas as well as interpersonal ties facilitated not only enlistment in the National Guard but also the stabilization of new recruits in the revolutionary army.

I thank Doug McAdam and Mario Diani for helpful critiques of earlier drafts of this paper.

In brief, social networks play a crucial role in the process of individual participation in social movements, and numerous other studies that emphasize this aspect can be cited (e.g. Oberschall 1973, 1993; Snow *et al.* 1980; McAdam 1982, 1988*a*,*b*; Rosenthal *et al.* 1985; Klandermans and Oegema 1987; della Porta 1988, 1995; Fernandez and McAdam 1989; Friedman and McAdam 1992; Kriesi 1993; Marwell and Oliver 1993; McAdam and Paulsen 1993; Diani 1995; Gould 1995; Klandermans 1997). The aim of this paper is not simply to provide further empirical evidence of the key role of social interactions in a given process of individual participation; it is rather to address the question of network intervention in this process. As I shall try to show, networks have multiple functions and intervene at different moments in the process of individual participation. Following the findings of scholars who have underscored the importance of networks for individual participation but who, at the same time, have stressed our still limited knowledge of the dimensions of networks that actually influence participation (Heckathorn 1993; Marwell and Oliver 1993; McAdam and Paulsen 1993; Gould 1995; Kim and Bearman 1997), this paper will seek to specify the various roles that networks play in the process of individual participation.

Why is it so important to disentangle the various dimensions of networks? As McAdam and Paulsen (1993) stressed a few years ago, although there is a growing body of studies attesting to the role of networks, they suffer from considerable theoretical inaccuracy that casts some doubt on the ultimate usefulness of this concept for the study of social movements. We are now aware that social ties are important for collective action, but we still need to theorize on the actual role of networks. Three theoretical reasons point up the need to clarify the concept of networks and their role in individual participation. First, specifying the dimensions of social networks gives us a better grasp of the mechanisms and dynamics that induce people to become involved in collective action, and in the end it provides us with a more complete explanation of the entire process of individual participation. To join collective action is a long process which involves both social structures and teleological decisions. Social networks intervene throughout this process, at the beginning by building or reinforcing individual identities that create potential for participation, and at the very end when individual preferences and perceptions (e.g. individual costs of action, chances of success, the risk involved) eventually prompt people to take action. Second, specifying the role of networks helps us to integrate structural and rationalist theories. While structuralist approaches emphasize the role of identities, values and social networks as enabling or constraining participation, rationalist explanations stress the role of human agency. These two theoretical traditions are less opposed to each other than it appears at first glance. To be sure, they are based on different philosophical traditions, but they in fact explain two different stages in the process of individual participation. While structuralists point to the formation of a potential for participation and recruitment through networks at the beginning of the process, rationalists have developed sophisticated models to grasp individual decisions, which come at the end of the participation process. The concept of social networks provides the theoretical link between these two distinct moments. One of the multiple functions of networks intervenes at the end of the participation process, when individuals define their preferences as to whether they will join collective action or otherwise. Individual decisions are shaped, at least in part, by interactions with other actors. Individuals incorporate and make sense of their multiple social interactions, which influence the definition of individual preferences. Thus, networks provide a bridge between structuralist and rationalist accounts. Third, specifying the role of networks allows us to bring meanings and culture back into the explanation of individual participation. Social networks are not only instrumental ties enabling or constraining participation: 'a social network is a network of meanings', as White (1992: 67) put it. Ties are imbued with stories. Therefore, social networks (as islands of meanings) shape the individual preferences and perceptions that form the basis for the ultimate decision to participate. Thus, networks shape both stable aspects such as values and identities and more volatile aspects such as perceptions and preferences.

In sum, specifying networks will strengthen our knowledge of collective action by clarifying mechanisms and dynamics, by bridging structure and agency, and by bringing meanings and culture back into our micro-models of collective action through a phenomenological conception of networks. After theoretical discussion of three functions of social networks in the process of individual participation, and after some brief remarks on method, I shall illustrate these functions by means of survey data on participants in two new social movement organizations.

THREE FUNCTIONS OF SOCIAL NETWORKS

Social networks intervene at different moments in the long process of individual participation. As many scholars have pointed out, people engage in collective action because they share certain norms and values related to a specific area of political contention. In this perspective, participation in collective action is an identification process (e.g. Freeman 1973; McAdam 1982; Morris 1984; Calhoun 1989; Fernandez and McAdam 1989; Andrews 1991; McAdam and Paulsen 1993; Whittier 1995; Melucci 1996). Since identities are created and shaped through social relations, networks play a crucial role. They build and reinforce the identities of individuals and provide them with a political consciousness that allows them to get ideologically closer to a given political issue. In this case, networks intervene in the early stage of the participation process. Social interactions are certainly not the only channels of identity and political consciousness building. Primary socialization and past experiences, amongst other factors, matter as well. However, social interactions play a key role in this respect. The cultural orientation of individuals is not a simple reflection of their social position; it develops in a web of social interactions. The social networks in which actors interact convey meanings (e.g. symbols, rituals, narratives) that build and solidify identities and shape the actors' cognitive frames, thereby enabling them to interpret social reality and to define a set of actions that involve them in this perceived reality (Somers 1992). Once individuals have been integrated into formal or informal networks, they find themselves in an interactive structure that enables them to define and redefine their interpretive frames, facilitates the process of identity-building and identity-strengthening, and creates or solidifies political consciousness towards a given protest issue. By favouring identification with certain political issues, this function of networks forms the initial condition for the establishment of the framing process that occurs between an individual and a social movement (Snow *et al.* 1986; McAdam and Paulsen 1993). In other words, this function of networks, which I call the *socialization function*, creates an initial disposition to participate.

To identify oneself with a cause, in our case with a specific political protest, is not a sufficient condition for an individual's potential to participate to be actualized. Collective action belongs to the category of human behaviour labelled 'non volitional': that is to say, the initial disposition to participate will remain latent or unrealized as long as there is no opportunity for it to be converted into action (Ajzen and Fishbein 1980). Social movement organizations, public demonstrations, riots and specific movement campaigns provide individuals culturally close to a given political contention with an opportunity to convert their dispositions to participate into concrete action. Social ties are one of the major channels through which potential activists are connected with an opportunity for participation. Again, social networks are not the only channels that can perform this task. For instance, movement organizations, by their own actions or advertisement, as well as media reports about movements, may also be important channels through which new supporters are attracted. However, networks play a mediating role by connecting prospective participants to an opportunity for mobilization and enabling them to convert their political consciousness into action. As many studies have shown, individuals with friends or acquaintances already involved in social movements are more inclined to take part in collective action (e.g. Snow *et al.* 1980; McAdam 1986, 1988*a,b*; della Porta 1988, 1995; Gould 1993*a,b*; Kriesi 1993). This role of social networks—what I call the *structural-connection function*—takes place before prospective participants join a social movement organization.

Before prospective activists actualize their potential for participation in a specific political contention—that is, after 'push' and 'pull' factors have intervened (respectively, socialization and structural linkages with the opportunity for mobilization)—they make a series of decisions. Joining collective action involves individual costs which vary according to factors such as the intensity of involvement, the type of protest, and the type of regime under which the action takes place. Whatever the costs, these always constitute a barrier against participation in collective action. Those who are ready to join a specific political contention undertake a decision-making process by assessing various parameters regarding the protest itself (e.g. the risks involved, the chances of success, the likelihood of government reform in the absence of protest) and their own willingness to take action (e.g. utility of their involvement in bringing about social changes). Rationalist scholars, who have underlined this aspect of collective action and developed sophisticated models of individual decisions (e.g. Olson 1965; Mueller and Opp 1986; Opp 1989; Chong 1991; Macy 1991; Sandler 1992; Marwell and Oliver 1993), try to explain behaviour with reference to universal human attributes (at least most of them). Structuralist scholars have been sceptical of this view of action, since it overlooks the impact of structural factors on human behaviour (e.g. institutional frameworks, social interactions, individual roles). In addition, some rationalists have themselves criticized collective action models which assume that individuals take isolated and autonomous decisions. In the light of findings by game theorists that individuals make interdependent decisions (e.g. Axelrod 1984)—'ego' as a rational actor must take into account what 'alter' does (or will do)—a number of social movement scholars have proposed collective action models which incorporate social interactions as well. The basic idea is that cooperative social behaviour is an outcome of rational self-interested actors, because they must consider others' intentions and actions. Gerald Marwell and Pamela Oliver have been among the first to analyse these matters and to combine individual and relational variables (Oliver 1984; Oliver *et al.* 1985, 1988; Marwell *et al.* 1988; Marwell and Oliver 1993). Their critical mass theory incorporates the influence of social networks into a decisional model. Other authors have developed new decisional models to carry this theory forward (e.g. Opp 1989; Macy 1991; Gould 1993*a,b*; Heckathorn 1993; Kim and Bearman 1997). All these scholars have stressed the crucial nexus between individual decisions and social relations: the decision to join collective action is influenced by the action of other participants. In other words, they emphasize a function of social networks which I call the *decision-shaping function*.

Although I take account of the final step of individual participation and the influence of social interactions in this stage of the process, I adopt a perspective different from that of the rationalist scholars mentioned above. Rational choice interpretations of the role of social interactions rely upon an instrumentalist conception of networks. This observation has already been made by Emirbayer and Goodwin (1994) in their stimulating paper on social networks and the role of culture and human agency. Rationalists conceive social influences in overly narrow terms: ego's behaviour is strategically adopted as a reaction against alter's intentions and actions. For example, the critical mass theory postulates that individuals decide whether to participate by looking at other people's behaviour, which enables them to anticipate the costs and potential outcomes of protest. Critical mass theorists define social networks only in instrumental terms. Contrary to the theses of the structuralists, who often overlook human agency in favour of social structures, agency is at the core of rationalist theories but is conceived in essentially instrumental terms. Individuals decide strategically according to the behaviour of others. Whilst a structuralist perspective usually encounters the problem of determinism, whereby agency and individual freedom do not exist or exist only to a very limited extent, a rationalist perspective entirely ignores the construction of meanings which arise from social interactions and shape individual freedom.

I put forward a phenomenological perspective that considers the constant work of definition and redefinition of the social world by individuals, as well as their self-positioning within this world, which at least in part influence their decision-making process. As Alfred Schutz (1967: 230) pointed out, 'it is the meaning of our experiences and not the ontological structure of the objects which constitutes reality.' Social relations create and sustain a structure of meanings that contributes to the definition of individual perceptions or preferences. Perceptions change according to events in a person's life, and according to external events, but also as a result of everyday interactions. Perceptions are then constantly redefined by individuals, and this process is largely shaped by social networks. They are shaped but not determined by social interactions. Far from merely reacting to interpersonal links and connections, individuals interpret such links and try to make sense of their interactions with others. They incorporate concrete interactions into their self and adapt the social knowledge they acquire from prior interactions to new information drawn from recent ones, thereby unleashing their own creativity. The way they formalize structures of meaning depends on this creative process of social learning, which takes place during moments of freedom (Emirbayer and Goodwin 1994). Preferences are then a product of the ability of individuals to make sense of the constant ebbs and flows of social interactions. Furthermore, as Pizzorno (1996) has pointed out, this product becomes meaningful to individuals once perceptions and preferences have been communicated and interpreted. This is a two-fold process which takes place during social relations, operating downstream when networks produce meanings that are integrated into the self and upstream when perceptions are communicated to others.

Thus, social networks also intervene at the very end of the process of individual participation by shaping the individual preferences or perceptions that form the decision-making process and bring potential activists to collective action. This function of networks occurs just before the individual enters collective action. It bridges the gap between structure and agency, and links, at least to some extent, structuralist and rationalist accounts of individual participation. Some scholars outside the rationalist research tradition have also pointed out the impact of networks on the decision to participate in collective action, but they are exceptions. Doug McAdam (1982) is among those who have gone farthest in specifying the decision-shaping function of networks. More recently, together with Ronelle Paulsen, McAdam has taken his reflections on the multiple roles of networks in the process of individual participation a step further (McAdam and Paulsen 1993). According to their microstructural model, social networks strongly shape the individual decision to participate. More specifically, the ultimate decision to participate is closely related to individual identities. People will join a social movement if this decision resonates with their identities, if someone can sustain their mobilization identity, if there are no countervailing identities, and so on. In their model, however, McAdam and Paulsen largely overlook the decision parameters stressed by rationalists, such as the effectiveness of the collective action or the risks involved in participation. Their microstructural model of recruitment emphasizes the crucial role of relational structures in the process of individual participation, but it ignores human agency.

In this paper, both human agency and social networks occupy centre stage. The latter are conceived in their structural role of, for example, bringing prospective participants closer to a protest opportunity, but also in cultural terms. As White (1992: 65) has put it, social networks are 'phenomenological realities'. They are islands of meanings which define and redefine individual identities through their interactions with other actors or groups, but also by shaping more volatile perceptions or preferences. In other words, this conception of social interactions as networks of meanings brings culture, but also human agency, back into the process of individual participation. Structural constraints and individual freedom are here closely interwoven in the cultural dimension of social interactions.

METHODS

Individual participation is not a unique and universal process. On the contrary, it varies according to numerous factors. Processes of individual participation under authoritarian regimes are certainly different then those that occur in democratic states. Repression, but also the liveliness of the civil society, modifies the processes of individual participation as well as the role of networks in these processes (e.g. Opp and Gern 1993). Interpersonal contacts play a greater role under repressive regimes. In political regimes of this kind, protest groups often take the form of clandestine organizations, and interpersonal ties help the covert recruitment of new supporters. Not only the political context, but also the types of protest activities in which individuals decide to become involved, occasion variation in the process. Joining a formal organization is not the same as committing oneself to a specific action campaign (e.g. the Freedom Summer Project) or a one-day street demonstration (e.g. the Hague peace demonstration of 1983). Similarly, the public visibility of social movement organizations and their action repertoire generate important variations in the participation processes. It is my intention in this paper to empirically assess the role of the three functions of networks mentioned above, but also the variations in participation processes. I shall not consider the influence of the political context (authoritarian versus democratic regimes) or the types of protest activities (formal organization versus more specific protest activities), although I would stress the influence of social movement organizations on individual participation. I shall focus on two characteristics of movement organizations that introduce variation into participation processes: their action repertoire (legal versus illegal forms of action) and their public visibility (high versus low). Cross-referencing these two dimensions yields a conceptual space comprising four distinct types of organization: legal movement organizations with high visibility (e.g. World Wildlife Fund, Greenpeace, Amnesty International), illegal organizations with high visibility (e.g. ETA, IRA, Rote Armee Fraktion), legal organizations with low visibility (small and local organizations like the Bern Declaration), and illegal groups with low visibility (small and clandestine organizations). These four situations should prove to be characterized by different participation processes in which the role of networks varies, particularly in their structural-connection function, but also in their decision-shaping function. For instance, networks should play a greater role in the recruitment process for movement organizations with low visibility (both legal and illegal) than they do in the case of groups with high visibility, for which other channels are able to bring potential members to the organization. Similarly, social connections should prove to be more important in the recruitment of new members, but also in shaping the individual decision-making process in the case of illegal organizations (both with high and low visibility). This type of political participation entails high risks; and for the assessment of the chances of success of terrorist actions or the risk involved in participation, social interactions should be crucial in bypassing the costs of this type of commitment. Several scholars have examined the role of networks in clandestine organizations (e.g. della Porta 1992, 1995), but studies have rarely examined the impact of public visibility on processes of individual participation. Here I shall compare two processes of individual participation in two organizations using a legal and peaceful action repertoire but with a clearly distinct degree of visibility in the public space.

The first organization arose from Protestant milieus in 1970 and belongs to the development-aid branch of the Swiss solidarity movement: the Bern Declaration.[1] This organization, which has about 18,000 members, is run by a small staff of professionals on a relatively low budget. Even though the Bern Declaration is present and quite active in both the French and German parts of the country, it is a fairly small organization with low public visibility.[2] The second organization chosen for comparison is a well-known association in the ecology movement with high public visibility: the World Wildlife Fund (WWF). The WWF has developed steadily since its inception (in 1961) to become one of the largest organizations in the Swiss ecology movement. With more than 210,000 members, almost 100 employees, and an annual budget of 28 million Swiss francs, the WWF is today not only one of the major environmentalist organizations in Switzerland, but one of the largest social movement organizations overall in the country. With regard to public visibility, I thus compare very distinct participation processes, and ask which network functions, specifically the structural-connection function, have differing impacts.[3]

Qualitative methods are better suited than quantitative ones for analysis of structures of meaning in social phenomena (e.g. Denzin 1989; Bryman 2000). Life histories or in-depth interviews are particularly able to capture structures of meanings. When individuals talk about themselves, they express the meaning of their practices and convey the subjective interpretation of their acts (Denzin 1989). I conducted in-depth interviews with members of the Bern Declaration, but unfortunately not with the WWF members. While I shall occasionally refer to the qualitative data set, so that rigorous comparison can be made between the two participation processes empirical illustration of the three functions of social networks in individual participation will essentially rely on quantitative data. The data are taken from two surveys of members of the Bern Declaration and the WWF.[4]

The survey data used raise the problem of retrospective bias, given that they were collected after individuals had joined the organization. Memory distortion is the major problem that arises when individuals are asked to respond to questions on past experiences and feelings. First, social psychologists tell us that memory fades, provoking selective recollections (e.g. Baddeley 1979). Moreover, this does not occur at random. Second, when individuals recall past events, they reinterpret them. This reinterpretation is done according to present experiences, the aim being to maintain social desirability and to reduce cognitive dissonance. For these various reasons, retrospective data pose validity and reliability problems. A better research design for the analysis of individual participation consists in interviews administered before and after individuals have joined the protest. However, this research design is in most cases impossible to plan in nonexperimental settings. How can the individuals who will join the protest be selected? Generally, they become visible to researchers only after they have participated. Very few scholars have been lucky enough to be able to use a before–after research design (see Klandermans and Oegema 1987; McAdam 1988*a*,*b*). Although the problem of retrospective bias is a serious one, I have indications that I can trust the data. First, most of the findings are consistent with previous studies, specifically those with a before–after research design.[5] Second, according to empirical tests conducted by Coen van Rij (1994) in his study of individual participation in trade unions, the reliability problem is less dramatic than one might think. Van Rij tested the reliability of a variety of questions, and like Alwin and Krosnick (1991) he argued that the reliability of retrospective data is not much lower than that of comparable non-retrospective questions.[6]

The final methodological remark concerns the dependent variable. Instead of assessing the role of the three functions of social networks on individual participation, I shall look at the intensity of participation. In other words, the aim of the paper is to understand how networks influence the intensity of participation in social movements, rather than concentrate on the simple fact of participating. The umbrella concept of participation covers various levels of commitment to social movements implying different degrees of effort. Scholars usually focus on participation as such rather than on the diverse forms that it can take.[7] To measure the intensity of participation, I use two concepts often emphasized in the literature. First, the notion of *effort* as operationalized by Oliver and Marwell (1992), who distinguish members who 'give time' from those who 'give money'. This allows us to separate people who engage in an active process of participation by spending time in a social movement organization from those who remain passive and limit themselves to giving financial support. However, this dimension does not distinguish among different levels of participation within the category of activists. The concept of *duration* proposed by Klandermans (1997), which I operationalized through the frequency of involvement, offers a means to separate two types of activists: those who are irregularly active (by collaborating on a specific campaign or participating in annual meetings) and those who participate on a regular basis. In sum, in the analyses that follow, I shall examine three different levels of participation and the corresponding categories of members: *subscribers* (passive members who contribute financially to the organization), *adherents* (irregularly active members), and *activists* (regularly active members).

THE ROLE OF NETWORKS IN TWO DISTINCT INDIVIDUAL PARTICIPATION PROCESSES

How do the three functions of social networks intervene in individual participation? What is the impact of each function on the whole process? How does the importance of these functions vary according to the public visibility of the opportunity for mobilization? These are the central questions addressed in this part of the paper, which uses the data described in the previous section to illustrate the theoretical arguments put forward above. Let us start with the role of the *socialization function* of networks, which, I argue, takes place at the beginning of the participation process. My hypothesis is not that networks are the only channel through which individuals are socialized to a specific protest issue; it is rather that embeddedness in formal or informal networks close to that issue helps individuals to create a salient identity which is an important cultural resource for joining the protest, and which facilitates the emergence of a political consciousness related to specific political issues (e.g. Andrews 1991; Kriesi 1993; McAdam and Paulsen 1993; Melucci 1996). As a corollary, I also hypothesize that individuals who have been strongly socialized and who identify closely with a protest issue are likely to become more intensely involved in a social movement.

These two hypotheses are confirmed by the survey data. First, very few members of the Bern Declaration and the WWF were not embedded in a dense relational structure before they joined the organization.[8] Most of them were already members of numerous social movement organizations (formal networks), and they had many interpersonal ties (informal networks) with individuals who were either already involved in the solidarity or ecology movements or ideologically close to the political issues addressed by those two movements. Of course, social networks are not the only channel of socialization, but this finding emphasizes the importance of prior embeddedness in networks for the creation of an initial disposition to participate. Thus, formal and informal networks as envelopes of meanings form a space of socialization and identity-building for the prospective members. It is interesting to note that, as far as formal networks are concerned, Bern Declaration and WWF members displayed a similar relational structure. Both types of participant were strongly rooted in organizations belonging to the new social movements, and within this movement family they were active in both ecology and solidarity groups (specifically, development-aid and human-rights organizations). The overlapping of political issues between solidarity and ecology movements that, about a decade ago, gave rise to the concept of 'sustainable development' constitutes an ideological bridge between the two types of protest. This cultural bridge enables these two networks to socialize individuals and provide them with a political consciousness towards solidarity and ecology issues. Besides sharing a similar embeddeness in the new social movements, Bern Declaration and WWF members were rooted to the same extent in conventional political and religious networks. The only significant difference between them was the larger proportion of WWF members belonging to youth and student associations. This difference is in part explained by the fact that the WWF organizes holiday camps for youngsters, which are publicized mainly through these types of association.

As argued above, inclusion in networks creates cultural proximity between an individual and a given protest movement, and hence affects the intensity of participation. Obviously, not all types of formal networks are able to build or reinforce the individual identities crucial for the creation of an initial disposition to participate. Only culturally close networks—that is, networks with similar cultural frames—can produce this initial disposition.[9] As Table 2.1 (Models 1) shows, individuals embedded in formal networks culturally close to the Bern Declaration and the WWF tend to participate at a higher level than individuals socially rooted in networks with no ideological connections with the solidarity or ecology movements.[10] In this initial stage of the participation process, social networks shape individual identities and create a positive association between the individual cognitive frames and movement cultural frames. Thus, only individuals embedded in culturally close networks and who have created identities that link culturally with the movement participate with higher intensity in both organizations. Life histories conducted with the Bern Declaration members showed that this phase of socialization occurs at the beginning of the process, and that the longer participants are involved in culturally close social networks, the higher their level of participation in the organization. It also reveals that individuals who do not have competing identities, that is, those who with mainly salient and meaningful embeddednesses, tend to engage at a higher level (Passy 2001*a,b*).

The only difference in this socialization function between the two participation processes examined relates to the role of interpersonal ties (informal networks). The latter increases the intensity of participation by both Bern Declaration and WWF members, but in the case of the WWF the impact is weaker and disappears once the formal networks are controlled for. Thus, while interpersonal ties play a role in the socialization process in the case of the WWF as well, formal networks

TABLE 2.1. *The impact of the socialization and structural-connection functions on intensity of participation (multiple regression)*

	Bern Declaration (Beta)				WWF (Beta)			
	Model 1	Model 2	Model 3	Model 4	Model 1	Model 2	Model 3	Model 4
Socialization function								
Formal networks								
Embedded in networks close to the movement	0.15***			0.16**	0.20***			0.16***
Embedded in formal networks (others)	−0.02			−0.01	−0.15***			−0.14***
Informal networks								
Embeddedness in informal networks	0.18***			0.12**	0.02			0.08
Structural-connection function								
Formal networks								
Recruited by formal networks		0.07	0.07	0.04		0.03	0.01	0.00
Informal networks								
Recruited by a member of the organization		0.24***	0.05	0.08		0.22***	0.10	0.13
Recruited by a subscriber			−0.06	−0.08			−0.05	−0.09
Recruited by an adherent			0.01	−0.01			0.02	0.00
Recruited by an activist			0.29***	0.25***			0.19**	0.16*
Recruited through weak ties			0.00	0.01			0.05	0.03
Recruited through strong acquired ties			0.12**	0.12*			0.03	0.03
Recruited through strong ascriptive ties			−0.09*	−0.07			0.00	0.00
R^2	0.06	0.07	0.16	0.21	0.06	0.06	0.09	0.13

* $p = 0.05$.
** $p = 0.01$.
*** $p = 0.001$.

are much more important. The socialization function plays a quite similar role in both processes and explains differential participation to the same extent. The explained variance of this function is the same for both the highly visible organization and for the much less visible one.

I now turn to the *structural-connection function* of networks as it operates in the two organizations studied. A number of works have shown that the linkage between the social movement organizations and prospective participants is more likely to occur through interpersonal (i.e. informal) ties than through organizational (i.e. formal) ones (e.g. McAdam 1986; della Porta 1988; McAdam and Paulsen 1993; Gould 1995). Accordingly, I hypothesized that individuals who have social ties with people already involved in a movement organization are more likely to become involved in that organization. Furthermore, this type of interaction yields different structures of meaning about political commitment. I thus expected the intensity of participation to vary according to the nature of the ties that link prospective members to their recruiters. More specifically, I first argued that, contrary to Granovetter's (1973) well-known theory of the role of weak ties for recruitment in the labour market, strong ties have a crucial impact on participation in social movements, mainly because they provide individuals with trust. As Pizzorno (1986) has pointed out, trust is crucial to the understanding of political behaviour in situations of uncertainty. Before people join a movement organization, they are often in a state of uncertainty because they lack information and knowledge about the organization. Recruiters are usually an important channel of knowledge about the protest. When recruiters are close friends (as opposed to acquaintances), potential participants tend to trust them and to be convinced that a particular organization is the one most appropriate for conversion of their political interests into a strong degree of commitment. Second, I assumed that the recruiter's level of participation in the organization affects that of prospective members: the more intense the involvement of recruiters, the stronger the commitment of newcomers. This is because centrally located recruiters are more apt to reduce the uncertainty emphasized by Pizzorno. Furthermore, core activists are usually 'true believers' better able to convince new members to contribute as much as possible to the organization's activities. Finally, the type of mobilization opportunity joined by prospective members should influence the role and, above all, the importance of the structural-connection function of networks in individual participation. As far as the public visibility of the organizations is concerned, I expected the role of networks to be less crucial for visible organizations than for less visible ones. Other recruitment channels exist for visible organizations like the WWF, which are able to attract new members through their own activities or advertisement and above all through the publicity given to their claims and actions by the media. By contrast, the media should be a less important recruitment channel for small social movement organizations with low visibility like the Bern Declaration.

The survey data largely supported these four hypotheses. First, social networks are important channels for the recruitment of participants in both organizations. More than half of the Bern Declaration and WWF members were connected to the opportunity for mobilization through social ties.[11] This percentage was slightly smaller in the case of the highly visible ecology organization. Nevertheless, even in this case, social interactions played a crucial role in connecting members to the protest. The media are also a fairly important recruitment channel for the WWF, at least compared to the Bern Declaration. About 30 per cent of the WWF participants were connected to the organization through this channel, while only 18 per cent joined the Bern Declaration in this way. Interpersonal ties seem to be more important than formal links in this connecting process, and this is particularly the case of the WWF, to which only a very small proportion of members were connected through formal links. By contrast, formal networks (specifically, religious organizations) played a significant role for the Bern Declaration, which has historical links with Protestant milieus.[12]

As Table 2.1 (Models 2) shows, for both organizations it is the fact of being recruited by informal ties rather than formal ties that increases the level of participation. However, as argued above, it is the nature of ties that affects the level of participation rather than the mere fact of being connected to the opportunity for mobilization through interpersonal ties (Models 3). First, at least in the case of the Bern Declaration, being recruited by a close friend (strong acquired ties) gives rise to strong activism. By contrast, recruitment through family ties (strong ascriptive) leads to lower levels of participation, while recruitment by acquaintances (weak ties) does not seem to affect the intensity of participation. It is important to note that the role of strong ties in this function of networks is more important for the less visible organization (the Bern Declaration) than for the highly visible one (the WWF). We know that trust is a critical factor behind participation in collective action, especially in situations of uncertainty. In highly visible organizations like the WWF, prospective participants are less prone to uncertainty because they know about the organization through the media, and through the organization's own activities, which are generally well publicized. Thus, the role of strong ties is less crucial in this type of participation process than it is in a process of individual participation, where prospective members know almost nothing about the opportunity for mobilization. In the latter case, strong ties seem to be more important than they are for highly visible organizations.

Second, Table 2.1 (Models 3) confirms that the level of participation depends on the position of the recruiter within the organization. Participants recruited by a core activist joined the organization at the highest level of commitment. In the case of both participation processes, being structurally connected to the opportunity for mobilization by highly committed participants substantially increases the level of involvement by new recruits. In fact, 'true believers' seem to be the recruiters most able to induce new members to enact the highest level of involvement. Nevertheless, this factor affects differential participation in the ecologist organization to a much lesser extent than it does in the case of the Bern Declaration. As I expected, for both processes of participation studied, the nature of ties is more important than the mere fact of being connected to the opportunity for mobilization through interpersonal ties. However, the impact of the structural-connection function of social networks on differential participation is of much less importance for the WWF than for the Bern Declaration.

This empirical finding confirms the hypothesis that public visibility affects the structural-connection function of social networks. This function is much more important when prospective members join an organization with less public visibility. As Table 2.1 (Models 3) shows, the explained variance of differential participation by this function of networks is larger in the less visible organization than in the highly visible one. For the less visible movement organizations, interpersonal relationships play a crucial role in structurally bridging potential participants to an opportunity for participation. By contrast, in the case of organizations with important media exposure, like the WWF, informal networks are also important, but to a lesser extent. For this type of organization, other recruitment channels intervene in this phase of the participation process, above all the media. The process of structural connection of prospective participants to the opportunity for mobilization is much more diffuse, that is taking various forms in the case of highly visible organizations than in that of less visible ones.

Although the socialization function of networks intervenes in a rather similar fashion in both processes of individual participation, mainly through formal ties culturally close to the opportunity for mobilization, and this function explains the same proportion of variance in differential participation in each process; the structural-connection function varies substantially from one process to the other. The variation observed in the latter function is reflected in the explained variance of networks in both participation processes. As Models 4 in Table 2.1 show, social networks play a weaker role in the highly visible organization than in the less visible one.

The *decision-shaping function* of networks intervenes in the later stage of individual participation. Individuals define preferences and perceptions concerning both a specific political protest and themselves. This decision-making process enables (or prevents) the conversion of the individual's potential for participation into actual action. Of course, numerous perceptions and preferences are involved in the decision process, and it is almost impossible to take all of them into account in micro-models of participation. I include in the present model four types of individual perception stressed by previous collective action studies: interest in the political issue (e.g. Marwell and Oliver 1993; Kim and Bearman 1997); the individual and the collective effectiveness of the action (e.g. McAdam 1982, 1986; Klandermans 1984, 1997; Oliver 1984; Opp 1989; Marwell and Oliver 1993); the ability of political authorities to solve the problem at hand (e.g. Piven and Cloward 1977); and personal availability, that is, the amount of time at a person's disposal to devote to collective action (McAdam 1986; Marwell and Oliver 1993).

With regards to the latter aspect, I consider only subjective availability to be a perception, treating objective availability as a factual observation. I do not take account of the risks involved in collective action, which have often been emphasized in the literature (e.g. McAdam 1986; Hirsch 1990), because participation in moderate and reformist organizations like the Bern Declaration and the WWF carries virtually no risks. I therefore assume that this perception does not play a significant role in the decision to join such organizations.

Evaluating this function of social networks is not an easy task. From a quantitative point of view, panel surveys are certainly the most appropriate way to do so, because they offer the advantage of measuring interactions at t1 and evaluating their effect at t2. Unfortunately, for the reasons given above I do not have this kind of data available. Another way to assess this function is to run a LISREL analysis which enables one to determine the indirect effect of social networks on individual participation. This method of evaluating the third function of social networks is somewhat artificial because it implies a dynamic view within a static design. However, using indicators of networks measured before involvement in both organizations (t1) and perceptions measured after an individual has become involved (t2), it at least yields an illustration of this function of networks, although it is not a real test of the theory.

I expected the entire set of perceptions considered in this model to be shaped by social interactions. More specifically, I predicted that the interest in the specific protest issue (i.e. development aid and environmental protection) would be an important intermediary variable in the decision-shaping role of social networks. It would influence the definition of the other perceptions included in this micro-model of participation in social movements. The interest in the protest issue is defined through the ebbs and flows of social interactions, and in turn shapes perceptions of the individual and collective effectiveness of the action, the ability of political authorities to solve the problem at hand, and, finally, personal availability. Thus, interest in the protest issue should play an important intermediary role in this third function of social networks. Social ties should therefore influence the definition of individual perceptions not only directly but also indirectly via interest in the protest issue.

The LISREL models presented in Figs 2.1 and 2.2 confirm the first hypothesis regarding the decision-shaping function of social networks.[13] Except for subjective availability, the full set of perceptions is significantly shaped by social networks. Table 2.2, which summarizes the impact of networks on individual perceptions and on differential participation as yielded by LISREL analysis, shows that of all the perceptions included in the model of individual participation, *individual effectiveness* is the one that is most strongly shaped by social interactions. Of course, as explained above, and as the correlation coefficients in Table 2.2 show, this perception, as well as all other types of perception or preference definition, are only in part shaped by social networks. That said, individual effectiveness is mainly affected

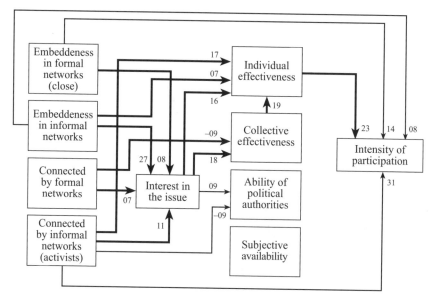

FIG. 2.1. *LISREL estimates of structural equations model of differential participation*
in the Bern Declaration (standardized solutions) (Degrees of freedom = 5;
Chi square = 6.809; Goodness of fit = 0.998; Probability = 0.235; N = 559)

by the interactions of prospective members with their recruiters, especially in the case of the Bern Declaration. In the less visible organization, the interaction between prospective members and their recruiters tends substantially to increase the sense that their participation in the protest serves to bring about social change. Thus, indirectly but strongly, recruiters influence the level of participation by increasing the feeling that if individuals engage in protest, their participation is not insignificant; on the contrary, it helps bring about social and political reforms. Life histories confirm the influence of this factor. Although prospective members usually knew virtually nothing about the organization, they joined it with a high level of participation because their recruiters provided them not only with information but above all the trust necessary to convert their political awareness into action. Even if the information about the organization was only partial or irrelevant, recruiters were able to heighten the individuals' perceptions of their own effectiveness (Passy and Giugni 2000; Passy 2001a,b). In highly visible organization (the WWF), the role of recruiters was less crucial in this respect. I pointed out above that the role of recruiters is much less important for this organization than for the Bern Declaration. This weaker impact in the case of the ecology organization clearly impinges upon the decision-shaping function.

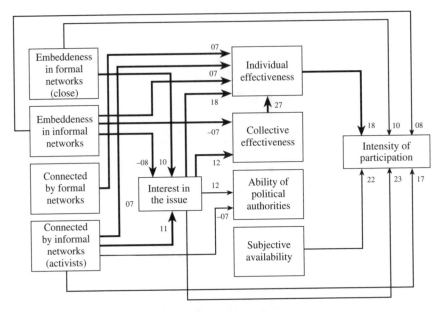

Fig. 2.2. *LISREL estimates of structural equations model of differential participation in the WWF (standardized solutions) (Degrees of freedom = 5; Chi square = 6.838; Goodness of fit = 0.998; Probability = 0.233; N = 524)*

As regards to the perception of *collective effectiveness* (i.e. the effectiveness of the organization in bringing about social change), we see that social ties influence this perception differentially in the two processes. For members of the Bern Declaration, this perception was partly shaped when they first came into contact with the opportunity for mobilization. This was not the case for the recruitment of the WWF members. It is again apparent how the weaker impact of interpersonal contact in the structural connection process impinges upon the definition of individual perceptions. In short, recruiters play a much less significant role in the organization with high public visibility.[14] The perception of collective effectiveness for WWF participants was developed, at least in part, during their prior embeddedness in interpersonal networks.

Finally, in both processes the perception of the ability of political authorities to solve problems pertaining to development aid (in the case of the Bern Declaration) and the environment (in the case of the WWF) is influenced by the interactions between prospective participants and their recruiters, who induced them to be more optimistic as to the role of the authorities in solving this kind of problem. The only perception that is apparently not shaped by social relations is personal availability. One explanation for this may be that social ties do not shape this perception, which directly relates to real personal constraints.

TABLE 2.2. *Direct and total effects of networks on individual perceptions and differential participation in the Bern Declaration and the WWF (standardized solutions)*

	Bern Declaration*					WWF**				
	Socialization by formal networks	Socialization by informal networks	Recruited by formal networks	Recruited by informal networks (activist)	Interest	Socialization by formal networks	Socialization by informal networks	Recruited by formal networks	Recruited by informal networks (activist)	Interest
Direct effects										
Interest in the issue	0.08	0.27	0.07	0.11	—	0.10	−0.08	0.04	0.02	—
Individual effectiveness	−0.01	0.07	0.03	0.17	0.16	−0.01	0.10	0.07	0.07	0.18
Collective effectiveness	0.06	0.06	−0.09	−0.05	0.18	0.00	−0.07	0.01	−0.02	0.12
Ability of political authorities	−0.02	0.04	0.01	−0.09	0.09	0.05	0.02	0.05	−0.07	0.12
Subjective availability	−0.02	−0.02	0.01	−0.03	0.05	0.02	−0.01	0.06	0.05	0.01
Intensity of participation	0.14	0.08	0.02	0.31	0.06	0.10	0.08	−0.05	0.23	0.17
Total effects										
Intensity of participation	0.15	0.13	0.03	0.35	0.12	0.12	0.08	−0.01	0.26	0.23

*Degrees of freedom = 5; Chi square = 6.809; Goodness of fit = 0.998; $P = 0.235$; $N = 559$.
**Degrees of freedom = 5; Chi square = 6.838; Goodness of fit = 0.998; $P = 0.233$; $N = 524$.

The second hypothesis regarding the decision-shaping function of networks is also supported by the LISREL analysis. First, social networks impinge upon the *interest* in the political issue. This finding confirms Kim and Bearman's (1997) and other scholars' assertions concerning the construction of interest (e.g. Marwell and Oliver 1993). Interest is a constructed perception which is not given. However, the important point here is that interest in a political issue strongly affects the definition of the other perceptions included in this participation model (see last column in Table 2.2, and also Figs 2.1 and 2.2). Political interest shapes the perception of individual effectiveness, of collective effectiveness, and of the ability of political authorities to bring about social change. These three types of perception are thus directly shaped by social networks, but also indirectly via the impact of interest in the issue. Thus, the decision-shaping function of social networks manifests itself in different ways.

Besides illustrating the two hypotheses regarding the decision-shaping function of networks, the LISREL analysis underscores another finding, which should be stressed if we are to gain proper understanding of the mechanisms driving individual participation in social movements and the role of social ties in the process. This concerns the extent to which social networks and individual effectiveness are interwoven. As Figs 2.1 and 2.2 show, of the set of perceptions included in the model, individual effectiveness is the best predictor of the intensity of participation.[15] This perception is strongly shaped by social ties, directly but also indirectly via two factors: interest in the political issue and perception of the organization's effectiveness. On the one hand, as we have just seen interest in the political issue is profoundly shaped by social interactions in both participation processes. This preference in its turn affects the entire set of perceptions of the model (except for subjective availability), but more strongly influences the effectiveness of involvement (individual and collective). Thus, as said, individual effectiveness is influenced indirectly by social ties via interest in the political issue. On the other hand, the perception of collective effectiveness is directly shaped by networks, but more weakly so than interest in the political issue and individual effectiveness. By contrast, this perception, which in its turn strongly influences individual effectiveness (see Figs 2.1 and 2.2), is closely determined by interest in the political issue. Once again, individual effectiveness is indirectly shaped by networks via the definition of collective effectiveness. This finding illustrates how the impact of social ties on individuals' perceptions manifests itself in different ways. Moreover, it shows that there is a privileged path (highlighted with bold arrows in Figs 2.1 and 2.2) leading to strong participation in social movements. Of all perceptions, individual effectiveness is the factor in the decision process that most closely influences the level of participation in both the Bern Declaration and the WWF. Prospective members with a strong feeling that if they engage in protest, their participation will serve at least to a certain extent to bring about social change and will actualize their potential for mobilization at the highest level of involvement. Individual effectiveness is also one of the perceptions of the model that is most influenced by social networks, directly but also indirectly via interest in the political issue and the perception of the organization's effectiveness. This last result highlights the close interweaving between social ties and individual effectiveness. In other words, it stresses the interconnectedness of relational factors and human agency, and demonstrates that both structuralist and rationalist accounts are indispensable to an explanation of individual participation.

CONCLUSIONS

Social networks matter, but they do so by performing various functions in the process of individual participation. They intervene in at least three different ways. First, they intervene in the socialization and construction of identities. In this function, networks yield structures of meaning that enable individuals to create (or to solidify) identities and to establish cultural proximity with a specific political contention, usually in the long run. Here networks create an initial disposition to participate by developing specific meaning structures. As we have seen, only social networks culturally close to a given protest issue are able to form this individual potential for participation. Close embeddedness in such relational structures tends to push prospective members to the highest level of participation. Second, networks intervene before prospective members join a social movement organization by providing those culturally sensitive to the issue with an opportunity to participate. Here networks structurally connect potential participants to a social movement organization. For this function of networks in particular, the structure of meanings arising from the relations between recruiters and recruits affects the intensity of participation. Trust, which is so important for entry into the public space (either through conventional action or through protest), is a key concept in the explanation of why certain types of social ties are more important than others for individual participation. Social ties provide individuals with specific meaning structures which significantly affect their perceptions of participation in social movement organizations. In this respect, close friends (especially in the case of organizations without salient public visibility), and participants already involved in the organization at the highest level of participation, are better able to provide prospective members with trust than other types of ties. Finally, networks intervene when people decide to join a movement organization. They influence the definition of individual perceptions which enable potential participants to decide on their involvement and its intensity. Again, networks as envelopes of meanings impinge upon the meanings of the action, which in turn affect individual participation.

Survey data provide empirical support for the theoretical definition of these three functions of networks in the participation process. As said, quantitative methods and data are not the most convenient basis for empirical assessment of these three functions of social networks, especially the decision-making one. Qualitative data would have shed clearer light on how social interactions provide

individuals with structures of meaning that help them to define individual perceptions and preferences. Moreover, qualitative data allow scholars to take serious
account of the notion of time, in that the definition of individual perceptions does
not take place once and for all but is a continuous process occurring in the ebbs
and flows of social interactions. Nevertheless, although the data set used here is
not fully convenient and certainly underestimates the weight of social ties in the
definition of preferences, it confirms that networks play an important role in this
phase of the participation process.

Social networks indeed matter, but the way in which they influence individual
participation varies according to the nature of participation processes. Here I have
compared two processes of individual participation which differ according to their
degree of visibility in the public space. As I hypothesized, the degree of public visibility affects the participation process and impinges upon the intervention of
social networks in this process. It especially influences the structural-connection
function of social ties. Whilst this function is crucial in the less visible organization, it plays a less important role in the highly visible one. For highly visible organizations such as the WWF, other channels can structurally bridge prospective
members with the opportunity for mobilization. The media play an important
role in this respect. In other words, the process of structurally bridging potential
participants to an opportunity for mobilization manifests itself in different ways
in highly visible organizations, which is not the case of organizations with low
public visibility. Whilst the nature of the organization causes variation in the participation process, other characteristics of mobilization processes give rise to variation in individual participation and in the role of networks. As said, the nature of
the political regimes in which political protest takes place and the type of social
movement activity in which prospective members engage should also shape the
participation process. In the future, scholars working in this area of research
should multiply empirical assessment of participation processes by highlighting
variations among them. This would help scholars to avoid the universalistic view
of social processes and achieve better understanding of the mechanisms that
underlie these processes (Tilly 1995a–d).

The specification of networks in the process of individual participation put
forward in this paper has also sought to avoid a universalistic and disembodied
view of social phenomena. Moreover, it should also help to avoid a catch-all view
of social ties in this process. More specifically, showing how social networks
intervene in the process of individual participation increases our knowledge of
collective action by shedding light on its mechanisms and dynamics. It enables us
to integrate the structural and rationalist perspectives so often seen as antithetical,
and it brings meanings and culture back into our micro-models of collective
action. The latter undertaking is possible once we consider social networks as phenomenological realities rather than treating them in instrumental terms (White
1992). Networks are important not only because they provide individuals with an
environment that facilitates recruitment to social movements but also because they

are envelopes of meanings able to create a structure of meanings about the future commitment of individuals. This conception of networks allows serious account to be taken of the concept of human agency—that is, individual freedom—in the participation process whereby individuals make sense and incorporate in their self their multiple and concrete interactions with others by giving free rein to their own creativity.

NOTES

1. The solidarity movement covers a wide range of organizations active in four issue fields: development aid, immigration and asylum, human rights, and antiracism. One of its peculiarities is the fact that people mobilize on behalf of others. For an extensive discussion of this movement see Passy (1998) and Giugni and Passy (2001).
2. The organization is fairly active in lobbying state representatives, as well as local and national administrations.
3. A simple but significant indication of the public visibility of the WWF is provided by a survey showing that the organization logo is the most widely known in Switzerland after Coca-Cola's (interview with a staff member of the Swiss section of the WWF).
4. The sample of members of the Bern Declaration comprised 646 respondents who returned a structured questionnaire sent to 1200 members of the organization. Subjects were selected at random in each of the two linguistic regions of Switzerland (German-speaking and French-speaking). I applied the same research design to the WWF survey, with one exception: given the small percentage of activists in the WWF as compared to the large number of members who simply give financial support to the organization, I inflated the number of activists. The WWF sample comprised of 670 members.
5. For example, the findings on the role of social and cultural characteristics and of social networks in the process of individual participation are consistent with these studies.
6. For example, he found that the variation in responses was rather low for factual information (year of joining a trade union); 46% of the trade unionists gave the same reply when they were interviewed twice, and in 25% of cases there was a variation of one year in their replies. He found similar results for attitudes (attitude towards trade unions): 92% of the trade unionists gave consistent answers between surveys conducted at different times.
7. For exceptions see Oliver (1984), McAdam (1988*a,b*), Kriesi (1993), Barkan *et al.* (1995), and Klandermans (1997).
8. About 11% of the members of the Bern Declaration and only 4% of the members of the WWF were not embedded in social networks (formal or informal) before joining the organization. See Appendix A for measures of covariates and Appendix B for descriptive statistics.
9. On cultural frames see Snow *et al.* (1986), Gamson (1992*a,b*, 1995), Snow and Benford (1992), and Tarrow (1992).
10. The formal networks closest in cultural and ideological characteristics that help socialize potential participants in the solidarity movement are new social movement

organizations and churches. On the one hand, because the solidarity movement belongs to the new social movements family, that is they mobilize along the same cultural cleavage (Kriesi *et al.* 1995), this movement family is well suited to socializing prospective members of the solidarity movement. On the other hand, historically many solidarity organizations have been born from Christian groups and they convey the notion of solidarity (Passy 1998). The culturally closest networks in socializing potential participants of the ecology movement are new social movement organizations, environmental parties, and student and youth organizations. Youth and students groups are particularly important for ecologist organizations which organize holiday camps for young people (e.g. the WWF). Many of those organizations increase young peoples' awareness of ecological issues and send them to holiday camps to clean rivers, beaches and so forth.

11. About 59% of the Bern Declaration members and 49% of the WWF members were connected to the organization through social ties.
12. Only 5% of the WWF members and 23% of the Bern Declaration members were structurally connected to the organization by formal networks.
13. To keep the models readable, Figs 2.1 and 2.2 show only statistically significant coefficients. LISREL models were run with AMOS software.
14. This statement finds further support when we compare the total effect of this factor (recruitment by informal networks) on both processes of participation (see Table 2.2).
15. The perception of individual availability seemingly plays a different role in each participation process. In fact, this indicator is not similarly measured in each process, so I cannot risk interpretation of this finding. Probably the variation between the two processes is due to the measurement of this perception.

APPENDIX A: OPERATIONALIZATION OF VARIABLES

Intensity of Participation (dependent variable)

A question was asked that covered the range of activities carried out in the Bern Declaration (Table 2.3) and the WWF (Table 2.4): (1) paying membership fees, (2) subscribing to the annual fund raising, (3) participating in campaigns, (4) attending the annual meeting, (5) helping with the organization of campaigns on a regular basis, (6) being a member of working groups, and (7) being a member of the central or local committees. The first two activities only involve financial contributions to the organization, the next two involve active participation on an irregular basis, and the last three call for active and regular participation. The variable has three categories:

(a) Subscribers: activities 1, 2, or both;
(b) Adherents: activities 3 or 4 but not more, regardless of whether they also engage in activities 1 or 2;
(c) Activists: activities 5, 6, 7, regardless of whether they also engage in one or more of the other activities.

Social Networks

Socialization

- Formal networks. Question: 'In the following list, are there organizations or movements to which you have belonged in the past?' List of types of organizations. For the Bern Declaration, networks close to the movement are identified by religious and new social movements. For the WWF, networks close to the movement are identified as youth and students groups, as well as new social movement organizations. The latter include the following thematic areas: ecology, antinuclear, development aid, human rights, political asylum and immigration, antiracism, peace, women, gay and lesbian.
- Informal networks. Question: 'Are your friends or acquaintances engaged/ interested in Third-World questions?' Ordinal variable of increasing level of engagement/interest.

Structural connection

- Formal networks. Question: 'Can you say how you came into contact with the Bern Declaration for the first time? Was it through … [list of potential recruiters]?' From this list I selected formal networks, that is, recruitment through churches and organizations for the Bern Declaration, and through firms ('the company where I work (or worked)') and organizations for the WWF.
- Informal networks. Question: 'Were there one or more persons you knew personally before you joined the organization (relative, friend, acquaintance), who were members and who encouraged you to join the organization?' I further specified the relation between recruiters and recruits according to two criteria:

  - (a) The nature of the relationship: strong acquired ties (close friends), strong ascriptive ties (relatives), weak ties (acquaintances, colleagues, neighbours);
  - (b) The level of involvement of recruiters in the organization (subscribers, adherents, activists).

Individual-level Variables

Perceptions

- Individual effectiveness. Question: 'How do you evaluate the contribution of your engagement in the organization (the Bern Declaration or the WWF)?' Ordinal variable of increasing effectiveness.
- Collective effectiveness. Question: 'Do you think that the action of the Bern Declaration is effective in ameliorating the situation of Third-World countries?' and 'Do you think that the action of the WWF is effective in

ameliorating the situation of the environment?' Ordinal variable of increasing effectiveness.

- Ability of authorities to bring about social change. Question: 'Here is a list of authorities, organizations, and citizen groups that worry about (or should worry about) the situation in Third-World countries. Can you indicate to what extent these authorities, organizations, and citizen groups are, in your view, able to ameliorate the situation of Third-World countries?' The same question was put to members of the WWF in regard to environmental protection. I first created two intermediate dummy variables, one by aggregating respondents who thought that the authorities (national or international) were either totally able or quite able to ameliorate the situation, the other by aggregating respondents who thought that citizen organizations were able or quite able to do so. I then created the dummy to be used in the analyses by combining these two intermediate variables. The latter equalled one when respondents thought that the authorities were unable to ameliorate the situation, while citizens organizations were able to do so.
- Subjective availability. This was the only variable that measured differently in both surveys. Question for members of the Bern Declaration: 'Of the following reasons, which are the ones that explain why you sometimes do not take part or, more exactly, that you do not take part to a greater extent?' Ordinal variable of increasing agreement with the reasons listed. I selected from the list the following reason: 'my available time is limited.' Question for members of the WWF 'Getting involved in a movement organization could be a time consuming activity. What is your perception of your time spent by being engaged in the WWF?' Ordinal variable of decreasing subjective availability.
- Interest in the issue. Question: 'What role do Third-World questions have in your life?' 'What role do environmental protection questions have in your life? Ordinal variable of increasing importance.

APPENDIX B: DESCRIPTIVE STATISTICS OF VARIABLES

TABLE 2.3. *The Bern Declaration survey*

Variable	Type	Minimum	Maximum	Mean	Standard deviation
Dependent variable					
Intensity of participation	Ordinal	1	3	1.34	0.62
Social networks variables					
Socialization					
Formal networks close to the movement	Ordinal	0	2	0.54	0.60
Other formal networks	Ordinal	0	7	0.52	0.98
Informal networks	Ordinal	1	4	2.51	0.90
Structural connection					
Organization (formal networks)	Dummy	0	1	0.35	0.48
Organization member (informal networks)	Dummy	0	1	0.36	0.48
Activist	Dummy	0	1	0.18	0.38
Adherent	Dummy	0	1	0.05	0.22
Subscriber	Dummy	0	1	0.13	0.34
Strong acquired ties	Dummy	0	1	0.14	0.35
Strong ascriptive ties	Dummy	0	1	0.06	0.24
Weak ties	Dummy	0	1	0.17	0.37
Individual-level variables					
Perceptions					
Interest in the issue	Ordinal	1	5	3.36	0.87
Individual effectiveness	Ordinal	1	5	2.71	1.12
Collective effectiveness	Ordinal	1	5	4.00	0.92
Ability of political authorities	Dummy	0	1	0.47	0.50
Subjective availability	Ordinal	1	5	1.87	1.17

TABLE 2.4. *The WWF survey*

Variable	Type	Minimum	Maximum	Mean	Standard deviation
Dependent variable					
Intensity of participation	Ordinal	1	3	1.93	0.90
Social networks variables					
Socialization					
Formal networks close to the movement	Ordinal	0	2	0.73	0.78
Other formal networks	Ordinal	0	7	1.79	1.18
Informal networks	Ordinal	1	4	2.85	1.73
Structural connection					
Organization (formal networks)	Dummy	0	1	0.09	0.32
Organization member (informal networks)	Dummy	0	1	0.34	0.47

TABLE 2.4. *Contd.*

Variable	Type	Minimum	Maximum	Mean	Standard deviation
Activist	Dummy	0	1	0.15	0.36
Adherent	Dummy	0	1	0.04	0.19
Subscriber	Dummy	0	1	0.20	0.40
Strong acquired ties	Dummy	0	1	0.15	0.35
Strong ascriptive ties	Dummy	0	1	0.16	0.37
Weak ties	Dummy	0	1	0.10	0.30
Individual-level variables					
Perceptions					
Interest in the issue	Ordinal	1	5	4.17	0.78
Individual effectiveness	Ordinal	1	5	3.31	1.15
Collective effectiveness	Ordinal	1	5	4.02	0.79
Ability of political authorities	Dummy	0	1	0.35	0.48
Subjective availability	Ordinal	1	5	2.73	1.28

3

Movement Development and Organizational Networks: The Role of 'Single Members' in the German Nazi Party, 1925–30

Helmut Anheier

INTRODUCTION

This chapter examines a critical aspect in the sociological analysis of social and political movements: the role that activists play in the initial organizational development and consolidation of those movements. Specifically, it looks at the impact and characteristics of movement entrepreneurs in the National Socialist Party in Germany (NSDAP) between its reestablishment in 1925 and its first major electoral breakthrough in September 1930. The results point up the crucial importance of these movement entrepreneurs during the party's early development as an organization. The analysis shows that activists embedded in the organizational networks of the right wing nationalist milieu were also those most likely to establish local party organizations. In the aggregate, their activities created the wider organizational infrastructure that the movement needed for its rapid expansion of membership after 1930.

As we shall see, the early Nazi activists were not isolated individuals; rather, they were typically part of an extended organizational network of the nationalist-militarist right wing of German politics and society. This fragmented and highly politicized 'movement industry' was largely a product of the crisis-fraught post-war years when militias of disbanded and regrouped army units (*Freikorps*) challenged the legitimacy of the new political order. By the early 1920s, however, the *Freikorps* and related associations had grown more isolated from the emerging

I would like to thank the (former) directors of the Berlin Document Center (BDC), Drs David Marwell and Dieter Krüger, for giving me access to party records, personnel files and other relevant BDC holdings in order to gather sociological data on early party members. I am indebted to Professor Dr Neidhardt, former Director of the Wissenschaftszentrum Berlin, for initiating and encouraging much of this research. I also thank Drs Vortkamp and Ohlemacher for their assistance in data collection and preparation. The Fritz Thyssen Foundation and the Wissenschaftszentrum Berlin supported this research.

democratic political system. Nonetheless, they continued to influence the national-militarist right wing of Germany's political spectrum and formed what Linz (1978) identified as the 'disloyal opposition' that plagued the Weimar Republic throughout its troubled existence.

While the Nazi movement may have been more marginal to mainstream national politics during the mid to late 1920s than at any other time during the Weimar Republic, the activists of the Nazi movement at local levels certainly were not. Throughout the period, Nazi activists continued to establish local party chapters and build networks between Party organizations and mainstream civil society. As we shall see, for these movement entrepreneurs the key to mobilization was the combination of three factors: their strong embeddedness in the networks of the Republic's disloyal opposition; a blanket rejection of the political mainstream (the '*System*' in Nazi terminology); and their 'normal', basically middle-class, profile (at least in a statistical sense).

Unlikely Success?

Judging from its rapid ascent to power, National Socialism was one of the most 'successful' social and political movements of the twentieth century. Initially fuelled by the political instability and social upheavals of the early postwar years, Nazi activists failed miserably in their first attempt to gain political power, the so-called 'Munich Beer Hall' uprising in November 1923. The Party was consequently declared illegal, and with Hitler imprisoned, the Nazi movement was left in some disarray. Many movement activists, however, went underground to establish clandestine organizations and local 'cells' or joined other right-wing groups, only to regroup soon after the NSDAP was refounded in February 1925 upon Hitler's release.

At first, the reestablished NSDAP, like the old one, represented a fringe element of Weimar politics. Ill-financed, marked by internal divisions and seemingly out of touch with the country's consolidating, though fragile, political culture, the NSDAP had nonetheless managed to position itself as the central institution of right-wing nationalism by the late 1920s. By September 1930, the NSDAP had grown into one of Germany's key political forces, gaining 18.3 per cent of all votes cast in the national elections, and in the following three years it managed to occupy and control all essential centres of political power. Thus, in just eight years, a movement located on Germany's political and geographical fringes came to rule the country and encountered little resistance against the establishment of a one-party dictatorship.

How was the phenomenal success of National Socialism possible? This is one of the most crucial questions in the study of Nazism, one that continues to occupy social scientists and historians alike.[1] Yet this chapter will approach this question neither primarily against the historical background in which the movement developed (Sternwell 1994; Lacquer 1996) nor from the perspective of political science

(Lespius 1978; Kater 1983), nor as a micro-sociology of Nazism (Kater 1985; Falter 1991; Mühlberger 1995; Brustein 1996). Rather, the chapter's primary concern is to examine the initial expansion and institutionalization of National Socialism as a network of local party chapters, organizations, and related associations.

We approach the organizational development of the party from the perspective of local party activists: the social movement entrepreneurs. The overall hypothesis is that these activists created and combined an important part of the organizational infrastructure upon which the NSDAP at first gradually, and later ever more force-fully, expanded into more and more areas of the country's social and political life. They did so by linking the organizational core of the Nazi movement, once estab-lished, to culturally and socially diverse networks of constituencies, often tran-scending narrow ideological, religious, and economic boundaries. By the late 1920s, the movement had managed to gain broad support that increasingly cut across the class structure and the political spectrum of Weimar Germany.

MOVEMENT DEVELOPMENT

By 1930, the NSDAP had become a '*Volkspartei*,' or people's party (Falter 1991; Brustein 1996) that would feed on complex voter structures and shifts among the electorate. Linz (1976, 1978) suggests that the underlying reasons for the success of national socialism lay neither in the divisive Weimar party system nor in volatile voter behaviour alone; they also resided in the 'prepolitical field' of local milieus, associations, networks, and movements.[2] Indeed, three patterns in the development of the Nazi movement underscore the importance of the prepolitical field: its development as a membership organization rather than as a political party based on votes; the re-formation of an organized disloyal opposition during the 1925 presidential elections; and the amplifying impact of strongholds earlier for later successes at the ballot box.

First, from a social movement perspective, it is important to bear in mind that the electoral success of the NSDAP came after its organizational development. By 1928, the Party had created a highly differentiated and comprehensive organiza-tion: a structure perhaps rather too complex and too large for the size of its mem-bership or the votes gained in elections. Next to the party apparatus itself, and the parallel structures of the SA and the SS, numerous other organizations existed. This structure emphasized individual participation in numerous local events, meet-ings, and quasi-military activities. The NSDAP as an organization was thus able to link the level of national and regional party politics to the everyday lives of party members and thereby managed to create a sense of community or '*Gemeinschaft*.'

Thus, for the first five years, the reestablished NSDAP was primarily a mem-bership organization that emphasized active member participation rather than voter maximization. With about 100,000 party members in some 1400 chapters and numerous party organizations, the party achieved just 2.6 per cent or 1 million of the valid votes cast in the national elections of May 1928. The relationship between membership numbers and voter numbers changed dramatically with the September 1930 vote: while membership increased by about one third to 129,000, the Party obtained a surprising 7.9 million (18.3 per cent) of the valid votes cast— an eight-fold increase on 1928. Consequently, the NSDAP, now the second largest party, suddenly changed from being a membership organization into a People's Party able to attract votes from population segments outside the narrower reservoir of nationalist voters.

Second, irrespective of the explosive growth of Nazism after 1930, the NSDAP was able to build significantly wherever right-wing nationalist constituencies had been either established or reinforced in the middle and late 1920s. The 1925 presidential election (the so-called 'Hindenburg election', thus named after the conservative candidate who won the election and later, in 1933, entrusted the chancellorship to Hitler) offers the clearest example of this phenomenon. This election brought with it the first successful gathering of the nationalist and antirepublican groups hostile to any form of democratic government. Falter (1991: 360–3) has found a very close correlation ($r = 0.82$) between the election results in 1925 and the results of the national elections between 1930 and 1933. In fact, two-thirds (67.2 per cent) of the variance in the NSDAP votes in the national elections between 1930 and 1933 are explained by the results for the Hindenburg election. In electoral districts where Hindenburg, the conservative candidate, had achieved above average proportions of votes cast, whether in Catholic and Protestant areas, whether in urban or rural, working-class or middle-class ones, the NSDAP was later significantly more successful than it was in the 'Hindenburg Diaspora' (Falter 1991: 360). Thus, the NSDAP made the most gains in areas that had early on experienced a broad-based formation of nationalist groups. The early organization of the 'disloyal opposition' proved vital for the Party's later successes.

Finally, a third pattern shows that Nazi strongholds, that is constituencies in which the NSDAP received above average support in elections prior to 1930, are the best predictors of electoral success in the national elections of the early 1930s (Falter 1991: 355, 439). In the September election of 1930, the variable 'Nazi stronghold' alone accounts for 38 per cent of the explained variance in the NSDAP portion of the votes cast, and for 28 per cent of the explained variance in votes gained. In other words, during the critical breakthrough phase of the NSDAP, the party grew stronger in local areas where it had already established itself as a serious political factor.

Resource Mobilization

The close connection between embeddedness in local milieus and early organizational development appears to have been critical for later movement success. For McAdam *et al.* (1988*a*,*b*); Neidhardt and Rucht (1993); della Porta and Diani (1999) and other theorists in the field, social movements are highly contingent phenomena. Their success not only requires the right cognitive-cultural framing structures to make movement concerns understandable and attractive to potential constituencies,[3] they also need sufficient grounding in local milieus, in particular existing organizations and networks, if they are to mobilize resources.[4] The 'active ingredient' in the Nazi movement, as in others, was the role of movement entrepreneurs, and the way in which they brought different organizations and their respective constituencies into the movement and also formed new ones.

Preexisting social structures facilitate the development of social movements because these are able to emerge along given institutional and organizational paths (Cattacin and Passy 1993; Neidhardt and Rucht 1993). These advantages spring from lower information and transaction costs for resources, and from the use of existing trust relations which facilitate member recruitment and retention. As regards National Socialism, the key social structure for its growth was the nationalist camp of right-wing politics, a complex and conflict-ridden organizational field. This arena constituted a veritable movement industry, and included a very broad spectrum of groups, ranging from small political parties and patriotic clubs, interest groups and youth groups to soldiers of fortune and paramilitary factions.

Converting and recruiting local leaders, and infiltrating their organizations, were the key to mobilizing the larger reservoirs of potential members.[5] On examining the population of a rural district in Bavaria, Zofka (1986: 60) showed that the Nazi movement was able to win over local villages by directly recruiting and mobilizing local opinion leaders. Koshar (1987) obtained similar findings for the city of Marburg, Hesse, between 1923 and 1933, where NSDAP members held offices and prominent positions in local and regional associations through which the party directly and indirectly gained access to other social, political, and economic spheres.

The cognitive-cultural framing and structural mediation of social movements, however, is only one of the preconditions for success. Of central importance is the presence of activists or movement entrepreneurs (McAdam *et al.* 1988: 716; Schmitt-Beck 1990; Thornton 1999). These are the 'active component' that facilitates framing and structural mediation. Like economic entrepreneurs, social movement entrepreneurs combine and coordinate 'inputs' for some gain. In contrast to economic entrepreneurs, their prime motivation is not to maximize monetary profits; rather, their aim is to maximize the number of members, and the movement's influence and success (see Anheier 2001*a* on the Nazi case). To this end, political entrepreneurs mobilize resources, connect groups, forge alliances, and seek to capitalize on political opportunities within and outside the movement (Gerhards and Rucht 1992). In fact, National Socialism initially offered a broad and open field for activists and volunteers that both invited and required participation. Besides the actual party organization, such opportunities were especially available in SA and SS formations, as well as in the various special party organizations: the National Socialist Student's Association, the NS Welfare Association,

the NS Women's Association, the German Cultural Association, the various professional NS-related associations for teachers, motorists, etc., and in numerous
other interest groups and branches.

The rest of this chapter will take a closer look at how movement entrepreneurs
contributed to the organizational development of National Socialism. Specifically,
it will explore the spread of the Nazi Party in organizational terms through the network of organizational relationships that provided the material as well as the arena
for movement entrepreneurs to operate.

THE SOCIOLOGY OF SINGLE MEMBERS

The empirical point of departure is the member registry for the city of Munich[6]
maintained by the NSDAP Party Secretary at headquarters from 1925 to 1930.
Together with nearly 5000 Munich-based members (Anheier and Neidhardt 1998),
the Registry includes a separate category of so-called 'single members,' that is,
NSDAP members who resided in localities with neither a party chapter (*Ortsgruppe*)
nor a district organization (*Gau*). In other words, single members lived in areas
outside the organizational-geographic reach of the Nazi Party.

Between 1925 and 1930, these single members were administered directly from
party headquarters in Munich. Once local chapters or district party organizations
had been founded, or once single members had moved to areas with party organizations in place, they were transferred to their relevant units. Did the 652 single
members listed in the Munich Registry include a pool of movement entrepreneurs
instrumental in mediating Nazi concerns in local milieus? And who connected the
movement to other organizations? Who were the single members? What is their
profile in terms of social background and organizational embeddedness? How
many were involved in the founding of local party chapters?

The single member registry includes 652 entries, with 12 names listed twice.[7]
Table 3.1 shows monthly changes in the number of single members from the beginning of 1925 to the end of 1930 (see also Fig. 3.1). The table highlights that the number of single members increased substantially after the reestablishment of the party
in February 1925. In 1927, the number of single members reached around 400—the
highest number—and dropped to almost 200 in the following years (Fig. 3.1). In
1930, the remaining single members were transferred either to regional party organizations (*Gaue*), local units, or the foreign office of the NSDAP.

In the first half of 1925, 151 single members joined the party, and another 186
followed until the start of 1926 (Table 3.1);[8] their numbers fell off thereafter.
Altogether, over half (58.4 per cent) of all new entries had occurred by the first
half of 1926: that is, within fewer than 16 months after the reestablishment of the
Party in February 1925. This means that in purely quantitative terms single members as a membership category were most important during the initial reorganization phase of the NSDAP between 1925 and 1927. Simultaneously, other changes

TABLE 3.1. *Development of single member status, NSDAP, 1925–30*

Biannual periods	Additions		Reductions		Balance period change	Number of members
	Entries	In-transfers	Exits	Out-transfers		
1925 I	151	0	1	5	145	145
1925 II	186	4	7	56	127	272
1926 I	105	32	23	67	47	319
1926 II	75	32	68	47	−8	311
1927 I	63	35	30	13	55	366
1927 II	49	72	31	62	28	394
1928 I	40	20	85	95	−120	274
1928 II	11	8	31	25	−37	237
1929 I	10	0	25	13	−28	209
1929 II	19	0	14	2	3	212
1930 I	28	0	18	0	10	222
1930 II	20	0	11	0	9	231
Total	757	203	344	385	Mean: 19	Mean: 266

to the stock of single members became more important. The number of those leaving the party rose but fluctuated considerably, typically reflecting the political performance of the party. For example, in the aftermath of the lost 1928 National Election, 85 single members left the party, which was a decline of 21 per cent in a total membership of 394 at that time.

Entries and exits were not the only factors that affected membership numbers. Transfers to other chapters are of special interest for our purposes. Such transfers usually happened when a group of Nazi supporters established a local party chapter. Transfers to local chapters also took place when single members moved to towns where local party organizations already existed. For example, single members moving to Berlin, Nuremberg, or Munich would be transferred to existing local chapters in those cities. On the whole, few such transfers occurred initially, but then the number rose until the middle of 1926: first to 56, then to 67, fluctuating thereafter (Table 3.1). By the end of 1927 there were only 13 transfers, but by one year later there were 95. After 1928, the number of transfers fell sharply as party chapters became more numerous across the country, and as regional party organizations assumed more responsibility for recruiting single members.[9]

Creating Local Party Chapters

According to the source material available in the BDC holdings, 45 (6.9 per cent) single members were instrumental in founding chapters. This percentage rises to 7.5 if those living outside Germany are excluded. It is highly likely that 137 further cases (21 per cent) were closely linked with the establishment of local

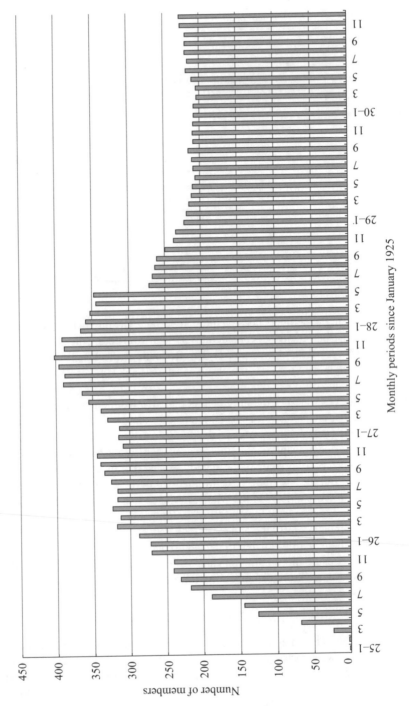

Fig. 3.1. *NSDAP single members, 1925–30*

chapters, although no explicit statement to that effect is to be found in the files available. This is typically the case if the Registry includes a handwritten note stating, for example, '*transferred to hometown chapter on 1 December 1926*,' and if it is clear from information in the files that a particular single member played a central role in the creation of the new local party chapter.[10] While about a quarter (27.9 per cent) of the single members can be either explicitly or implicitly connected with the establishment of local chapters, there is no indication of such activities in the sources available at the BDC for 351 (or 53 per cent) of them. The BDC files contain no other information in this respect for another 118 members (16.1 per cent).

The single members made up a very small proportion of overall party membership. At the end of 1925, the NSDAP had 27,117 members; a number that grew to 49,523 in 1926 and to 72,590 in 1927, and again increased in 1928 to 108,717. By the time of the September election of 1930 the party had around 130,000 members (Schäfer 1957: 11). At no time between 1925 and 1930 did single members represent more than 1 per cent of total membership. In 1925, when the number of single members reached its peak, their share of the total NSDAP membership amounted to 1 per cent. It dropped to 0.7 per cent in 1926, to 0.5 per cent in 1927, and had fallen to below 0.2 per cent by 1930 (Table 3.2).

Nonetheless, the relatively small number of single members made a comparatively large contribution to the organizational development of National Socialism. According to the *Partei-Statistik* (*Party Statistics*) (NSDAP 1935: 175), 607 local chapters existed in Germany by the end of 1925. By 1928 the number had risen to 1378, and by 1930 to 4964 chapters.[11] Table 3.2 shows that, according to the Party Statistics, at least 771 chapters were founded in the period between the end of 1925 and the end of 1928. This period coincides with the phase when single

TABLE 3.2. *Single members and NSDAP party chapters, 1925–30*

	1925	1928	1930
Members	27,117	108,717	130,000
Single members	272	209	231
Single members as percentage of all members	1.00	0.19	0.18
Party chapters	607	1,378	4,964
New party chapters (net)	771	3,586	
Transfers of single members to party chapters	370	15	
Foundings of party chapters by single members	179	3	
Single members foundings in percentage of all new foundings	23.22	0.1	
Single members foundings in percentage of total foundings	3.45	12.99	3.67

members were most frequently transferred to newly established chapters (see Table 3.1). In fact, about 95 per cent of all transfers to local chapters took place during those years.[12]

Table 3.2 suggests that the founding activities of single members may have accounted for nearly a quarter (23.6 per cent) of the 771 additional new chapters created between the end of 1925 and the end of 1928.[13] Relative to the 1378 chapters that existed in 1928, the share of single member creations still amounts to 13.2 per cent. In other words, although single members represented less than 1 per cent of total membership after 1925, they contributed significantly to the party's establishment. After 1928, the importance of the single members for the organizational development of the party sharply declined—a process that mirrored the growing role of the regional party structures. As the party became more of an 'organization' and less a 'movement,' its continued expansion may have had less need for this particular type of local activist. The results in Table 3.2 support the contention by McAdam *et al.* (1988*a*, *b*) that political entrepreneurs play a central role in the initial building phase of movements, and then lose their critical importance in the course of institutionalization (see also della Porta and Diani 1999: 151–2).

Spatial Distribution of Single Members

The Nazi movement belonged to a period when mobilization efforts had to rely on direct contacts (speeches, meetings, and rallies), postal communication, and travel by public transport, in particular trains and trams. Figure 3.2 shows the relative concentration of single members in Bavaria, especially around Munich, for the period 1925–6.[14] This pattern corresponds to the prevailing centrality of the Munich NSDAP in southern Bavarian and Swabian communities until the late 1920s, and it explains the almost radial pattern of single member locations in this part of the country during 1925–6. Otherwise, Fig. 3.2 shows concentrations in the spatial distribution of single members in Franconia north of Nuremberg, where the NSDAP already had taken hold and had been present in the form of clandestine organizations during its prohibition between 1923 and 1925 (Pridham 1973). There are lighter concentrations in central Germany (Halle-Merseburg, Saxony), the Swabian Alps, and in parts of West Prussia. Single members are relatively less frequent in those parts of the country in which regional party organizations were already in place by 1925. This is most markedly the case of Baden, an area in Southwest Germany adjoining the French border, where the Party achieved early successes in establishing local and regional organizations (Grill 1983). In such cases, the regional party organization (*Gau*), rather than Munich headquarters, would administer any single members residing in the area. Hence, we may expect the spatial concentration of single members in the vicinity of existing Nazi strongholds, as shown for Munich in Fig. 3.2, to be replicated in areas like Baden as well.

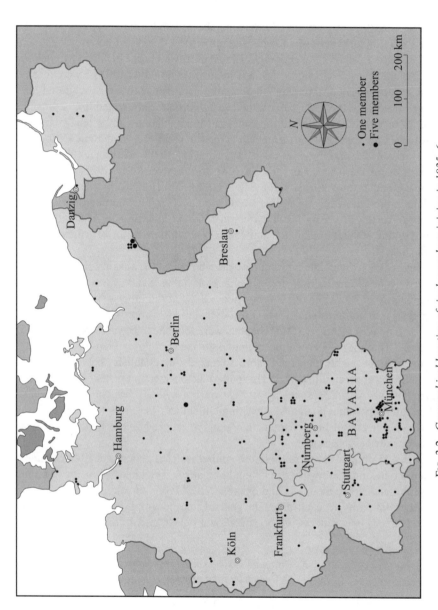

FIG. 3.2. *Geographical location of single members joining in 1925–6*

The relative concentration of single members in and around areas in which the Party was already established increased rather than decreased between 1925 and 1930. Table 3.3 shows the geographical distance from home towns to Munich for each of the respective cohorts.[15] Single members who joined in 1925 were located at a greater distance from Munich and were geographically more scattered than later cohorts: for the 1925 cohort, the average distance amounted to 262 km; for the 1926 cohort the distance diminished to 156 km, and to 126 km one year later. Moreover, the spread of the distances decreased: while the standard deviation was 251 km in 1925, and the inter-quartile range 344 km, these distances shrink considerably for the next cohorts (Table 3.3). In other words, in 1925, the average single member took at least half a day to get to Munich (250 km there and back), while in the following years most single members could commute by train from their home town to party headquarters in Munich: in 1926 half of them already lived within 100 km of that city, and 75 per cent within a radius of around 200 km from it.

Figure 3.3 presents the approximate distribution of the various chapters established by the 1925 cohort of single members. It shows that they were founded predominantly in Bavaria, with a very wide scatter in the other areas. This pattern provides important insights, if we consider that in 1925 approximately 17 per cent (104) of all the existing NSDAP chapters were founded in Bavaria (NSDAP 1935: 175–6). This means that single members located in closer vicinity to NSDAP strongholds probably managed more frequently to establish chapters than did those living at greater distances. This pattern is reflected in the historical development of the NSDAP, especially in Bavaria but also in Franconia. Vice-versa, the spatial distribution suggests that single members were less frequent *and* less successful in establishing chapters in regions where the NSDAP had an altogether lower presence at that time.

The single members were therefore neither isolated geographically nor cut off from the institutional world of National Socialism. The opposite seems to be the case, in fact: single members and existing NSDAP organizations were located in relative proximity to each other. In general, the geographical pattern of single member locations reflects the organizational development and consolidation of

TABLE 3.3. *Distances of single member locations from Munich by cohort (in km)*

Cohort	Average distances		Distance variations		Cases (N)
	Mean	Median	Standard deviation	Interquartile range	
1925	262	156	251	344	322
1926	156	105	176	117	165
1927–30	126	78	150	103	108

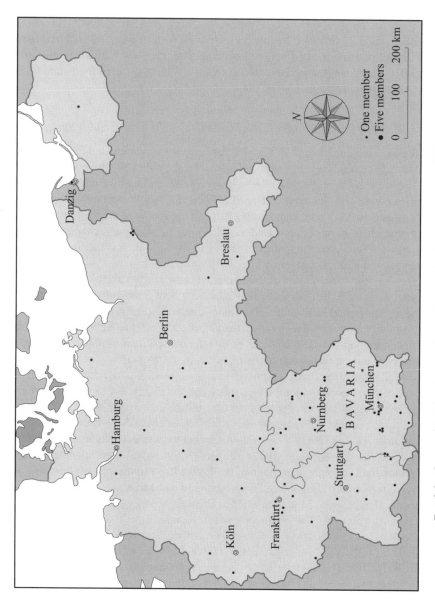

FIG. 3.3. *Geographical location of chapter founded by single members in 1925*

the party administration. Indeed, the Party's organizational growth via single member activities followed mainly an interstitial pattern whereby chapters were established in areas located between existing structures and networks; only at a second level did single member activities gain new, 'virgin' territory distant from established party strongholds.[16]

Broad-based, Middle Class Movement of the Lost Generation

Of the 652 single members, 70 (or 10.7 per cent) were women, and 53 (or 8.1 per cent) lived abroad. The youngest member was 16, the oldest 82. The average age of the single members at the time of admission was 32, and half were 28 or younger. Every second single member was aged between 23 and 38, and only 10 per cent were older than 50. This means that the single members were primarily part of the 'lost generation' born between 1890 and 1900 whose youth was characterized by nationalist fervour, the calamities of the First World War, and the long years of economic and political instability after 1918.

How does the social profile of single members differ from that of the population in general? Table 3.4 shows that single members were represented in all branches of the economy; and in 16 of the 26 economic branches, the relative percentage of single members never differs by more than 2 per cent points from the relative share for the entire population.[17] This means that the occupational profile of the single members in almost two-thirds of the branches is approximately similar to that for the overall population. Table 3.4 also indicates the relative under-representation of the agricultural sectors among single members. Relatively few (8 per cent) of all single members—compared to 22.4 per cent for the entire population—worked in agriculture. The under-representation of this sector coincides with an overrepresentation of retailing: every fourth single member worked in this branch, compared to one in 12 for the entire population. The retail business was especially hard-hit by the prolonged economic depression of the 1920s. In particular, small shopkeepers proved a fertile recruiting ground for both right wing and antisemitic movements generally (Falter 1991; Mühlberger 1995; Brustein 1996).

Three main results flow from comparison based on the 1925 census between the social class composition of the single members and NSDAP membership as a whole, as well as the entire population (Table 3.5).[18] First, single members were more likely to be economically active than the population at large (36 vs. 13 per cent without stated occupation), but somewhat less so than the Nazi membership overall (13 vs. 5 per cent without stated occupation). Second, single members, like the Nazi party generally, were primarily a middle class movement: two out of three single members were of lower middle and middle class status compared to one in every two Nazi members, and 42 per cent for the economically active population. Correspondingly, the share of lower class members was much smaller among single members than among both the party and the population. Third, the share of members

TABLE 3.4. *Economic branch distribution for single members and population, 1925*

Branch	Single members		BDC sample[a] (%)	Population[b]	
	N	%		%	N
Unemployed, no occupation	71	12.0	9.7	9.1	5662.444
Agriculture	48	8.1	16.3	22.4	13,994.133
Forestry, fishing	8	1.4	0.6	0.6	379.123
Industrial manufacturing	47	7.9	10.4	1.8	1104.523
Mining	5	0.8	0.9	3.8	2367.932
Quarrying	4	0.7	0.8	2.3	1464.750
Iron and metal	15	2.5	5.1	5.1	3178.157
Machine building	9	1.5	2.0	4.2	2601.690
Electronics	4	0.7	1.2	1.6	979.291
Chemical industry	3	0.5	0.1	1.2	760.822
Textile industry	3	0.5	0.5	3.0	1849.912
Paper and printing	5	0.8	0.8	1.5	958.594
Wood processing	8	1.4	4.1	3.0	1884.336
Food and tobacco	17	2.9	4.8	3.8	2350.944
Clothing and fashion	14	2.4	2.6	3.9	2418.491
Building and construction	25	4.2	4.7	6.2	3861.839
Retail and wholesale	149	25.2	19.4	8.3	5172.689
Insurance	3	0.5	0.2	0.4	221.889
Transport	27	4.6	4.5	6.7	4162.546
Gastronomy	12	2.0	2.0	1.6	1004.817
Administration and military	31	5.2	2.5	2.8	1762.148
Education and religion	24	4.1	1.5	1.5	931.579
Judiciary and interest assoc.	1	0.2	0.3	0.3	198.424
Art and culture, journalism	14	2.4	1.2	0.4	263.138
Health and social welfare	37	6.3	2.7	1.5	964.705
Domestic services	8	1.4	1.1	3.1	1910.257
Total	592	0.0	100.0	100.0	62,409.173
		592	N = 40,801		

[a]Brustein–Falter membership sample, 1925–33.
[b]Potentially economically active population and their family members.

of upper middle and upper class status was four times higher among single members than among the population, and twice the share of the overall Nazi membership.

Thus, the data suggest a social profile of the single members with four main characteristics: they were predominantly men of the 'lost generation,' from middle-class backgrounds, residing in cities or small towns rather than rural communities, and represented in all economic branches and occupations. In sum, their social profile, with the exception of the greater representation of upper middle and upper class members, was no different from what sociologists have identified for the Nazi membership as a whole (Kater 1971, 1983; Mühlberger 1991, 1995; Fischer 1995; Brustein 1996).

TABLE 3.5. *Social class characteristics of single members,
total membership, and population*

	Single members, 1925–30		Membership, 1925–32[a]		Population[b]	
	%	% excluding 'No occupation'	%	% excluding 'No occupation'	%	% excluding 'No occupation'
Lower class	21	24	40	42	35	55
Lower middle and middle class	54	62	50	53	27	42
Upper middle and upper class	12	14	5	5	2	3
No occupation	13	—	5	—	36	—
Total	100	100	100	100	100	100
N	562		39,812		62,410,619	

[a] Brustein (1996: 20; Fig. 1.3).
[b] Potentially economically active population and their family members; 1925 census.

Single Members and Organizational Memberships

What does the social profile mean for organizational development? Was it aided by the political and organizational embeddedness of single members? Clearly, given that they were of higher status than average members and the population at large, single members most likely had more economic and status-related resources available to them. Yet what were the 'paths' and the social networks through which single members facilitated and effected the spread of National Socialism?[19] To answer this question, we must go beyond the standard membership profile and look at the organizational memberships of single members.

With the exception of a few cases, single-members were neither well-known nor prominent. The case of Dr Emil Kirdorf is an exception. After a personal meeting with Hitler, the well-known 80-year-old industrialist joined the party as a single member in August 1927 and helped establish first contacts between Hitler and leading business circles in the Rhine-Ruhr area (Deuterlein 1982: 285–6). More typical are the cases of single members who devoted their work to the party, sometimes at great personal cost and often without receiving adequate financial or political rewards, let alone greater social mobility. In general, we find a broad spectrum of personal experiences among single members, ranging from the unspectacular to the tragic, and from the idealistic to the careerist, yet they all involve the use as well as the creation of organizations and networks in the development of the Nazi Party.

Living in the small town of Solln in Hesse, and born in Munich, Hermine G. is an example of the passive, unspectacular single member. As a war-widow she joined the party in November 1919 after a random encounter with Hitler, and she did so again on 4 April 1925 shortly after the reestablishment of the party. In the following years, she supported the establishment of the Solln Party chapter and founded local chapters for the NS women's association in Solln and surrounding towns.

The tragic-idealist case is exemplified by Egon L. from the Western town of Trier, who, after a brief military career (1889–96), worked as a merchant in the book trade. As company leader on the Western front in the First World War, he was severely wounded and left disfigured, with some of his facial features destroyed. A tireless activist, he soon became a district leader of the *Deutschvölkische Schutz-und Trutzbund* (see below) and also joined the Nazi Party. In 1924, he was sentenced to six months imprisonment by the English military command in Cologne for his political activities, and was subsequently deported to Bavaria. After moving to Pasing near Munich, he worked as a manager in a publishing house, yet soon became unemployed. He then worked as a freelance writer for the nationalist press but became increasingly impoverished. With the Party declared illegal, he ran the local chapter of the '*Völkische Block*' (People's Block) as well as various covert organizations like the '*Trambahngesellschaft Pasing*' (Trolley Society Pasing) or the '*Siebener-Ausschuß*' (Committee of Seven). All of these were soon merged into the Party after its reestablishment in 1925, and he founded the local Party chapter in Pasing. His party activities did not enable Egon L. to overcome his personal and financial difficulties: he later lived on public welfare payments and only after 1933 found part-time work in the National Propaganda section of the Party.

The case of Max K., a butcher from a small town in upper Bavaria, exemplifies the careerist type of single-member. After being active in the *Freikorps* movements following the First World War, he joined the party as a single-member in the Würzburg area in August 1926 and moved to Munich a year later, where he joined the local SS. He was involved in building the Gern-Neuhaus chapter on the city's outskirts, and managed to become a paid Party employee as a driver. After 1933, Max K. rapidly moved up the SS hierarchy and received high Nazi awards like the *Totenkopfring* or the *Julleuchter*. He died at the age of 67 in May 1944.

Alfred D., born in 1894 in Franconia, joined the air force as a volunteer in the First World War, and returned in 1918 to join the *Freikorps Oberland* and the *Einwohnerwehr*, spending the next two years fighting in various uprisings in Bavaria, the Ruhr, and Silesia. He joined the Nazi Party in 1923 and took part in the Beer Hall Putsch by organizing weapons and ammunition from dissolved *Einwohnerwehr* groups around Munich. With the Party declared illegal, he joined a clandestine organization, the *Grossdeutsche Volksgemeinschaft*, and founded local chapters in several places. After the reestablishment of the Nazi Party, Alfred D. rejoined it, together with some of his comrades from the *Gruppe Oberland* and the *Grossdeutsche Volksgemeinschaft*. In 1926, he moved to Auerbach in North-East Bavaria to establish a Nazi chapter and to practise as an architect, but he was soon driven away by political opponents who called for his business to be boycotted. In search of new opportunities, he resettled in the town of Lauf in Franconia, and in 1928 became one of the cofounders of the local Nazi chapter there, in addition to running the local SA chapter. His career was cut short in 1935 when, after being prosecuted for false testimony and homosexual conduct, he was sent to prison and expelled from the Party.

For about 75 per cent of the single members, the available sources at the BDC indicate no membership of any organization other than the Nazi Party.[20] About 12 per cent were members of one other organization, and 13 per cent of two or more. The great majority (350) of the 397 organizational memberships held by single members were in related right-wing nationalist groups. Some of these memberships were in organizations of Germany's immediate political past, like the *Freikorps* and their successor organizations, others were in covert organizations founded while the Nazi party was illegal, and yet others were in general nationalist-militarist groups. The organizations not related to the right-wing nationalist camp included professional associations, students associations, sports clubs, art clubs, consumer associations, the German Alpine Society, the Red Cross, the German Medical Association, walking clubs, or the local volunteer fire brigade.

The primary locus of membership in the right-wing nationalist camp suggests that the movement may have 'fed' on preexisting membership structures and clusters which the single members helped channel into the reestablished Nazi party. Ties with other 'bourgeois' associations of Germany's civil society may well have enhanced this process by extending the reach of single members for recruitment purposes. Indeed, as Table 3.6 shows, the number of organizational memberships was closely related to the successful establishment of local party chapters. Whereas only 2 per cent of single members for which no other organizational membership can be reported created party chapters, 12 per cent of those with one membership, and 37 per cent of those with four or more, did so. That the relationship is not linear suggests that other elements may have played a role as well, such as personal networks (Anheier and Ohlemacher 1996), socio-demographic factors (Anheier 2001*a*), local party politics (Lepsius 1978; Anheier and Neidhardt 1998) and religious factors (Hamilton 1982).

Several right wing nationalist organizations were prominent among single members. These organizations display a complicated and often inter-related 'genealogy,' suggesting both cross-cutting membership clusters and continuity in

TABLE 3.6. *Memberships and chapter creations by single members*

	Number of Memberships (%)				
	None	One	Two	Three	Four and more
No founder	98	88	78	87	63
Explicit founder	2	12	22	13	37
	100	100	100	100	100
Total *N*	475	81	40	23	32

the membership cadre. Most of these associations were initially founded between 1918 and 1923, with their roots in the *Freikorps* movement following the First World War, and many were declared illegal at one time or another. They ranged, however, from terrorist groups like the *Organization Consul* to paramilitary groups like *Bund Bayern und Reich*, and from the antisemitic *Thule Gesellschaft* to politically motivated veterans associations like the *Stahlhelm*. Specifically:[21]

1. *Alldeutscher Verband* (All-German Association; one membership among single members): founded in 1891 as a nationalist membership organization advocating procolonial and militarist policies, it represents in many ways the oldest and most influential part of the organized right wing in Germany until the early 1920s. The *Verband* encouraged the formation of *Freikorps* after the First World War in order to oppose downsizing of the Army and the decommissioning of arms. It was instrumental in the founding of the *Völkischer Schutz- und Trutzbund* and other antisemitic groups, and maintained links with terrorist organizations like *Organisation Consul*. By the mid 1920s, the *Verband* had lost its influence as other groups gained importance, in particular the NSDAP.

2. *Völkischer Schutz- und Trutzbund* (National Protection and Defence Association; 13 memberships among single members): founded in 1919 as a parallel, allied organization to the *Alldeutscher Verband*, this was an antisemitic, nationalist membership association fighting against the 'Jewish Republic' and using the print media for massive propaganda campaigns. The organization was aided by leading right wing publishers, some of whom had close links with the *Münchner Beobachter*, the predecessor of what became the major Nazi newspaper a few years later (Anheier *et al.* 1998). The *Bund*, with over 110,000 members in 1920, was declared illegal in 1922 and its members were largely absorbed by the NSDAP, together with the network of clandestine organizations that it had created between 1923 and 1925.

3. *Völkischer Block* (People's Block; 12 members) and *Groß-deutsche Volksgemeinschaft* (Greater German People Community; 13 members): these were membership associations serving as covert organizations while the NSDAP remained illegal. As such they became 'holding pools' for members from a variety of other nationalist fringe groups as well, in particular the successor organizations to the *Freikorps* movement like *Bund Oberland* and the *Einwohnerwehr*. Members of the *Völkischer Block* and the *Groß-deutsche Volksgemeinschaft* were rapidly reabsorbed by the NSDAP after 1925.

4. *Bund Oberland* (11 members): the successor organization to the *Freikorps Oberland*, a militia group that fought in various uprisings in Munich (1919), the Ruhr (1920), and Silesia (1921). When the *Freikorps Oberland* was dissolved in the summer of 1921, the *Bund Oberland* was established in Munich, and included members from other *Freikorps* as well. Close cooperation with NSDAP (and SA) began, and a joint organization was

formed in 1923: the *Deutsche Kampfbund*, which participated in the Beer Hall Putsch later that year. Declared illegal, the *Bund* reconstituted itself as a covert organization, the *Deutscher Schützen- und Wanderverband* (German Shooting and Walking Association). In May 1925, many members joined the *Stahlhelm* (see below), and merged with the NSDAP in 1926.

5. *Freikorp Epp* (10 members) and *Gruppe/Freikorps Ehrhard* (one): two *Freikorps* founded in 1919 who exerted significant influence among the German military and in the nationalist political camp. Many of their members became instrumental in the founding and operating of successor organizations like the *Einwohnerwehr* (Epp group), *Organisation Concul, Wikingbund*, but also the early SA. Single members were part of several other Freikorps: Hinterpommern, Franken, Halle, Landshut, Baltikum, Bamberg, Anhalt, or Oberland.

6. *Einwohnerwehr* (People's Defence; 10 members): units were created throughout Germany between 1919 and 1921 as local, antisocialist militias to forestall political uprisings and protect the population against looting. With large weapons depots under their command, the *Einwohnerwehr* in Bavaria alone had about 300,000 members organized on military lines and with an organizational structure that was later adopted by the Nazi Party. The *Einwohnerwehr* units were dissolved in the summer of 1921, and the *Bund Bayern und Reich* became their main successor organization. However, many local units in Bavaria persisted and soon reestablished themselves as SA chapters within the NSDAP in 1922–3 and, again, after 1925.

7. *Bund Bayern und Reich* (Union Bavaria and Empire; seven members): established in 1922 from a secret society, the *Organisation Pittinger*, which had assumed protection of the secret weapons depots of the *Einwohnerwehr* in Bavaria, by the end of 1923, the *Bund* had become the largest paramilit-ary, pro-Monarchist formation in Bavaria and included affiliated organiza-tions like *Reichskriegsflagge* (Imperial War Flag; three members) and the *Vaterländischen Vereine München*. After 1923, both groups moved close to the NSDAP, and the remainder of the *Bund* began to cooperate closely with other monarchist organizations, merging with the Bavarian *Stahlhelm* section in 1929.

8. *Stahlhelm* (Steel Helmet, seven members): founded in 1918 as a veteran asso-ciation for soldiers returning from the First World War, this was a country-wide organization with close ties to the *Freikorps* and *Einwohnerwehren*. Antirepublican and antidemocratic, it pursued nationalist policies and began to exclude Jews from membership as early as 1924. By 1928, *Stahlhelm* had over 300,000 members and included a youth wing, a women's branch and a social welfare fund. Throughout the 1920s *Stahlhelm* was an umbrella organ-ization for nationalist veterans associations ideologically close to the Nazi Party and the SA. After 1933, *Stahlhelm* became a *de facto* part of the SA, and fully merged with it in 1935.

The following three organizations were located on the extreme nationalist right. They seem to have figured less among single members in 1925–7, but they had constituted the secretive-elitist core of Nazism as an emerging movement industry since 1918:

9. The *Thule Gesellschaft* was a lodge-like formation founded in 1918, and banned a year later, that served as the initial organizational core of the emerging Nazi movement. Its 1500 members included many future Nazi leaders, and some of the rituals of the future Party were first introduced at the secretive meetings of the Thule Society.

10. *Organisation Consul* was a clandestine organization that emerged in 1920 from the *Freikorps Ehrhard*. Its 5000 members were administered under the cover of the 'Bavarian Wood Processing Society' and engaged in terrorist activities, murdering several high-ranking politicians, including Finance Minister Erzberger in 1921 and Foreign Minister Rathenau in 1922. After 1923, it dissolved but its members joined the *Bund Wiking* and the *Neudeutscher Bund*.

11. *Bund Wiking* (Viking Union; one member) was founded in 1923 by leading members of the *Freikorps Ehrhard* and the *Organisation Consul* as an extreme antirepublican, paramilitary unit. Its goal was the overthrow of the Weimar Republic and the establishment of a new political-nationalist system under its own leadership. Members worked closely with the NSDAP until the organization was declared illegal in 1926, when they joined the Party, SA and SS and other units such as *Stahlhelm*.

This complex movement industry provided the terrain on which the Nazi Party could develop, and on which movement entrepreneurs among the single members could operate. Unfortunately, data limitations and missing information do not allow complete reconstruction of the network that linked individuals and organizations. Nonetheless, for 99 of the single members with at least one membership, it has been possible to identify 83 named organizations in which they held memberships. The organization-member network so constructed among 99 members and 83 organizations includes 218 ties, and has a density of 3 per cent.

This Boolean network was subjected to a hierarchical cluster analysis (HICLUS)[22] to detect structural patterns in memberships. Of course, given data limitations, the results can only be taken as illustrative of the larger network structure that may have existed among single members. Moreover, the network structures are not based on contemporaneous links but are a summary picture of associational affiliation among single members in the period under consideration.

Seven of the major right wing nationalist organizations emerge as the building blocks of the associational infrastructure created by the single members (Fig. 3.4). They are typically linked through common genealogy and activities (not shown), but also through membership clusters of links among people as well as organizations. The seven organizations link a total of 61 single members directly or

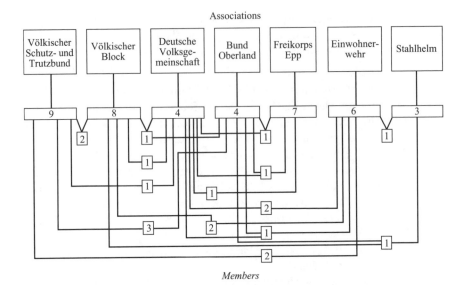

FIG. 3.4. *Network structure of memberships in right-wing associations*
among single members

Note: Number indicates number of members in set or superset.

indirectly. For example, the *Völkischer Schutz- und Trutzbund* has nine members among the single members who belonged to this organization alone. At the same time, there are an additional eight members who are linked both to this organization as well as others: two links with the *Völkischer Block*, one with the *Deutsche Volksgemeinschaft*, three with the *Bund Oberland*, and two with the *Einwohnerwehr*. In addition, *Völkischer Block* and *Deutsche Volksgemeinschaft* are linked by one member, *Deutsche Volksgemeinschaft* and *Einwohnerwehr* by two, as are *Einwohnerwehr* and *Völkischer Block*.

The end result is a complex membership structure among members and organizations—the associational infrastructure of National Socialism. What single members did was to use and combine elements of this system into the emerging Nazi party. Where this system was in place, single members were more likely to succeed in establishing party chapters, where it was absent or less developed, they were less successful, as Table 3.5 suggested. It was embeddedness in preexisting social networks that facilitated both their success in establishing local chapters, and in the aggregate, the organizational development of the party.

CONCLUSIONS

The purpose of the foregoing analysis of the single members of the NSDAP has been to furnish better understanding of the organizational development of

National Socialism in the second half of the 1920s. Of course, it is not claimed that the activities of the single members represented *the* key to success of the NSDAP. Nonetheless, they contributed in important ways which are non-obvious and easily overlooked. The data indicate that a relatively small number of national socialists, that is, those most tightly integrated in the ethnic-national arenas, managed to establish a considerable proportion of the newly created chapters and consequently consolidated the institutional base and strength of Nazism at local levels.

The importance of single members was most pronounced when the party was reestablished; and in a certain sense single members as a membership category lost their relevance as the NSDAP emerged as an organization. Single members helped the party gain interstitial terrain between strongholds by gaining footholds in communities that hitherto had had no local party organization in place. The relative geographical proximity of single members to existing party institutions highlights the central role played by organizational and personal networks in establishing the party. The organizational embeddedness of single members in the organizational infrastructure of Nazism aided their efforts to establish and anchor the party locally. The networks among nationalist, right wing organizations, and among members and Nazi sympathizers, provided the foundation on which the large and ambitious party organization was constructed. These early efforts helped make the Hindenburg effect and other path-dependent successes possible.

The results have two implications for the sociology of social movements. First, they underscore the importance of local activists and political entrepreneurs for the spread and development not only of participatory and democratic movements but also of authoritarian ones displaying a strong professional and hierarchical structure and a charismatic leadership. Second, the findings enable us to qualify traditional 'mass society' types of arguments about the marginality of activists of radical movements (Kornhauser 1959; Lipset 1960; Linz 1967). The local Nazi entrepreneurs did not arise from a social vacuum; rather, they originated mostly from already existing organizations and social networks. Single members who established chapters were part of complex associational infrastructures that included wide sections of the antirepublican and antidemocratic movement industry and only had sporadic ties to organizations operating in other sectors of society. It was not the social isolation of NSDAP members *per se*, but their embeddedness in an organizational field consisting of 'concentric' rather than 'cross-cutting' circles (Simmel 1955), and, initially, largely secluded from the rest of German civil society, that provided favourable opportunity structures for mobilizing protest into the institutional paths of the NSDAP. The success of social movements like National Socialism is therefore facilitated by the way and the extent to which their core organizations (here, the NSDAP) succeed in building links to related causes, organizations and networks.

NOTES

1. Research on the development of National Socialism has moved away from universal and monocausal explanations. Following the seminal work by Linz (1976, 1978), research increasingly emphasizes the complex and conditional causal structure behind the success of National Socialism. As Falter suggests (1991: 364–74), none of the main explanations proposed can account on its own for the breakthrough of national socialism: neither the *class-based attempt* by Lipset (1960), which argues that the initial success of the NSDAP was due to the electoral support provided by a disenchanted, impoverished middle class, nor Bendix's (1952) idea of the *radicalization of 'apolitical' population segments* which sees the decisive success factor in the mobilization of non-voters and the young, nor Burnham's (1972) *theory of political–religious nationalism*, in which the middle-class Protestant block carried the deciding vote for the NSDAP.
2. Likewise, Hamilton (1982) and Falter (1991: 374–5) propose that factors such as local social structures and cultures should be included in explanations of the rise of Nazism.
3. See Anheier *et al.* (1998) for the Munich NSDAP and the Nazi press; and Goffman (1974) and Snow *et al.* (1986) more generally on the importance of framing.
4. See Anheier and Ohlemacher (1996), and Anheier and Neidhardt (1998) for the Nazi movement; Diani (1995), and della Porta and Diani (1999), more generally.
5. Hitler's strategy to refuse formal cooperation with any of the right-wing national associations opened the way for the infiltration and undermining of these organizations and clubs that rapidly gave the NSDAP a central organizational and political position in the extreme right camp (Gill 1983).
6. The *Berlin Document Center*, where the Registry is located, houses extensive personal records and related documents confiscated by US troops in 1945. Among these records is a nearly complete set of NSDAP membership cards, the membership records of the SA, the SS, and the Race and Settlement Main Office records, the National Culture Chamber, the NS Federation of Teachers, correspondence from major party organizations, and the records of the Supreme Party Court (Browder 1972; Kater 1977). The Munich Registry, arranged by city district and consisting of 22 bound ledgers, includes handwritten entries stating name, address, age, occupation, dates of joining and leaving the party, information on dues paid, and a separate set of comments (Anheier and Neidhardt 1998). Using membership number and date of birth as key identifiers, the various holdings of the BDC were searched for information on individual members and then collated into individual dossiers, yielding a systematic data set on their social and political profiles.
7. This deals with the single members who joined the party in a community without a chapter, then left, and subsequently rejoined the party as single members in another town.
8. In Table 1, entries (652 cases) and reentries (105 cases) are combined. Withdrawals (144 cases), reexits (9 cases), and expulsions (181 cases) are handled in the same manner.
9. Table 1 also shows that the number of transfers *from* other party organizations was essentially a phenomenon of the second and third year after the initial reestablishment. These transfers took place in two phases: approximately 47% of all transfers occurred between July 1925 and December 1926, and a further 41% in the 12 months from July 1927 until June 1928. Exits divide into distinct periods: one in the second half of 1926, when 21% of single members left the party, and the other in the first half of 1928 when there was

a drop of 22%. During 1926, two-thirds of the exits were due to party expulsions, probably in connection with the so-called '*Fürstenabfindung*', or the policy debate on treatment of aristocratic property which sparked heated internal disputes and cleavages within the NSDAP. Generally, we find that the reduction in membership through exits was mostly due to exclusion and 'purges' within the NSDAP, and resulted less from voluntary withdrawals by individual members, which indicates a relatively high level of commitment among single members to the party's cause and mission.

10. Single members established two chapters abroad, in the USA and Austria. These single members stayed in the central membership administration in Munich.

11. In comparison, two years after the takeover in 1935, the NSDAP had 21,283 chapters with nearly 2.5 million members (NSDAP 1935).

12. The chapters established by single members could not be dated with certainty in many cases. The assumption is that there is a connection between the date when the chapter was founded and the transfer of the single members from the Munich party headquarters.

13. Significant data problems suggest that the comparison should be treated with great caution, and that it serves to indicate the importance of single members in relative terms rather than absolute ones. The data problems stem from missing information about chapter closures and mergers, which are not recorded in the 1935 *Partei Statistik*. Consequently, the results should be interpreted as showing that the single member establishments constituted a certain percentage in the period from 1925 to 1928 of established chapters, because data on chapter closures and mergers could not be obtained.

14. Single members living abroad are not included in Fig. 3.2, nor are cases listed in the Registry for purely administrative reasons. For example, some applicants erroneously applied for membership to Munich headquarters directly, rather than through local chapters; such cases were treated as single members on a temporary basis until the party administration was able to clarify the matter with the local party chief.

15. Distances are air distances based on geographical latitude and longitude. Members residing abroad were excluded from these calculations.

16. Hedström (1994) and Hedström *et al.* (2000) also found substantial correlation between territorial proximity and organizational diffusion when examining the development of the Swedish unions and Social Democratic Party.

17. Population data are based on the 1925 census of professions and economic activities (Statistisches Reichsamt 1927).

18. The coding scheme follows the social class classification developed by Mühlberger (1991, 1995) and refined by Falter (1991) and Brustein (1996); see Brustein (1996: 185–7, Appendix A: 201–2, footnotes 69, 70, 73–4) for a fuller description of the coding procedure used.

19. One key factor often identified in the literature on the development of National Socialism, namely religious affiliation (Burnham 1972; Linz 1976; Hamilton 1982; Falter 1991), cannot be examined because of missing data in the source material.

20. The number of memberships held by single members was probably higher both among the right-wing movement industry and within organizations of civil society, in particular local associations and religious organizations. The empirical information presented in this section is therefore based on an under-count of actual memberships.

21. The summary descriptions of the various associations are based on extended treatment of Nazi-related groups and militias in *Münchner Stadtmuseum* (1993: 47–70; 83–96); see also Rudlof (1992).

22. HICLUS is a clustering programme developed by De Boek and Rosenberg (1988) and Van Mechelen *et al.* (1999). It is a two-way/two mode method for examining the structure of relationships between objects (here: organizations) and attributes (individual members) by looking for equivalence (i.e. placing objects/attributes with similar relationships in the same set) and hierarchy (i.e. detecting set-superset structures).

Part II

Interorganizational Networks

4

Networks in Opposition: Linking Organizations Through Activists in the Polish People's Republic

Maryjane Osa

INTRODUCTION

Equality can lead to despotism, Tocqueville repeatedly warns us. Under democracy, the tyranny of the majority is prevented through the exercise of press freedom and civil association (de Tocqueville 2000: 489–95). Where these freedoms are denied, dictatorship rests easily. In nondemocracies, individuals' isolation can be bridged when unexpected opportunities arise or when people make novel use of institutions; in rare cases, social associations form and become an instrument against oppression. This chapter examines how oppositional networks develop when deprived of the legal framework taken for granted in democratic states. As Tocqueville advised, overcoming isolation is the first step toward freedom. However, many missteps may be required before a challenge to dictatorship can succeed.

The consensus among social movement researchers working within the political process framework is that movement emergence depends on three broad factors: political opportunity, organizational networks, and cultural framing or other interpretative processes (McAdam 1999: viii). Many empirical studies confirm that these factors are associated with the incidence of social movements (Kitschelt 1986; Diani 1996; Rucht 1996; Klandermans 1997). However, the evidence is drawn primarily from studies of social movements in democratic states. In democracies, civil rights are constitutionally protected, the mass media is uncensored, and dissent is tolerated. However, in nondemocratic states, the political system is relatively closed, dissenters are persecuted, and the media is controlled. Will the political process model hold for these limiting cases?

Non-democratic systems include a variety of types: military dictatorships, monarchies, one-party states, and Leninist (or state socialist) regimes, to name a few. Yet, with the exception of traditional monarchies, they share an important characteristic: these societies lack a mechanism for regular, legitimate transfers of power sanctioned by those subject to the state. As a result, the basis of rule in nondemocracies always involves a much higher degree of coercion than that in democratic states. The Leninist regime is considered to be one of the most repressive nondemocratic states. Unlike bureaucratic authoritarian states which may have autonomous trade unions or competitive political parties, in a Leninist country, political authority is monopolized by the Communist Party; public information and economic planning are also under the Party's control.

The institutions of repression and the structure of the Leninist state place serious constraints on all three of the conditions associated with movement emergence. First, political opportunities are limited because the state does not permit institutionalized access to policy-makers, the media, and the courts. Second, the sphere of civic association is restricted to a narrow range of non-political organizations, and social activity is channelled into officially sanctioned organizations. Many forms of association are illegal. Third, policy debates are attenuated through government control of the media and adherence to the 'party line'. The public sphere is replaced by an 'official' one (Jowitt 1992: 287–9). Since dissenting views cannot be diffused through the mass media, cultural definitions of issues, actors and events cannot be openly contested (cf. Gamson 1988). Yet protest and mobilization do occur in even the most restrictive political environments. One of the ways in which challengers circumvent state power is through social networks.

In Leninist regimes, people rely on their network capital in situations where, in liberal democratic countries, the market or the government would supply resources. Because of 'the inherent rigidities and shortages of communist bureaucracies,' people are forced to turn to their networks for normal undertakings such as house-building (Sik and Wellman 1999: 225–32). The use of networks is necessary even to access corruption in the system. For example, one must know *which* official to approach with a bribe and what sort of payment is expected for the service desired. This type of information is only available from trusted members of one's social network.[1]

Social movement research has shown that networks can act as 'mobilizing structures' that facilitate waves of mobilization and the formation of social movements in democracies. In Leninist regimes, there should be an even stronger positive relationship between networks and mobilization because networks must substitute both for organizations and mass media. There are a number of ways in which networks can help overcome these obstacles to collective action. First, opposition networks provide channels through which uncensored information circulates. They circumvent the state censorship controls by passing along written materials and gossip. Networks structure the diffusion of information. Second, networks use social contacts for raising money, locating, and sharing the material resources necessary for mobilization. Third, as networks expand, the risks of illicit association become shared and the individual risk incurred in oppositional activity is reduced. Fourth, the sharing of risks, information, and material enhances social solidarity and increases the likelihood that a collective identity will emerge. Fifth, as networks expand and take on a more oppositional identity, they begin to substitute for a public sphere. New organizations articulate a variety of positions and pose alternative tactics for confronting the state. Interactions within the network form a context for micromobilization processes: frames and counter–frames are proposed, and adopted or rejected as the population of organizations grows or diminishes. In all these ways, social networks provide leverage to overcome the repressive capacity of the state and to provide the necessary foundation for mobilization by opposition groups.

East Europeanists have explained dissident movements in Poland, Hungary, and Czechoslovakia prior to 1989 as the result of a growing 'civil society' in the Leninist countries (Ost 1990; Bernhard 1993; Arato 2000). Their views are seemingly similar to my networks argument; nevertheless, there are substantial differences between the two approaches. I will sketch out three points of divergence.

Civil society proponents start from the premise that the East European dissidents' programme 'for the reconstruction for [sic] civil society was born in Poland in the mid- and late-1970s' (Arato 2000: 45). At that juncture, prominent East European intellectuals considered reform of the Leninist system impossible; they embraced instead the idea of an autonomous civil society as an alternative sphere for oppositional activity. Rather than struggling for political power, post-1976 activists advocated increasing independent social and cultural activities to thereby decrease the state's span of control over society. Scholars' civil society narratives focused mostly on organizations created by these dissidents, neglecting other groups that, although less politically acceptable, may have been active. By contrast, I start from the premise that the discourse of civil society was, above all, a political theory of the opposition. Using the (relentlessly empirical) methods of social structural analysis, I am able to draw a sharp distinction between the dissidents' political programme and the empirical reality of the oppositional network to which they contributed. I reject the premise that civil society was suddenly 'reconstituted' in 1976. Based on extensive data gathering, I have documented oppositional network development in Poland from the mid-1950s through the Solidarity period (Osa 2001, 2003).

Second, despite lengthy discussions about 'the concept of civil society,' there remains some confusion and diversity in how the concept is applied, for example, in studies of democratization (Seligman 1992). It is generally accepted that civil society is a 'sphere of social autonomy' between the public (state) realm and that of private life (Keane 1988; Habermas 1989). But the definition provides little guidance as to which social formations should be studied as the relevant part of 'civil society'. For example, under what conditions can churches be considered part of the private realm and when do they form part of civil society? A networks approach, alternatively, begins with the boundary specification problem (Laumann *et al.* 1983). At the outset, the network analyst working in the nominalist mode sets the network boundaries so that they are analytically relevant to the research problem. Guided by theory, the analyst specifies a decision rule for inclusion (of actors, relations, events) prior to data collection.

Finally, 'civil society' is treated as a dichotomous variable in most of the literature. Civil society is posited either as present/absent or weak/strong (Bernhard 1996). What marks the threshold for the civil society to act as a causal force? This issue is not addressed in the literature. The networks approach, on the other hand, focuses on network structure as an explanatory variable. Network theory states that differently structured networks will have different properties; thus, we can assume that some types of networks will be better than others for facilitating collective action (Laumann and Pappi 1976; Gould 1991). In other words, not all types of networks or 'civil societies' are well suited for mobilization. What network characteristics are likely to facilitate movement emergence? Why are some networks less vulnerable to repression than others? These are the questions that can be addressed by applying a networks analytic approach.

In this chapter, I will investigate six interorganizational networks comprised by 'civil society' groups. Three networks evolved during the late 1960s protest wave; three other networks included the formation of Solidarity. I analyse the internal evolution of 'civil society' by examining network changes over time. Correlating network structures and protest mobilization, I can suggest how differently configured networks may affect movement formation. A caveat: the empirical data presented here allow me to say something concrete about network development during two periods of oppositional mobilization. Political opportunity conditions and cultural contributions to movement formation are treated elsewhere (Osa and Corduneanu-Huci 2003; Osa 2003).

Data and Methods

Network data were collected for the years 1966–70 and 1976–81 in order to analyse the social structures that developed during two protest waves (see Fig. 4.1).[2] Contentions in the mid-1960s began with Church-state conflict in 1966, followed by student unrest in 1968 and labour strikes in 1970. The second wave started in 1976 with labour insurgency, then a pause, followed by the strikes in July and August 1980 that led to the formation of Solidarity. My primary concern is to identify and analyse the oppositional networks that developed during these confrontations with the regime. Secondarily, I will use the data to speculate on the relationship between oppositional network developments and protest cycles in nondemocracies. The limitations of the data do not allow me to make a causal argument regarding the latter relation.

The data set consists of membership information for a set of 'social influence associations,' organizations whose goals are directed towards changing or preserving social conditions, and not primarily towards fulfilling the recreational or affiliative needs of its members (Knoke and Wood 1981: 31). I defined the 'opposition domain' as the organization set that includes all known social influence associations unaffiliated with (or unsponsored by) the Communist party which engaged in public social action during a given period. Civil association was severely restricted in communist Poland, so there are relatively few groups in the

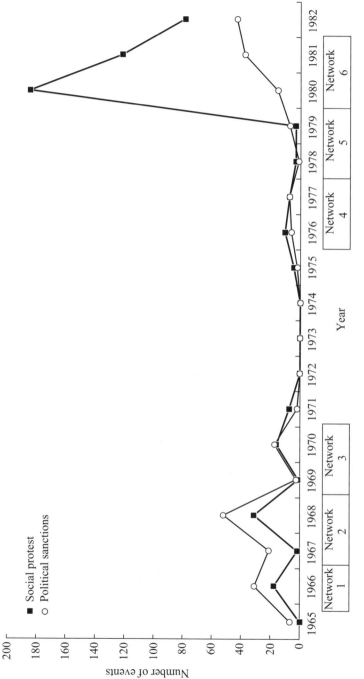

FIG. 4.1. Social protest and repression: 1965–82

data set.[3] Consequently, the opposition domain organization set is not a sample; it is the entire population. The set includes both formal and informal organizations. Although membership requirements were usually more stringent for the formal organizations, both types of groups held meetings, planned objectives, delegated tasks among the members, and worked towards specific, internally generated goals. I refer to all groups in the set as 'organizations' for convenience.

For this study, I used membership information to create six affiliation sets, or 'networks'. Networks 1–3 covered the mobilization period of the late 1960s; networks 4–6 were drawn for the late 1970s (see Fig. 4.1). Although I begin with two mode data (individuals, organizations), I focus only on the ties among organizations for practical and theoretical reasons. First, the large number of individuals in the data set ($N = 1720$) makes analysing the interpersonal networks unwieldy. In addition, each member is assumed to be tied to all others in the organization; there are no data on the directionality of intra-organizational ties. In other words, the membership data are not sufficiently fine-grained to capture the important contents (e.g. friendship, animosity, and rivalry) of interpersonal relations. Second, both political process and resource mobilization theories emphasize the importance of ties among organizations as conduits for the resource exchanges that underlie mobilization (Curtis and Zurcher 1973; Laumann *et al.* 1978; Killian 1984). Individuals with overlapping memberships form the connective tissue of the interorganizational network.[4] These data are also useful for analysing subgroup cohesion and the relational structure of the network.

The empirical analysis is organized with reference to four key concepts. First, each organization was coded according to its *social/ideology category*. Polish opposition organizations formed around a nucleus of individuals who shared either some social characteristic (e.g. youth, occupation) or ideological commitment (Catholicism, Marxism). The basis for group identity and solidarity is indicated by its social/ideological categorization. The purpose of this coding is to provide a qualitative indicator of 'groupness' which complements the structural indicators of the network analysis. It is a measure for what Charles Tilly and Harrison White refer to as 'catnets' (Tilly 1978: 62–4; Pharr 1990: 92–3; White 1992). Second, in my study, the variable *strength of ties* is used to evaluate subgroup cohesion. My operationalization of this concept diverges somewhat from the common usage because the data do not allow me to specify directionality of ties (Lin *et al.* 1981; Knoke 1990: 237–8). However, my data set does indicate how many members are jointly shared by any organizational pair. The strength of the tie, then, is conceived as the level of affiliation overlap: low (one or two members shared between the organizational pair), medium (three to four shared members) or high (five or more shared members). Third, for the purposes of this study, I distinguish between *cliques* and the less restrictive formulation, *subgroup*. A *clique* is defined as a maximally connected subgroup consisting of at least three nodes. Since diffusion is a major process underlying social mobilization, the *subgroup* definition I adopt does not require all possible ties between a set of points to be actual; rather, it is based on the idea of reachability: that contacts between all points can be made by going through intermediate points in the subgroup (Wasserman and Faust 1995: 257–8). Finally, in comparing networks, I use a measure of *network centralization* rather than *network density*. Comparisons of densities of different size networks are not valid because network density is limited by size. This is because the number of relations (ties) an agent (node) can sustain declines as the size of the network increases. However, centralization measures can be usefully compared. While network density describes 'the general level of cohesion in a graph; centralization describes the extent to which this cohesion is organized around particular focal points' (Scott 2000: 89). Mobilization is facilitated when the network is relatively centralized, and hard to sustain when it is not.

ISLANDS OF OPPOSITION: THE 1960s PROTEST 'WAVE'

Divide ut regnes. It is ironic that the Polish United Workers' Party (*Polska Zjednoczona Partia Robotnicza*—PZPR) would resort to this classical strategy to maintain social control. After all, the Leninist imperative to create socialism by transforming society underlaid the establishment of political institutions and policies in the Polish People's Republic during the 1950s (Seton-Watson 1950; Brzezinski 1967). Equality was to be established by eliminating private property, restricting access to higher education for the children of the intelligentsia, and collectivizing agriculture. The PZPR pursued these goals with a vengeance. And yet, class and regional distinctions never completely disappeared. By the 1960s, the regime had lost the battle in the countryside; private farming—not the state farms—was the major source of agricultural output. Intellectuals' offspring matriculated in the universities. Urban–rural antagonisms flourished. With the battle for ideological purity lost, the Party made use of society's resurgent 'bourgeois' tendencies to prevent the emergence of a cohesive social structure that could oppose its rule. Despite massive social protests in the 1960s, the Leninist regime successfully prevented coalition-building among oppositional groups. First, the authorities exploited social cleavages to 'divide and rule'; this prevented mobilization in one community from diffusing throughout the social system, to spark a true cycle of protest (Tarrow 1998*a,b*). Second, the state effectively 'contained' protest by increasing repression each time mobilization commenced.

Protest events were exceeded by the number of state sanctions from 1966 to 1970 (see Fig. 4.1). Each set of protests was mounted by a different community: church and state were in conflict in 1966, students demonstrated in 1968, and workers struck in 1970. In what follows, I describe the protests mounted by each sector in the 1960s pseudo-wave. Then I analyse the organizational development in this period. I conclude this section with some observations regarding the barriers to network expansion and social movement formation.

Protest Events: 1966–70

Culture was the battleground for church-state conflicts in 1966. At issue was the commemoration of an anniversary of political and religious significance. Traditionally, Poles trace their history as a people from 966 AD when Miesko I established the first Polish kingdom. Needing the political support of the Pope to oppose the encroaching Germans, King Miesko ordered his pagan subjects to convert to Roman Catholicism (Vlasto 1970: 115; Davies 1982: I, 61–76). Thus, the claim of political sovereignty was established simultaneously with 'Poland's baptism'. One thousand years later, Catholic religious leaders planned massive pilgrimages and outdoor ceremonies to commemorate the millennium of Catholicism in Poland. But the Communist government wanted to emphasize a thousand years of Polish statehood and ignore the historic (and nationalistic) religious connection.

Church-state conflict started in 1965 when, in the spirit of the Second Vatican Council and in preparation for the millennium, the Polish episcopate wrote an open letter to the German bishops inviting them to participate in the ceremonies. Poland's communist authorities expressed outrage that Polish bishops would engage in 'foreign policy' and act in a conciliatory manner towards Germans (Raina 1995: 33–6). PZPR officials used the overture for propaganda purposes and they did not allow the full text of the Episcopal letter to be published. By distorting the Polish bishops' message of forgiveness, the Party tried to stir up anti-German sentiments against the Church on the eve of the millennium.

Religious authorities had started preparations in 1957 with the 'Great Novena of the Millennium,' a programme of pastoral mobilization leading up to the 1966 celebration (Osa 1996). The Church defined the millennium in spiritual and national terms, stressing Roman Catholicism's contributions to Polish history and culture. The Leninist regime presented itself as the culmination of the long historical development of Polish statehood, which led inexorably to socialism. Polish communists avoided talking about the Russians. Spontaneous social protests came about when political authorities tried to impede the religious ceremonies; religious adherents and by-standers resisted state attempts to suppress the Catholic millennial activities.

Protest in 1966 was clothed sumptuously in symbols: pilgrimages turned into marches and demonstrations when police tried to block processions of the Black Madonna icon. Nationalist symbols such as the Polish eagle wearing a royal crown, the red and white of Polish sovereignty, yellow and white for the Pope, blue and white for the Blessed Mother—all were used in context to express demands for religious freedom and the right of cultural expression. During street demonstrations in Warsaw's Old City, protesters shouted, 'We demand freedom!' 'Down with the Communists!' 'We forgive you!' and 'Long live Cardinal Wyszyński!' (Raina 1994: 402). The authorities, party officials, and police, were targets of popular anger. But despite the tense situation, for example, in Warsaw during the Millennial celebrations, demonstrations never turned violent. As one participant noted, 'this was a group returning from the millennial ceremonies, people in whose ears had just run the words of the Primate (Cardinal Wyszyński) on love, peace, and forgiveness' (Raina 1991: 265).

State repression only strengthened the resolve of believers to honour the Black Madonna and celebrate the Millennium of Polish Catholicism in the manner prescribed by the Church hierarchy. Nevertheless, government propaganda was successful in preventing other opposition groups, notably those of the secular left, from protesting state harassment of the Church. The official press portrayed the bishops as anachronistic and, in their overture to the Germans, antipatriotic. Reflecting on the controversy ten years later, opposition leader Adam Michnik wrote that 'the truth is that I can find in (the letter to the German Bishops) absolutely nothing that could justify the surprisingly hostile reaction it elicited in otherwise quite civil people. Nor can I find anything that might explain the unexpected susceptibility of these critics to the demagogic arguments of officialdom' (Michnik 1993: 87). Although the blunt powers of the state were not sufficient to shut down Catholic ceremonies, control of the media allowed authorities to shape public opinion by playing on long-simmering prejudices of 'otherwise quite civil people'.

For Catholics, 1966 was an important anniversary for Polish Catholicism; for radical students and the secular left, the year marked the tenth anniversary of the mobilization of 1956. Students at Warsaw University asked Professor Leszek Kołakowski to give a public lecture on the state's failure to live up to the promises of deStalinization that formed Gomulka's platform in 1956. Kołakowski's lecture initiated a wave of renewed interest in systemic reform on the part of students and segments of the cultural intelligentsia. For this he was quickly expelled from the PZPR. Throughout 1967, a core group of Warsaw University students nicknamed 'Commandos,' organized discussion groups and 'political salons'. Initially, they confined their activities to the University campus, attempting to transform some 'official' (i.e. Communist controlled) campus organizations into independent student associations. The Polish students also related to the 1960s youth culture; and while they were sympathetic towards student movements in France and West Germany, they responded avidly to the Czechoslovak students' attempts to democratize socialism (Friszke 1994: 224–67).

Gomulka's ruling faction of the PZPR was vulnerable. On the one hand, First Secretary Gomułka worried that the economic decentralization underway in Hungary and Yugoslavia, and the democratic reforms within the Czechoslovak party would lead to social demands for change in Poland. On the other hand, Gomułka was pressured from within the Party by a growing nationalistic faction (so-called 'partisans') led by security chief Moczar (Bethel 1969). As Gomulka's power base constricted, he relied more heavily on the Soviet comrades for support; this opened him up to the nationalist challenge at home. The First Secretary's rigidity and ineptitude in dealing with Poland's economic situation alarmed technocrats and working people alike. Thus, the authorities' reactions to protest in 1968 reflected intra-party conflicts as well as external pressures.

Although government informers had infiltrated the 'Commandos' early on, it was not until the spring of 1968 that conflict between students and state authorities became public. The proximate cause was Gomułka's order to shut down the production of *Forefather's Eve*, a play by nineteenth century Romantic poet, Adam Mickiewicz. Gomułka worried that the Soviets would take offence at the anti-Russian subtext stressed in this revival of Mickiewicz' drama. Students, actors, writers, and artists participated in a demonstration on the night of the last performance. The demonstration was broken up by police, who selected members of the Commando group for arrest. Student activists were first fined, and then kicked out of University. This led to increased mobilization on the part of activist students and their supporters among the secular left and cultural intelligentsia. Protests spread from Warsaw to academic centres in eight other cities. It took three weeks for state authorities to bring an end to the student mobilization (Hoover, Poland Collection).

State repression was immediate and multifaceted. First, an immense propaganda campaign was started in the media that depicted students as irresponsible, spoiled, and under the influence of outside agitators. The media proclaimed that the expulsions of 1600 students from the universities was appropriate and necessary. Second, Gomułka's opponents within the party started an 'anti-Zionist campaign'. They asserted that students' leaders and their professors were mostly of Jewish background and they were being manipulated by Israel and West Germany (?!). This unleashed a disgraceful antisemitic campaign that was directed against the students as well as many high-placed party members. Historians estimated that two-thirds of the Jews who had survived the holocaust in Poland emigrated as a result of this administrative pogrom (Pelczynski 1980: 391). This initiative was also a subtle way of challenging Gomułka, since his wife was Jewish. Finally, party authorities orchestrated counter-demonstrations by workers brought out to support the regime. They carried banners that read, 'Students to their studies, writers to their pens!' and 'Purge the party of Zionists!' (Michnik *et al.* 1995: 172). Although worker support of the regime was a sham, the inconvenience of being shipped off from their factories to demonstrations left them with the conviction that 'what the hell, here we are working—and (the students are) out there playing around and making trouble' (Michnik *et al.* 1995: 158). In short, the state exploited social prejudices along a number of dimensions: generational (presenting students as spoiled children), class (pitting the educated segment of society against the blue collars), and ethnic (playing on ethnic stereotypes and reviving a barely hidden antisemitism). Consequently, social support for the student movement was limited.

Students and their supporters faced serious legal repercussions. Members of the student organizations received 3–7 year prison terms. Others were fined, lost their jobs, or were forced to emigrate (Friszke 1994: 250–1). Thus, when working class mobilization started on the Baltic coast in 1970, the 1968 activists were sidelined.

The 1970 protests resulted from government economic decisions. Facing serious budget shortfalls, the state needed to reduce its subsidies to consumers. Price hikes on meat were announced on 12 December 1970, as Polish families were preparing for the Christmas holidays. The unexpected decision was opposed by workers in Gdańsk: at seventeen facilities work was immediately suspended. The largest walk-out was at the Lenin shipyards, where workers demanded the rescission of the increases. The shipyards director and the officials at the District Party headquarters refused to consider workers' grievances; protests spread through Gdańsk, ultimately turning violent. The District PZPR headquarters was burned, and the prison vandalized. Protesters were killed and wounded in street fighting between demonstrators and security forces. On Tuesday, 15 December, the strikes and demonstrations spread to the neighbouring Baltic port city of Gdynia. The confrontations grew larger. On Thursday, First Secretary Gomułka authorized military intervention and approved the use of live ammunition. In Gdynia, military police fired on unarmed demonstrators, killing fifteen. Protests erupted in two other coastal cities. This spread of civil unrest led to a crisis within the PZPR. Anti-Gomułka forces within the Party consulted with the Kremlin; Breszhnev advised Gomułka to seek a solution through political rather than military means (Ascherson 1982: 102). This both infuriated and undermined the Polish First Secretary, who experienced a minor stroke. The Central Committee took advantage of Gomułka's temporary incapacity to remove him and appoint Edward Gierek as the new First Secretary. But despite the change in leadership and government public relations efforts, work stoppages and other protests continued. In February, the PZPR restored the old meat prices and protests ended. This only postponed the crisis: the state was constrained to keep meat prices at the December 1970 level, despite worsening economic conditions.

Network Development: 1966–70

Catholic associations, the mainstay of the opposition domain, were the only known, active groups in 1966. The 'Catholic pyramid' consisted of four intellectuals' organizations established during the 1956 round of mobilization (Osa 2001). Other 'civil society' groups were suppressed by the regime in the late 1950s, but the Catholic groups survived. The legal basis for the operation of the latter groups was the 1956 Church-State Agreement (Stehle 1965: 306–10), and Cardinal Wyszyński made it clear that state repression of the associations would engender a major church-state crisis. Although they benefited from Church protection, the Catholic clubs were independent organizations (see Fig. 4.2).

Three of the groups produced Catholic periodicals: one weekly paper (*Tygodnik Powszechny* [TGP]) and two monthly magazines (*Znak*, ZNK and *Więż*, WEZ).[5] (They had limited distributions and were, of course, subject to state censorship.) The pages of the Catholic journals featured essays, articles, and commentaries written by prominent Catholic intellectuals, both from Poland and abroad.

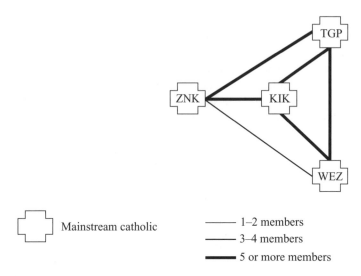

The fourth group was a multipurpose club for Catholic intelligentsia (*Klub Inteli-gencij Katolików*, KIK) that had branches in six cities. Most of the members and contributors to the Catholic publications also belonged to KIK.

The Catholic organizations in Network 1 (Fig. 4.2) form a clique structure: that is, they are maximally connected. In addition, there is substantial membership overlap between the organizations, indicated by the thickness of the lines. Four of the rela-tions have the strongest ties, with five or more members shared in common (KIK–ZNK, KIK–TGP, KIK–WEZ, and TGP–ZNK). All of KIK's relations are strong ties since KIK functions as somewhat of an 'umbrella' organization, including individuals from all the other groups. WEZ's medium tie (3–4 members in common) to TGP and weak tie (1–2 shared members) to ZNK is mostly due to geographical distance: WEZ is located in Warsaw, and the other two groups are in Kraków.

Now consider the relation between the network and the set of protest events that took place in 1966. There is seemingly a strong correspondence. Prochurch protests occurred as a result of governmental interference with religious demon-strations; the only organizations the opposition domain are the Catholic organiza-tions. Yet any connection between the formal organizations and the unplanned protests was indirect. Catholic intellectuals (especially those from WEZ) criti-cized Cardinal Wyszyński's Great Novena as too nationalistic, too traditional and divergent from the progressive, ecumenical spirit of Vatican II. Nevertheless, once the regime engaged church leaders in a series of confrontations, the Catholic intel-ligentsia closed ranks. Lay Catholics who participated in the Great Novena cere-monies gathered at KIK; TGP and ZNK published a number of articles that explored Polish Marian traditions and their 'historic' (read: national) significance.

The sociogram presented in Fig. 4.3 shows the configuration of the 1967/8 organization set, Network 2. The domain grew through the addition of three student organizations, two of which were linked to the Catholic pyramid. The student activists at the centre of the 1968 events were from the group called 'Commandos' (*Komandosy*, KOM). A second group that formed in response to the March events was called *Taternik* (TAT). This was a small group of students who were concerned that state propaganda was presenting a wildly inaccurate picture of the students' grievances and actions. TAT dedicated itself to smuggling out documents, photographs, and other information on the March events to the West where the materials could be published and distributed. A final group, 'The Movement' (*Ruch*, RUC), was separate from, and ideologically dissimilar to, the other student groups. RUC was a semiconspiratorial group which included some left-leaning members and some mainstream Catholic youth; they opposed Russian domination and openly embraced Polish nationalism. RUC's goals and tactics were subversive: members planned robberies and other criminal acts to finance their efforts to overthrow the state. Disputes within the group over ideology, tactics, and personal bids for power led to its disintegration once the arrests began in 1969.

The sociogram depicting Network 2 shows a 75 per cent increase in the size of the domain ($N = 7$). All of the increase is due to the addition of the student groups. Even though the youth groups were newly formed, they were connected to the Catholic milieu through Commandos' contacts with ZNK.[6] TAT was a group that emerged from KOM; it had an indirect link to the Catholic circle. RUC appears as an isolate.

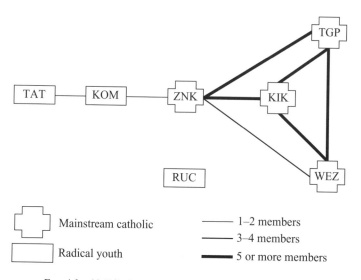

Fig. 4.3. *1967/8 Organization to organization ties (N = 7)*

The relation between protests and organizations in Network 2 is direct. KOM was the main instigator of the student movement, organizing demonstrations, petition signing, and rallies. The Catholic Znak group of Parliamentary deputies[7] took up the students' cause in their 'Interpellation' addressed to the Prime Minister (Karpinski 1982: 120). Nevertheless, this mini-network broke down quickly under the pressure of state retaliation against the student activists.

Finally, the domain configuration in 1969/70 (Network 3) is shown in Fig. 4.4. There are no new groups; instead, the domain has begun to contract. KOM activists were put on trial in early 1969; in 1970, TAT leaders were imprisoned; and RUC members were sentenced in 1971. At the end of the 1960s 'wave,' the only remaining occupants in the opposition domain were (again) the Catholic 'pyramid' of groups: KIK, ZNK, WEZ, and TGP.

Network 3 has no relation to social protest in 1970. Although the bloody demonstrations that occurred in the Baltic region resulted from labour insurgency, no strike or workers' organizations appear in the data set. Workers' committees had been formed in the enterprises, but these were under Party control. In the late 1960s, no organized opposition groups existed in Gdańsk and Gdynia (Friszke 1994: 263). The violent protests that took place in December of 1970 were unplanned and directed towards reversing the price hikes. Although workers later demanded more autonomy and a free press, they did not question the leading role of the PZPR, the socialist system of production, or the alliance with the Soviet Union. Most of the workers' demands centred on fixing the problems of socialism: they supported Yugoslav-style 'workers' self-management' and a decentralized

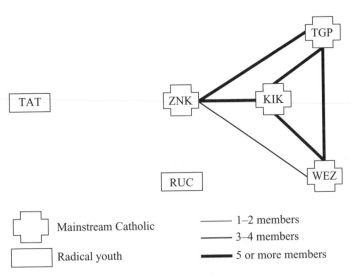

Fig. 4.4. *1969/70 Organization to organization ties (N = 6)*

economic system. Indeed, many strike leaders were party members. While the coastal workers sought a better model of socialism and improved treatment by those in power, they supported the system—while still harbouring a bitter antipathy towards the party apparatus (Friszke 1994: 264–5). Thus, the appearance of a new leader who promised to improve working conditions and who restored the former meat prices brought an end to labour actions before the insurgency could establish a formal, organized presence.

To sum up: Catholic associations formed a stable clique which was the only element that persisted from one mobilization to the next. There were two reasons for this. First, these groups were protected by religious authorities whose standing 'Joint Committee' provided a mechanism for negotiating with the government. Second, the groups were internally more cohesive than other organizations in the domain because members of the Catholic organizations shared deep convictions and values. By contrast, the student organizations were intense but ephemeral; they were easily repressed by the authorities.

The late 60s formed a 'pseudo wave' because the government prevented protest activity from accelerating and expanding in 'a phase of heightened conflict across the social system' (Tarrow 1998: 142). Street confrontations between police and religious celebrants in 1966, student marches in 1968, and labour insurgency in 1970—each surge of protest was contained through the manipulation of public perceptions by state-controlled mass media and by coercion. The authorities used their power directly, imprisoning opponents, and indirectly, exacerbating social cleavages to divide and rule. Thus, the repeated attempts at social mobilization from 1966 through 1970 illustrate the difficulties and high barriers faced by challengers in a non-democratic system.

SOLIDARITY: IN OPPOSITION'S WEB

In the early 1970s, First Secretary Gierek attempted to improve living and working conditions by reorienting the state's economy. His regime's policy shifted away from the autarkic development which concentrated on heavy industry and towards a more integrated approach stressing trade and expanded consumption. The capital investment for Gierek's ambitious programme came from Western banks. When poor harvests and increased energy costs led to an economic downturn, a crisis loomed because of ballooning debt payments on foreign bank loans. But a half decade of economic growth and social quiescence gave the government authorities confidence that they had finally secured legitimacy for the regime. Consequently, Gierek's Politburo believed the time was right to make the tough decisions that would bring consumer prices more closely in line with production costs (Lepak 1988).

Protest Events: 1976–81

Meat prices had been frozen since 1970 as a result of worker opposition to higher prices and the violent strikes that toppled the Gomulka regime. By 1976, continued government subsidies for food could no longer be sustained. The decision was made to quickly implement a new price schedule for foodstuffs, rather than phase in price increases and risk mounting social opposition. On 24 June 1976, government officials announced that food prices would increase on average by 60 per cent as of 27 June. The government called up special units to patrol the streets of Gdańsk to deter protest. They also conscripted 'politically suspect' individuals for emergency duty in the army. Nevertheless, on Friday, the morning of the 25th, work stoppages were widespread. Factory walk-outs led to violent demonstrations in several cities. In Warsaw, the Ursus factory workers tore up a railway track and stopped international traffic. In Radom, rioters looted stores and set the provincial party headquarters on fire. By that evening, the Prime Minister went on television to announce that 'after consultations with the working class,' it was decided that the price hikes should be suspended pending further review (Bernhard 1993: 46–75).

Over the weekend, the security services took their revenge. Hundreds of demonstrators were rounded up, arrested, and beaten while in custody. Trials were peremptory; punishments were harsh, including jail time, fines, and loss of employment. Although outrage at the disproportionate response of the authorities grew, this did not lead to further protest. Instead, activists focused on creating linkages between social communities by organizing a 'Workers' Defense Committee' (*Komitet Obrony Robotników*, KOR) to coordinate aid and legal assistance for incarcerated demonstrators and their families.

KOR sought the prisoners' release through open letters to the government and by encouraging supporters in the West to put pressure on Polish authorities. KOR members organized a centre to accumulate and analyse information regarding employment conditions and actively cooperated with foreign journalists. Well-known members such as Adam Michnik wrote articles for the Western press publicizing conditions in Poland. KOR activists collected signatures on petitions, calling on legislators to establish a special commission to investigate the excesses of the security forces.

Under this pressure, the government declared an amnesty in spring 1977 and freed the remaining detainees. By the end of the summer, KOR's original mission had been accomplished. Internal discussions were held about how to evolve; in September, the opposition group adopted a new name: Committee for Social Self-Defense (KSS–KOR).[8]

In October 1978 an unexpected event occurred which deeply affected Polish politics and culture. The Cardinal of Kraków, Karol Wojtyła, was elected Pope. News of Wojtyła's election was met in Poland with astonishment and national pride, even among Party members. But Wojtyła's elevation created a dilemma for Poland's communist rulers. Soviet Premier Brezhnev insisted that Gierek downplay the situation, even refuse Wojtyła a visa for his return to Poland (Szulc 1995: 322–3). Gierek resisted the suggestion. The Polish First Secretary knew a Polish Pope was too big an event to ignore. Unlike his predecessor Gomułka, who tried to constrain the Church's Millennium ceremonies, Gierek took a 'hands off' approach. Strategically, this was probably his best option: if the government had tried to prevent the Pope's 'Pilgrimage to the Homeland,' the regime would have faced massive demonstrations and relentless criticism at home and abroad. Yet the absence of police or any indication of state power from the mass gatherings at which the Pope spoke contributed to a sense of hope and possibility that encouraged the opposition. Contemporary observers and later commentators agreed that the Papal pilgrimage to Poland in 1979 created a 'psychological earthquake' in society that inspired great numbers of people to action not long thereafter (Szajkowski 1983: 72; Kubik 1994: 139).

A year after the Pope's visit to Poland, an administrative ruling effected the redistribution of available meat supplies, making choice cuts available only at expensive 'commercial shops'. No announcement of price rises accompanied this move, but consumers drew their own conclusions from the worsening meat shortages. A wave of strikes followed this 'unannounced decision' (Lepak 1988: 197). By July 1980, 51 plants in all corners of Poland had wrested concessions from management and another seventeen were on strike (Ascherson 1982: 130–1). The situation was most serious in Lublin where 'the railway men had welded an engine to the rails along the line leading to the border with the Soviet Union' (Wałęsa 1987: 116). Railroad workers were particularly militant because management had reneged on concessions won during an earlier strike. After Gierek's direct intervention, the strike was settled with economic and work rule concessions.

In August, shipyard workers in Gdańsk went on strike. Although negotiations with party and enterprise officials promised a speedy conclusion to the work stoppage, employee demands escalated beyond immediate economic concerns. Strike leaders, pressured by rank-and-file workers and sympathy strikers to continue the labour action, demanded the erection of a monument to honour workers slain in 1970. They established an Inter-factory Strike Committee to coordinate labour resistance. Finally, the strikers called for direct negotiations between their representatives and government officials who would be authorized to make political concessions, notably the establishment of free, independent trade unions. On 31 August, the Gdańsk Accords were signed. This agreement authorized the first autonomous labour union organization to operate in a communist country, independent from the Party. The union was named 'Solidarity'. During the next three months, Solidarity branches were formed in every type of workplace—from steel mills, to health clinics, to university offices—even the police wanted an union representation. Farmers began to organize a 'Rural Solidarity'. Although the government had signed the Gdańsk Accords in August, the authorities balked at its implementation. Solidarity activists were drawn into repeated confrontations when they tried to get the government to fulfil its promises. Conflicts intensified and spread across the social system, becoming a true protest cycle. Contention was halted only through a massive military operation on 13 December, 1981. 'Soft' leaders in the Politburo had been replaced by military men, led by General Wojciech Jaruzelski. Under a threat of Soviet invasion, Jaruzelski's men devised an operation to round up the national leaders of Solidarity and to freeze social action through the declaration of martial law (www.solidarnosc.org.pl). Thus ended the Solidarity's legal existence in the Polish People's Republic (PRL).

Network Development: 1976–81

Although civil society scholars contend that the 'reconstitution' of a public sphere began with the formation of KOR in 1976, my research documents the continuous presence of independent associations during the preceding two decades. While the opposition domain contracted following state repression of the student movement in 1968, my data show that resurgence of this arena actually began prior to the labour unrest in June 1976, and *not* with the founding of KOR afterwards.

Three organizations were created before the strikes in 1976. The liberal group, Movement of Free Democrats (*Ruch Wolnych Demokratów*, RWD), was established in July 1974. RWD's goal was to monitor the Polish government's implementation of the Helsinki Accords, to which Poland was a signatory. RWD sought democratic reforms over the long term, using human rights as a focal point for extending citizenship rights. Two nationalist groups formed just before the strikes in 1976. The Polish Independence League (*Polskie Porozumienie Niepodległościowe*, PPN) desired to reorient Poland's foreign policy, away from the USSR and towards NATO. The PPN nationalists promoted an 'antitotalitarian' programme; their short-term goal was to gain freedom of speech and the press. In the long term, PPN hoped to move Poland toward a multiparty democracy (Friszke 1994: 490–9).

A second nationalist organization was founded a month after PPN. Independence Current (*Nurt Niepodległościowe*, NUN) was a semi-clandestine cell of nationalists who sought to separate Poland from the policies and influence of the USSR. Because of personal tensions among competing members of the group, it dissolved by 1978, its members dispersed among a number of other nationalist groups.

The Workers' Defense Committee (KOR) was organized when the government retaliated against the strikers in June 1976 (as mentioned in the previous section). KOR was the first, and most important, proponent of a 'civic' or 'antipolitical' orientation (Lipski 1985; Bernhard 1993; Friszke 1994: 338–451). Much has been written on this organization, and the famous activists who belonged to it are well known in the West. My brief discussion is intended only to highlight the factors that distinguished KOR from other organizations in the opposition domain.

KOR had expanded rapidly. Whereas most opposition organizations were headquartered in one of the major cities, with perhaps a few branches elsewhere, KOR became active nationally in short order. After KOR transformed itself into the Social Self-Defense Committee, KSS-KOR, the group broadened its scope while keeping its ideological programme deliberately ambiguous. The group emphasized human rights, the development of independent culture, and social justice. KOR eschewed open political aspirations, and dedicated itself to supporting the independent activities of 'society'. Among KOR's members were individuals from the secular left organizations of the 1950s, the 1960s student movement, and both progressive and mainstream Catholic associations. KOR included social democrats, liberals, and nationalists. Through its many publishing activities, KOR provided a major impetus for the underground press.

In March 1977, a number of KOR activists formed a new organization to engage the government more explicitly on the issue of human rights, the Movement in Defence of Human and Citizens' Rights (*Ruch Obrony Praw Człowieka i Obywatela*, in database: ROP). ROP members were heavily influenced by Catholic social doctrine and determined to act politically in accordance with Catholic ethics.

The Students' Solidarity Committee (SKS) was established in May 1977. This new student group was more moderate than those formed during the 1960s. In general, the data set for Networks 4–6 included many fewer 'radical youth' groups because students and working class youth were joining more broad-based organizations in the 1970s.

The structure of the 1976/7 domain (Network 4) was more complex than it had been in the 1960s (see Fig. 4.5). The number of organizations had almost doubled since 1970. There was greater diversity among groups. Three new social/ideology categories were represented: liberal, nationalist, and 'civic'. While the Catholic organizations continued to form a strong clique with KIK as the central node, the enlarged opposition domain included a second organization equalling KIK in centrality: KOR. Network 4 exhibited several advantages over the 1960s networks. First, its centre was a triad: KIK–KOR–ROP. This is a more stable structure than if a single, dominant organization served as broker to the network. Second, the domain was organized in such a way as to make rapid growth likely. The Catholic pyramid was a stable resource base that contributed members to new organizations (esp. PPN and KOR). Network growth now took place outside of the Catholic sector, in previously unmobilized sectors.

In 1976, the relation between the protest arena and the opposition domain was somewhat ambiguous. Workers, the source of social protest in 1976, were still unrepresented by formal labour organizations. Yet the non-violent protests that forced the government to offer an amnesty in 1977 were organized by one of the most central organizations, KOR. Figure 4.1 shows the small surge of protest events in 1976/7 that reflect these activities. But the same illustration reveals a new trend: although the security services applied violent measures against strikers, the number of repressive sanctions did not match or exceed protests. Elsewhere, I have argued that governmental and party unit changes coupled with economic decentralization reduced state capacity significantly (Osa 2003). As a result, the state became less capable of deploying massive repressive forces against dissidents.

Turning next to Network 5 (1978/9), we see that the size of the domain increased by 90 per cent (see Fig. 4.6). Because so many new organizations were formed, I will discuss only the most significant new groups.

The nationalist sector was quite active. It lost one organization (NUN), but added four new groups: Polish National Party (*Polskie Stronnictwo Narodowe*,

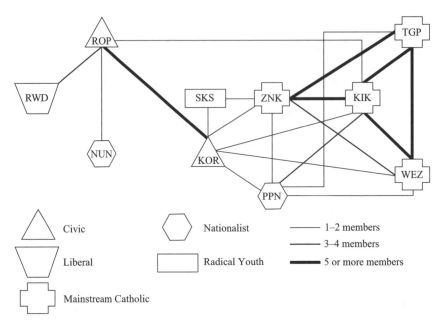

FIG. 4.5. *1976/7 Organization to organization ties (N = 10)*

PSN), the Young Poland Movement, Catholic traditionalists in ZNA, and the influential Confederation for Independent Poland (*Konfederacja Polski Niepodległej*, KPN). Led by Leszek Moczulski, KPN was an overtly nationalist group whose members believed that socialism's days in Poland were numbered, that the country should separate from the Soviet bloc and establish a multiparty democracy. Moczulski's followers were considered to be right-wing radicals; KPN members were often targeted by the secret police.

The 'civic' sector had also expanded. Four new civic organizations were added, of which the Society of Scientific Courses (*Towarzystwo Kursów Naukowych*, TKN) was the most important. TKN, also called the 'Flying University,' was organized by academics and cultural figures who wished to stimulate unfettered discussion on sensitive topics. Courses took place in private apartments on a rotating basis to discourage police repression; hence the name, 'Flying University'. TKN encouraged the open debates that are necessary for the development of competing political and cultural analyses critical to movement framing and micromobilization.

The most significant founding was the establishment of the Free Trade Union group (*Wolne Związki Zawodowe*, WZZ). This was an organization of labour activists who had participated in the strikes of 1970 and 1976. It was a kind of exploratory 'working group' established outside of the enterprises to consider

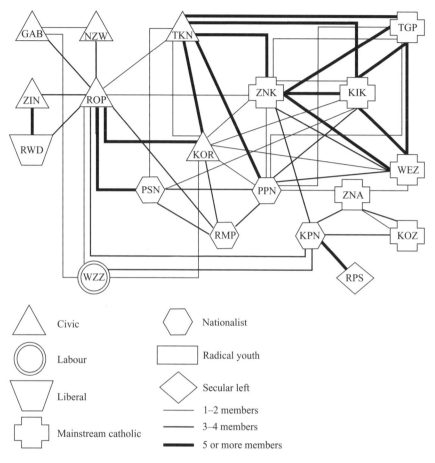

FIG. 4.6. *1978/9 Organization to organization ties (N = 19)*

ways of creating a broad-based independent labour movement. WZZ had strong ties to KOR. Most of the early Solidarity leaders were members of WZZ.

Structurally, Network 5 is the most complex thus far. First, the mean degree centrality rose from 3.8 (for the 1976/7 network) to 5.3 for Network 5. This means that the average number of ties for an organization had increased by 40 per cent. Second, network centralization increased by 5 per cent over Network 4 to 36 per cent. The increase in centralization is due to the fact that while Network 4 was coordinated by two organizations, Catholic KIK and civic KOR, Network 5 (1978/9) was organized around five prominent organizations: the Catholic groups KIK and ZNK, and the civic nodes ROP, KOR, TKN. Third, the nationalist groups were increasing in prominence. Nationalist organizations accounted for 44 per cent of the growth in the size of the domain. Two nationalist organizations, KPN and PPN, exceeded the mean centrality scores. In short, all these measures indicate that while the network was expanding, it was also becoming better integrated. The number of 'strong ties' grew, groups representing various social/ideology categories were strongly tied to organizations outside their sectors, and brokerage roles were shared between the older Catholic core groups (KIK, ZNK) and the recent 'civic' associations (KOR, ROP, and TKN). These structural developments created a domain which was robust and well organized to facilitate rapid mobilization.

But what about the relation between the oppositional domain and the protest arena? No protest events were recorded for 1978/9. Yet papal Masses in June 1979 drew crowds of up to a million people—not exactly good news for the government. All of the organization and planning for these events was left to the Church hierarchy and laity. They were responsible for site preparation, crowd control, clean-up, etc. While I have no direct evidence that opposition groups were involved, certainly the individuals who were members of these civil society associations also participated in the events surrounding the Papal pilgrimage.

Finally, our last organization set, Network 6, shows the configuration into which Solidarity was born (see Fig. 4.7). Although size of the opposition domain again increased (this time by 21 per cent), the rate of growth slowed significantly. The slower growth in the number of organizations resulted from the huge expansion of one organization: Solidarity. Network 6 exhibits a number of significant changes. First, the labour sector expanded and became the central focus of the opposition domain. Labour organizations were linked most strongly to nationalist, Catholic, and 'civic' organizations. This pattern of external ties reflected the internal divisions within the labour movement between traditionalist/nationalist elements and the more anti-clerical, democratic socialist proponents. Second, the nationalist category also expanded to comprise 26 per cent of the network. Third, the 'civic' sector consolidated. Fourth, Rural Solidarity (*Solidarność Rolnych Indiwidualnych*, SRI) represented the addition of the agricultural sector to the opposition domain.

Network 6 shows a development towards even greater complexity in 1980. Overnight, Solidarity became the most central organization (degree 14). Solidarity appeared as the hub of a wheel structure with organizations representing every social category revolving around it. And yet, the network as a whole was not organized in a centre-periphery pattern. Rather, the wheel structure was embedded in a broader network with multiple foci. KIK, TKN, and KOR formed a second tier of central nodes that anchored the Solidarity wheel within the broader oppositional domain. This had positive implications for resource and information flows, mobilization potential, and resilience in the face of state repression.

Network 6 had a strong, direct connection to events in the protest arena. Figure 4.1 shows the enormous upsurge in protest events that began with the summer strikes in 1980 and ended with the imposition of martial law in December 1981. The sudden upsurge had two components. First, protest events resulted from

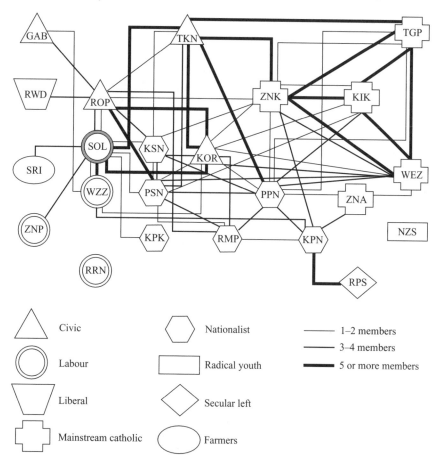

FIG. 4.7. *1980/1 Organization to organization ties (N = 23)*

economic dissatisfactions and the inability of the union to negotiate conclusive agreements with the enterprise directors and government. Economic discontent fuelled public rallies, marches, demonstrations and work stoppages. Second, the government's reluctance to implement the Gdańsk Accords, for example, delaying legal registration of the union, led to political protests organized not only by Solidarity, but also by other supportive groups. Together, these two trends resulted in broad-based and rapid mobilization. Nevertheless, protest activity peaked in 1980; demobilization had begun even *before* martial law was imposed.

Unlike the 1960s pseudo-wave, in 1980–1, the repressive capacity of government was consistently surpassed by the mobilization capacity of the society. Partly this was due to low morale within the party/government apparatus and the state's diminishing resources and declining organizational efficacy. But it was also due to a growing number of radical nationalist groups which drew the attention of the security forces. Party leaders had to repress radical groups like KPN that directly challenged the socialist content of the state and the alliance with USSR. Not to do so would antagonize their bosses within the Kremlin. Labour activists were not ideologically as dangerous as the nationalists; they were also better protected because of their embeddedness in a well-organized opposition domain and their prominence in international public opinion. Thus, when the crackdown came in December 1981, it had to be carried out by the Generals, who turned out to be effective villains—but ineffective rulers.

CONCLUSIONS

Nondemocratic states are not subject to oversight by independent journalists or jurists. Their methods for repressing dissent are diverse and many: for example, press censorship, secret police surveillance of citizens, restrictions on travel, forced conscription to military service, and the deployment of informants and spy networks. The absence of collective action and civic association in an authoritarian state is the norm. Yet, the barriers to autonomous social action are sometimes surmounted, protests are organized, and occasionally social movements emerge. Under difficult, risky conditions, people do form organizations which challenge state power.

This chapter has examined developmental patterns in the oppositional domain using network data from Poland during two waves of protest: the 1966–70 'pseudo-wave,' and the 1976–81 wave culminating in the formation of the Solidarity trade union. The empirical study addressed two questions: Why are some networks less vulnerable to repression? What network characteristics facilitate movement emergence? We found that the presence of opposition organizations, even when the domain experienced growth, was not sufficient to cause a social movement to form. Examination of the oppositional activity in 1966–70 showed how the state used its coercive powers and its ability to manipulate extant social cleavages to prevent coalition formation within the domain and the initiation of a protest cycle. By contrast, the second wave showed that networks during the 1976–80 period exhibited characteristics that rendered the opposition domain less vulnerable to repression and better able to facilitate social mobilization. Figures 4.8 and 4.9 illustrate the trends in protest activity and network development for the two periods.

Analysis of network development yields a number of strong findings in the Polish case that challenge the conventional explanations for Solidarity. But the Polish analysis also provides a basis for hypotheses that can be applied to cases of mobilization in nondemocratic states more generally. First, I will enumerate my conclusions about the Polish case and then I will conclude with possible generalizations.

In the literature on democratization in Poland, insufficient attention is given to the role of the Catholic milieu in sustaining organizations that posed a continual challenge to state dominance of public life. The foregoing data analysis has shown that the Catholic 'pyramid,' four associations of Catholic intelligentsia, acted to anchor to the opposition domain and provide a foundation for growth and diversification.

The network analysis also reveals contributions to movement formation in 1980 that are not emphasized in the literature on Solidarity. First, the organizational domain expansion that occurred prior to the founding of the union created a web of structural supports to sustain the new organization through its tentative early period (see Figs 4.6 and 4.9). Second, the 'civic' orientation of highly central groups provided a nonideological formulation for cooperation that promoted coalition-building among diverse organizations. By emphasizing overarching themes such as human rights, national culture, and social autonomy, the civic groups oriented political discourse away from divisive issues. They also reduced the antagonisms between more ideologically defined subgroups such as nationalists and secular left ('revisionists') by using symbols to reference political ideas rather than by proposing substantive collective action agendas (Osa 1997). Finally, the nationalist sector, although dismissed by political commentators and activists as politically marginal, increased in size and network prominence throughout the 1970s. Nationalist groups were important contributors to radical protest actions and acted as a buffer to the labour sector. Nationalists drew the attention of the authorities who were forced to divert repressive resources away from civic and labour groups in order to suppress the anti-Soviet programme of the nationalists.

The general finding of my study is that network development is related to the protest arena in the following way: protest peaks arise when the interorganizational structures in the opposition domain reach their highest degree of development, that is their most complex form.[9] 'Complexity' is measured by the size of the domain, the number of cliques in the structure, the level of membership overlaps, and the number of brokers. This suggests that as the measures of network structural complexity increase, there will be a greater likelihood of sustained protest mobilization.

The analysis of social movement emergence in Poland suggests some factors that may apply to other cases of high-risk collective action in nondemocracies. I conclude with three related propositions: For a movement to emerge in an authoritarian setting, supporting structures (such as oppositional networks or external allies) must be in place prior to large scale collective action. To overcome the repressive state's ability to fragment the opposition, ideologically neutral groups must generate inclusive master frames that allow sectoral differences to remain latent. Finally, the presence of marginal, radical groups (e.g. rebels or national separatists) can benefit mainstream opposition groups as long as the government sees the mainstream opposition as a less dangerous alternative than the radicals.

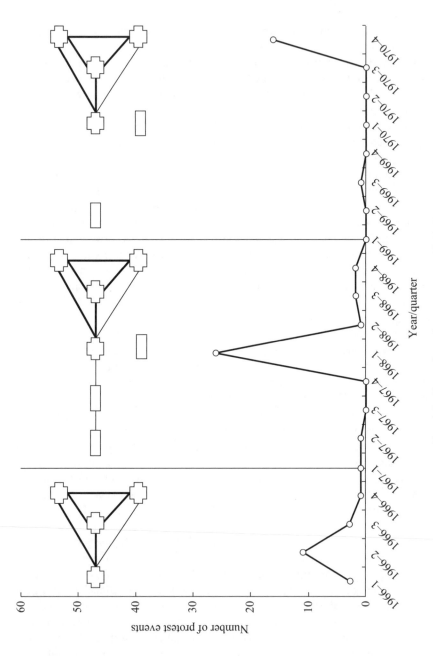

FIG. 4.8. *Networks and protest events, 1966–70*

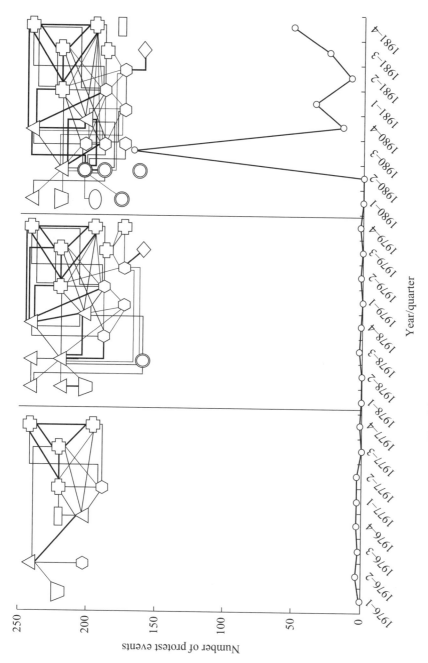

FIG. 4.9. *Networks and protest events, 1976–81*

NOTES

1. A little visa problem that was solved by the gift of a pound of coffee to a police official in 1988 opened my eyes to this aspect of social networks 'behind the Iron Curtain'.
2. Polish Opposition Membership Database, © 2000 Maryjane Osa. For information on data collection procedures, see Osa (2003).
3. Since most of the organizations in the data set were illegal groups, complete membership lists are unavailable. I obtained the names of activists through cross-checking different sources including: secret police records, organizational archival papers, group publications, activist memoirs published in the West, and historical accounts of the opposition published in Poland after 1989.
4. The study utilizes a set of procedures described by Breiger (1974) for the empirical analysis of membership networks, also called affiliation sets. This approach investigates the intersection of persons and the groups to which they belong, or persons and the events in which they participate. The affiliation sets thus describe two mode networks where 'connections among members of one of the modes are based on linkages established through the second mode' (Wasserman and Faust 1995: 291).
5. Because of space limitations, my descriptions of the organizations will be brief. For further information on the organizations, see Friszke (1994) or Osa (2003). To facilitate my discussion of the interorganizational networks, I will refer to the groups by their three-letter computer identification codes instead of their Polish names.
6. There is anecdotal evidence to suggest that KOM was linked to KIK and WEZ as well, but there are no records documenting shared members; consequently, those ties are absent from the sociogram.
7. These individuals are included in the ZNK member lists.
8. For simplicity's sake, I will refer to this group throughout the text as 'KOR,' as that is the code for the organization in my database.
9. Three other networks not included in this chapter (1954/5, 1956/7, and 1958/9) also follow this pattern (Osa 2001).

5

'Leaders' or Brokers? Positions and Influence in Social Movement Networks

Mario Diani

Social scientists from a structuralist perspective have often addressed the question whether actors' power and influence correlate with their network position (Freeman 1979; Cook *et al.* 1983; Marsden 1983; Knoke and Burt 1983; Bonacich 1987; Knoke 1994; Mizruchi 1996). Although this hypothesis has generated several empirical studies,[1] it has hardly been considered, let alone tested, in social movement research. This is somewhat paradoxical, as the widespread recognition of the importance of the relational dimension of social movements (Gerlach and Hine 1970; Oliver 1989; Diani 1992*a*; Tilly 1994; McCarthy 1996; Melucci 1996) should have paved the way to a reformulation in the light of network concepts of issues of power, influence, and ultimately leadership within social movements. Instead, despite rare exceptions (Barker *et al.* 2001), the analysis of power dynamics, and in particular of leadership, has hardly been at the core of social movement analysis of late (Lofland 1996: 212–14; Klandermans 1997: 132–5; della Porta and Diani 1999: ch. 6).

Movement leadership has traditionally been viewed as a dyadic, asymmetric relationship between a leader, be it an individual or a movement organization, and its supporters—again, either members of a specific movement organization, or people sympathizing with a given cause (Klandermans 1989: 215–24, 301–14; 1997: 132–5; McAdam *et al.* 1996; Melucci 1996: ch. 17; della Porta and Diani 1999: ch. 6). This was consistent with long established conceptions of leadership (Gouldner 1965; Camic 1980), but failed to capture the experience of left-libertarian movements: their members not only tend to be either weakly related to specific organizations (in the case of individuals) or formally independent from each other (in the case of organizations), but often reject authoritative leadership

In one way or another, Alberto Melucci, Giovanni Lodi, Mark Brown, Roberto Fernandez, Ann Mische, Charles Tilly, and Doug McAdam all helped with this project. Previous versions of this argument were presented at the Social movement sessions of the 1997 ESA conference (Essex) and the 1998 Sunbelt conference (Sitges).

figures as a matter of principle (Pearce 1980; Diani and Donati 1984; Brown 1989; Lichterman 1995: 196).

However, movement actors' rejection of formal leadership roles does not automatically eradicate the problems leaders used to tackle, or the need for the functions they used to perform. Available accounts of social movements' internal dynamics show how their members struggle to reconcile their aspiration to autonomous and independent action with persistent needs of coordination and public representation (Melucci 1996: 344–7). A relational view of social movement leadership (Melucci 1996: 335–8; see also Downton 1973) suggests that leadership roles need not entail control over a unified organization, or explicit recognition of charisma from followers. They may also, far less obtrusively, result from certain actors' location at the centre of exchanges of practical and symbolic resources among movement organizations. This will not generate domination, if by that we mean actors' capacity to impose sanctions over others in order to control their behaviour, but rather varying degrees of influence.[2] The latter may consist, for example, of actors' ability to promote coalition work among movement organizations, or of their being perceived by media and political institutions as movement 'representatives'.

With a few exceptions (Diani and Donati 1984; Rosenthal *et al.* 1985, 1997; Staggenborg 1988; Mushaben 1989; Schmitt-Beck 1989; Diani 1995; Schou 1997), analysts of movement networks have paid scant attention to this line of inquiry. In this chapter I draw upon data on network dynamics in the environmental movement in Milan in the mid-1980s to explore the relationship between network position, influence, and SMOs' properties. First, I discuss possible alternative conceptualizations of influence within social movement networks: what kinds of influence do different indicators of structural position in a network measure? In particular, how do we account in network terms for different activities such as alliance-building and intermediation between different movement sectors? Second, I ask if incumbency of core positions within a movement network actually imply some capacity to act as a 'movement representative' in the public sphere. Finally, I contrast a standard explanation for SMOs' differential location in movement networks, based on the amount of organizational resources, to another, emphasizing the role of the social capital generated by activists through their multiple memberships.

MEASURING INFLUENCE IN SOCIAL MOVEMENTS: NETWORK CENTRALITY AND SOCIAL BROKERAGE

The capacity to build alliances and coalitions has been found to increase interest groups' influence over public authorities in key policy domains such as health, energy, or labour (Laumann and Knoke 1987: 387; Knoke 1990*b*: 208; Knoke *et al.* 1996), although the extent to which such findings may be generalized to other policy areas is still uncertain (Knoke 1990*b*: 212). Evidence on environmental politics in Italy similarly suggests that protest initiatives promoted by coalitions of SMOs are likely to have a broader scope, and to target higher-level political institutions, than initiatives promoted by individual groups.[3] At the same time, establishing and maintaining alliances is inherently costly and problematic (Staggenborg 1986; Zald and McCarthy 1987; Knoke 1990*b*: 209; Hathaway and Meyer 1994; Balser 1997). Therefore, SMOs' capacity to convince prospective allies to devote part of their scarce organizational resources to cooperate with them may be safely regarded as proof of their influence in the movement sector (Downton, 1973).

There are actually several ways to measure actors' location within social movement networks, and therefore their potential influence (Freeman 1979; Cook *et al.* 1983; Marsden 1983; Bonacich 1987; Knoke 1990*a*). The simplest is the number of ties which actors receive from other actors in the network (in the language of social network analysis, in-degree [Freeman 1979]). This measure of network centrality (or *prestige*: Wasserman and Faust [1995, ch. 5]) suggests that an SMO will be central in its network to the extent that other SMOs identify it as a partner in alliances.[4]

From a different perspective, we can also capture SMOs' influence by assessing their capacity to relate to different sectors of a movement, and therefore their potential role as communication links. Differences in specific goals, strategic and tactical options, and broader attitudes may often discourage communication and cooperation between SMOs. Networks of 'restricted access' (Marsden 1983: 690) may develop accordingly. Under these conditions, the capacity to develop linkages with SMOs that are not directly communicating constitutes an important asset. In particular, when pronounced ideological differences exist within a movement, SMOs placed in intermediary structural positions may be expected to be particularly influential, possibly more than SMOs having the same number of ties, but concentrated within specific movement factions. However, the influence that originates from intermediation processes within movement networks may not necessarily lead to the assumption of explicit leadership roles. The dynamic which we are interested in is probably best captured by the concept of 'social broker'. A broker may be defined as an actor connecting other actors which are not directly related to each other (Boissevain 1974: 148; Marsden 1982; Burt 1992). From the perspective of this chapter, brokers' most crucial property lies in their capacity to connect actors who are not communicating because of some specific political or social barrier, rather than the mere absence of practical opportunities (Gould and Fernandez 1989; Fernandez and Gould 1994). In the case of the Milan environmental movement in the mid-1980s, barriers consisted mostly of the well-known differences between conservation and political ecology traditions (Rucht 1989; Dalton 1994; Diani 1995). It is on such occasions that brokerage is crucial for the survival of chains of interaction, and therefore for the connectedness of a network as a whole.[5]

EXPLAINING CENTRALITY AND BROKERAGE
ROLES IN MOVEMENT NETWORKS

We may explain differences in SMOs' network location, and therefore in their potential influence, in the light of both actors' (in our case, organizational) properties.[6] Among the former, consistently with the basic tenets of resource mobilization theory (Zald and McCarthy 1987), the size of organizational resources may be expected to be particularly influential on both centrality and brokerage measures. Larger resources render an SMO more visible, and more capable of working on several issues simultaneously. Possibilities for multiple collaborations, some of which may even cut across barriers within the movement sector, may thus develop. Resources also allow the appointment of professional staff, which may be expected to control greater political skills than the average movement activist. This may result in SMOs being better equipped at promoting successful campaigns on which other actors may converge (thus increasing their centrality), and/or at mediating between divergent interests and world views (Staggenborg 1988), thus increasing their brokerage potential.

Second, both centrality and brokerage may depend on SMOs' capacity to cover not just more numerous, but more diversified issues than others. Previous research suggests a strong correlation between the scope of associations' agendas, their presence in different policy domains, and their involvement in coalition activity (Knoke 1990*b*: 209–10). In the case of environmental movements, organizations who regularly address both urban ecology issues (traffic, pollution, etc.) and more classic conservation issues might find themselves more centrally located than SMOs addressing—no matter how broadly—only one of these major areas of concern. This is not simply because their potential pool of allies is broader; but because the greater flexibility of their profile may allow them to play more easily the role of movement agencies, which other SMOs with more specific concerns may refer to when appropriate (Lichterman 1995: 203–8; Melucci 1996: ch. 17).

Third, one might expect organizations that have been very recently established to play more peripheral roles in social movement networks. Alliance building depends on factors such as a relatively consolidated organizational structure, the spread of information about the organization and its perception by prospective allies as a relevant political actor, its public visibility. This cannot be achieved overnight. At the same time, beyond a certain threshold, the impact of the length of the period in existence may be expected to decrease.[7]

It may also be worth looking at the role of activists in generating additional channels of communication. Through their overlapping memberships, movement activists develop submerged linkages, which connect SMOs even when public mobilization is not in progress (Whittier 1995; Melucci 1996).[8] These bonds are also a reflection of how activists perceive different SMOs as close, or at the very least, as mutually compatible. Linkages generated by activists' multiple involvement may be regarded as a specific form of social capital,[9] which creates a favourable ground for interorganizational cooperation (Diani 1995: 133).

Data and Methods

Data for this study were collected among environmental organizations in the Milan metropolitan area in 1985 and early 1986 (Diani and Lodi 1988; Diani 1995: 193–6). Italian environmentalism in the 1980s did not differ substantially from its foreign counterparts in Northern Europe or the USA (Lowe and Goyder 1983; Jamison *et al.* 1990; Dalton 1994). Anti-nuclear groups and political ecology organizations had developed alongside more established conservation associations in the late 1970s to early 1980s. The mid-1980s had also witnessed the foundation of local Green Lists and the spread of informal grass-roots groups, mostly operating at the neighbourhood level (Diani 1995: ch. 2).

All informal groups and semi-bureaucratic organizations mobilizing on environmental issues, that defined themselves *and* were perceived by other SMOs as part of the movement, were included in the unit of analysis. Interviews were conducted with representatives of 42 organizations.[10] A 42 × 42 asymmetric alliance matrix was then built by assuming the existence of a linkage any time an SMO identified another as a regular partner in mobilization campaigns.[11] The density of the resulting matrix was 0.050, corresponding to an average of 2.1 ties for each organization.

In-degree scores were computed directly on the alliance matrix. Differences in the main traditions of environmental action represented the basis for the definition of movement subgroups, preliminary to the evaluation of brokerage roles. Environmental SMOs were allocated to different subgroups depending on their proximity to a political ecology (20 SMOs) or a conservation tradition (22 SMOs).[12] Gould and Fernandez's (1989) algorithm was then applied to the alliance matrix, and a raw brokerage score was computed, by summing up two of Gould and Fernandez's measures for brokerage across different groups, the *representative* and the *gatekeeper*.[13]

Three independent variables measure organizational properties: 'membership size', a proxy for organizational resources (local membership size, in the case of local branches of national organizations; no membership—and therefore no organizational resources apart from activists' personal contribution—was assumed in the case of totally informal groups); 'multiplicity of issues' addressed, a dummy variable with value 1 when an SMO was regularly active on both nature protection and urban ecology; 'period in existence', again a dummy variable with value = 1 when the SMO had been established after 1982, that is, less than three years before data collection took place.

Relational properties for the latent network—degree and brokerage scores[14]— were computed on a 42 × 42 symmetric matrix of interorganizational ties, based on the core activists' overlapping memberships. A linkage was assumed to exist any time two SMOs shared at least one of their core members. The density of the resulting matrix was 0.057, corresponding to an average of 2.3 ties for each SMO. Information for this matrix came from individual questionnaires distributed among SMOs' core members, those who gave the biggest contribution to run the organization and could therefore be expected to be more influential on alliance-building decisions.[15] About 197 activists, out of an estimated 400, returned the questionnaires.

Centrality in the Environmental Network

If leaders are leaders also because of their capacity to link to third parties, and thus to act as representatives of their followers, then SMOs with high centrality scores should be more frequently linked to relevant external actors than the more peripheral SMOs. This was actually the case in Milan. The most central SMOs were more likely than others to have access to the media. As Table 5.1 shows, the average centrality of SMOs who reported regular contacts to the national media was significantly higher than that of groups who had connections to local media only.[16] The most central groups were, in other words, more likely to be perceived by media and external observers as the actors entitled to speak up on behalf of the movement as a whole.[17] Likewise, while virtually all SMOs were engaged in collaborations with local councils, only a smaller number was involved in regular collaboration and consultation with higher bodies like the Milan provincial or the Lombardy regional council. Involvement in this type of ties was also found to be positively correlated with centrality in the movement alliance network (Table 5.1).

A closer look at the most important campaigns in Milan in the mid-1980s provides further illustration of the role played by the most central SMOs in the alliance network. These included the Milan branches of major conservation associations WWF and Italia Nostra, and of their political ecology counterpart Legambiente, but also the South Park Campaign, a local umbrella organization claiming the creation of a protected green belt in the Southern Milanese periphery. Other SMOs on lower, but still remarkable scores (3–4) were the Milan branches of major animal rights groups LIPU (Italian League for the Protection of Birds) and LAC (League for the Abolition of Hunting), along with two local branches of Legambiente, active in neighbouring towns in the Northern belt of Milan (Cinisello and Cologno), and the Milan Green List.

TABLE 5.1. *Average in-degree scores for SMOs with/without regular linkages to public institutions and national media*

	Regular linkages	No regular linkages	$p > F$
Public institutions	3.2	1.4	0.07
National media	2.6	0.4	0.04

These groups were indeed behind many of the most significant initiatives in the area. WWF, Italia Nostra, and Legambiente were the chief promoters of the campaign which succeeded in reducing private cars' access to the city centre in 1985—arguably the most relevant mobilization in the city for years. They were also supportive of initiatives related to energy policies and nuclear power issues, and only a few years later would have been backing animal rights organizations' unsuccessful attempt to achieve a global ban on hunting.[18] As for more informal, grassroots groups, the most central among them were protagonists in some of the most visible campaigns in the Milan peripheries: that for the creation of the South Park, in which the Green List was also involved, and that pursuing similar goals in the Northern periphery (Legambiente branches in Cologno and Cinisello). In sum, while none of the most central organizations was able to exert explicit domination over other environmental groups, they could be safely regarded as the most influential set of actors in the Milan network at the time. From different perspectives and in different capacities, they were able to both set the movement's agenda and be perceived from the outside as its *de facto* representatives.

But what accounts for network centrality? Model 1 in Table 5.2 includes resources and multiplicity of issues as explanatory variables of in-degree scores. Only the former are significantly—and positively—related to centrality. The fit of the model improves significantly ($p < 0.001$) when we bring a network variable into the equation. There is a clear, positive relation between SMOs' centrality in the latent network (as reflected in degree scores) and their centrality in inter-organizational exchanges (Model 2). The relationship holds and there is no improvement to the model when we control for the period of foundation: SMOs established after 1982 seem to have the same chances of playing a central role in the movement's campaigns as their older counterparts with similar organizational and relational resources (Model 3).

TABLE 5.2. *OLS coefficients predicting in-degree scores (square root) in the Milan environmental alliance network (N = 42; standard errors in parentheses)*

Models	1	2	3
Resources	0.04^{**} (0.01)	0.03^{**} (0.01)	0.03^{**} (0.01)
Multiple issues	-0.19 (0.29)	-0.43 (0.27)	-0.44 (0.27)
Degree scores in the latent network (sqrt)	—	0.47^{**} (0.13)	0.48^{**} (0.13)
Established after 1982	—	—	-0.16 (0.24)
Constant	0.82^{**} (0.16)	0.37^{*} (0.19)	0.46^{*} (0.23)
Adjusted R^2	0.30^{**}	0.46^{**}	0.45^{**}

$^{*}p < 0.05.$

$^{**}p < 0.01.$

SMOs which happen to be at the core of flows of communication to other groups, generated by their activists through their multiple memberships, are also likely to play central roles in networks of alliances. This does not imply necessarily multiplicity of ties between SMOs: as a matter of fact, of the 87 pairs of organizations linked by an alliance, only 24 also shared one or more core activists. Rather, centrality in the latent network means that through the opportunities for informal communication and networking created by their activists' multiple commitments, SMOs may increase their appeal to the rest of the movement, and find themselves in a more favourable position to attract alliances, even if their resources are not impressive. Among the core groups in the Milan case, the South Park Campaign provides the best illustration of this process: it was established by people who were also active in other SMOs in the area, but none of the latter organizations were among the Campaign's direct allies. Rather, consistently with the argument that interorganizational alliances in general are facilitated by indirect connections (Gulati 1995), adhesion to those groups provided militants of the South Park Campaign with the opportunity to establish ties to still other environmental groups, which then established alliances to the Campaign. In this process, the SMOs which the South Park activists were members of played the role of 'social relays' (Ohlemacher 1996) in that they provided the context in which distant actors established ties.

BROKERAGE IN THE MILANESE NETWORK

The distribution of brokerage scores differs remarkably from that of in-degree scores. Brokerage is extremely concentrated: the four SMOs scoring highest on Fernandez and Gould's indicators (the Milan branches of Legambiente, WWF, and Italia Nostra, plus the South Park Campaign) are involved in 56 brokerage relations out of 75 (75 per cent); 30 SMOs play no brokerage roles at all. In contrast, the four SMOs highest on in-degree (interestingly, the same four) receive only 47 per cent (41/87) of ties in the network; only 15 SMOs are not identified by other SMOs as partners in any alliance.

The coincidence of the top four brokers and 'leaders' might lead us to expect no significant differences between in-degree and brokerage measures as far as SMOs' capacity to develop ties to national media and political institutions, and therefore their role as informal representatives of the movement, is concerned. Data suggest, however, a quite different picture. Being involved in several, a few, or no brokerage linkages shows no relation to SMOs' chance of having access to the national media (Table 5.3). There are, in contrast, significant differences between levels of brokerage scores and access to higher level of political institutions. However, even in this case, the assumption of a positive relationship between levels of brokerage and increasing visibility in the media and political arenas finds no support, as SMOs playing some limited brokerage role are actually

TABLE 5.3. *Regular linkages to public institutions and national media*
for SMOs with different brokerage scores (N = 42)

	Brokerage scores			Fisher's exact test
	Nul	Low	High	
Public institutions				
Regular linkages	12	0	3	0.02
No regular linkages	18	8	1	
National media				
Regular linkages	22	6	4	0.72
No regular linkages	8	2	0	

more weakly connected to media and institutions than those playing no brokerage roles at all.

Despite the overlap among the very core SMOs (which I will discuss in the conclusions), these data point at quite different functions being performed by SMOs with some leadership and by those with some brokering capacity. Movement 'leaders' (i.e. the most central SMOs) attract the scarce resources internal to the movement towards certain campaigns rather than others, and also stand a better chance of representing the movement in the broader public sphere, in its dealings with the media and core political institutions. In contrast, playing a brokerage role does not seem to affect the public profile of SMOs in a significant way, if not for the very core organizations. The most important function of brokerage is within the movement network, as it allows the establishing of communication across different subgroups of the movement and in this sense facilitates the integration of otherwise heterogeneous organizations.

Figure 5.1 facilitates our understanding of these different dynamics by showing the structure of the Milan alliance network, consisting of 37 SMOs (five were dropped from the figure as they neither sent nor received any alliance tie). The centre of the network comprises of the four SMOs scoring highest on both indicators (N1, N8, N10, N17), plus the Milan Green List (N16), the South Milan branch of WWF (N23) and a Cyclists' association, Ciclobby (N6), who worked closely with the major groups on the occasion of the referendum against private cars. Clusters of groups at the top, bottom, and right of the network are largely defined on a territorial basis, as they consist of actors operating in the Western Milan neighbourhoods (top, N15, N34, N38), the Northern Milanese periphery (right, N42, N18, N2, N3, N9, N20, N31, N32, N29), and the Southern periphery (bottom, N19, N21, N22, plus the South Park Campaign and the South Milan WWF—N17 and N23—who are however at the centre given their more diversified connections). The left part of the network consists mainly of conservation and animal rights organizations, plus two libertarian organizations with both interests in conservation issues and ties to the Milan Green List (N25 and N30).

Diani

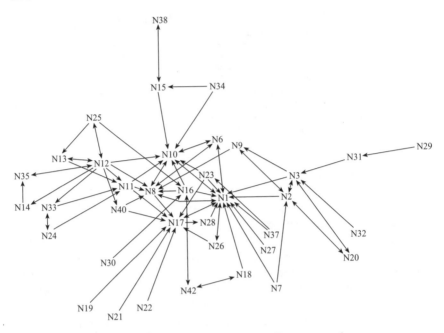

FIG. 5.1. *The Milan environmental alliance network*

While density is higher at the centre of the network, at least two of its peripheral components (the conservation/animal rights and the North Milan ones), and possibly three (if we include the Western neighbourhoods network, which is however far smaller) display substantial levels of interaction. These remain even if we drop the four most central groups from the network (Fig. 5.2). The internal connectedness of the movement network, however, disappears. The South Milan network collapses altogether, as no ties are left among its other components. The fragmentation corresponds to a large extent to the conservation versus political ecology divide (exceptions being the smallest network, West Milan, one animal rights group (N7) and the North Milan branch of WWF (N9) in the North Milan network). No systematic alliances seem to relate political ecology and conservation groups in the absence of a very restricted number of core organizations who are able to promote initiatives which may attract a more heterogeneous support. One should not neglect, however, the role of local brokers: in the North Milan, local branches of Legambiente in Cinisello and Cologno (N2 and N3) engaged in activities like the campaign for the creation of the North Milan Park, or the protection of a local eighteenth century villa threatened by developers, along with the local WWF branch. On this ground they provided a potential link, and an opportunity to the creation of broader solidarities, between the local WWF branch (N9) and their other partners (N20, N31, N32), groups with a distinctive left-wing profile, and strong linkages to other protest movements.[19] On the other hand, groups

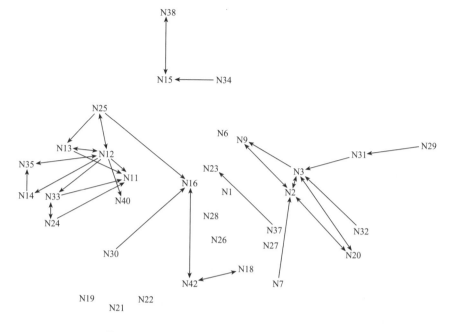

FIG. 5.2. *The network without the four top brokers*

with a clear public profile and a long tradition of campaigning may not necessarily be able to play brokerage roles. For example, bird protection group LIPU and anti-hunting LAC had a leading position in the field of animal rights; this resulted in a remarkable number of SMOs identifying them as partners in alliances as well as in them enjoying some access to major media and institutions. However, they only attracted alliances from similar conservationist groups; their brokerage power—and therefore their contribution to the overcoming of traditional barriers within the movement—was null.

A logistic regression offers some explanation of the reasons why some groups played at least some brokerage role, while others did not (Table 5.4). Model 1 shows both organizational resources and the capacity to cover a variety of issues as significant predictors of brokerage roles. In contrast to what we found out in our analysis of in-degree scores, adding relational properties[20] to the model (Model 2) does not increase its explanatory power at all. Consistently with what emerged in the case of in-degree scores, controlling for period in existence does not modify the pattern, either.

The implications of this evidence should not be overemphasized, given the extreme skewness of the distribution of brokerage scores and therefore the substantial difference between high and low scoring brokers. However, the profile of

TABLE 5.4. *Logistic coefficients predicting brokerage capacity in the Milan environmental alliance network (N = 42; standard errors in parentheses)*

Models	1	2	3
Resources	0.04* (0.02)	0.05* (0.02)	0.05* (0.02)
Multiple issues	1.09* (0.50)	1.19* (0.55)	1.25* (0.56)
Brokerage role in the latent network (0/1)	—	−0.28 (0.55)	−0.27 (0.57)
Established after 1982	—	—	0.49 (0.50)
Constant	−1.22** (0.32)	−1.19** (0.33)	−1.53** (0.50)
p > Chi2	0.00	0.01	0.01

*$p < 0.05$.

**$p < 0.01$.

the four most central brokers appears—with one exception—largely consistent with the results of the logistic regression.

A distinctive trait of the 'big three' (Legambiente, WWF, and Italia Nostra) vis-à-vis other environmental SMOs with some degree of bureaucracy was their ability to develop permanent structures (Rovelli 1988; Farro 1991). While other groups (including animal rights lobbies LIPU and LAC) had a number of local branches and substantial membership, Legambiente, WWF, and Italia Nostra, were the only ones with anything like a national rank-and-file structure. In 1991 their local branches were estimated to 444, 230, and 200, respectively, while among other SMOs only LIPU (slightly) exceeded 100 (Diani 1995: 36). More important, they had for different reasons established strong ties to specific sectors of public opinion, which rendered them an obvious reference point for people with high environmental concerns. Over a twenty years span, Italia Nostra and WWF had targeted teachers and school pupils, either through educational activities (mainly Italia Nostra) or voluntary work camps (mainly WWF). Although established in 1980 only, Legambiente could rely upon the extensive infrastructural network of ARCI, the cultural association of the Italian Left, of which it was originally a branch. The three major groups therefore could not only act as mobilizing bodies in their own right, but also as agencies, providing other environmental groups with information and expertise.

The three bureaucratic brokers actually combined attention for a broad range of issues with substantial organizational resources. Legambiente was born as an umbrella organization for local and/or single-issue groups of various sorts. The national headquarters ran their own campaigns, which local chapters might or might not support, without any hierarchical dependence between the two. The connection was rather provided by the regional offices of the organization, which acted as agencies, with the task of supporting campaigns promoted by the national headquarters, and helping local groups in their more modest actions.[21] Greater diversification of issues ensued, and with it, more diversified opportunities for alliances across the board. WWF and Italia Nostra were—and still are—closer to the classic model of the conservation public interest association. However, already in the 1970s they had innovated on a purely conservationist profile. They had developed an interest in urban ecology issues, and become more open to consider the inclusion of protest politics in their action repertoire. Although this had been more pronounced for WWF than for Italia Nostra, even the latter had shown increasing sympathy for antinuclear protest action, while still preferring its conventional lobbying techniques (Diani 1995, ch. 2).

None of these traits (organizational strength, combined with an inclusive profile and a broad range of topics addressed) applied to animal rights groups like LAC and LIPU. Although their interests were not necessarily restricted to animal welfare, that was clearly their major focus. Having been active for almost a decade both LIPU and LAC had a quite established organizational identity, which may have discouraged groups of different persuasions from regarding them as possible partners. This was even more pronounced for other animal rights groups like LEAL or ENPA. A more distinct profile and a certain degree of reluctance to engage in broader initiatives surely did not help the conservation groups' adoption of brokerage roles. Nor did the fact that their organizational structure was weaker, and less articulated, than that of the 'big three'.

Among the local branches of SMOs with national profile, brokerage seemed to be higher for SMOs active on a broader range of issues, and/or which operated at least partially as 'movement agencies'. The Park South Campaign represents, however, a clear exception to the 'rule'. As a local, informal group, it could not rely upon organizational structures that allowed it to act as a movement agency. As a single-issue campaign, it did not aspire to cover a broad range of issues. However, its specific issue was broad enough to accommodate a range of local concerns. The creation of a park in a heavily industrialized area like Milan appealed to both conservationist positions and radical critiques of industrialism and unregulated urbanization. The Legambiente branches in Cinisello and Cologno also elicited support from diverse sectors of the movement by promoting initiatives on urban issues with both a political and conservationist side. There appears to be some scope within movement networks for brokerage by actors who cannot act as 'movement agencies', provided they can launch campaigns on broad and encompassing—if clearly local—issues.

DISCUSSION AND CONCLUSIONS

The Milanese case suggests that centrality (in our case, in-degree) and brokerage measures reflect different dynamics within movement networks. The former comes closest to conventional forms of leadership, as organizations identified by many other SMOs as partners in alliances are also more likely to be connected to media and political institutions, and thus in the best position to act as 'representatives' of the movement in the broader public sphere. In contrast, occupying a brokerage position in the movement network does not imply necessarily a public role; brokerage positions are however crucial for the integration of the movement network, given their incumbents' capacity to attract support from SMOs with different world-views. In the absence of core brokers, the Milanese movement would consist of noncommunicating sectors narrowly defined by neighbourhood boundaries, or reference to specific issues. Although alliances to the brokers may develop on the occasion of different specific campaigns, and therefore need not imply direct collaboration between the peripheral parties involved, nonetheless the presence of a restricted number of actors towards whom most interactions converge greatly facilitates the transformation of an aggregate of individual, largely isolated groups, into a connected movement network, as it opens up channels of potential communication and mutual recognition.

It is therefore advisable to differentiate movement leadership from movement brokerage, especially as the two are also accounted for by partially different factors. Centrality in a movement network (as measured by in-degree) is not a function of organizational resources only. It is also a function of the networking capacity, generated by individual activists through their multiple memberships. The embeddedness of movement organizations in networks, based on their activists' behaviour, draws our attention to the existence of specific movement structures, more persistent and less volatile than those consisting of ties between SMOs.[22]

At the same time, though, evidence presented here does not merely confirm the existence of two parallel networks within social movements. It also allows us to better specify the interdependence between the two: what happens in the complex web of overlapping commitments created by activists bears directly on organizational behaviour, and shapes organizational opportunities for alliance and cooperation. Linkages created by activists are not a mere facilitator of sustained individual involvement (McAdam 1988 *a,b*; McAdam and Paulsen 1993); nor do they represent simply the basis for the development of subcultural activities and communitarian lifestyles. Submerged latent ties operate as a distinctive form of social capital which affects SMOs' position in alliance networks. For SMOs, alliance-building is often a costly and risky operation. It implies the recognition of commonalties and points of convergence between actors with distinct agendas, often competing, and sometimes positively distrustful of each other (Hathaway and Meyer 1994; Melucci 1996; Rochon and Meyer 1997). By creating new bridges through their multiple personal involvements, either directly or indirectly, movement activists facilitate the spread of solidarity (and, plausibly, mutual trust) among different groups and organizations. This finding is consistent with recent developments in the study of alliance-building among business organizations (e.g. Podolny and Page 1998; Ebers 1999; Kenis and Knoke 2002).

In contrast, personal ties to other SMOs do not appear to matter for the assumption of brokerage roles, which is rather accounted for by the combination of organizational resources and capacity to cover a broad range of issues. While centrality in alliances seems to require that the claims of specific SMOs to leadership be somehow supported and validated by interpersonal linkages, a more neutral profile seems to facilitate potential brokers. Brokerage requires 'neutral spaces' (Boissevain 1974) where actors with different perspectives can find a point of convergence, rather than the intergroup solidarity that the very fact of sharing activists implies. The semi-bureaucratic structure of most movement brokers, and the range of topics they address, seem to facilitate the activation of ties to SMOs with heterogeneous orientations. In turn, this opens up opportunities for communication (and possibly, collaboration) within the movement network, which would not otherwise be available (see Figs 5.1 and 5.2).

To sum up: (a) measures of network centrality and network brokerage capture different features of social movement networks; (b) while the former can be taken as indicators of movement leadership in the more conventional sense, given their incumbents' linkages to public actors, the latter identify crucial positions for the connectedness of a movement network; (c) while network centrality is accounted for by a combination of organizational properties and social capital, movement brokerage seems to depend exclusively on organizational traits. But how to account for the fact that at least in the Milan case, despite differences in leadership and brokerage roles, still the top brokers are also (in three cases out of four) the most visible leaders in the network? This is at odds with most theorizing on brokers, and its emphasis on their semi-marginality. It may be useful to conclude by briefly addressing this issue.

The overlap between incumbents of the top centrality and brokerage positions may be at least partially due to the particular structure of the Milanese movement, which in turn was shaped by the specific political and cultural conditions in which the movement developed.[23] Italian environmentalism grew as a distinct social movement in the early 1980s, that is at the end of what had been probably the most sustained series of collective action campaigns in Western democracies since the end of the Second World War (Tarrow 1989; della Porta 1995). In the 1970s, the emerging political ecology organizations had failed to develop systematic linkages to groups in the conservationist tradition like Italia Nostra or WWF. This had been largely due to their different location with respect to the dominant political cleavages of the time. The left-right cleavage was at its highest 'salience': it operated, in other words, as a substantial line of divide between individual and organizational actors. This rendered cooperation between the early environmental organizations difficult. In that context, brokerage roles were mostly played by informal groups of concerned scientists and intellectuals rather than by formal movement organizations. A central figure in these groups was, among others, the late scientist and leftist political figure Laura Conti. Her scientific qualifications allowed her to raise environmental issues within the scientific community and to be regarded as an authoritative, reliable figure even by the moderate conservation associations; at the same time, her political skills and political persuasions (she also served as an MP in the ranks of the Communist Party) made her a mentor for the earliest generation of political ecologists (Poggio 1996).[24]

In the 1980s, in contrast, the reduced salience of the left–right cleavage and more favourable conditions for environmental action—in particular the growth of sectors of public opinion interested in quality of life, personal health, and self-realization, and greater attention from political elites to environmental issues (Diani 1995: ch. 2)—facilitated the emergence of a different pattern of linkages. A structure developed, in which a restricted set of core organizations, representative of the variety of orientations within the movement, promoted joint visible campaigns and also acted as bridges between more peripheral, and often isolated, groups (Diani 1995: ch. 7; Figs 1 and 2). This pattern of relationships—and the peculiar political conditions underpinning it—may account for the partial overlap of SMOs capable of attracting consensus on their own campaigns (and therefore high on in-degree) and SMOs more skilled at roles of intermediation (and therefore high on brokerage scores). This was not due to the fact that differences between different sectors of environmental action had disappeared. On the contrary, SMOs close to a conservation perspective still substantially differed from their political ecology counterparts in a variety of areas (Diani 1995: 48–63). However, in the 1980s those differences did not act as positive barriers to interorganizational cooperation. Major SMOs with different ideological persuasions were rather inclusive in their choice of allies, and reluctant to emphasize ideological differences. In broader terms, instrumental styles of action largely prevailed over both radical, political, and expressive countercultural ones (Diani 1995: ch. 2). Starting a cooperation with a group holding a different orientation to the environmental question did not usually generate negative reactions from one's traditional allies. In such a context, the need for brokerage functions, played by actors different from those occupying other central roles, may not have been particularly strong.

These remarks point at a problem which has been largely unexplored so far, the relation between the shape of social networks, and the configuration of political opportunities. We may in particular ask ourselves whether connected, centralized structures of the type described here should be regarded as typical of political phases in which the salience of ideological conflict is comparatively low. Under changed political conditions, the picture might be rather different. Ideological and cultural differences might generate greater potential for fragmentation within a movement, and restrict actors' access to each other (Marsden 1983). The need for distinctive brokerage functions might accordingly increase. A deeper division of labour between major SMOs might also emerge (Zald and McCarthy 1987; Mushaben 1989; Rucht 1989). Some might specialize in the promotion of action campaigns, and in the mobilization of support from within specific movement subsectors. They might score high on centrality measures, yet within their movement fractions. Others might prove better at playing brokerage roles, thanks to their greater intermediation skills. As the Italian case in the 1970s suggests, when other types of political cleavages shape the forms of political activism, the integration of the different components of an emerging movement, cutting across the most salient cleavages, appears more problematic. It is under these conditions that the peculiarity of brokerage roles may be expected to be highest.

NOTES

1. These include intra- and inter-organizational behaviour, elite structure, party forma-
   tion, and interest representation (Laumann and Pappi 1976; Laumann and Knoke 1987;
   Mizruchi and Schwartz 1987; Knoke 1990*a*; Fernandez 1991; Nohria and Eccles 1992;
   Brass and Burkhardt 1993; Padgett and Ansell 1993; Knoke 1994; Krackhardt and
   Brass 1994; Mizruchi and Galaskiewicz 1994).

2. Knoke (1990*a*: 3–7) discusses the difference between domination and influence from
   a social network perspective.

3. Of the 320 protest events reported in the major daily *la Repubblica* between 1988 and
   1997, 72 were promoted by coalitions. Of these, 83% targeted national or even international institutions, as opposed to 68% of the events promoted by single SMOs;
   likewise, 62% of the issues addressed had a national or international scope, versus
   50% of issues addressed by individual SMOs (both differences significant at 0.001
   level) (Diani and Forno forthcoming).

4. The concept of in-degree fails to take into account that, while the number of allies an
   SMO may rely upon obviously matters, the linkages and the structural position of its
   allies are also crucial. Bonacich's concept of 'prominence' (Bonacich 1972; Knoke
   and Burt 1983) captures this dimension. Being related to others who in turn control a
   large number of ties, prominent actors may be expected to have easier access to crucial resources and information. As it were, though, our analysis yielded identical
   results regardless of whether in-degree or prominence measures were used.

5. Brokerage is both conceptually and methodologically preferable to the comparable
   measure of betweenness (Freeman 1979), which does not take differences between
   actors into account, and also requires symmetric data (Wasserman and Faust 1995:
   188–92).

6. Boissevain (1974: 147–8) distinguished between first order resources (the skills,
   money, etc., that actors directly control) and second order resources (the set of ties
   which allow actors to access those resources, actually controlled by other actors to
   whom they are connected).

7. For example, in their analysis of environmental associations in Britain, Lowe and
   Goyder (1983) found no systematic evidence that long-established conservation associations played a greater role than groups formed in the late 1960s/early 1970s.

8. Rosenthal *et al.* (1985, 1997), Fernandez and McAdam (1988), and Carroll and Ratner
   (1996) analyse the structure of social movements as a reflection of the activists' multiple memberships. The theoretical sources of this approach may be found in Simmel
   (1955) and Breiger (1988).

9. Coleman (1990); Edwards *et al.* (2001). For applications of the concept to social
   movement analysis: Minkoff (1997); Diani (1997).

10. These were based on semi-structured questionnaires and lasted between 60 and 90 min.

11. Regularity of collaboration was assessed on the basis of respondents' perceptions
    rather than on 'objective' criteria—which would necessarily mean very different
    things for different organizations.

12. Conservation groups differed from political ecology ones in their issue priorities (Diani
    1995: 55–6), and in their core activists' socio-demographic profile (p. 58), political
    background (pp. 68–9), framing of the environmental question (pp. 76–7), and linkages
    to non-environmental organizations (p. 91). Evidence on the Milan alliance network
    also confirms that differences between traditions actually affected interorganizational

exchanges: two-thirds of linkages (56/87) took place within movement sectors, and only one third across them, despite theoretical opportunities for exchanges across sectors slightly outnumbering those for exchanges within sectors (880 vs. 842).

13. The third of Gould and Fernandez's (1989) measure of brokerage across subgroups, the liaison type, did not apply here as the unit of analysis was partitioned into two subgroups only.

14. In the case of symmetric data, representative and gatekeeper brokerage scores are identical.

15. Only members of the executive board were interviewed in the case of semi-bureaucratic organizations, while all regular members of informal grass-roots groups were in principle contacted.

16. Regularity of linkage was once again assessed on the basis of respondents' perceptions rather than 'objective' criteria. 'National media' include the local sections of major national newspapers, sometimes the national sections of the same papers, and the regional offices of the major public and private radio and television networks; 'local media' consist of neighbourhood weekly newspapers and local radio stations.

17. To some extent this may also be a self-reinforcing process: attention paid by media operators to the most visible SMOs may well encourage less influential SMOs to contact the former as a result of the former's perceived public role (Kielbowicz and Scherer 1986).

18. A referendum which took place in Spring 1990 recorded an overwhelming majority in favour of the abolition of hunting, yet the result was not validated due to a turnout slightly below the 50% threshold (Diani 1995: 43).

19. Even in the mid-1980s members of these groups were particularly active in both the traditional left (11% vs. 4% of activists of other ecology groups, $p = 0.10$) and in radical protest movements (14% vs. 4%, $p = 0.03$).

20. Modelled here as a dichotomous variable measuring whether an SMO occupied a brokerage position in the latent network, or not (13 out of 42 did).

21. The structure of Legambiente has since then changed, with the national headquarters getting an increasingly high profile (Donati 1996).

22. The assumption of the volatility of movement networks is recurrent in the literature (Klandermans 1997). Individual affiliations, however, tend to display a substantial degree of continuity over time (Diani 1995, ch. 4).

23. Cook *et al.* (1983: 278) have long emphasized the importance of looking at the conditions under which certain patterns of network ties are likely to emerge. In the field of social movements, however, this problem has rarely been the focus of specific attention. For preliminary explorations see Diani (1995, ch. 7) and Balser (1997).

24. Staggenborg (1988) offers interesting examples of individual brokers within the American prochoice movement.

6

Community Embeddedness and Collaborative Governance in the San Francisco Bay Area Environmental Movement

Christopher Ansell

In recent years, students of policy formation, planning, and public administration have become interested in a management strategy called 'collaborative governance' (Gray 1989). In this approach to governance, public agencies, and public officials openly and inclusively engage various stakeholders in a process of dialogue and mutual adjustment about problems of common concern. Stakeholders are generally seen as having different, even antithetical interests. But the strategy puts faith in the idea that through dialogue, stakeholders may identify unanticipated opportunities for positive cooperation or at least ways to mitigate the costs of adversarial relations.

In economic sociology and organization theory, another body of literature has developed around the importance of 'embeddedness' in shaping governance structures. Following Granovetter (1985), this literature argues that the 'embedding' of economic activity in social relations allows exchange to be organized with less reliance on either formal contracts or organizational hierarchy. Network embeddedness enhances the ability of organizations to manage interpersonal or inter-organizational exchange through informal and relational mechanisms, like norms of trust and reciprocity (Uzzi 1996; Gulati and Gargiulo 1999). This embeddedness perspective is close in spirit to the argument put forward by social capital theorists that dense horizontal networks among independent civic associations are necessary for the cultivation of an autonomous civil society (Putnam 1993).

Communitarianism is one idiom through which the two sides of this discussion are brought together (Sandel 1996). It is through 'communities'—typically though not necessarily territorial in nature—that the conditions enumerated in both the collaborative governance literature and in the embeddedness/social capital literature are to be found. The necessity of including the stakeholders most directly affected by public actions and the requirement of face-to-face deliberation entailed by the notion of 'communicative rationality' are seen as best promoted through decentralized planning and policy decisions (Barber 1984; Williams and Matheny 1995).

The dense embeddedness of territorial communities is seen as providing the trust and social capital necessary to overcome political polarization. Within communities, embeddedness and collaborative governance should march hand-in-hand.

The attractiveness of this view depends in part upon a presumed relationship between political mobilization and territorial communities. An implicit presumption of the communitarian idea is that commitment to place is more likely to lead to integrative policy debates than commitment to issue. In the evolution of social movements and interest groups, cross-local mobilization around certain issues or interests leads to a 'disembedding' of associations from territorial communities. These associations become focused on narrow goals that they pursue unchecked by the more integrative concerns of any community, resulting in adversarial politics. The vertical and sectoral nature of representation is accentuated over the horizontal and integrative.

A contrasting view sees this disembedding as a process of modernization in which interest representation is freed from the parochial passions of communal politics and where subordinated interests free themselves from the informal coercion of local political fiefdoms. Freed from the informal personalism of local communities, these associations become professionalized, and consequently, more open to rational deliberation. The first view sees territorially embedded associations as more favourable towards collaboration, while the second view sees issue-based associations as more inclined to collaboration.

Similar tensions run through social movement theory. New social movements often express anti-bureaucratic, 'small-is-beautiful,' communitarian views. For these social movements, grassroots mobilization means 'community organizing' (Lichterman 1996). These movements exemplify the ideals of civic participation, developing the dense horizontal networks celebrated in civil society arguments. Furthermore, the grassroots organizing of social movements can be seen as necessary for 'opening up' the policy process, forcing public agencies to adopt a more inclusive policy style (Dryzek 1996). New social movements, in particular, are seen as the critical advocates of direct participatory democracy and collaborative governance can be seen as an administrative form of this participation. These affinities suggest that collaborative governance may be particularly likely to emerge in political arenas where new social movements are active.

Other perspectives on social movements, however, would suggest that they would be less likely to engage in collaborative governance. Social movements embrace 'outsider' strategies of grassroots mobilization and direct action in contrast to the 'insider' lobbying strategies embraced by interest groups (Staggenborg 1988; Walker 1997). In addition, while social movement organizations may be densely networked together, these networks may be primarily subcultural or countercultural (Melucci 1989). Such networks serve to mobilize and sustain opposition to the dominant culture and the status quo (Fernandez and McAdam 1988; Lo 1992). A venerable tradition within social movements and within social movement theory views collaboration with the state and societal opponents as leading to cooptation and deradicalization (Michels 1959; Piven and Cloward 1977).

This tension can also be restated in a communitarian idiom. In the first version, the communitarianism of new social movements is something they advocate as a plan for politics and society as a whole. In the second, the social movement is itself the community, which defines itself in opposition to the surrounding main-stream community.

Seen through this communitarian lens, the hypothetical relationship between embeddedness and collaborative governance becomes somewhat more provocat-ive. How does embeddedness in a particular territorial community or a particular issue-oriented community affect social movement attitudes towards collaboration? How does embeddedness in a social movement subculture affect the attitudes of groups towards collaboration? In this chapter, I examine these questions through an investigation of one social movement community defined in both territorial and issue-related terms—the San Francisco Bay Area environmental movement.

The San Francisco Bay Area is home to a progressive and well-established envir-onmental movement. It is a region famous for its progressive politics and social movement activism. It is also a region both richly endowed with natural resources and increasingly pressured by urban development. These factors combine to produce a local environmental movement with surprising organizational depth and diversity. The movement varies from local groups working to preserve small neighbourhood natural areas to associations working to protect natural resources on a global scale. Bay Area environmental organizations range from strictly volun-teer groups with small, informal memberships to well-staffed professional organizations with sizeable budgets. The vibrant, well-established, and diverse character of this movement make it an interesting community in which to explore some of the issues associated with the relationship between embeddedness and collaboration.

VARIETIES OF EMBEDDEDNESS

Embeddedness has predominantly come to mean the embedding of a person or organization in a set of social relations or networks. Building on distinctions drawn in network analysis, Gulati and Gargiulo (1999) usefully distinguish between positional, structural, and relational embeddedness. A major measure of positional embeddedness is centrality. Presumably, the more central an organi-zation is within a network of relationships, the more it is deeply embedded in that network. This measure should capture the full ambiguity of the attitude of social movements towards cooperative modes of governance. If social movements create an oppositional dynamic, higher centrality should lead towards a less san-guine view of collaboration. If social movements provide the basic infrastructure of civil society, then greater centrality may promote a more favourable atti-tude towards collaboration. Of course, it is very possible that both these effects could be pulling in different directions and consequently 'wash out' the effect of centrality.

Network theory identifies several measures of centrality (Freeman 1979). While these measures are often highly correlated in practice, they capture slightly different meanings of positional embeddedness. Degree centrality refers to the number of ties that a nodal actor sends to other actors (outdegree) or receives from other actors (indegree). In this context, degree centrality indicates whether an SMO has a particularly dense or impoverished set of relationships with other actors in the community. High outdegree suggests that an organization is actively networking with other groups. High indegree indicates that an organization is prominent or perhaps powerful—other organizations seek its advice, resources, or influence. Closeness centrality indicates the distance of one particular actor to all other actors in the network (as measured by path length). Actors with high closeness centrality can presumably more easily and directly connect and interact with other actors in a network. High closeness centrality means that an actor can easily influence and extract resources from the full network. Betweenness centrality refers to the degree to which an actor is on the path 'between' other actors in the network and can thus presumably mediate relationships between those actors. Thus, the centrality measure comes closest to measuring the degree to which an actor operates as a powerful broker within a network.

Relational embeddedness, according to Gulati and Gargiulo, refers to the degree of cohesion in a social network. In studying social movement embeddedness, cohesion might refer to the degree to which the network is closed in on itself and thus operates like a subculture or counter-culture. One measure of this is the degree to which actors are involved in cliques with other actors in the social network. In network terms, a (maximal) clique is a group in which every member has a relationship to every other member of the clique. In open networks, cliques may be rare and where they exist may be quite small. As a network becomes more closed, we should expect the number and size of cliques to increase. The more cliques of large size that an actor is a member of, the more that actor is important to the closure of the network as a whole.

Structural embeddedness is operationalized by Gulati and Gargiulo as structural equivalence. In network analysis, actors are structurally equivalent when they have a similar pattern of ties to third parties. Borgatti and Everett (1992) have observed that structural equivalence is not a pure measure of structural position, but rather captures aspects of both network position and network proximity. This is clearly a disadvantage if one wants to isolate the importance of network position. However, it may be an advantage when trying to operationalize embeddedness. Arguably, the concept of embeddedness presumes the importance of direct dyadic interaction (through which face-to-face interaction operates) *and* the importance of indirect ties (that promote the generalized norms of trust and reciprocity to the network level). In other words, embeddedness implies not only the importance of belonging to a concrete set of dyadic relations, but also of belonging to a broader network of ties. Like the clique model, structural equivalence identifies actors that belong to the same network. But the clique model identifies membership in specific 'subgroups' by identifying where networks have become relatively closed. In contrast, structural equivalence identifies common networks in terms of both direct and indirect ties. Structural equivalence identifies network communities that are not closed.

Following Granovetter, I use the term *embeddedness* to refer to the idea of integration into particular networks. Both the social capital and communitarian literature, however, also point to the way in which organizations are rooted in particular communities. Therefore, we also need to consider how social movement organizations are situated in their communities temporally and socially. And we need to examine the kinds of communities they are rooted in—territorial versus issue-based communities.

Temporally, we are concerned with the length of time that a person or organization has been situated in a particular communal context. Presumably, the longer a person or organization has been situated in a given context, the more they have been socialized into the norms of that context and the more they have had time to develop informal, locally-specific knowledge and strategies for working in that context.

Socially, we are concerned with the degree to which an organization is open to and interpenetrated by its surrounding environment. Many social movement organizations, for example, have only a very limited demarcation from informal social networks. On the other hand, bureaucratization and professionalization may draw increasingly sharp boundaries between organizations and their environments. This boundary increases the autonomy of organizations from their social context (Udy 1962). In the context of social movements, we can distinguish between those organizations that organize and support themselves through strong interconnections with their immediate context versus those that gain relative autonomy from that environment.

In territorial terms, we are concerned with how narrowly or widely social movement organizations define their territorial focus. Are they primarily focused on protecting a local natural resource (a specific wetland, coastline, forest, etc.)? Or do they understand the entire world to be potentially within their ambit (wetlands, coastlines, forests, etc.)? The assumption here is that the more local the territorial scope of an association, the more it may have face-to-face relations on the basis of territorial residence and proximity. As territorial scope expands, organization might still be organized through face-to-face networks, but these will be less associated with ties of neighbourhood and residential proximity. As territorial scope expands, we expect people to be brought together around shared interests or attitudes. It is also useful to further distinguish whether social movement organizations understand themselves to be operating primarily in terms of place-oriented or issue-oriented communities.

Finally, in terms of issue-oriented communities, we know that the environmental movement is composed of a great many specialized though overlapping issue foci. Because of their concern with certain issues, the critical reference groups for environmental associations may be specialized policy communities. It is highly plausible to expect that attitudes towards collaboration may vary from issue to issue as the specificities of certain policy debates and solutions vary. The environmental justice movement, for instance, might be highly conflictual while policy debates in recycling might be much more cooperative.

THE SURVEY

A survey of the Bay Area environmental movement was conducted during the spring of 2000, with most of the surveys being administered during the months of March and April. For the purposes of this study, the 'Bay Area' encompasses the nine counties that belong to the Association of Bay Area Governments: Alameda, Contra Costa, Marin, Napa, San Francisco, San Mateo, Santa Clara, Solano, and Sonoma. The survey was administered on environmental groups with an office or an outpost, however informal, in the Bay Area. The preliminary list of environmental groups was composed from three sources available on the internet: the Bay Area Progressive Network, Bay Area Action's Ecocalender directory of Bay Area environmental groups, and Yahoo's listing of environmental groups for each of the nine counties. I then examined the websites links of many of these groups to identify other groups involved in environmental issues. The resulting list included 174 organizations.[1] Eventually, we collected 70 completed surveys.[2] While this response rate seems low in comparison with the total population surveyed, we found that a large number of organizations in our initial sample were either impossible to contact or actually moribund. It is quite reasonable to conclude that this data contains a selection bias towards more active and better-established organizations, though the surveyed organizations still represent a wide variety of organizational types.

The survey itself asked a range of questions eliciting information on organizational characteristics, relations with other environmental organizations, and attitudes towards collaboration. With respect to collaboration, I made a decision in the design of the survey to focus on general attitudes towards collaboration with government and with groups with opposing interests.[3] The following questions best capture the general attitude towards collaborative governance: 'How valuable is close collaboration with government agencies in solving environmental problems?'; 'How useful is it to enter into dialogue with groups or segments of the population whose values, interests, or goals are strongly opposed to your own?'. Answers were coded from 1 to 5, with 1 indicating that the respondent thought that collaboration with government agencies or dialogue with opposing groups was 'a waste of time' and 5 indicating that it was 'very valuable' (see Table 6.1).

The survey also asked a battery of questions to elicit the dimensions of network embeddedness and to identify how organizations related to the Bay Area community. With respect to network embeddedness, the survey elicits information only on

TABLE 6.1. *Summary measures of variables
measuring propensity to collaboration with
government agencies and dialogue
with opposing groups*

	Collaboration	Dialogue
Minimum	1.00	1.00
Maximum	5.00	5.00
Mean	3.903	3.659
Standard deviation	1.086	1.170
N	62	63

interorganizational networks, or what Diani calls the 'visible' network (Diani 1995).[4] Interorganizational network relations were elicited by asking respondents to identify, from the full list of 174 organizations, the organizations with whom they had 'directly worked'.[5] 'Directly' was defined as 'groups with whom your organization had personal contact' and was included to discourage the inclusion of organizations with whom they had had only indirect contact through common membership in an alliance or umbrella group. 'Worked' was defined as contact ranging from 'informal consultation to formal alliance'. This information was then coded as a 70×70 asymmetric matrix.

I then calculated the measures of degree, closeness, and betweenness centrality that would be used to assess positional embeddedness (all analyses were conducted using the UCINET V package: Borgatti *et al.* 1998). Because the data is asymmetric, the measures included indegree and outdegree centrality as well as incloseness and outcloseness. A single measure is produced for betweenness centrality. I also used the clustering routine CONCOR (Breiger *et al.* 1976) to estimate structural equivalence, which served as my measure of structural embeddedness. I began by allowing the procedure to produce two consecutive splits, yielding four blocks. I then used block membership as a dummy variable in my subsequent linear regression analysis. I will return in the discussion below to how I subsequently refined this analysis. Finally, I conducted a clique analysis on the data. I first established that the largest cliques in the network were seven-member cliques (i.e. there were no cliques with greater than seven members). There were 13 seven-member cliques, most of them with overlapping memberships. I then took the number of seven-group cliques to which an organization belonged as an indicator of how much that organization contributed to the closure of the network as a whole.

A question about the year of foundation located each organization temporally in the environmental movement. Since we know that new organizations may be created by activists with long careers in the environmental movement, the survey also asked how long the respondent had been working in the environmental movement in general and in the Bay Area environmental movement in particular.[6]

With respect to the integration of each organization in the local Bay Area community, the survey asked about the reliance of the organization on volunteers, the number of full-time staff, and the number of members. The more that organizations rely on volunteers and the more they are membership organizations, the more I regard them as open to the local environment. I regard organizations as more autonomous from their local communities if they are run primarily by full-time staff and do not utilize volunteers or have a membership base. The survey also asked if the organization adopted any of the following techniques to recruit members: word of mouth, advertising, personal contacts, door-to-door membership campaigns, and mailings. As mobilization techniques, I consider word of mouth and personal contacts to depend on a strong rootedness in the local community. These are techniques that presume reliance on an extended informal network. In contrast, advertising and mailings are impersonal means of recruitment. Door-to-door campaigns are intermediate between informal and formal. The survey also asked about whether the group's financing came from any of the following sources: membership dues, services provided, government grants or other public funding, grants from private foundations, or charitable donations from private donors. Here, the reasoning is that organizations that depend on resources from membership and, to a somewhat lesser extent, from charitable donations from private donors, are more embedded in the community than those who derive funding from services or government/foundation grants.

A second measure of linkage to the local community is affiliation with larger state-wide, nation-wide, or international organizations. Arguably, the stronger the external control or authority of the extra-local organization, the less the local group is tied to and responsive to the local community. The survey sought to elicit the character of this relationship by asking whether the surveyed organization would describe itself as a branch office, a chapter, an affiliate, or a member of this external group.[7] For example, a branch office is generally more under the control of a central organization than a chapter and consequently, in theory, is relatively less strongly tied to and responsive to the local context. While recognizing that these terms are inevitably somewhat vague and variable in their interpretation, the strength of linkage to the local community is judged as follows: independent organizations (no external affiliation) are most locally rooted, followed by members, affiliates, chapters, and branch offices.

Territorial jurisdiction was ascertained by asking organizations to identify the label that best captured the scope of their territorial involvement: neighbourhood, town or city, county, East Bay, Peninsula, South Bay, North Bay, Bay Area, Northern California, California, the West, the USA, or the World. I also coded an 'In-Bay' dummy variable to include all responses that indicated that the best label was either neighbourhood, town or city, county, East Bay, Peninsula, South Bay, North Bay, or Bay Area.

To ascertain the ties of groups to issue-oriented communities, the survey presented respondents with a broad list of issues and asked them to identify those issues their group worked on.[8] Each issue was then coded as a dummy variable. In addition, I coded the total number of issues that a group worked on, since we often hear that 'single issue' groups will act differently than groups working on a broad range of issues. Since even quite small groups worked on quite a few issues, I also sought a way to represent patterns of linkage to multiple issue domains. I used correspondence analysis to identify the commonalities in the patterns of issue linkage across all issues, utilizing the scores produced by this procedure as an indication of similar issue communities.[9]

The survey also sought to determine whether a group identified more closely with its territorial community or with its issue community. The survey first asked whether the group felt itself to be part of a larger community of groups with complementary goals. Of course, nearly everyone answered yes. The following question then asked the respondent whether they would describe this community primarily in terms of 'territory' or a 'group of people working on a particular issue irregardless of place'. A third option allowed them to identify this community as 'a group of people working on a particular issue in a particular place'.

Finally, the survey asked about which of the following strategies the group adopted to deal with environmental issues: a legal strategy, direct action, education and research, cultivation of public awareness, formulation of new policies or regulations, monitoring of existing legislative or policy implementation, lobbying congress, state legislatures, county boards of supervisors, or municipal councils, or lobbying international, federal, state, or local agencies. This question was partly designed to help distinguish social movement strategies (direct action, cultivation of public awareness) from interest group strategies (formulating policy and lobbying legislative bodies and agencies). In addition, it was expected that organizations adopting legal strategies would have quite adversarial attitudes, while organizations that specialized in lobbying agencies would have more collaborative attitudes (as potential insiders).

RESULTS OF THE ANALYSIS

With respect to attitudes towards collaboration with public agencies, a linear regression analysis found that structural network embeddedness (structural equivalence) did positively affect attitudes towards collaboration, while relational network embeddedness (cliques) had a negative impact. Affiliations with groups outside the Bay Area also negatively affected the attitudes towards collaboration. At least as operationalized, other indicators of being rooted in the local community (temporal, territorial) or in particular issue-oriented communities were substantively and statistically insignificant in relation to collaboration. With the exception of outcloseness centrality, the measures for network centrality (positional embeddedness) were also insignificant. As will be discussed below, however, outcloseness seems to capture something very similar to structural embeddedness.

As for the degree to which organizations are tied to the local community, the most important finding was that organizations with affiliations to organizations outside the Bay Area have a less favourable attitude towards collaboration with government agencies. On the other hand, the character of the relationship to these external organizations does not appear to matter. Branch organizations are no less favourable towards collaboration than chapters, etc. Contrary to what we might expect from Staggenborg's (1988) or Walker's (1997) analysis of the professionalization and bureaucratization of social movements, neither membership base, nor modes of recruiting members, nor reliance on volunteers or staff size seem to have had any significant impact on collaboration. However, those organizations that derived funding from government grants (not surprisingly) did have a more collaborative attitude towards government agencies than those that did not. But contrary to expectations, organizations that adopted legal strategies were actually more favourable towards collaboration. Also contrary to expectations, neither the adoption of direct action strategies nor the adoption of lobbying strategies (including lobbying of agencies), had any significant influence on the attitude towards collaboration.

Perhaps the most interesting findings were the results for structural and relational network embeddedness. In my initial CONCOR analysis, I produced four structurally equivalent blocks.[10] With membership in these blocks coded as dummy variables in the linear regression model, one of the blocks (Block 1) proved quite positive (substantive and statistical significance) to collaboration. To examine the robustness of this finding, I then analysed a more aggregated (two-block) and more disaggregated (eight-block) model. When Block 1 was aggregated with Block 2, the relationship with collaboration declined substantively and statistically. When Block 1 was further disaggregated into two blocks, the relationship between one of the resulting blocks (Block B) and collaboration was sharper (the positive substantive relationship increased and statistical significance was somewhat improved). For the other block, the relationship was still positive, but no longer statistically significant.

Given my predilection for larger blocks, I decided to keep these groups together in presenting my image matrix analysis. But before presenting that analysis, let me report the findings for relational embeddedness. Recall that relational embeddedness measures the cohesion of the network and that I operationalized individual contributions to network closure as the number of cliques of which each organization was a member. The modest (though highly significant statistically) negative impact of this variable on collaboration supports the argument that the more subcultural or countercultural the social movement, the less it will view governmental collaboration in favourable terms. The multivariate results for the variables discussed above are reported in Table 6.2. The finding that one block of structurally equivalent organizations was quite favourable towards collaboration obviously raises questions about the nature of this block in contrast to the other blocks. The following image matrix (Fig. 6.1) helps to understand the distinctiveness, in network terms, of Block 1.

TABLE 6.2. *OLS coefficients predicting propensity for collaboration with government agencies (N = 62; standard errors in parentheses)[a]*

Block 1	0.94^{**} (0.24)
Public grants	0.66^{**} (0.22)
Legal strategies	0.45^{*} (0.22)
Outside affiliations	-0.59^{**} (0.22)
Clique	-0.10^{**} (0.03)
Constant	3.61^{**} (0.21)
Multiple R^2	0.46^{**}

$^{*}p < 0.05.$
$^{**}p < 0.01.$
[a] Block 1 was coded 1 if the organization was in Block 1 and 0 otherwise; public grants was coded 1 if the organization reported receiving funding for public grants and 0 otherwise; legal strategies was coded 1 if the organization reported utilizing legal strategies and 0 otherwise; outside affiliations was coded 1 if the organization reported an affiliation outside the Bay Area and 0 otherwise; clique reports the number of seven-member cliques to which an organization belongs. It varies from 0 to 13, with a mean of 1.3 and a standard deviation of 3.122.

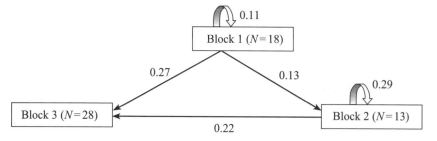

FIG. 6.1. *Image matrix of the Bay Area environmental movement. Cutoff for reporting image matrix links: average density of entire network = 0.10*

To some extent, the image matrix suggests a classic core–periphery structure for the Bay Area environmental movement. Block 3 is the core block. Blocks 1 and 2 send ties to Block 3 that are unreciprocated. From this perspective, Blocks 1 and 2 represent relatively peripheral groups. Both are integrated, however, into the broader Bay Area movement by their own efforts to network with core actors. The ties sent by peripheral Blocks 1 and 2 to Block 3 are fairly dense: the density of ties is over twice the density of network as a whole. In contrast to these peripheral blocks, Block 4 appears to be isolated from the movement as a whole and to lack internal cohesion.

Yet the image matrix also suggests that the structure of the movement departs in some interesting ways from a classic core–periphery structure.[11] Most importantly, Block 1 sends links not only to the core (as in a classic core–periphery structure), but also to the other peripheral block (Block 2). If Block 2 did not also send ties to Block 3, Fig. 6.1 would suggest a movement with two distinct cores.

A second departure from the classic core–periphery structure is that the peripheral blocks are themselves internally cohesive. In such a structure, peripheral groups seek relations with the core, but not among themselves. Here, in contrast, the image matrix reveals that the two 'peripheral' blocks—1 and 2—are internally cohesive. This is particularly true of Block 2. The density of within-block ties in Block 2 is nearly three times the density of the overall network. This suggests that Block 2 has some cliquish tendencies. In contrast, Block 3—the block you might expect to be most cliquish—does not appear particularly cohesive.

In this modified core–periphery structure, Block 1 appears distinctive. Not only is it internally cohesive, but it also sends ties to both Blocks 2 and 3. My initial inclination was to see Block 1 in a sort of brokerage role, providing a bridge between Blocks 2 and 3. Yet this does not really appear to be the case. Block 1 is sending ties to Blocks 2 and 3, but not receiving them. A broker would be receiving ties (cf. Diani 1995: 123, and in this book). Nor is it possible to conclude, as I initially did, that Block 1 integrates the movement as a whole because it is the only block that has strong ties to the two other main blocks. Yet the fact that Block 1 has both a degree of internal cohesion and ties to both other blocks is important. Block 1 groups send a large quantity of ties to other blocks. While Block 1 groups are peripheral, they appear strongly oriented towards 'networking'. This impression is reinforced by examining outcloseness centrality—the measure of closeness centrality based on just those ties that organizations send to other organizations. If outcloseness centrality is substituted for Block 1 in the multivariate equation, it has a statistically significant positive association with attitudes of collaboration (as reported in Table 6.4, the zero-order correlation between outcloseness and Block 1 is 0.277). If both are included in the regression, Block 1 remains highly significant while outcloseness centrality loses its statistical significance.

Before exploring this 'networking' strategy more fully, it is important to see whether these findings also hold for the other dependent variable—the degree to which groups were willing to engage in dialogue with groups holding opposing values and perspectives. My analysis produces similar findings: Block 1 also proves to be favourable towards dialogue with opposing groups (see Table 6.3). Again, I experimented with more and less aggregated blockings. In this analysis,

TABLE 6.3. *OLS coefficients predicting
propensity to dialogue with opposing groups
(N = 63; standard errors in parentheses)*

Block B	1.31** (0.33)
Sustainable development	1.11** (0.32)
Urban sprawl	− 1.02** (0.34)
Outside affiliations	0.58* (0.24)
Clique 1[a]	− 0.82** (0.32)
Constant	3.25** (0.19)
Multiple R^2	0.40**

*$p < 0.05$.
**$p < 0.01$.
[a] In Clique 1, groups who were a member of at least
one of the 13 seven-member cliques were coded 1;
all other groups were coded 0.

only one of the two partitions of Block 1—Block B ($N = 11$)—is significantly related to propensity to dialogue. The following analysis uses Block B, rather than Block 1, because Block B provides a better fit than Block 1 in a bivariate model and also seems to considerably sharpen up the multivariate model.

In this analysis, affiliation with an external group again proves to dampen enthusiasm for dialogue, but financial support from public grants and recourse to legal strategies does not have any significant influence. The number of seven-member cliques an organization belonged to proves to be only marginally significant. However, a recoded clique measure (Clique 1) proved more powerful and is included in the multivariate model. Using propensity to dialogue as the dependent variable, other variables operationalizing various forms of network embeddedness and the linkage of the groups to territorial and issue-oriented communities were reexamined. In bivariate analyses, involvement in four issues areas—renewable resources, sustainable development, urban sprawl, and wilderness—has an important influence on inclination to dialogue. In the multivariate model, only sustainable development and urban sprawl remained robust. Involvement in the issue area of sustainable development had a quite positive influence, while involvement with the issue of urban sprawl seemed to significantly dampen this positive spirit.

Having now established the overall relationship between the structure of the network and the inclinations of environmental groups to engage in collaboration with public agencies and dialogue with groups with different perspectives, we can now investigate more closely the nature of the different blocks of organizations identified above. By examining the zero-order correlations between block membership and other survey variables, Table 6.4 provides a detailed profile of each of the blocks. These profiles allow us to pose a general question about the findings of this network analysis: is block membership really a proxy for other variables? In particular, is Block 1 (or Block B) simply identifying a group of nonradical environmental groups? While it might still be interesting to understand why these groups are structurally equivalent, such a finding would vitiate the preliminary finding that *the characteristics of the network* explains attitudes towards collaboration and dialogue. Based on the zero-order correlations between survey variables and blocks (Table 6.4), we can sketch the following profiles of blocks:

1. Block 2 organizations seem to be *professional issue-oriented advocacy groups*. These organizations are the least place-oriented (-0.199) and the most issue-oriented (0.130) of any of the blocks. They appear to rely more heavily on staff (0.199) than on volunteers (-0.137). They do not rely on word of mouth (-0.265^*) or personal contacts (-0.185) to recruit members, nor do they raise money through services (-0.256^*). Their focus is not local and they are the least focused on environmental protection within the Bay Area of any block (In-Bay $= -0.210$). Their strategies focus on lobbying legislatures (0.278^*) and public agencies (0.211). They tend to have had more negative experiences with public agencies than other blocks (-0.234) and their relation with these agencies tends to be conflictual (0.261^*). These groups appear to rely significantly on a strategy of networking with other groups (outdegree $= 0.290^*$). While none of the blocks is particularly cliquish, Block 2 has the greatest tendency in this regard (0.155).

2. The profile of Block 4 is in many respects the opposite of Block 2. Groups in this block are largely *local, volunteer-based environmental groups*. These organizations do not have significant staff resources ($- 0.163$) and tend to rely instead on volunteers (0.199). Their focus is localized. Their action is oriented towards counties (0.198), the Peninsula (0.186), and especially, the North Bay (0.337^{**}). While they have a strong focus *within* the Bay Area (0.353^*), they are not particularly focused on the Bay Area as a whole (-0.092). Of all four main blocks, they are the most place-oriented (0.112) and the least issue-oriented (-0.180). They do not generally target public agencies for lobbying (-0.172), though their experiences with public agencies have been better than those of other blocks (0.158). These local organizations are relatively isolated (as shown in Fig. 6.1): they make relatively little effort to network with other groups (outdegree $= -0.266^*$); nor are they the target of networking (indegree $= -0.276^*$). They are the least cliquish of all the blocks (-0.181).

3. Block 3 (core) groups are probably *membership-based environment groups with significant organizational resources*. These groups have both staff (0.198) and members (0.144). They recruit members through word-of-mouth (0.236^*) and door-to-door campaigns (0.248). Support from foundations (0.323^*) rather than dues (-0.013), however, appears to be their main source of revenue. These organizations are the least focused on lobbying legislatures (-0.211) or public agencies (-0.187) of any of the blocks. As suggested in Fig. 6.1, many other Bay Area groups want to network with

TABLE 6.4. *Pearson correlations between block membership and survey variables*

Variables	Blocks						N
	A	B	1	2	3	4	
Date founded	0.177	0.043	0.157	−0.101	−0.092	0.043	70
Number staff	−0.108	−0.106	−0.162	0.188	0.198	−0.163	69
Number members	−0.067	−0.111	−0.138	0.078	0.144	−0.114	69
Volunteer	0.061	−0.036	0.012	−0.137	−0.050	0.199	70
Word of mouth	0.068	−0.139	−0.069	−0.265*	0.236*	0.048	70
Advertising	−0.197	0.126	−0.045	−0.022	0.052	0.003	63
Door-to-door	0.201	−0.135	0.041	−0.185	0.248	−0.175	63
Personal contacts	0.132	0.000	0.096	−0.149	−0.013	0.068	63
Dues	0.123	−0.046	0.046	0.007	−0.013	−0.046	70
Service	0.071	0.032	0.076	−0.256*	0.050	0.116	70
Public funding	0.029	−0.100	−0.063	−0.077	0.072	0.061	70
Foundations	−0.211	−0.248*	−0.351**	0.058	0.323**	−0.074	70
Private donors	0.136	−0.048	0.053	−0.015	0.083	−0.160	70
Neighbourhood	0.092	−0.120	−0.036	0.010	0.000	0.033	70
County	0.086	0.097	0.139	−0.228	−0.090	0.198	70
Peninsula	0.014	−0.166	−0.128	−0.183	0.122	0.186	70
North Bay	−0.092	−0.120	−0.163	−0.132	0.000	0.337**	70
South Bay	0.156	−0.049	0.067	−0.074	−0.052	0.069	70
East Bay	−0.128	0.069	−0.031	0.036	0.035	−0.049	70
Bay Area	0.101	0.220	0.253*	−0.217	0.015	−0.092	70
In-Bay	0.078	−0.048	0.013	−0.210	−0.107	0.353**	70
Place-oriented	0.137	−0.052	0.054	−0.199	0.028	0.112	67
Issue-oriented	0.014	−0.008	0.003	0.130	0.023	−0.180	66
Legal action	0.106	−0.044	0.036	0.120	−0.036	−0.124	70
Direct action	−0.010	0.124	0.097	0.029	0.036	−0.195	70
Education	0.048	0.118	0.131	−0.129	−0.029	0.020	70
Awareness	0.120	−0.092	0.006	−0.059	0.018	0.032	70
Policymaking	0.019	−0.077	−0.051	−0.004	0.047	0.002	70
Monitoring	−0.048	0.039	0.000	0.110	−0.058	−0.039	70
Legislatures	−0.086	0.069	−0.002	0.278*	−0.211	−0.010	70
Agencies	0.067	0.143	0.165	0.211	−0.187	−0.172	70
Best experience	−0.005	0.003	−0.001	−0.008	−0.116	0.158	63
Worst experience	0.191	0.126	0.237	−0.234	−0.092	0.084	59
Cooperative	0.064	0.163	0.181	−0.080	−0.148	0.061	61
Conflictual	−0.153	−0.121	−0.206	0.261*	0.096	−0.179	59
Frequency	−0.159	0.024	−0.083	0.170	−0.105	0.057	69
Incloseness	0.058	−0.440***	−0.327**	0.075	0.201	0.042	70
Outcloseness	0.023	0.314**	0.277*	0.228	−0.207	−0.298*	70
Indegree	−0.137	−0.110	−0.185	0.060	0.323**	−0.276*	70
Outdegree	0.036	0.408***	0.365**	0.290*	−0.358**	−0.266*	70
Clique	−0.063	0.072	0.017	0.155	−0.004	−0.181	70

* $p < 0.05$.
** $p < 0.01$.
*** $p < 0.001$.

Block 3 groups (indegree $= 0.323^{**}$). But Block 3 groups do not appear to aggressively network with other groups (outdegree $= -0.358^{**}$).

4. Instead of profiling Block 1 as whole, I will focus on the sub-block with the highest propensity to collaboration and dialogue—Block B. In sharp contrast to Block 3, Block B does not rely on foundations for financial support (-0.253^{*}). Of all the Blocks, Block B appears to be the collection of groups whose scope of action is most focused on the Bay Area per se (0.220). This association between these groups and the Bay Area as a whole is, in fact, statistically significant for the larger Block 1 from which Block B is derived (0.253^{*}). However, Block B is neither particularly place- (-0.052) nor issue-oriented (-0.008). Nor does it have a characteristic strategic profile, though it does have a tendency to work with public agencies (0.143). The relationship between these groups and public agencies tends to be cooperative (0.163). Yet the most distinctive characteristic of Block B is its networking profile: it cultivates strong networks with other groups (outdegree $= 0.408^{***}$) and maintains strong access to the entire Bay Area environmental network (outcloseness $= 0.314^{**}$). However, this access is unilateral. These groups are very far from being central players in the Bay Area environmental movement (incloseness $= -0.440^{***}$).

These profiles are not sharply etched in the data. The correlations between block membership and the survey variables are only statistically significant for a few variables. While it is legitimate to suggest that Block B is somewhat more cooperative than the other blocks, it also appears more likely to engage in 'direct action' than the other blocks. More importantly, neither of these variables is statistically significant. Based on the survey, there is little evidence that block membership is simply a proxy for the moderatism of the block members. In contrast, the correlations between membership in block B and the network variables in Table 6.4 are highly statistically significant (especially incloseness and outdegree).

Block 1 groups are not central players in the Bay Area environmental movement. They are on the periphery of the movement. Yet by their own initiative they are solidly linked to other Bay area organizations. How then should we explain, in network terms, why they are open both to collaboration with public agencies and to dialogue with groups with contending perspectives? The analysis suggests two points. First, Block B groups operate like niche organizations that presuppose a more extensive organizational network that they may 'plug into' for purposes of mobilizing various issue-oriented or place-oriented communities. Second, these groups are constituted in such a way that they work according to a 'network logic' rather than an 'organizational logic'. I suspect that the size and scope of the Bay Area Environmental Movement provides a basis for a variety of organizational and issue niches. The niche organizations of Block B rely and depend on the reservoir of resources, people, and institutions that constitute the core of the movement— particularly those in Block 3 (the *membership-based environmental groups with significant organizational resources*). These core organizations operate according to an 'organizational logic'—they seek to develop and maintain resources and support through the development of organizational capacities. They administer on-going programs and coordinate relatively complex organized activities. To support these programs and activities, they routinize fund-raising. While they are by no means autarkic, this organizational logic cultivates an internal focus on maintaining and improving the organization's own programs and administration. In contrast, niche organizations are constituted as nodes in a more extensive network. They do not seek to administer or maintain extensive programs. Instead, they focus on trying to operate within a broader organizational field of existing organizations and social networks. Resources are mostly external to the organization.[12] These are lean organizations that prize flexibility of manoeuvre. Program planning or routinized fund-raising are less important than the ability to recognize and take advantage of strategic opportunities as they arise.

In February and March 2001, in-depth interviews were conducted with eight of the 11 groups in Block B in order to probe this argument. With three partial exceptions, we found that a strategy of networking was a critical aspect of mobilization for these groups. One fairly prominent group (A), for instance, described a strategy of mobilization in which they create coalitions through personal contacts and meetings. These coalitions are built up over years and can then be rapidly mobilized as issues arise. A second group (B) indicated that networking was an essential strategy and that they worked with other organizations on every project. These networks are built strategically by partnering with organizations that its members trust. A third group (C) says you cannot be effective unless you work with other organizations and that there was no issue on which it did not collaborate with other organizations. Networking was 'ubiquitous'. This group suggested that it would sometimes work with other groups even though it had nothing to gain, because that was the norm of the environmental movement. A fourth group (D) reported that networking was 'the most important strategy at our disposal'. The person interviewed—a board member active in the Bay Area environmental movement over the last 30 years—reported that she had 'probably worked with every organization in the bay area at one time or another'. A fifth group (E) indicated that networks were the only way of building broad support on issues and the interviewee reported that 'My job is to relate all over the place.' The final three groups suggested that networking had a more modest role in their organizations. Group F reports that networking is important but other groups do not provide much support. The interviewee suggested that he was not currently in a 'network-building' mode and that he was not very deliberate about networking. Group G claims that 'local, national, and international networking' is one of their main activities, but that they were more important for moral support than for specific projects. The interviewee claimed that the group did not actively seek to build coalitions. Finally, Group H does work regularly with other organizations, but finds cooperation often lacking (partly because of the nature of the issue the group works on).

These organizations operate with quite limited staffs and resources, yet seem relatively unconcerned about funding. All of them seemed to be adept at piggybacking on resources available in the larger community. Group A, whose committed but low paid staff worked at home to save money, noted that it specifically sought to work in coalitions in order to maximize the effect of their resources. They receive a substantial amount of pro bono help. Group B tries to 'leverage' their resources through partnerships. Group C shares expenses with related organizations (e.g. joint hosting of events). With few fixed costs aside from its newsletter, Group D says that it stretches its existing resources by working with groups or agencies that have resources to share. Group E stopped raising funds two years ago. Group F indicates that the funds required for their activities are minimal, but that they stretch resources by getting people involved who occupy strategic positions in the community. Group G is a one-person operation without funding, which means that 'networking is all he has'.

A few of the organizations explicitly noted the synergy between networks and large organizations. Group B says that a loose network gets more done, but you also need the expertise that established organizations can provide. Group C suggests that networks are better on single issues, especially when there is a well-defined focus. Larger organizations provide the money to get a message out. Diversity of organizational strategy is one of the key strengths of the environmental movement. Group D indicates that you need a mix of networks and organizations because they focus on issues with different scopes. Networks tend to focus on local issues while established organizations work on broader issues of state and national significance. Group G notes that both decentralized direct action networks and mainstream groups are necessary to appeal to different segments of the population.

Why might these groups that rely heavily on networking be more oriented towards collaboration and dialogue with other groups? Although the argument cannot be substantiated with the current survey evidence, my view is that niche organizations that rely heavily on a 'network logic' are by nature more inclined to engage other groups. By their very nature, they are oriented towards collaborative action with other groups. Group A, for instance, noted that its approach has always been to work with government institutions and engage in legal processes, knowing that there are good people in agencies who want to do the right thing. Group D provided numerous examples of how her organization has used political channels and other groups to change state and national laws. Group E notes that it is open to working with all parties. Group G notes that while they loathe hunting, they understand that hunting groups can be powerful allies that reach different constituencies.

At the same time, the tensions generated by networking strategies were quite visible in the interviews. Group A claims to have been very disappointed with other environmental organizations that have wanted to compete with them rather than work together. Group B indicates that it must cautiously build networks with groups that its members trust. Group D indicates that it 'always' networks with organizations and individuals who agree with their position on the issue at hand.

Group F notes that other groups have not really offered much concrete help. Group G notes that they have encountered problems in working with other groups because they do not share the same perspective. He notes an internal debate in his organization concerning whether they should network only with groups that understand their message or with groups that have a different perspective in the hopes that they might change how they think. Group H claims that other environmental groups have sometimes been uncooperative, leading to unnecessary legal battles.

CONCLUSIONS

This paper began by posing a hypothetical relationship between embeddedness and collaborative governance. In the research conducted for this paper, collaborative governance was not measured directly. I suspect that understanding actual patterns of collaborative governance would require a much more issue-specific and processual research design. My goal in this paper, however, was to see whether embeddedness could explain something about the general propensity to embrace collaborative governance. Therefore, the proxy for collaborative governance used in this study was attitude towards collaboration, and more specifically, attitudes towards collaboration with public agencies and dialogue with opposing groups. The paper found evidence that embeddedness does shape attitudes towards collaboration with agencies and opposing groups.

Yet the main thrust of the paper has been to elaborate different types of embeddedness and ultimately to ask what types of embeddedness encourage collaboration. Following Gulati and Gargiulo, I distinguished between positional, relational, and structural forms of network embeddedness. In the introduction to the paper, I also framed the question of embeddedness in a more general communitarian perspective. From this perspective, I suggested that groups strongly linked to territorial communities, who value place above issue, are likely to be more inclined to adopt collaborative attitudes. But I also noted the opposing perspective: that professional, issue-oriented groups were more open to negotiation and compromise (and hence collaboration). It is also plausible that social movement communities that operate as subcultures or counter-cultures may be less oriented to cooperation.

With respect to the view that place-based rather than issue-based organizations have more collaborative attitudes, I find mixed support. I find little *direct* support for this argument. Organizations oriented to place appeared no more likely than organizations oriented to issues to be collaborative. Nor does the age of the organization or the length of time its leaders have been part of the local community—possible indicators of accumulated social capital—appear to have any significant influence on attitudes towards collaboration or dialogue. Yet the analysis does indicate that organizations unaffiliated with larger state-wide, nation-wide, or international organizations—who by implication are more strongly linked to the local community—do have more collaborative attitudes and are more likely to engage in dialogue with groups that have opposing perspectives. Some suggestive (but not statistically significant) evidence from Table 6.4 indicates that the least place-oriented and most issue-oriented block (Block 2) experienced more conflictual relations with public agencies than the most place-oriented and least issue-oriented block (Block 4). Yet this finding is not strong and we must take account of the fact that the issue-oriented groups were more intimately engaged in working with public agencies. Other evidence on issue orientation suggests that attitudes towards dialogue will depend on the issue: groups concerned with sustainable development were more favourable towards dialogue, while the urban sprawl community was less favourable.

The most interesting findings from the survey relate to the nature of network embeddedness. As least in analysing attitudes towards collaboration, this study found little support for various measures of centrality (positional embeddedness) as the critical measure of embeddedness. Frankly, based on the findings of previous studies and on my own sense that centrality is an intuitively direct operationalization of the idea of embeddedness, this was a surprise. Indegree and outdegree centrality, the individual measures best representing the importance of 'dense' social networks, were not significant. While closeness centrality did show some explanatory promise, structural and relational embeddedness were ultimately more successful explanatory variables.

Relational and structural embeddedness help to delineate how embeddedness in social movement networks might affect attitudes towards collaboration and dialogue. Relational embeddedness is intended to capture the cohesion of networks and I have used it here to capture the subcultural or counter-cultural dimension of social movement networks. I have reasoned that subcultural or counter-cultural networks are more closed than other networks, a dimension I measure by examining membership in cliques. Network closure is theorized, in turn, as producing less openness towards external parties and, consequently, dampened enthusiasm for collaboration and dialogue with these parties. And indeed, this was found to be the case for both collaboration with public agencies and dialogue with opposing groups.

It is clear, however, that not all structurally equivalent blocks are similarly prone towards collaboration and dialogue. I found that membership in only one of the four blocks I initially analysed predicted positive attitudes towards collaboration and dialogue and that only one subgroup within this block was unambiguously favourable towards collaboration and dialogue. Analysing the relationships between blocks, however, indicated that the block with favourable attitudes towards collaboration and dialogue was the block with a strong propensity to adopt a 'networking' strategy. The groups in this block were distinguished by the fact that they had a low indegree, but a high outdegree. They were clearly not central players in the Bay Area environmental movement, but they were remarkably well integrated into the Bay Area environmental movement through their own unilateral efforts to network (high outcloseness). These groups are peripheral actors, but they know how to plug themselves into and utilize the resources of the broader network. The interviews suggest, though do not confirm, that this 'networking logic' is related to a greater openness to working with all types of organizations and persons on a collaborative basis.

In this study, relational embeddedness locates organizations that tend to be closed to collaboration and dialogue outside the in-group (clique), while structural equivalence locates organizations open to outside collaboration. It is noteworthy that relational and structural embeddedness have provided a better explanation of attitudes towards collaboration and dialogue than the commonly adduced distinction between 'outsider' direct action strategies and 'insider' lobbying strategies.

NOTES

1. Since my intention was to focus on the subset of voluntary and non-profit organizations that engage in political activity broadly defined—i.e. activity designed to sway public policy in particular directions—I dropped organizations from the list that are *primarily*: (1) commercial; (2) educational (except in a broader political sense); (3) journals, magazines, newsletters; (4) governmental; (5) research organizations; (6) recreational; (7) land trusts; (8) recycling organizations; and those organizations for which environmental issues are distinctly peripheral to their main mission. When in doubt, I retained the organization.

2. At the outset of the project, an early version of the survey was tested on several organizations. Based on this experience, a number of survey questions were rewritten in order to improve interpretability and to reduce the time it took to administer the survey. We also arrived at a method for administering the survey: we personally contacted the organization and sought to administer the survey to the highest 'executive' position in the organization. 'Top executive position' means the person with overall responsibility for day-to-day management and policy-making. For example, we sought to survey the Executive Director, the President, the Chairman, etc. Because of their busy schedules, it was not always possible to survey these leaders. But we followed this guideline whenever possible. Once contact was made, we forwarded the survey to this person by fax, mail, or e-mail. When possible, we then conducted the survey in person (usually over the telephone), though this was not always possible either. A cover letter that accompanied the survey promised anonymity for the organization in any presentation of the survey results. We found it quite difficult to get these organizations to respond to the survey, especially since many of them are run by small, overworked staffs or volunteers. Often it proved exceedingly difficult just to establish contact with these organizations. Once contact had been made, however, we aggressively followed up by telephone and e-mail with any organizations that expressed an initial willingness to complete the survey.

3. This approach was not ideal because, as respondents told us in completing the survey, their attitudes towards collaboration varied depending on the public agencies and interest group opponents in question. In an early phase of designing the survey, I considered asking questions about relationships with specific agencies and specific groups. But this approach proved difficult for two reasons. First, I believed it quite important to keep the primary independent variable (embeddedness) distinct from the dependent variable (collaboration). Thus, it was useful to think of collaboration more as a general attitude

than a network relation. Second, our early field test of the survey convinced us that collecting a successful sample meant that we had to greatly streamline the question-naire. Asking about relations to specific agencies or opposing groups was, from this perspective, infeasible.

4. In his study of the Italian environmental movement, Diani (1995) has clearly shown that interpersonal ties among activists (the 'latent' network) may yield quite a differ-ent view of movement networks.

5. The relationship 'directly worked' could certainly be usefully disaggregated. Krackhardt, for example, finds that advice networks yield a significantly different image of an organization than do friendship networks (Krackhardt 1992). Preliminary testing of the survey, however, suggested that respondents were impatient with the net-work questions on the survey. We decided to keep the question as simple as possible.

6. For example, if a director with a great deal of experience moved to a newly founded group, then founding date would probably give a misleading characterization of the local social capital or contextual knowledge accessible to the group.

7. If respondents were not sure, we used the following distinctions to guide them: (a) a 'branch office' is a direct administrative extension of a central organization and the branch office ultimately reports to (and derives its authority from) that office; (b) a 'chapter' has been 'chartered' by a parent organization and is similar to other chapters organized and governed by the same charter; but the chapter is generally self-governing (elects its own officers) and through voting or delegation contributes to the governance of the parent organization; (c) an 'affiliate' is also self-governing and participates in the governance of a larger 'umbrella' organization to which it belongs; (d) it differs from a chapter in that it is not constituted by a charter and thus is typically constitutionally different from other affiliates; (e) 'member' implies the weakest relationship between a local group and a larger organization. Your group subscribes to a larger organization, but does not actively participate in its governance.

8. The issues are air quality, animal rights, coastline preservation, endangered species, environmental education, environmental justice, fisheries, global warming, natural areas protection, nuclear safety, ozone, parks and recreation, pesticides, recycling, renewable resources, rivers or watersheds, sustainable development, toxics, trans-portation, urban sprawl, water quality, wetlands, wilderness, and wildlife.

9. Correspondence analysis produces a measure similar to structural equivalence on two-mode relational data (here, the two modes are organizations × issues). In this case, I identified the correspondence between the patterns of issues that organizations indic-ated that they worked on. The analysis then creates scores that dimensionalize the distances between these correspondences. See Wasserman and Faust (1995: 334–43).

10. I had some substantive predilection for more aggregated blocks, since structural equivalence was supposed to identify common network membership in open networks rather than in closed subgroups. See Table 6.4 for a profile of the blocks generated by CONCOR, in the light of the survey variables.

11. It is interesting to compare the image matrix for the Bay Area environmental movement with the one produced by Diani for the 'visible network' of the Milan environmental movement (1995: 123). The Milan movement appears to be a more straightforward core–periphery structure.

12. This finding mirrors Diani's conclusion that high outdegree is uncorrelated with organizational resources in the Milan environmental movement (1995: 105–8).

Part III

Networking the Political Process

7

Contentious Connections in Great Britain, 1828–34

Charles Tilly and Lesley J. Wood

When eighteenth century British activists started inventing the social movement, they had little idea what a peculiar and influential political form they were fabricating. They fashioned a new sort of campaign: the sustained challenge to authorities on behalf of a relatively well defined program in the name of an aggrieved population by means of coordinated public performances displaying the worthiness, unity, numbers, and commitment of the program's supporters. As they took shape in Great Britain, social movements regularly came to include associational founding and recruitment, public meetings, processions, demonstrations, petition drives, and statements to the press. Although it took half a century for this configuration of activities to become standard politics, and longer than that for it to acquire the name social movement, the configuration's emergence marked a new stage in British popular politics.

The social movement certainly had peculiar properties for its time. It emerged in a day when popular politics divided mainly between direct action, on one side, and appeals to patrons, on the other. Britain's violent, often vindictive eighteenth century forms of direct action included rough music, donkeying, window breaking, pulling down of dishonoured houses, and seizure of high-priced or sequestered grain. They also had positive counterparts such as parading heroes in chairs or placing candles in windows for public celebrations. Although the direct petition to King or parliament had some standing as an appeal to patrons by middle-class Britons, ordinary people more often asked local notables to bring their troubles to the authorities' attention.

In this context, it was peculiar for people to start making claims by the means we now recognize as belonging to social movements: forming special-interest associations, holding public meetings, organizing petition drives, marching, lobbying, making statements for public consumption, and so on. These new means abandoned both direct action and appeals to local patrons, despite the fact that either of the old strategies often continued to produce results in the short run. The new means, in contrast, had no prospect of realizing people's claims in one or two iterations. They only worked—if they did!—over the long run and after repeated efforts. They often neutralized themselves, furthermore, by provoking counter-movements on the part of opponents.

Yet social movement strategies turned out to have wide appeal. The new bundle of political forms, the social movement, centred on campaigns in support of or opposition to publicly articulated programmes by means of associations, meetings, demonstrations, petitions, electoral participation, strikes, and related means of coordinated action. It provided an opportunity to offer a sustained challenge to powerful figures and institutions without necessarily attacking them physically, but also without kowtowing to them. It said, in effect, 'We are here, we support this cause, there are lots of us, we know how to act together, and we could cause trouble if we wanted to.' It asserted the consequential presence of new political actors and/or political programmes.

Why, how, with what correlates and consequences did social movements become so prevalent in Great Britain and elsewhere? This paper takes up only one causal strand in that complex fabric of cause and effect. It concentrates on the inter-dependence of (a) widening adoption of social-movement forms and (b) increasing centrality of parliament (more precisely, the House of Commons, and by extension parliamentary elections) to Britain's popular politics. The overall argument on which the paper builds runs as follows:

1. Britain's enormous increase of military expenditure from the Seven Years War (1756–63) onward significantly enhanced tax-authorizing parliament's leverage in national politics.
2. Parliament used its enhanced powers by acting more decisively and effectively on matters that directly affected the welfare of ordinary people, even in the face of royal and noble opposition.
3. The crown and royal patronage became less central to most forms of national politics, especially those directly involving popular interests.
4. Despite a narrow parliamentary electorate, as a consequence, parliamentary debates, legislation, and election both more frequently took up issues of concern to ordinary people and incited popular responses.
5. Because propertied males affiliated with the state church wielded disproportionate weight in parliament and in national politics at large, people outside that small category more often faced threats than benefits to their interests from governmental action.
6. Yet some members of parliament sought popular support as a counterweight to factions based on landed wealth, and therefore made alliances (intermittent or long term) with popular political leaders.
7. Organized popular forces therefore discovered that they could gain political weight through a combination of (a) displaying support for advocates of their interests and (b) threatening to disrupt the routines of elite politics.

8. Populist political entrepreneurs experimented incessantly, probing the existing political system for soft spots, adapting established forms of claim-making to new participants, occasions, or issues, and devising new tactics as opportunities presented themselves.

9. Repeated interactions among popular claimants, objects of claims, authorities, and parliament (especially the House of Commons) established the social movement as a standard way of making sustained claims at a national scale in Great Britain.

10. Although the process was well under way by 1828, the major national campaigns of 1828–34—notably the vast mobilization that preceded and produced 1832's Reform Act—consolidated both social movement politics and the position of the Commons at the centre of popular claim making.

Schematically, the argument says that parliamentarization and the expansion of social movement politics reinforced each other. Earlier work (Tilly 1995*a–d*, 1997) has made the general case for such a line of argument. This paper amplifies earlier analyses by looking more closely at changes in the forms, participants, and objects of popular claim making during the seven turbulent years from 1828 to 1834. It adds a comparison of three significantly different political regions to previously documented national trends. Building on the recognition that claims of X on Y or vice versa establish relations among political actors and among categories of political actors, it uses formal network analyses to document its major empirical claims. After a summary sketch of social movement activity in Great Britain from the 1780s into the 1830s, it proceeds to a closer examination of 1828–34.

THE RISE OF SOCIAL MOVEMENTS IN GREAT BRITAIN, 1787–1834

Although we could trace elements of social movement activism back to the libertarian campaigns of John Wilkes in the 1760s and the anti-Catholic campaign of George Gordon in the 1780s, crystallization of Britain's social movement repertoire greatly accelerated with national campaigns against the slave trade, then against slavery itself. In collaboration with activists in other Western countries, British antislavery movement organizers played a major part in abolishing both slave trading and slavery itself through most of the Atlantic world. Heroic activists sometimes campaigned publicly against slavery in major regions of slave-based production, including the British colonies. Crucial campaigns, however, first took place mostly where slaves were rare but beneficiaries of their production were prominent. For the most part, antislavery support arose in populations that benefited no more than indirectly from slave production.

The British version of the social movement's story begins in 1787. British Quakers, Methodists, and other antiestablishment Protestants joined with more secular advocates of working class freedoms to oppose all forms of coerced labour. A Society for the Abolition of the Slave Trade, organized in 1787, coordinated a vast national campaign, an early social movement.

At first glance, the central role of Manchester, Lancashire, the industrial revolution's first great metropolis, in that campaign looks strange. Textile production in Manchester depended heavily on cotton produced by slaves in the Americas. But in Manchester, both masters and workers trumpeted the superiority of freedom over slave labour, despite disagreeing bitterly over what sorts of freedoms workers should actually enjoy.[1] In 1788, Manchester's citizens sent to parliament a petition against the slave trade endorsed by a reported 10,639 citizens, about two-thirds of its adult male population. Even at the risk of paying more for cotton produced by free labour, they agitated for the end of slavery. During the winter of 1787–8 abolitionists organized multiple public meetings in the city, typically leaving a copy of the petition in place for signature or endorsement with an X after the meeting.

Manchester's initiative set the city against the leaders of Liverpool, the main port through which slave-produced cotton entered England. In the name of economic progress and property rights, Liverpool's leaders objected to the antislavery activism. Manchester's example, however, had the wider resonance in Great Britain. Perhaps 100 thousand people throughout Britain put their names to abolitionist petitions in 1787–8. At the same time, other associations, public meetings, and petition drives were agitating for parliamentary reform as well as for repeal of restrictions on political rights of Catholics and of Protestant Dissenters (non-members of the state-backed Anglican Church such as Baptists and Methodists).

During the next two decades, British activists rounded out the social movement repertoire with two crucial additions: the lobby and the demonstration. Lobbying began literally as talking to Members of parliament in the lobby of the parliament building on their way to or from sessions. Later the word generalized to mean any direct intervention with legislators to influence their votes. British activists also created the two forms of the demonstration we still know today: the disciplined march through streets and the organized assembly in a symbolically significant public space, both accompanied by coordinated displays of support for a shared programme.

Of course all the forms of social movement activism had precedents, including elite public meetings, formal presentations of petitions, and the committees of correspondence that played so important a part in the American resistance to royal demands during the 1760s and 1770s. They drew heavily on organizational repertoires already prevalent among activist Dissenters such as the Quakers. But between the 1780s and the 1820s British activists (religious and secular) created a new synthesis. From then to the present, social movements regularly combined associations, meetings, demonstrations, petitions, electoral participation, lobbying, strikes, and related means of coordinated action.

Within Great Britain, parliament began responding to popular pressure with partial regulation of the slave trade in 1788. By 1806, abolition of the slave trade had become a major issue in parliamentary elections. In 1807, parliament declared illegal the shipping of slaves to Britain's colonies. From that point on, British activists demanded that their government act against other slave-trading countries. Great Britain then pressed for the withdrawal of other European powers from the slave trade. At the end of the Napoleonic Wars in 1815, the major European powers except for Spain and Portugal agreed to abolition of the trade. Under economic and diplomatic pressure from Britain, Spain and Portugal reluctantly withdrew from officially sanctioned slave trading step-by-step between 1815 and 1867. From 1867 onward, only outlaws shipped slaves across the Atlantic. With Brazil's abolition of slavery in 1888, slavery lost all legal standing in Western Europe and the Americas.

Meanwhile, the social movement form had been consolidating outside the purview of antislavery politics. During the great wars of 1792–1815 with France, not only British advocates of democratic reform but also their proregime opponents widely adopted associations, public meetings, demonstrations, electoral campaigns, pamphlets, and petitions as means of conveying their messages. Severe wartime restrictions on association and assembly slowed the pace of social movement mobilization until the postwar years, but through the wars reformers and workers continued to rail publicly against corruption and capitalist exploitation.

In the company of eighteenth century style attacks on machines, enclosures, and exploitative employers, the immediate postwar years (1816–20) brought a great surge of social movement mobilization on behalf of political reform and workers' rights to organize. Even the vastly popular campaign of support for Queen Caroline, the estranged wife of new King George IV, in 1820–1 occurred largely through meetings, processions, and demonstrations. Electoral campaigns attracted wider and wider participation in social movement style. In Ireland (from 1801 part of a fragile United Kingdom), Daniel O'Connell and his allies were organizing the mass-membership Catholic Association to break down the exclusion of Catholics from national politics and parliament. At the same time, Protestant Dissenters within Great Britain were campaigning for expansion of their own restricted political rights. Literati, political activists, and officeholders alike commonly interpreted the swelling of popular campaigns as the Rise of the Crowd. They disagreed sharply, to be sure, on whether the crowd's rise threatened liberty or promised liberation (Morgan 1988; Herzog 1998; Plotz 2000).

Several of these social movement campaigns culminated in the years from 1828 to 1834. In 1828, as a response to widespread agitation, parliament's repeal of the seventeenth century Test and Corporation Acts opened up political participation for Protestant Dissenters. In 1829, under even greater pressure from campaigns and counter-campaigns, parliament staved off threatened insurrection in Ireland by reducing restrictions on Catholic political participation—balancing that measure by narrowing the franchise in Ireland and banning the massive Catholic Association. By far the greatest social movement mobilization, however, centred on demands for parliamentary reform: widened eligibility for membership in parliament, an expanded franchise, equalization of existing representation, and increased public accountability for parliament itself.

The Reform Act of 1832 made modest concessions in all these directions. Although historians keep debating whether, to what extent, and how popular demands promoted the passage of the Reform Act (see, e.g. Price 1999: 264–73; Archer 2000: 70–2), they generally agree that the popular participation in social movements oriented to the Reform in 1830–2 exceeded anything Great Britain had ever seen before. At a minimum, massive popular mobilization gave parliamentary supporters of the Reform such as Thomas Babington Macaulay plausible grounds for their arguments that modest concessions would hold off revolution. They could, after all, point to the spectres of France and Belgium, where revolutionaries had installed new regimes in 1830. Radical societies, political unions, and workers' associations allied uneasily in a turbulent national campaign. Widespread involvement of organized workers in the 1830–2 campaign made the Act's virtual exclusion of workers from the vote a more salient public issue in 1832–4, when parliament often sided with the propertied on such questions as the Poor Law. Precisely because of the example of the Reform movement, the victory of parliament, and the expanded space of representative politics made established local assemblies crucial arenas for communication with national authorities. A great deal of contention during those later years simultaneously began in local assemblies and/or concerned the proper membership and conduct of local assemblies.

THREE REGIONS FROM 1828 TO 1834

Let us close in on a major moment in the social movement's consolidation, the seven years from 1828 to 1834. Those years cannot show us the long-term interplay between Parliamentary change and social movement development. But they allow us to witness a momentous break: mass mobilization promoted the Reform Act of 1832, which in turn altered relations between British subjects and the seats of national power. In order not to render an already complex analysis utterly incomprehensible, the evidence to follow will employ a crude distinction between 1828–31 ('before' the Reform Act, which actually passed in June 1832) and 1832–4 ('after' the Act). The evidence comes from a more general study of contentious politics in Great Britain from 1758 to 1834.

The study as a whole catalogues 8088 'contentious gatherings' occurring in (a) Southeastern England (Kent, Middlesex, Surrey, and Sussex) during 13 scattered years from 1758 to 1820 and (b) Great Britain (England, Wales, and Scotland) as a whole during the seven years from 1828 to 1834. Contentious gatherings are occasions on which a number of people (in the instance, 10 or more) outside the government gathered in a publicly accessible place and made visible collective claims bearing on the interests of at least one person outside their own number. The machine-readable catalogue contains truncated, edited textual transcriptions

TABLE 7.1. *Distribution of contentious gatherings*
over time and space

	Kent	Lancashire	Middlesex	Great Britain
1828–31	192	273	1166	4045
1832–4	101	187	1454	2839
Total	293	460	2620	6884

of such events reported in *Gentlemen's Magazine, the Annual Register,* or the *London Chronicle* for 1758, 1759, 1768, 1769, 1780, and 1781; in those publications as well as the *Times* of London for 1789, 1795, 1801, 1807, 1811, 1819, and 1820; and in *Gentlemen's Magazine, Annual Register, Morning Chronicle, Times, Mirror of parliament, Hansard's Parliamentary Debates* or *Votes and Proceedings of parliament* for 1828–34.[2]

Within that set, the present analysis deals with contentious gatherings occurring in the counties of Kent, Lancashire, and Middlesex, and sometimes in Great Britain as a whole, aggregated into the two periods 1828–31 and 1832–4 (Table 7.1).

As a rough index of mobilization and demobilization, contentious gatherings declined significantly from 48 to 34 per year in Kent, dropped slightly from 68 to 62 per year in Lancashire, rose from 292 to 485 per year in Middlesex, and diminished mildly from 1011 to 946 per year over the whole of Great Britain. The three counties displayed different patterns of mobilization and demobilization as functions of their dominant activities. Kent was a region of capitalist agriculture, Lancashire Britain's prime concentration of capitalist industry, and Middlesex the densest part of London and environs.[3] The three counties by no means exhaust the variety of Great Britain in the 1830s, but they offer an opportunity to see whether parliamentarization and social movement expansion operated differently in agrarian, industrial, and urban environments.

Evidence to come indicates that after the massive parliament-centred mobilizations of 1828–31, agrarian Kent subsided not only into lower levels of public contention but also into more parochial forms of claim making. To the extent that social movement politics existed in Kent after the Reform, it split between popular efforts to open up local power structures and elite appeals to national authorities. Although workers continued to figure more prominently in popular contention in Lancashire than elsewhere, both Lancashire and Middlesex moved more definitively than Kent toward a system of public claim making strongly centred on parliament. That claim making increasingly took social movement forms.

Our machine-readable descriptions of contentious gatherings include separate records for (1) whole events, (2) sources consulted, (3) each distinct individual named in our accounts, (4) each separate location involved, (5) participating formations (any person or set of persons the sources describe as acting distinctly from others), (6) individual actions by those formations transcribed as stylized verbs, and (7) coders' and editors' comments on the event and/or its sources. Here we concentrate on whole events, participating formations, and the verbs of individual actions. Some verbs (e.g. 'exit') are intransitive; they have no objects. In the whole data set, just over half of the verbs have objects—formation A does X to formation B. A 'group of silk weavers,' for example, may *cheer* a Member of parliament. In this case, we call the Member of parliament (MP) object of a claim. We regard all such claim making as establishing a relation at two levels: between the particular parties involved in the contentious gathering at hand, and between the *categories of political actors* involved more generally. Thus we take the illustrative case as evidence not only of a concrete relation between the silk weavers of London's Spitalfields district and their local MP, but also of a more general relation between members of trades (silk weavers, in the instance) and MPs as a class of actors. The present analysis focuses exclusively on relations among categories of actors. It uses formal network methods to identify relations among categories.

A rough tabulation of the claim objects in 1828–31 and 1832–4 for our three counties and Great Britain as a whole therefore provides a first hand indication of whether we have any changes in the orientation of contention 'before' and 'after' the Reform Act to explain. We do. Table 7.2 provides that information. For ease of computation, we have based the figures for Great Britain as a whole on an unbiased 10 per cent sample of all 20,853 claims.

Royalty, Gentlemen, and Government represent the centres that, according to our account of parliamentarization, were already losing sway during the half-century or so before 1828, and continued to lose ground as a consequence of Reform. Royalty means the king and his immediate family, who had stood at the centre of national patronage politics during the eighteenth century, but had suffered diminished influence after 1760 as the parliament gained power. Gentlemen (nobles, peers, and gentry) and Government (high officials of the realm) were likewise

TABLE 7.2. *Selected objects of claims, 1828–34, as percentage of all claims*

Object	Area							
	Kent		Lancashire		Middlesex		Great Britain[*]	
	1828–31	1832–4	1828–31	1832–4	1828–31	1832–4	1828–31	1832–4
Royalty	5.6	14.0	3.2	2.0	6.1	3.4	5.9	6.1
Gentlemen	1.3	0.0	0.0	0.0	0.4	0.1	0.5	0.0
Government	0.0	0.0	0.6	0.0	0.9	0.0	1.1	0.0
Ministers	1.9	3.2	3.6	0.7	6.4	6.4	3.6	7.8
MP	12.5	9.7	5.5	10.5	6.6	14.1	9.5	13.9
Other parliament	25.0	23.6	24.4	25.7	12.9	22.8	20.7	24.9

[*]10% sample of all claims; includes Kent, Lancashire, and Middlesex.

losing their centrality in public politics. (The House of Lords also became more peripheral in the process, but that more complex story deserves telling elsewhere.) Increasing responsibility of Ministers to the parliament rather than the king signals a shift rather than a diminution of Ministers' political weight. MPs and parliament, in our account, became more crucial to popular politics, while Ministers acquired increasing ties to both of them.

Table 7.2 confirms the relative decline of Royalty, Gentlemen, and Government, on one side, the relative rise of MPs and parliament, on the other. But Kent, the rural county, behaves differently from Lancashire and Middlesex, the industrial and urban counties; in Kent, Royalty becomes a more frequent object of claims after Reform, while MP and parliament lose some of their prominence. (Royalty likewise gains slightly over Great Britain as a whole.) It is as if the rural elites—both in Kent and elsewhere in Great Britain—tried the parliament, lost, and turned back to Royalty while their industrial and urban counterparts were moving enthusiastically into a parliamentary regime.

Changes in occasions for claim making amplify that picture. A rough classification of occasions for contentious gatherings distinguishes:

1. *Violent gathering*: attacks on poorhouses, affrays of hunters with game wardens, public shaming of renegade workers, pulling down of dishonoured or dangerous houses, beating of informers, and other direct applications of force.
2. *Other unplanned gathering*: nonviolent market conflicts; responses to the arrivals of dignitaries, heroes, or blackguards; popularly-initiated public celebrations of major events and other instances of assembly and claim making without substantial prior planning.
3. *Election meeting*: gatherings to endorse candidates, hear campaign speeches, or attend elections themselves.
4. *Authorized assembly*: offering demands, complaints, or expressions of support with respect to others in regularly constituted bodies such as vestry meetings, wardmotes (i.e. ward assemblies), and city councils.
5. *Association meeting*: similar claim making in official sessions of explicitly named associations, including religious, economic, and political organizations.
6. *Other public meeting*: previously announced discussions of public issues open to the general citizenry (or sometimes the 'respectable inhabitants') of a locality.
7. *Other*: organized celebration, delegation, parade, demonstration, strike, or turnout.

No event qualified as a contentious gathering unless our sources provided direct evidence of at least one public, contentious claim—we demand, we support, we condemn, we humbly pray, and so on. We called a claim 'contentious' if its realization would have (positively or negatively) affected the interests of at least one person outside of the claiming formation. That meant excluding many gatherings at which people discussed public issues. The sources, for example, announced thousands of public meetings that we excluded for lack of reported claims on people outside their own participants. In this classification of gatherings that did qualify, categories overlap; for example, 'other' public meetings often followed closed meetings of associations. Some contentious gatherings began as meetings, but then someone started a brawl; this classification treats such events as violent. Since violence increased the likelihood that our sources would mention a gathering and that they would describe claim making activity, the catalogue exaggerates the relative frequency of violent events. Because of selectivity in the sources, the catalogue also greatly under-represents industrial conflict—turnouts, strikes, and public struggles within trades. Comparisons with other sources, however, provide no indication that the catalogue's selectivity biases comparisons over time (see Tilly 1995, Appendix 1).

The categories permit distinctions among:

(1) the violent confrontations and other unplanned gatherings that had prevailed in eighteenth century contentious gatherings, but became less frequent after 1800;

(2) the authorized local assemblies of residents, parishioners, ratepayers, or electors that persisted from the eighteenth to the nineteenth centuries but became increasingly important as arenas for debate of national political issues, and

(3) the elections, association meetings, other public meetings, and 'other' forms that formed primary sites for social movement activity.

As we will see, violent and unplanned gatherings continued to decline significantly over the short interval from 1828 to 1834 while the second and third categories (authorized assemblies and public meetings) continued to increase. Meanwhile, the relative prominence of authorized public assemblies varied significantly from county to county.

Figures 7.1–7.4 summarize before/after differences in the distributions of contentious gathering types for the three counties and for Great Britain as a whole. In agrarian Kent, violent events of 1828–31 included multiple incidents of the 1830 Swing rebellion, in which landless labourers burned hayricks, attacked threshing machines, and sometimes clashed directly with farmers and repressive forces as they urged substantial farmers and local officials (sometimes successfully) to take measures against falling wages and unemployment. Violent events and other unplanned gatherings did not disappear in Kent after 1831, but they diminished from 34 to 27 per cent of all contentious gatherings. In Kent, the shares of associational and other public meetings also diminished. Before 1832, Kent had not only hosted the earliest phase of the Swing rebellion, but also fostered multiple meetings and counter-meetings organized by associations supporting and opposing Catholic rights. The partial resolution of that issue in 1829 and the partial parliamentary reform of 1832 left the regularly scheduled meeting of residents and officials Kent's principal occasion for popular claim making.

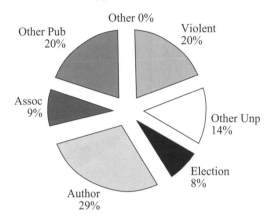

Event types, Kent 1828–31

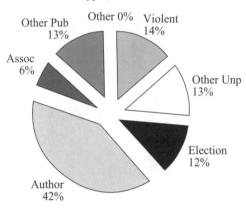

Event types, Kent 1832–4

FIG. 7.1. *Event types in Kent, 1828–34*

Lancashire, pioneer of antislavery mobilization, already had long experience with associational meetings before 1828. A significantly higher share of its 1828–31 contentious gatherings (20 per cent) than of Kent's (9 per cent) arose from associational meetings. That proportion grew larger in 1832–4. As in Kent, nevertheless, authorized local assemblies loomed larger after the Reform Act's passage than before; in Lancashire, too, citizens took to addressing authorities by means of previously announced and publicly sponsored meetings. Similarly, violent and other unplanned gatherings lost ground, as rough confrontations between workers and masters or authorities gave way to nonviolent routine politics.

In Middlesex—essentially London—we see a place where the 'before' of 1828–31 already resembles the 'after' of 1832–4 in Lancashire. Violent events and

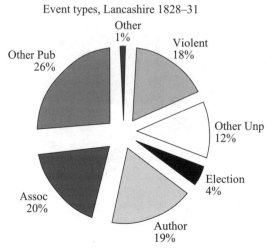

Event types, Lancashire 1828–31

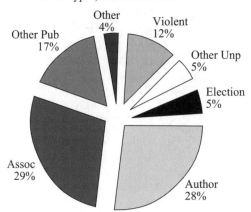

Event types, Lancashire 1832–4

FIG. 7.2. *Event types in Lancashire, 1828–34*

other unplanned gatherings nevertheless sank from 22 per cent to 12 per cent of London's total contentious gatherings while associational meetings increased to more than a third and authorized public assemblies gained moderately. London shows us the widespread use of issue-oriented general public meetings during the 1828–31 mobilizations around Test and Corporation Act repeal, Catholic Emancipation and, overwhelmingly, Reform. Between 1832 and 1834, Londoners continued to make claims during electoral campaigns and by means of various sorts of demonstrations. But they gathered mainly to deliberate, then pass resolutions, send petitions, or otherwise communicate their will to public authorities.

A look at Great Britain's totals makes clear that Kent represented changes in the country as a whole more faithfully than did Lancashire or Middlesex. True,

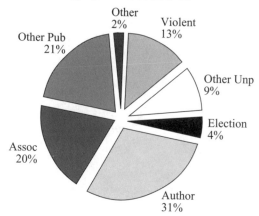

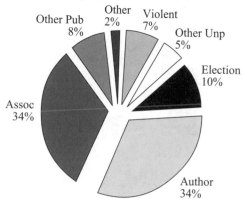

FIG. 7.3. *Event types in Middlesex, 1828–34*

associational meetings figured more prominently nationally than in Kent both before and after Reform. But on the whole, the shift toward authorized public assemblies and electoral gatherings already apparent in Kent describes a national trend as well. After the massive mobilizations of 1828–31, Great Britain at large settled into more routine versions of authorized claim making. Increasingly, Britons formed associations to pursue collective interests. They then voiced those interests especially by participating in electoral campaigns and pressing local authorities to convene assemblies of constituted bodies, assemblies in which local people deliberated on the day's public issues. As the people of Kent retreated toward relatively exclusive assemblies and attacks upon them, the people of Lancashire and Middlesex continued in the social movement mode of unauthorized

Event types, Great Britain 1828–31

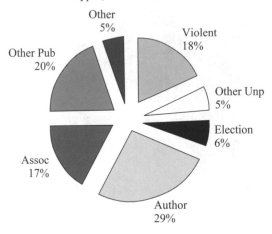

Event types, Great Britain 1832–4

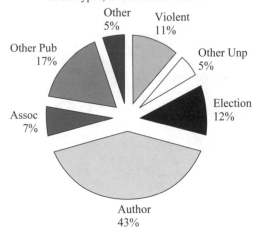

Fig. 7.4. *Event types in Great Britain, 1828–34*

public assemblies, special interest associations, and raucous participation in elections. The sort of politics displayed by Lancashire and Middlesex actually became more central to relationships among Great Britain's major political actors. To see that more clearly, we must examine relationships as such.

CLAIM MAKING NETWORKS

In this analysis, we represent relationships not among individuals or concrete groups, but among *categories* of individuals and groups. The entire data set included about

12,000 different concrete formation names, as given in our sources. Here we group them into just 16 categories grouping together actors that occupied, according to earlier analyses (Tilly 1997), similar positions in the British national polity of the 1830s. The 16 categories with examples are:

- *Church*: Catholics, Protestant Dissenters, and Society of Friends
- *Constables*: beadles, keepers, and New Police
- *Crowd*: assemblage, mob, and multitude
- *Electors*: delegation, electors, and freeholders
- *Government*: gentlemen, King's Ministers, and nobles
- *Inhabitants*: house occupants, inhabitants, and populace
- *Interest*: advocates of free speech, Benefit Societies, and farmers
- *Locals*: churchwardens, local officials, and supporters
- *Officials*: alderman, Common Council, and Common Sergeant
- *Other*: associates of prisoner, individual name, others
- *Pariahs*: Irish, poachers, and poor
- *Parliament*: Commons, Lords, and Member of parliament
- *Repressive*: city marshal, police, and troops
- *Royalty*: King and Government, Majesties, and Queen
- *Trade*: chief mate, employers, and master
- *Workers*: artisans, labourers, and weavers

Let us be clear: the categories do not summarize our best judgments of a formation's social composition, but the name assigned to it by reporters in the publications from which we drew the catalogue. Two important qualifications follow. First, the same individuals could appear in different formation categories from one CG to another; individual members of a formation called Workers in one event, for example, sometimes showed up as members of other formations called Church, Crowd, Inhabitants, Interest, or Pariahs. Second, formations vary in social homogeneity: the category parliament includes persons much more similar to each other than the category Inhabitants. All this is as it should be: we are examining *in whose name* and *on whom* sets of people made public collective claims in Great Britain during the years from 1828 to 1831. The categories group together sets of claimants and objects of claims that occupied similar positions in British public politics of the 1820s and 1830s.

In a similar fashion, we aggregated the verbs our accounts used to describe actions by formations within contentious gatherings. The full data set includes about 2000 different verbs, reduced here to just eight categories (again with samples):

- *Attack*: batter, battle, and decry
- *Cheer*: applaud, cheer, and thank
- *Claim*: appeal, depute, and petition
- *Communicate*: advertise, bicker, and hear petition

- *Control*: arrest, donkey, and rebuke
- *Deliberate*: address, chair, and meet
- *Enter*: abandon, march, and proceed
- *Other*: adjourn, breakfast, and turn out

In our three counties, the proportions of all verbs for the whole period 1828–34 constituted by these categories appear in Table 7.3.

Deliberation (the meeting, resolving, moving, and seconding of organized public assemblies) increased significantly in all three counties after the Reform; the deliberately called public assembly became a dominant setting for making of collective claims. Yet some indicative differences appear among counties. Despite the attack-centred Swing rebellion of 1830s, Kent's frequency of attacks actually rose after 1831; those attacks, increasingly verbal rather than physical, divided between those initiated especially by citizens excluded from local political deliberations and those directed by public assemblies toward national governmental actors or institutions. By comparison with other counties, nevertheless, Kent's formations did a good deal of cheering, mostly in support of local notables and royalty. Control and attack reached their peaks in Lancashire as a consequence of repeated confrontations between working class gatherings and forces of order, on one side, between workers and enemies within their own trades, on the other. Middlesex claimants put more of their energy overall into the characteristic acts of social movements: claiming, communicating, and deliberating. Over Great Britain as a whole (including the three counties singled out here), the most remarkable shift between 1828–31 and 1832–4 increased the share of deliberative verbs from

TABLE 7.3. *Frequencies of major verb categories, 1828–34, by county*

Verb category	Area							
	Kent		Lancashire		Middlesex		Great Britain[*]	
	1828–31	1832–4	1828–31	1832–4	1828–31	1832–4	1828–31	1832–4
Attack	6.9	17.2	14.9	13.8	13.0	12.2	11.5	10.7
Cheer	26.3	23.7	8.1	7.2	19.7	18.1	17.5	17.5
Claim	30.0	15.1	32.1	20.4	15.4	7.3	22.9	17.9
Communicate	6.9	7.5	3.6	9.9	7.2	6.8	5.7	5.1
Control	13.1	8.6	17.2	18.4	14.8	7.9	12.4	10.7
Deliberate	11.9	18.3	9.4	21.7	23.2	40.9	20.2	29.5
Enter	3.1	5.4	6.5	5.3	3.6	2.8	6.3	2.6
Other	1.9	4.3	8.1	3.3	3.1	3.9	3.4	6.0
Total	100.0	100.0	100.0	100.0	100.0	100.0	100.0	100.0
Number of actions	160	93	308	152	1420	1014	402	234

[*]10% sample of all actions; includes Kent, Lancashire and Middlesex.

20.5 to 29.5 per cent of the total. The public meeting and its decorum became the principal site of collective claim making.

We could read the overall pattern as a temporary shift from the intense social movement mobilization of 1828–31 toward a common aftermath of social movement surges: heightened activity by associations and constituted public bodies. (The shift was only temporary: during the later 1830s, for example, Britain's industrial regions produced the vast social movement mobilization called Chartism.) In Middlesex after 1831, claiming gave way to deliberating, as authorized assemblies and associational meetings provided the occasions for more than two-thirds of all Middlesex contentious gatherings. Even more so than in Kent and Lancashire, public deliberation became Middlesex's standard form of collective claim making. These broad differences lead immediately to questions about who did what to whom, and how that changed from before to after the Reform. An analysis of claim making networks helps answer those questions.

Here we concentrate on just two verb categories: *attack* and *claim*. Although they include verbal and symbolic actions as well as physical damage and seizure, attack verbs represent the older forms of direct action on behalf of local interests. Claim verbs indicate the use of relatively formal collective means in the social movement vein. For each of the verb categories taken separately, we have constructed matrices displaying the frequency with which members of the 16 formation categories carried on actions having other formations for their objects. (We now aggregate the previously distinguished Gentlemen, Government, and Ministers into a single entity—Government—just as we lump together MP and Other parliament.) Before looking more deeply into the structure of those matrices, we draw the more frequent relations thus identified in each county and period as simple networks. Figures 7.5–7.10 show relations occupying at least 0.5 per cent of all transitive actions occurring in the locality for Attack and Claim verbs in Kent, Lancashire, and Middlesex separately for 'before' and 'after' the Reform Act: 1828–31 and 1832–4.

A significant contrast between agrarian Kent, on one side, and industrial-urban Lancashire and Middlesex, on the other, reappears in these network diagrams. As in the tabulations of claim objects, these more refined analyses show us Kent's recession from nationally oriented, parliament-centred mobilization in 1828–31 to more parochial and/or elite politics in 1832–4. In Lancashire and Middlesex, we see continuation of popular participation and a further move toward centring claims on parliament. The Attack diagram for Kent 1828–31 reveals a configuration oriented toward named individuals (the principal component of Other), but including (mostly verbal) attacks on the parliament and particular MPs as well as on the national establishment (Government). By 1832–4, Government has disappeared as a major object of attack in Kent, but local assemblies continue to attack parliament. Kent's attacks of 1832–4 still swirl around named individuals, mostly local leaders of one sort or another. In both Lancashire and Middlesex, crowds figure just as prominently among attacks as in Kent, but pair more regularly with

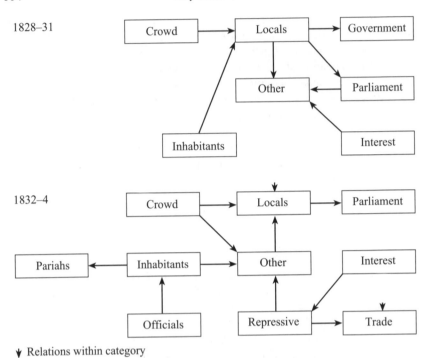

1828–31

1832–4

▼ Relations within category

FIG. 7.5. *Attack relations among categories of actors, Kent 1828–34*
(0.5% + of all relations in place and period)

repressive forces—that is, not regular local peacekeepers but exceptional crowd-busters such as troops and marshals.[4] There Lancashire and Middlesex divide, with attacks proliferating in industrial Lancashire after 1831, but narrowing to the pair crowd–repressive in metropolitan Middlesex.

Claim relations, characteristic of the public meetings we have already seen gaining importance, tell a somewhat different story. In Kent, 58 per cent of all contentious gatherings in the prereform mobilization of 1828–31 began as public meetings of one sort or another. In Fig. 7.8 we see that during the same period parliament formed the centre of Kent's public claim making, despite competition from local office-holders, national government figures, and royalty. After the Reform, assemblies of Kent inhabitants continued to address parliament on occasion, but royalty and government gained relatively. In this regard, Lancashire and Middlesex differed not only from Kent, but also from each other. During 1828–31, the claim making patterns of Lancashire and Middlesex strikingly resembled each other, with inhabitants sometimes making claims on royalty, but inhabitants and everyone else joining to make claims on parliament.

During 1832–4 the two counties split apart. Lancashire's people continued to centre their claims on parliament, but separate clusters linked: (a) inhabitants,

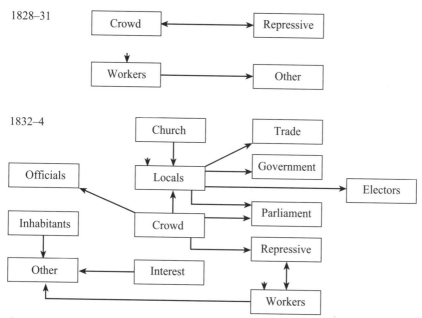

Fig. 7.6. *Attack relations among categories of actors, Lancashire 1828–34*
(0.5% + of all relations in place and period)

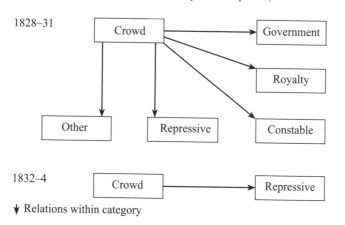

Fig. 7.7. *Attack relations among categories of actors, Middlesex 1828–34*
(0.5% + of all relations in place and period)

electors, and others, (b) locals, officials, and crowds. Despite parliamentarization, Lancashire's local politics remained rambunctious and partly independent of national affairs. Lancashire's social movements bifurcated. In Middlesex, the pattern of orientation to the parliament that characterized 1828–31 contentions stayed in place with almost no alteration whatsoever. Middlesex remained the national centre of social movement politics. From the perspective of parliamentarization as well, Middlesex led the way, Lancashire followed to some extent, but Kent dragged its feet.

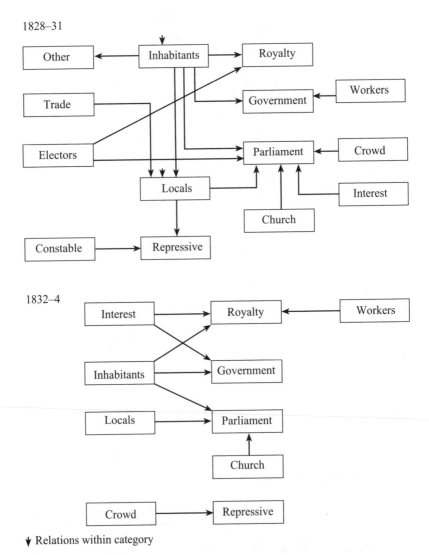

Fɪɢ. 7.8. *Claim relations among categories of actors, Kent 1828–34 (0.5% + of all relations in place and period)*

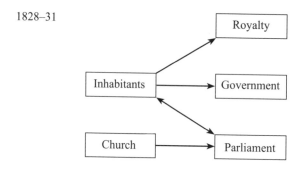

1828–31

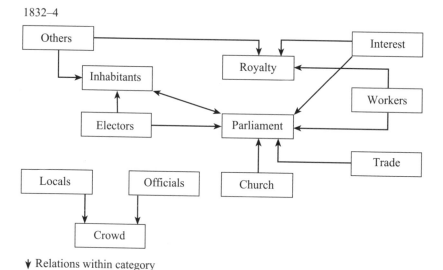

1832–4

▼ Relations within category

FIG. 7.9. *Claim relations among categories of actors, Lancashire 1828–34*
(0.5% + of all relations in place and period)

THE CENTRALITY OF MAJOR ACTORS

If the evidence on one-step relations between contentious actors and their objects clearly identifies parliamentarization as a continuing trend during the period of Reform, it does not pinpoint parliament's place within the larger set of relations that connected all actors. Our analyses so far have dealt only with direct relations, as when Inhabitants assemble to petition parliament. Network techniques make it possible to ask how closely connected any actor was to other well connected actors, as when Crowds bedevil Officials, who turn to Constables, who in turn harass Crowds. More precisely, we examine *objects of claims* to determine the extent to which they are the termini of claim making chains in which intermediate claimants themselves are major objects of claims directed at them alone. Instead of looking at Attack and Claim separately, we lump all sorts of claims together. The idea is to determine whether the Reform mobilization produced significant shifts and regional differences in the relative prominence of different objects of claims.

Using Ronald Burt's Structure programme, we measure this sort of centrality by means of three-step relation strength (Table 7.4). The measure is an eigen-vector measure varying over actors from 0 (an actor receiving no relations at all) to 1 (an actor constituting the only object of claims for every other actor). On the double bet that (a) claims reverberate beyond a single step of relationship and (b) every category of political actor in Britain of the 1830s could reach the national level through fewer than four steps of relationship, we weight the relations by prox-imity, up to three steps. The procedure measures exclusive relations received by a particular formation. It represents the proportion to which i has an exclusive rela-tion from j, including relations to itself, for example inhabitants making claims on other inhabitants. As a measure of centrality, this variable estimates the extent to which actor i is the object of exclusive relations from everyone. As it should, relational strength gains more from exclusive relations with powerful players than exclusive relations with weak players. To that extent, it measures not only central-ity, but also power.

Our one-step network diagrams have already shown us parliament receiving more claims from powerful actors than any other object did. Table 7.4's three-step measures permit refinement of the earlier observations. In Kent, we witness the emergence of a distinctive popular politics in which appeals to the king retained

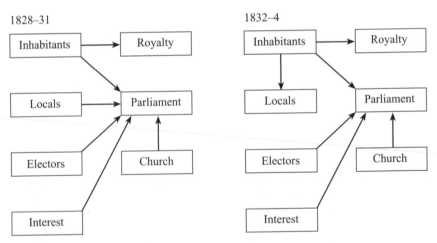

▾ Relations within category

FIG. 7.10. *Claim relations among categories of actors, Middlesex 1828–34*
(0.5% + of all relations in place and period)

prominence after 1831, while repressive forces such as troops and marshals battled with local citizens. As hinted earlier, crowds show up as persistent nodes of claim making in Middlesex before 1832 and in Lancashire throughout the period, but not in Kent for either period. In Lancashire, we see a popular politics centring not only on crowds but also on masters and skilled artisans (Trade) rather than workers presenting themselves as workers.[5]

As an understandable consequence of intensifying local–national connections, locals (e.g. churchwardens, clergy, committees, local officials, parishioners, supporters, and wardmotes) appear as the sorts of brokers we might reasonably expect in Kent and Middlesex, but not in Lancashire. In Kent and Middlesex, these intermediaries played crucial parts in the politics of assembling and addressing national holders of power. In Middlesex, officials (which means essentially officers of London's municipal administrations) occupied similar positions in the major mobilizations of 1828–31, but then lost prominence in the post-Reform politics of 1832–4. In parallel, Middlesex citizens centred their appeals of 1828–31 not only on parliament but also on the king's ministers and other high officials. With the passage of Reform, the appeal to high governmental officials declined in importance to the overall structure of claim making. That decline in the centrality of Government occurred in all three counties.

Nevertheless, the major news of Table 7.4 arrives in the line devoted to parliament. In all three counties and Great Britain as a whole, parliament figured

TABLE 7.4. *Three-step relation strengths of major actors, 1828–34, by county*

Actor	Area							
	Kent		Lancashire		Middlesex		Great Britain[*]	
	1828–31	1832–4	1828–31	1832–4	1828–31	1832–4	1828–31	1832–4
Church	0.024	0.000	0.007	0.000	0.008	0.004	0.014	0.005
Constable	0.018	0.024	0.022	0.009	0.039	0.022	0.069	0.063
Crowd	0.080	0.060	**0.178**	**0.186**	**0.135**	0.088	**0.132**	**0.129**
Electors	0.042	0.036	0.000	0.040	0.020	**0.108**	0.028	0.028
Government	0.086	0.023	0.059	0.038	**0.109**	0.084	0.084	**0.128**
Inhabitants	0.013	0.036	0.073	0.075	0.043	0.021	0.051	0.028
Interest	0.028	0.000	0.015	0.000	0.050	0.017	0.022	0.015
Locals	**0.182**	**0.228**	0.089	0.039	**0.133**	**0.150**	0.051	0.052
Official	0.000	0.006	0.000	0.013	**0.158**	0.037	0.050	0.028
Pariahs	0.008	0.021	0.013	0.012	0.033	0.046	0.011	0.029
Parliament	**0.285**	**0.298**	**0.200**	**0.339**	**0.245**	**0.331**	**0.327**	**0.364**
Repressive	0.046	**0.105**	0.032	0.065	0.096	0.088	0.061	0.047
Royalty	0.041	**0.114**	0.029	0.017	0.060	0.039	0.041	0.067
Trade	0.000	0.049	**0.134**	0.038	0.063	0.030	0.046	0.019
Workers	0.076	0.000	0.077	0.058	0.050	0.009	0.015	0.000

Bold = Relation strength > 0.100. 0.000 = No formations in this category.
*10% sample of all claims; includes Kent, Lancashire, and Middlesex.

more centrally in claim making than any other class of formations. Parliament only gained in centrality after the Reform. By 1832–4, in Kent, Lancashire, and Middlesex alike parliament was attracting close to a third (0.298, 0.339, and 0.331) of all the claims it could, in principle, have attracted. Yet the three counties show us three somewhat different variants of parliamentarization:

1. In agrarian Kent, considerable persistence of local politics coupled with adoption of standard arrangements in which regularly convened assemblies of residents and local officials sent appeals to the king's close collaborators or, especially, to parliament.
2. In industrial Lancashire, division between: (a) the local politics of workers, tradesmen, and crowds and (b) the national politics of local assemblies communicating with parliament, assemblies more often involving special-interest associations (especially work-based associations) than in Kent or Middlesex.
3. In Middlesex, the fullest coincidence of social movement politics with Parliamentary foci—crowds, authorized assemblies, special-interest associations, and public meetings on one side, parliament on the other, with local officials often in between.

Figure 7.11 recalls the general meaning of parliamentarization. Consistent with the relation-strength analysis, it centres on objects of collective claims. Broadly speaking, parliamentarization entails shifts of claim making from the local to the national scale, and from indirect national representation through various patrons to direct national representation of both local and national actors. More concretely, in this scheme local power holders and members of local communities continue to *make* claims, but become less frequent *objects* of claims. At the national scale, royalty, nobility, and great patrons likewise become less frequent objects of claims as parliament becomes the focus of national claim making. In terms of this scheme, our three counties followed different trajectories between 1828 and 1834. Figure 7.12 summarizes. After several decades during which politics moved in a parliamentary direction in all three counties, Kent actually veered back slightly toward local and/or indirect claim making after 1828. Lancashire continued its long movement toward national and direct politics, but remained in a more local position than Middlesex. The national centre, Middlesex, had led Great Britain's parliamentarization long before 1828. It continued to do so thereafter, ending the years from 1828 to 1834 concentrating a large part of its claim making on the parliament itself.

This analysis has not fully untangled the causal web between parliamentarization and the proliferation of social movement politics. In order to get at the general relations among actors, furthermore, we have neglected the demonstrating, petitioning, lobbying, pamphleting, electoral campaigning, and day-to-day organizing that constitute the actual texture of social movements. But the increasingly crucial place of public meetings in Britain's popular politics (which the

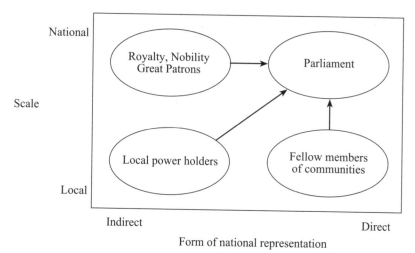

FIG. 7.11. *Parliamentarization as changing objects of claims*

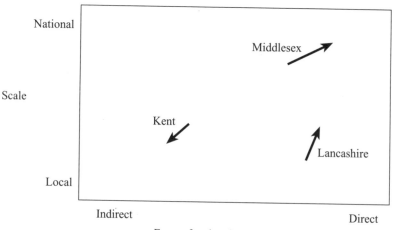

FIG. 7.12. *Differences in parliamentarization among Kent,
Lancashire, and Middlesex, 1828–34*

evidence presented here documents amply) represents a major cause, effect, and
component of the social movement's rise to prominence.

Social movement politics emerged, as we have seen, to different degrees and in
somewhat different versions in agrarian, industrial, and urban regions. Those differences confirm that something more was happening than the mere mechanistic
adoption of new political prescriptions from the top down. British people created

their new forms of politics through struggle. In the process, they forged new relationships to national centres of power.

NOTES

1. Manchester masters contested, for example, any rights of free labourers to form unions and to strike. In common with their fellows elsewhere in Britain and North America, they advocated individual-to-individual contracts as the basis of employment (see Steinfeld 2001).
2. For technical details and closely related research, see Munger (1979, 1981*a*,*b*); Schweitzer (1979); Schweitzer and Simmons (1981); Tilly and Schweitzer (1982); Steinberg (1999*a*,*b*).
3. A full 38% of the catalogue's 6884 contentious gatherings from 1828 to 1834 occurred in Middlesex, a proportion inflated by London-centred sources, yet still indicative of London's primordial place in national politics.
4. The category Constable brings together different varieties of regularly established local police; Middlesex attacks of crowds on constables in 1828–31 consisted largely of resistance to Robert Peel's New Police.
5. Many workers participated in formations here classified as Crowds, but we persist in using the names our sources assigned to formations rather than second-guessing the sources. We treat the assertion and attribution of public names as consequential political acts, expressions of political identities (see Jenson 1993; Tilly 1998*a*,*b*).

8

Networks, Diffusion, and Cycles of Collective Action

Pamela E. Oliver and Daniel J. Myers

This chapter shows how different 'network' arguments about how protest spreads imply quite different underlying mechanisms that in turn produce different diffusion processes. There is considerable ambiguity about the relationships among networks, diffusion, and action cycles and the way these can be identified in empirical data. We thus both seek to unpack the 'network' concept into different kinds of processes, and then show how these different network processes affect the diffusion processes we are studying. We sketch out some formal models to capture some of these distinctions.

This chapter extends recent work (Oliver and Myers forthcoming) that develops diffusion models of protest cycles, and focuses on discussing links between network concepts and diffusion concepts in understanding protest cycles. We conceive of social movements as diffuse action fields in which actions affect other actions and the action repertoires of the different actors coevolve through time and through interaction with each other. Movement activists and regimes engage in strategic interactions, each responding to the actions of the other. Different organizations within a movement respond to the actions of others, as successful tactical innovations and movement frames diffuse to new organizations. News media cover or fail to cover particular protests, and thus encourage or discourage future protests. Each of these processes affects the others, in a complex, multifaceted set of interactions. Over time, the action set of each actor evolves in response to the actions of the others and, thus, the whole field is one large coevolving environment in which the characteristics and actions of any actor is constrained and influenced by the characteristics and actions of all other actors in the environment.

One central concern about understanding diffusion and networks in protest waves is that we do not actually have straightforward data about the underlying social networks or mobilization processes. Protest event data usually just contain records of the timing and location of events along with some (often incomplete) information about the participants in the event, their forms of action, and their stated claims or other rhetoric (McAdam 1982; Olzak 1992; Kriesi *et al.* 1995;

Tilly 1995a–d). Rarely, if ever, will the data contain information on the social relationships or communication processes that were involved in organizing and mobilizing that event. Lacking this kind of data, we want to know whether different patterns of social organization will give rise to different patterns in protest event data, and how what we already know about how protests get organized might influence our analysis of protest event data.

After a brief review of the interplay between diffusion concepts and network effects, we develop some important distinctions among different processes often lumped together as 'network effects'. We then develop preliminary models for three empirically important network processes in movements: the flow of information, the flow of influence, and the construction of joint action. All of these models are built on a core modelling 'engine' which we explain. Our models of information flow are most complex, as we stress on the importance of two kinds of networks: broadcast networks, and node-to-node networks. Finally, we show how the models we are constructing are capable of representing the strength of network ties, not just their presence or absence, and of permitting network ties themselves to evolve and be dependent on other processes.

DISAGGREGATING PROTEST WAVES TO GET AT MECHANISMS OF DIFFUSION

The ideas of cycles of protest, diffusion, and network effects are often discussed without making clear distinctions among them. Diffusion is the process whereby past events make future events more likely. In 'classic' diffusion models, there is a transmission of some innovation between people, and it is impossible to have any diffusion without some kind of contact or network tie between individuals. But this equation between networks and diffusion arises because of the assumption of permanent and irreversible 'adoption' in classic diffusion models, an assumption that is inappropriate for the diffusion of collective action (Myers and Oliver 2000; Oliver and Myers forthcoming). Individuals and groups or populations can and do protests or riot on multiple occasions, and the performance of an action by an individual or group often makes a repetition of that action more likely. One could insist on using the word 'diffusion' only when demonstrably *different* people are protesting or rioting, but this definition is problematic for at least two reasons. First, empirical data on protest events almost never contain sufficient detail to distinguish clearly between new actors and repeaters. If repeated events of the same type occur in the same geographic area (e.g. riots), the rioters are quite likely a mixture of previous and new participants. Available data generally provide only numerical counts of numbers of participants and perhaps the names of a few key leaders. They would never provide sufficient detail to track exactly how many new people are entering a form of action and where they came from. Data of that level of detail are only available in detailed case studies of well-structured events, not in data across a large number of events or more amorphous events. The second reason is theoretical. The reinforcement process, whereby an actor's own actions and its consequences influence that actor's future actions, is theoretically almost identical to a diffusion process, whereby one actor's actions and their consequences influence other actors' future actions. Most of the same processes and factors are involved in the repetition of actions by the same actors and the adoption of actions by new actors. Either way, the 'diffusion' effects of an action are mediated by whether the action is repressed, whether it gets media coverage, whether it affects policy, and so forth. The only difference is that actors presumably know about their own actions and its immediate consequences, while others cannot be affected by a group's actions unless they know about them. Only the 'network processes' themselves are different between self-reinforcement and diffusion to other actors. Because protest is a repeatable, reversible action, diffusion models of protest must focus on the spread of actions, not the spread of actors (Myers 1996, 1997, 2001).

An additional distinction needs to be made between diffusion and cycles. Diffusion processes tend to generate waves or cycles of events, but not all waves of events arise from diffusion processes. Waves of protest can also arise from rhythms and from common responses to external events. A major event such as a disaster or an act of war may trigger independent responses in many locales. Rhythms are what the term 'cycle' most often means in other contexts, periodic rhythms of physical or social life that structure time. The ordinary rhythms of life structure protest just as they structure any other activity, so that protest generally occurs when people are awake and around the constraints of work, school, and political schedules. Beyond these quotidian rhythms are the rhythms of protest itself. There is a recovery or regrouping interval after most actions before a group is ready to act again. At a minimum, people must eat and sleep. Big events such as marches on Washington necessarily require relatively long intervals between them for organizing the logistics. Ritualized protests are often held at regular intervals. The presence of rhythms and external shocks does not, however, mean that diffusion processes are absent. Empirical research has often demonstrated diffusion processes in the spread of information about a major event (Shibutani 1966) and Myers (1996) found clear evidence of diffusion effects within the 'long hot summers' of the 1960s riots and after the assassination of Martin Luther King, Jr.

Finally, we need to recognize the importance of diffusion processes nested within other diffusion processes. Long multi-year protest waves are the accumulation of smaller protest waves arising from particular campaigns and the smaller-scale diffusion processes that occur within them. McAdam (1983) showed that the bursts of activity in the civil rights movement followed tactical innovations. The diffusion of collective action across national boundaries also shows evidence of waves within waves, a general wave of mobilization that transcended national boundaries, and nation-specific waves (Kriesi *et al.* 1995). Similarly, a broad social movement is always made up of smaller campaigns in particular localities or involving particular issues. These smaller campaigns usually arise either from a burst of repeated actions by one group or in one locality, or the diffusion of a particular movement issue, frame, or tactic between groups or localities. The term 'network' is often used in both cases, but in the former, it tends to refer empirically to the existing social and political ties within a community that permit a set of people to act in concert, while in the latter, it refers empirically to communication channels through which information is spread between different local networks.

Specifying these nested diffusion processes is theoretically critical, as it is clear that big protest waves are built from smaller campaigns that have their own logics, while influencing each other in the larger wave. These campaigns implicate network processes. A wide variety of network forms are involved in campaigns. The most basic is a series of events around the same issue involving the same people in a single locale. If no new people are brought in, this is a simple case of repetitive action by the same actors, a pure 'reinforcement model' process, in which the consequences of earlier actions influence the rate of subsequent actions by these same people, but there is no interpersonal diffusion process involved. However, if these events become larger over time, then we would say that some kind of between-person diffusion has occurred. Of course, even if the number of participants stays constant, there could well have been turnover in the participants. We have developed an approach that is capable of being modified to capture these waves within waves, but we will not be developing such modifications in the scope of this chapter.

SPECIFYING NETWORK EFFECTS

As we dig into the mechanisms of diffusion, it is important to specify the very different kinds of 'network' relations that are involved in different kinds of diffusion. A very wide range of specific phenomena has been lumped together under the rubric of 'network effects' or 'social ties'. If we are going to understand the role of network effects in diffusion, we need to unpack the concept. There are at least three distinct (although related) processes that occur through network ties: communication, influence, and joint action. The relation among these three processes is somewhat hierarchical. A communication tie provides a basis for disseminating information that something has occurred. An influence tie provides a basis for one actor to affect the opinions or actions of another actor; influence requires communication but involves additional social processes beyond mere communication. Joint action may be considered an extreme case of influence, in which initially separate actors come to make joint decisions and act in concert. Influence requires communication, but not all communication entails influence. Joint action requires both communication and influence. It is important to recognize the concept of joint action because empirically researchers may not be able to distinguish multiple acts from concerted joint actions. Many protest event series exhibit huge 'spikes' in which a very big action 'suddenly' occurs or many different actors 'suddenly' engage in the same kind of action at the same time, and these spikes cannot possibly be modelled with standard diffusion models. However, we will show that a model of 'hidden organizing' outside the view of the data collectors can quite readily model such spikes. This chapter will provide detailed discussion of some of the issues involved in each of these three kinds of processes, and outline some approaches to formal modelling of each. In each case, we will give special attention to the question of how the process might be reflected in observed empirical data on protests. However, before moving to these three sections, it is important to consider some other distinctions and dimensions among network processes.

Dimensions of Proximity or Connection

Information and influence flow through social networks. But there are different ways in which actors can be 'connected'. There are at least three dimensions to network proximity that are relevant to the study of social movements: spatial, organizational, and other social. These may be expected to play different roles in protest and social movements.

Spatial/social: Movement actions are space-bound: people often congregate in the same place at the same time to act in concert. Riots and 'spontaneous' protests most often diffuse spatially: individuals become aware of the riot or protest because they are near it. However, there is no 'pure' space, and space itself is always socially organized. Neighbourhoods are usually segregated by class, ethnicity, or race, and are often segregated by political orientation, so that different 'kinds' of people are found in different kinds of public spaces. Social etiquette rules about class or ethnicity or gender, as well as language differences may create communication barriers that are the practical equivalent of great distances. A wide variety of routine social structures can create network ties. For example, Oberschall (1989) shows that early sit-ins in North Carolina after the first Greensboro sit-in diffused as black colleges played basketball games against each other. The mass media also have a decided spatial component. Mass media have clear geographic and linguistic catchments. Although there is 'national' news, which is usually broadly available, that 'national' news always has a bias toward events occurring near the site of publication or broadcast (Mueller 1997; Myers and Caniglia 2000). Myers (2000*a*) found for example that although large riots diffused nationally, presumably by way of national news coverage, smaller riots diffused within the boundaries of television broadcast ranges. Prior to electronic communication, collective disturbances diffused along transportation routes and took longer to diffuse (Rudé 1964; Hobsbawm and Rudé 1968; Charlesworth 1979; Myers 2000*b*).

Movement/organizational: Even within spaces, the participants in particular actions usually have additional ties to each other beyond mere proximity. Between spaces, actions may be coordinated through political/movement ties between movement organizations. Local chapters of the same national organization would be expected to have high political ties. Different organizations with similar political/movement goals would tend to have positive ties, although they would also have some elements of competition between them. There obviously has to be some actual mechanism of communication between spatially dispersed elements of the same organization, such as organization newsletters, or telephone calls or e-mail among members. But these actual mechanisms of communication are most often invisible to the protest events researcher, who merely notes that events were organized in five different cities by local chapters of the same organization.

Relational/social: Movement organizations may have ties to nonmembers through their members' 'other' social relationships and memberships. These other ties include kinship and friendship, attendance at the same school, membership in the same recreational club or religious congregation, employment at the same workplace, or membership in some secondary association that has no direct relation to the movement. In many cases, these 'other' ties become the basis for recruitment into a movement organization or its actions, as well as for increased support for the movement's opinions (Ohlemacher 1996). Movements whose members have social connections to the larger society through many different social ties are likely to be better able to mobilize support than those that lack such ties. However, as we consider influence models below, it will become apparent that these external ties can have both 'positive' and 'negative' effects on movement mobilization.

In the work that follows, we will not be able to explore the effects of these different kinds of proximity, but have set up general schemes that should be able to capture the structures that the different kinds of relations would imply.

Sizes of Networks and Numbers of Actors

If we are looking at the total numbers of participants in collective action, we often conceive of the network diffusion as reaching down to individual people. But it is well established that most people enter protest movements as parts of relatively cohesive groups, and that whole groups make decisions together about whether to participate in particular actions. This means that it is often most reasonable to think of the 'actors' as groups, not individuals. But when this is so, we will then also want to be able to consider the 'size' of each of these actors, which is the number of people it mobilizes. Although capturing this complexity in its totality is beyond the scope of this chapter, we will discuss how our models can be modified to deal with group size issues.

Network Structures and Collective Action

Network theorists have devoted a fair amount of attention to measuring and categorizing qualitative differences in network structures, as well as quantifying the position of any one actor in a qualitatively-defined network (Knoke and Kuklinski 1982; Wasserman and Faust 1995). The same number of ties in a network has different effects depending upon their distribution, so that star-like structures in which one central person has links to other actors who have no links to each other are, for example, quite different from circles in which each actor has exactly two ties to other actors and all actors are connected. Similarly, cliques can be defined within larger networks. Unless one wants to stay at the level of the case study, however, it is difficult to use these concepts in the study of the diffusion of collective action across a large and complex population. Instead we need to have summary measures of a movement group's network ties. In this chapter, we will give some simple examples of how structural effects can be incorporated, but will not pursue this dimension in any depth.

The Basic Model

In this model, each actor has a probability p_k of acting at each time period. The number of people who actually act at each time period varies stochastically around the mean p_k, where N is the number of actors. Each actor's p_k may change across time as a function of the past actions of themselves or others. Elsewhere (Oliver and Myers 2001), we explore the question of the form of the underlying model for the diffusion of collective action. Plausible models for mobilization cycles that go up and down are not straightforward. Collective action always declines, and the question is whether this should be specified as arising from a natural tendency within actors that occurs regardless of outside influences, or whether it is a process of outside factors such as repression. Addressing these questions is beyond the scope of this chapter. Here, we will simplify the individual decision model and focus only on the upswing or accelerative phase (Oliver *et al.* 1985) of a protest cycle, where the feedback effect from others' actions is entirely positive. This underlying model does not produce event distributions that look like real protest cycles, which always come down again, but it will give us a basis for evaluating network effects.

Models in this chapter are developed using the Stella simulation programme from High Performance Systems, Inc.[1] The program has a graphical interface to represent differential equations. An appealing feature of Stella is that it generates a list of the equations implied by the graphical connections.[2] The programme can handle one- or two-dimensional arrays with sizes constrained only by the capacity of the computer. The acting probability and other characteristics of each actor are captured by one-dimensional arrays, while network links and inter-actor influences are captured by two-dimensional arrays. The programme accepts hot links to inputs and outputs, so it is possible to set up a who-to-whom matrix of network linkages in a spreadsheet that can be read by the programme. All of the models in this chapter could readily be programmed in some other way, but we have found Stella to be a very useful development tool as it hugely reduces the ratio of programming to thinking in the process of model development.

For analysis, we have set up several fixed network configurations as well as a random network controlled by a random number generator and can choose between network configurations with a user-controlled switch. For this chapter, the arrays are fixed at size 10, which is large enough to show some of the effects of random variations, but small enough to be manageable in a development phase. Substantively, an N this small could be understood as actions in different cities or by different groups in a movement. Representing a city of a million inhabitants as a matrix would tax our computer systems and be unlikely to be informative. The more reasonable way to proceed for representing large populations is to conceive them as subgroups with varying sizes, where the group's size is another variable in the model. Such an extension is beyond the scope of this chapter.

Baseline Model with No Communication

For baseline comparisons, we begin with a group of N actors who have no awareness of each other. Each group may randomly emit an action. We tally the plot of all actions. Initially, we have all actors with the same low probability. Because actors do not influence each other, this probability does not change. Because of its random component, each iteration of this model produces a slightly different outcome plot. Figure 8.1 shows plots of the baseline model for a system of 10 actors. Even though there is a constant probability of action, because it is a random model, there are varying numbers of actors at any given time, and the frequency plot exhibits a spiky sawtooth form with waves typical of protest event plots. The cumulative count, however, shows a different story: in a purely random model with a constant probability, the total rises essentially linearly with time. We will be using the total counts across five periods in subsequent models because they damp out some of the random variations of one-period counts. These five-period counts are roughly equivalent to the kinds of patterns you would get if you aggregate daily event counts to weeks, or weekly counts to months. This is shown in the bottom panel of Fig. 8.1. Note that this purely random process generates cycles and even small diffusion-like S-curves in the cumulative count.

To model information diffusion effects, we have to provide some specification of how one actor's probability of acting is affected by the actions of others. Here, we will assume that the tendency to repeat this action is a function of how many others are doing it. Although verbal theorists can relax into vague discussions of positive effects, and even quantitative empirical researchers can just specify a regression coefficient on the lag of prior action, when we write a mathematical model, we have to say exactly how we think people respond to others' actions, and this is not at all clear from empirical research. Shall we assume that others' actions always increase our own probabilities, no matter what? And, if so, in what functional form? Linearly in a power relationship? With rising and then falling marginal returns? Or should we assume that actors respond not to the absolute level of others' actions, but to whether it is increasing or not? The former assumption, that

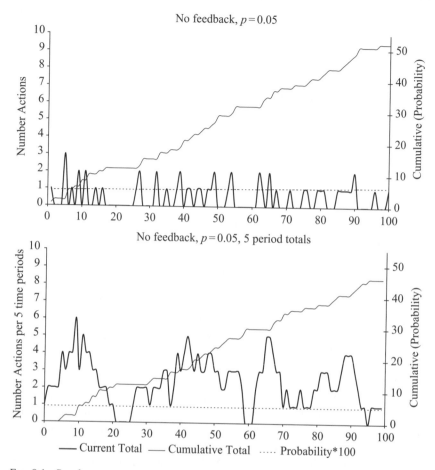

FIG. 8.1. *Random processes produce apparent cycles. Top panel is number of events per time period, bottom panel is 5-period moving average (used in other models)*

actors respond to the level of others' actions, would arise if there is an accelerating production function or if actors' behaviour is principally determined by influence or imitation processes. However, in the long run, such models produce unanimous action in which everyone is protesting with certainty forever, something that never happens. The latter assumption, that actors respond positively to the increases in others' actions, and negatively to decreases, would arise from an S-shaped production function that first rises then falls, which seems consistent with an underlying process in which initial action obtains benefits, but there are declining marginal returns to action after it has been at a given level for some time. Our initial work with this second model indicates that, while interesting, it produces volatile results that are very sensitive to initial conditions, which makes it unsuitable as a platform for investigating network effects.[3] For this reason, in this chapter we use models employing the assumption that actors respond to the level of prior action.

The model we use assumes that actors respond to the total level of others' action in a diffusion-like fashion. The basic elements of this model are: p_t = probability of acting at time t; n = number of actors—a random process determines whether each actor actually acts on a given trial; $r_{k(t)}$ = recent total number of actions across all actors within the past k trials, at time t; and k = the number of trials considered.

The algorithm for changing the probability of action as a function of past actions is

$$p_t = p_{t-1}(1 + w_1 (kn - r_{t-1}) (r_{t-1})/n),$$

where w_1 is a weighting coefficient on the feedback term. Actors simply respond to the total of others' actions, which means that 'full information' is assumed so that there are no network effects. This simple model produces an S-shaped growth in the probability until a probability of 1.0 is reached, when it stabilizes with everyone acting. The weighting factor determines how quickly this happens; if the weighting factor is small enough relative to the time span of the model, the probabilities may remain essentially unchanged for the duration of the model. The distribution of current action exhibits random variation around an S-shaped rise until unanimous action is reached; unanimous action is an absorbing state. The cumulative distribution is S-shaped until unanimity is reached, and thenceforth rises linearly. In Fig. 8.2 we show examples of the effect of feedback from others' actions in this algorithm. The plot of cumulative protests clearly shows the S-shaped growth pattern diagnostic of a diffusion process in the first phase, until unanimous action is achieved, and then it becomes a linear curve like any other constant-probability model. We have parameterized the baseline model so that it has a low level of action if there is no feedback and a relatively rapid rise toward unanimity if there is 100 per cent feedback through all possible network ties. This will give us a backdrop against which to consider the effects of various network constructs. The upper panel shows the current action rate as well as the cumulative event count and the probability for a homogenous group in which everyone's initial probability is 5 per cent and the feedback weight is 0.005. The lower panel provides two variants of the initial probability of action. In the homogeneous case, all actors begin with a 5 per cent probability of acting; in the heterogeneous case, actor 1 has a 40 per cent chance of acting, while the other nine actors each have a 1 per cent chance. The average probability is about the same in the two cases. The lower panel compares the homogeneous and heterogeneous cases for the full feedback and zero feedback models. When there is no feedback, the heterogeneous group has slightly more action, due to the one high-probability actor. When there is full feedback, the heterogeneous group reaches unanimous action a little more slowly than the homogeneous group.

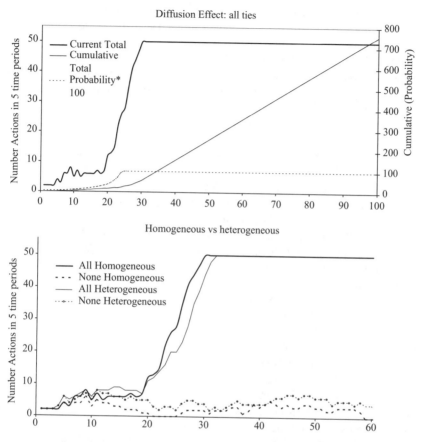

FIG. 8.2. *Diffusion in networks with all ties. Top panel shows diffusion in a homogeneous group (all have $p_0=.05$) with all ties present. Bottom pane contrasts all ties with no ties for homogeneous and heterogeneous groups (one actor has $p_0=.4$, all others $p_0=.01$). Feedback weight is .005.*

INFORMATION FLOWS

When ideas or actions are diffusing between actors, the 'thing' that is transmitted is information. Broadly speaking, there are two types of networks through which information may flow, node-to-node and broadcast. Node-to-node paths are the kind usually implied by the use of the term 'network'. Actor A communicates with actor B, who communicates with actor C, and so forth. Many network analysts examine the efficiency of communication across node-to-node networks with different properties, such as overall density of ties, the tendency to cliquing, or the extent to which communication is channelled through a few key actors. By contrast, a broadcast network involves a single communication source that is directly received by a very large number of people. In our era, this is the mass media. But previous eras also had broadcast communication on a smaller scale, in the form of town criers and travelling messengers.

Although hard-core network analysis focuses on the effects of network structure and chains of indirect ties (Knoke and Kuklinski 1982; Wasserman and Faust 1995), any 'network' analysis of communication in protest waves in the modern era is sterile if it does not treat the mass media. Large numbers of people who otherwise have no connection at all can be 'connected' by their responses to a common news or entertainment source. When the actions of one group are covered in the mass media, communication effects can spread as far as the media are broadcast, without prior connection between the actors. Myers (1996, 2000*a*) shows that large riots that received national television coverage increased riot propensities nationally, while smaller riots increased riot propensities within their local television catchment areas. Protest event data based on newspapers, especially if it is drawn from a single 'national' news source, is, by definition, data on the events that can be assumed to have been communicated to a broad population.

But, of course, the news media are not unbiased samplers of events. They are rather intentional actors who select news stories for reasonably well-defined reasons, and it is well established that the size and disruptiveness of an event increase its probabilities of news coverage, as does the proximity of the event to the news organization (Snyder and Kelly 1977; McCarthy *et al.* 1996; Mueller 1997; Myers and Caniglia 2000). More recent research also suggests that news media cover some kinds of issues much more than others (Oliver and Myers 1999; Oliver and Maney 2000). The media themselves are subject to diffusion processes, both within one news organization, and between them. If a news organization has already published several stories about a particular issue, it is less likely to publish another because it is not 'news,' although there is some evidence that for at least some issues, the recent publication of one article about an issue will raise the probability of another article about the same issue, as the news organization follows the 'story'. Between news organizations, once one outlet picks up a story, other outlets may pick it up. If enough outlets begin to cover the story, it becomes news, and the media will begin actively seeking more stories on the same theme. The result is the 'media attention cycle' which has been shown to under-represent movements at the beginnings and ends of their cycles, and over-represent them in the middle, when the issue is 'hot' (Downs 1972; Cancian and Ross 1981; McCarthy *et al.* 1996).

Even though the mass media play a central role in our era, node-to-node networks are also important. Social ties between groups increase and deepen information flows beyond the information presented in the mass media, as posited in the classic 'two step' model for media influence on attitudes. Social influence appears to flow principally through social connections, not the mass media, so that we expect information coming only through news sources to be much less effective in changing opinions and orienting people toward action than information coming through social ties.

In the real world, patterns of diffusion and the ways diffusion uses different networks are messy, to say the least. In fact, the different kinds of networks patterns not only operate at the same time, but also are affected by one another. Recently, a number of scholars studying media coverage of protest and demonstrations have noted that larger events are more likely to get media coverage—and more of it (Snyder and Kelly 1977; McCarthy *et al.* 1996; Mueller 1997; Oliver and Myers 1999; Myers and Caniglia 2000; Oliver and Maney 2000). This means that the larger a protest group's local network is and the stronger the ties in that network, the larger its events will be and the more press coverage it will receive.

When the press covers a protest event, the protest issue and tactic are projected to other potential actors thereby invoking a completely different kind of network. In this way, recruitment through personal networks can piggyback on media coverage. Even if activists in one city have no direct communicative ties with activists in a second, they may be inspired to invoke their local network to produce an imitative event once they hear about the first event through the mass media. Thus the media operates directly through its distribution network to mobilize additional individuals to join existing protest groups and it can also invoke networks indirectly by mobilizing a node in a different activist network that will activate its local network.

Other carriers of diffusing protest also interact with local networks and the media to reinforce and extend their influence. For example, some protest has been tied to travelling activists who give speeches or engage in direct attempts to organize. These activists do not just wander aimlessly, but select targets based partially on the likelihood that their efforts will be successful—as indicated by some level of local organization which has the network ties to support the protest activity. Indeed, these activists may even be called upon by existing organization to come and help rally the troops. Furthermore, media coverage of the speeches and meetings helps to draw new recruits into the fold of potential activists and the ensuing actions give the media more to report.

The messages delivered to individuals by their personal contacts and by the media can also reinforce each other during the critical time when the individual is presented with an opportunity to decide whether or not to act (Oliver 1989). If, when approached by a friend or colleague and asked to act in support of civil rights, and the recruit has recently been watching the news about church burnings, that recruit may be more likely to respond to the personal network. The importance of the cycles of influence among distinct kinds of networks cannot be ignored.

When information is not carried by the mass media, node-to-node network ties determine the targets of action, flows of resources, and flows of information. Spatial, organizational, or relational ties between actors may permit them to know about information not carried in the mass media. Chains of direct ties can indirectly link actors with others who are quite distant from them and lead to the widespread diffusion of information. When indirect ties are involved, it is possible to track the diffusion over time through successive circles of influence or along well-defined physical paths. Crowd actions in the past have diffused across time from a point of origin along major transportation routes (e.g. Rudé 1964: 25; Shibutani 1966: 103–6). Individuals received communication about developing riots (Singer 1968) and sit-in campaigns (Morris 1984) by direct communication from prior acquaintances. Announcements at church services spread the word about the Montgomery bus boycott (Morris 1984). Activists encounter new ideologies and tactics at conferences with other activists (Rothman and Oliver 1999). Such effects are especially noticeable in prior centuries (Charlesworth 1979), or in the earliest phases of more recent movements. Once action has begun and receives mass media coverage, it becomes difficult to empirically assess the basis of communication and influence flows without directly asking each actor involved, and even when asked, actors may have been subject to multiple sources of relatively redundant information.

Modelling Network Ties with No Media Coverage

Suppose we have a taboo issue that the news media refuse to cover. Or, perhaps, instead of being 'taboo,' it is one of those positive and uplifting kinds of action which lack news value because it is not conflict-oriented and not linked to institutional politics (Oliver and Myers 1999; Oliver and Maney 2000). To add network effects to the baseline model we create a who-to-whom network matrix with entries that are zeroes or ones. A matrix with all 1's is the 'everyone affects everyone' model and produces the same results as a model in which people's actions are affected by totals. Conversely, a matrix with all 0's produces the same result as the independent probabilities model. Because the underlying model is a growth model, where there is no decline, if actors are influenced by others' actions (or their own) there is a gradual increase in the probability of action and, thus, in the average level of total action, but the rate at which the action increases is a function of the density of communication. Between the 'full information' model and the 'no information' model lay the models in which there are some connections between actors. Theoretically, it is important to specify whether the diagonals are 1s or 0s, that is, whether people increase their action as a function of their own actions as well as of others' actions, but exploring these subtleties is beyond the scope of this chapter.[4]

This model can be used to assess the effects of varying network structures. Because it is stochastic, even for exactly the same determinate who-to-whom relationship matrix, there will be different results on each iteration of the model, depending on random fluctuations in exactly who acts when. We may use Stella's ability to use a seed for the random number generator to fix this process and compare network structures. Figure 8.3 compares one random and three fixed structures including a 'star' network in which all ties are through actor, a cliqued network in which all ties are within cliques (1, 2, 3 vs. 4, 5, 6 vs. 7, 8, 9, 10), and a bridged cliqued network in which there is an additional tie between 3 and 4, and

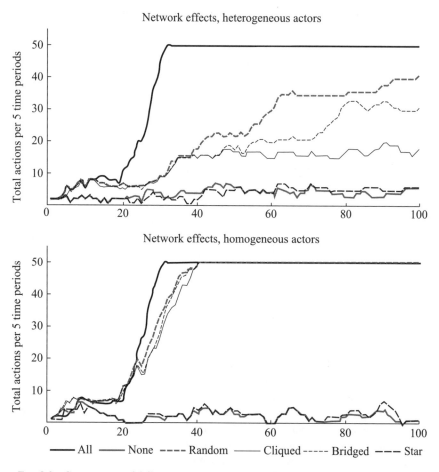

FIG. 8.3. *Comparison of different patterns of network ties in the diffusion of action for heterogeneous and homogeneous groups*

between 6 and 7. In this model, different random networks vary widely in their results, and the variability of results due to network ties is even greater when the initial probability distribution is heterogeneous. The particular random network in this figure is slightly more effective than the bridged clique network, which in turn is slightly more effective than the fully cliqued network. The 'star' network in this example fares little better than no feedback at all: this arises because the non-stars only have information about one actor's actions and so the total level of action is too small to lead to much increase through feedback. In an influence model, shown later, a star can have a much bigger impact on action.

This approach can be readily generalized to much larger network matrices (e.g. 100×100), but these are quite difficult to analyse without prior theory of what kinds of structures are relevant or interesting. Obviously, the approach of using a full matrix of who-to-whom ties becomes computationally impossible with very large groups such as the tens or hundreds of thousands in city populations, and seems most appropriate for modelling the relationships between groups.

Modelling Protest and the Media

Protesters generally seek news coverage as the mechanism for having influence on a wider public and the authorities. Protests that receive no news coverage are often construed as failures. Protests that receive news coverage are likely to be invigorated, and activists are likely to prolong their activism and emit more total protests if they have received news coverage. But, of course, the news media do not cover all protests that occur, and their coverage is dependent on the amount of protest. There are 'media attention cycles,' which are diffusion cycles: news media tend to ignore a protest campaign in its small initial phases and then, when they do begin to cover it, there is a flurry of coverage for a while until it becomes 'old news,' and then coverage dies down again.

Adding media effects into a model requires specifying how the media work. This is a complex problem, which will need to be the subject of a separate analysis. We need to consider both how the media affect protest, and how protest affects the media. In this chapter, we will assume that the media are simply a channel of communication, so news coverage of events affects protest by conveying to actors information about the protest rates of others. This means that we will assume that media coverage acts just like full feedback or network communication, in terms of the algorithm for the effect of others' actions on an actor's probability of acting. In terms of the relation between protest and the probability that the protest receives news coverage, there is some information from recent empirical work. We know that there are issue attention cycles that may be functions of factors exogenous protest, or may be set off by protest; an issue attention cycle raises the probability that an event will be covered. In addition, we know that the probability of an event being covered increases with its size, and recent large events may draw a higher rate of coverage to immediately subsequent events. There are also 'news hole' effects, so that there is a limit on the amount of action that can be reported on one day. Myers and Caniglia (2000) found, for example, that the *New York Times* under-reported riots at the peak of a riot cycle: even though they reported that there was a lot of rioting going on, any particular riot was less likely to be mentioned when there were many riots happening.

In this chapter, we cannot provide a full analysis, but illustrate a possible approach to such a problem by showing the effects of several kinds of media factors separately. We begin by showing the effect of a flat percentage of news coverage on the rate of 'adoption' of action compared to full information. Figure 8.4 shows the rate of action diffusion with news coverage at a constant 50 and 20 per cent probability as compared with the full information model (equivalent to

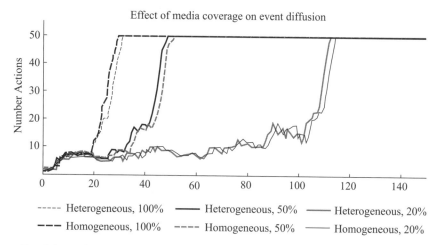

FIG. 8.4. *Media coverage as flat percentage provides communication, which promotes event diffusion. There is little difference between heterogeneous and homogeneous groups.*

100 per cent probability of news coverage). In this initial model, the specification is that the news media has a single probability of news coverage. If it 'covers' action at all, it covers all the action that is occurring on that round. A more detailed specification would say that the media could be differentially sensitive to different actors, so that actors could have different probabilities of coverage or that different proportions of those acting on a round could be covered. That would yield different patterns of results.

Figure 8.5 shows how the diffusion of action is affected when the probability of news coverage is not a flat percentage, but increases with the size of the action, for example, the number of actors. The 'functional' relation is parameterized so that actions involving all ten actors have a 50 per cent rate of coverage, while the probability for smaller actions is proportionately smaller. This dependence of news coverage on event size markedly slows the spread of action.

In most research, newspapers are the source of data and thus only news coverage of action is empirically observable. Figure 8.6 shows both action and news coverage of action when the probability of news coverage is a constant 50 per cent (upper panel), and when the probability of news coverage is 50 per cent for the largest actions (involving all ten actors) but is proportionately lower for smaller actions. Two patterns are clear is these figures. First, if the probability news coverage is proportional to the size of the events, diffusion is delayed relative to a constant probability of coverage, because the earlier smaller events (involving just one or two actors) are less likely to get news coverage. Additionally, the apparent level of protest from news coverage is even lower than the actual level, due to the lower probability of coverage. Second, note that the cycles of news stories differ

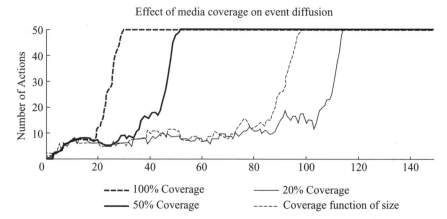

FIG. 8.5. *Comparison of action diffusion when news coverage rate is 100%, 50%, 20%, or a function of number of actors. Homogeneous groups.*

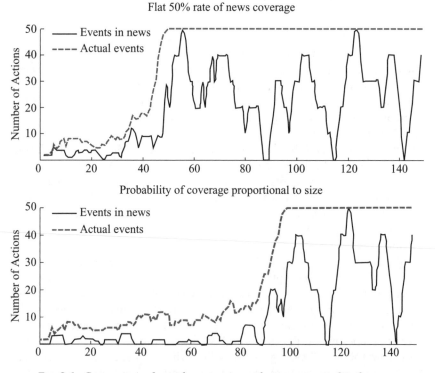

FIG. 8.6. *Comparison of actual event series with events reported in the news. Top panel shows a flat 50% coverage rate. Bottom panel shows coverage proportional to the number of actors. Homogeneous groups.*

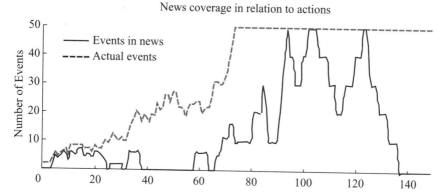

FIG. 8.7. *Independent issue attention cycle can distort apparent protest cycle. Dashed line shows actual events, solid line shows events reported in the news.*

markedly from the cycles of action. This is especially true when the probability of coverage is a function of event size. But even after action has reached unanimity, random fluctuations in news coverage give the appearance of protest cycles where there are none. However, in both these cases, news coverage does successfully track the difference between high-action and low-action periods.

There is substantial reason to believe that the news media's probability of covering protest is often determined not by the characteristics of the protest, but by external events or political cycles (Oliver and Maney 2000). In Fig. 8.7, the probability of news coverage is exogenously determined as a sine function, that is, a wave that goes up and down independently of protest levels. As before, past news coverage of protest raises future protesting. In this example, there is an early news cycle that helps to spark a diffusion process. Then the news coverage dies down while the protest is still rising. Coverage comes and goes again later when action is unanimous. Because very often the news coverage of protest is the only 'data' we have about protest, it is very important to recognize how easy it is for news cycles to be unrelated to protest cycles, and it is obviously important to do a more detailed study of how protest and news coverage relate to each other.

INFLUENCE

There are many network theorists working on influence models which assume that people's attitudes are shaped by those of the people to whom they have network ties, and in particular that the degree of influence will be affected by the homogeneity/heterogeneity of the opinions in the networks to which one is tied. If virtually all of one's acquaintances share the same political perspective, one's mobilization level or attitude extremity will be greater than if one's acquaintances vary in political perspectives (Pfaff 1996; Kim and Bearman 1997; Soule 1997; Van Dyke 1998; Chwe 1999; Sandell 1999). This suggests that there is an interesting dynamic in the way networks affect mobilization. The same factors that create higher influence (all one's acquaintances are similar) are likely also to reduce the extent to which a group has network ties into nonmovement organizations. Thus relatively closed, politicized networks tend to increase diffusion through self-reinforcement processes, while relatively open networks have more potential to foster diffusion through mobilizing new participants, although the force of such a diffusion effect is likely to be weaker. Of particular concern is whether a group is relatively inbred, with ties only to itself or to other movement groups, or whether it has ties out into the general population of people who are not already mobilized. For example, Ohlemacher (1996) develops the concept of the social relay to distinguish the networks in two communities, one in which the protesters were relatively isolated, and the other in which protesters had substantial ties to non-protest organizations in the community: the relatively isolated protesters were viewed as more radical and failed to generate a broad mobilization, while the protesters with substantial non-protest ties built a broader, less marginalized, mobilization.

We may begin to model these processes by adapting Gould's (1993*a,b*) influence model, in which each person's probability of action is affected by the average of the action level of all the others to whom she/he is tied. If there are zero network ties, each person's probability stays the same; if there are 100 per cent of all possible network ties, everyone's probability fairly rapidly converges to the same probability, with the initially higher probabilities dropping and the initially lower probabilities increasing. If we put a simple who-to-whom matrix in this system, network ties affect the speed with which these processes occur, but not the final outcomes. We can see how this works by setting up a two-clique network with radically different initial values of opinions. If the cliques are completely unconnected, they will each reach their own equilibrium, as in the top panel of Fig. 8.8. Here, then, we have the gap between the isolated radical terrorist cell, for example, and the larger population. The radical cell can maintain its radicalism, but at the cost of having no influence on the larger population. If there are any bridges between the networks, however, influence will 'leak' across the system and the two cliques will move toward each other and will ultimately reach system-wide equilibrium, as in the middle panel of the figure. However, the move toward equilibrium can take quite a while to happen and, in the mean time, there can be radical disjuncture between subnetworks. These two cliqued cases may be compared with the bottom panel, which shows how one random network fairly rapidly converges to a system-wide equilibrium. In this particular case, it happens that one actor has no ties to other actors and so remains unchanged while everyone else converges toward equilibrium.

Network analysts usually treat the structure of network ties as fixed and unchanging. But, of course, movement actors devote a great deal of effort toward

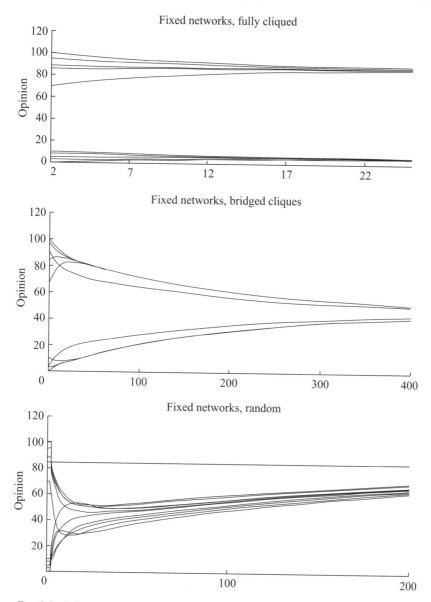

FIG. 8.8. *Influence processes in cliqued, bridged and random networks. Network ties fixed. (In the random network, one actor happens to have no ties to others.)*

creating new ties, and even the less planned forms of social interaction create new ties. In a formal modelling approach, it is quite feasible to make the ties themselves change over time in response to prior interaction. We may demonstrate this with a modified influence model. Instead of fixed present/absent ties, we begin with a who-to-whom matrix in which each entry is the probability that two actors will come into contact and influence each other. In this model, a matrix of 0,1 network ties is generated on each round probabilistically as a function of the given probabilities of influence. In addition, we add a feedback to these probabilities so that if a contact actually occurs (i.e. if there is a 1 in the matrix, even if it arises from a low probability of occurrence) that contact raises the probability of future contact by a given amount. To demonstrate how this model works, we set up an

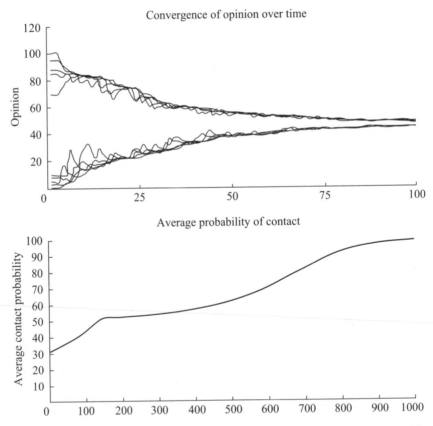

FIG. 8.9. *Network ties are probabilistic and can be increased by contact. Each clique of five actors initially has 50% probability within clique and 5% between cliques. Upper panel shows opinion convergence as actors come into contact. Lower panel shows that the average probability of contact gradually rises across many time periods*

input matrix with two cliques, each of which has a 50 per cent probability of making contact within the clique and only a 5 per cent chance of making contact between cliques. As before, we give the two cliques widely different starting values on the opinion measure. As Fig. 8.9 demonstrates, this model also generates convergence toward an equilibrium value, although it happens more slowly and with random fluctuations around the trend. As the bottom panel of Fig. 8.9 indicates, the average overall density of ties within the network gradually increases as well, approaching saturation as a limit. The irregular shape of the plot exhibits the influence of the cliquing. There is an initial rapid increase in the average contact probability arising from increases within cliques. After this phase, there is a classic S-shaped diffusion curve arising from the gradual increase in the probability of contact between cliques, which accelerates in the middle of the process, and then slows again as the network approaches saturation.

JOINT ACTION

An important phenomenon in any sphere of social action is that individuals come together to form collective actors, and smaller collective actors come together to form larger collective actors. When people organize themselves into groups, they do not show the random patterns of individuals acting independently, but very different patterns that arise from coordinated action. In evaluating protest event data, it is important to recognize that the 'actors' producing the event plots can be of widely different sizes and, in addition, can often be shifting around, grouping and regrouping themselves into temporary coalitions and alliances. No existing models of the diffusion of action have addressed the ways in which these patterns affect the observable event distributions. We cannot provide a detailed analysis of this problem, but we present here one example of it in the empirical data, and show how that kind of phenomenon can be modelled.

Movement Networks and the Problem of Protest 'Spikes'

The typical protest wave is more 'spiked' than standard diffusion models can possibly capture. That is, the empirical waves rise and fall much more quickly than can be accounted for by models of interactor transmission. One possible explanation for this pattern is that much of the protest event data is drawn from media sources and the attention cycle bias makes the peaks of action appear more extreme than they are. Another reason may be the failure to account for repeated actions by the same actor in network models. The density of connections drives diffusion between actors between them. If networks were conceived as operating across time, the network connections to self would increase the overall density of connections within the population and perhaps account for some of the steepness of the empirical curves for protest distribution.

In some cases the 'spike' is generated by a major external shock that has provoked a common response, without explicit coordination. When this occurs, however, the response will be something that requires relatively little coordination and has become a standard action form within a particular population. Identical actions involving complex coordination or novel tactics would not be expected to arise simultaneously in diverse locales simply from an external shock, without explicit coordination and communication through networks. The initial day of rioting after the assassination of Martin Luther King, Jr occurred in a context in which black urban populations were familiar with the 'riot' as an action form. The wave of protests at the beginning of the 1991 Gulf War bombings followed a build-up of mobilization in which it was 'understood' that everyone would protest if the war started.

Pulling out diffusion effects in these cases of closely connected events requires thinking clearly about the nature of the event and the type of coordination involved. In the USA 1960s riots, there was clear evidence of diffusion of small riots to nearby communities within the next day or two. For major protests in Germany, where the demonstrations are generally held on weekends, particularly Saturdays, there would be a seven or more day lag for diffusion effects to occur. That is, there are good reasons to expect different time lags for different kinds of events.

Other problems arise from using the news media as a data source when they are also one of the actors in the process. When the data source is one national news source, it is likely that there will be smaller regional diffusion effects that are not captured in the news source. What appears as a spike in the news accounts may simply be a failure to report the smaller events building up to and following a major event, and media attention cycles may exacerbate this spiking. (In subsequent work with our media models, we can investigate these possibilities.) Myers' riot data is based on newspapers, but was compiled from a large collection of local newspapers by a clipping service and, as a consequence, had much more information about smaller and more localized riot waves. Nevertheless, even Myers' data shows greater peaking than would be predicted by most diffusion models, so there is clearly more work to do.

Joint Action as a Source of Spikes

Many spikes in protest distributions arise from joint action that has clearly been organized. Sometimes this organization is overt and can actually be located in news sources, if it is looked for. Other times it is covert. We examined two data series available to us, Ruud Koopman's data on new social movements' protests in Germany and Kelley Strawn's data on Mexican protests, and identified a large number of cases in which similar events occurred almost simultaneously in multiple locales, often with no prior warning or build-up of action. It is obvious in most of these cases that there has to have been prior communication and coordination, whether or not it is visible in the data sources. There is clearly some sort of network diffusion process operating, but something else is diffusing other than the final action. Instead, it is an ideology or action plan that is diffusing and the simultaneous coordinated action that follows is an observable expression of a different diffusion process. From a diffusion modelling perspective, such 'multiple event days' create apparent discontinuous spikes in the flow of events.

We have modelled a simple process that generates a 'spike'. Actors have a constant low probability of emitting protest actions. But in addition, actors are organizing. They are linked to other actors through their networks. Each actor has a probability of 'organizing' other actors (which is also assumed to be the probability of acting at the end). Actors 'organize' only those to whom they have a network tie. Each receipt of organizing raises an actor's probability of participating in the 'big event' at the appointed time, as well as of organizing other actors. (In this initial model, these two probabilities are treated as the same, but they could be readily differentiated.) But nothing 'happens' at the big event until the appointed day, when everyone acts at once. In this example, we assume that Actor 1 is the organizer and starts with a 100 per cent chance of organizing/acting, while all the other actors begin with a zero per cent chance of organizing/acting. Each time an actor receives an organizing contact, his/her probability of acting rises 1 per cent. At the specified time period (time = 100 in this example), each actor acts or not with the accumulated probability. This model produces a result that looks like Fig. 8.10. We have added random noise of a low probability of acting, to show how hidden organizing looks against a backdrop of random action. This discontinuous spike is the product of more gradually diffusing influence that is raising the probabilities of action. Figure 8.11 shows these probabilities rising for several different network configurations. The results in Fig. 8.11 differ dramatically from each other: the three random networks have widely different results, and the cliqued

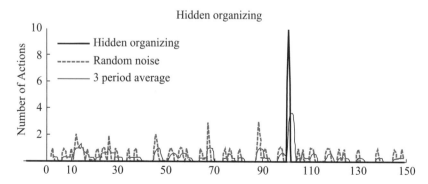

FIG. 8.10. *Hidden organizing, against a backdrop of random noise. Random networks*

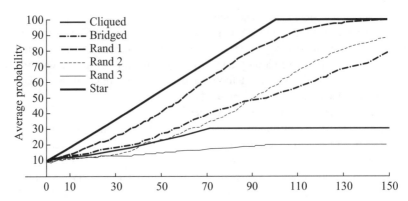

FIG. 8.11. *The average probability which is rising in hiding varies tremendously with network structure. Because of the skew in starting values, it is connection to Actor 1 that is especially important*

and bridged networks are different from each other. In this model of hidden organizing, the 'star' model is most effective. The size of the 'big event' differs markedly depending on the network organizing it.

Figure 8.12 shows how the effects of network structure can be seen in this process by calculating and plotting the average probability within cliques. Only the bridged cliques show an 'interesting' plot where the spread of organizing through the bridges can be seen. Full cliques have zero probability outside the organizer's clique, while random networks rarely show much cliquing. In a star network, the average probabilities for all the non-stars are about the same. A similar technique of examining different subgroups within a larger network could be used for the information and influence models, as well. It is important to note that the effects of different network structures vary greatly depending on how the network 'works'. Information flows, influence flows, and hidden organizing appear to be impacted differently by different network structures.

This particular specification of hidden organizing assumed that actors were building up to an appointed day, which is the appropriate model for big demonstrations. An alternate specification would be that actors organize until they have mobilized a large enough critical mass, that is, until some size criterion is achieved; this alternate approach would seem more appropriate for the hidden organizing behind a coup or revolution. Hidden organizing mechanisms can be incorporated into an influence model or a communication model. In empirical cases, this behind-the-scenes organizing is occurring simultaneously with other actions. However, it would be expected that actors might have limited resources, which might lead to a decline in other forms of action as organizing increases. Modelling this would require some algorithm for how actors choose between organizing and acting, a complexity that is beyond the scope of this article. Another issue to explore is

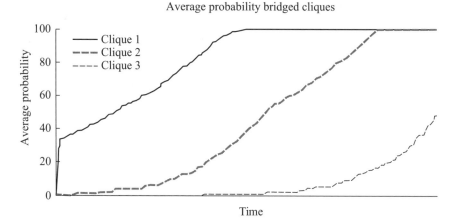

FIG. 8.12. *Probability of organizing for a big event. Network structure can be seen in the average probability within cliques. Here the spread of organizing through the bridges can be seen. Full cliques have zero probability outside the organizer's clique. Random networks show wide variablity in the degree of cliquing*

whether these coordinated actions foster subsequent actions via a diffusion effect, or whether all possible actors act in concert, and action falls off afterwards.

DISCUSSION AND CONCLUSIONS

The term 'network' needs to be unpacked if it is to move beyond vague heuristic and actually structure research into social movements. We find that attempting to specify network effects in formal models forces us to grapple with the difficult questions of exactly what we think these effects are and how they work, and how they relate to concepts of diffusion. The models we are working with in this chapter are of a particular sort that is rarely attempted in sociology. We are not analysing empirical data and fitting regression coefficients. And we are not specifying elegant deductive models and deriving their formal properties. Both of us have done both of these in other works. But in this project, we are struggling with what empirical data patterns actually look like, and trying to model the underlying processes that could be giving rise to these patterns. This chapter has sketched an approach to this problem and has shown how the flows of information, influence, and joint action can be modelled and how these different processes can yield widely different results.

As we have worked on this problem, we have come to recognize that any empirically valid model needs to have a substantial random or stochastic element. Random fluctuations from constant probabilities produce the kind of spiky, jagged plots of event counts over time that are characteristic of empirical data. These same random fluctuations frequently produce 'waves' of events, especially when they are aggregated across a few time periods. Once we made the shift to stochastic modelling, we have been forced to confront the huge effect which simple random variation produces in our models. Even with a fixed set of network ties, random fluctuations in who happens to act when can produce large effects on the pace with which action or influence diffuses. Random variations in which actors are tied to each other in a network can produce even larger differences in results. Substantively, this means that sheer chance appears to play a large role in affecting the trajectory of a protest cycle. It will take some time to absorb the theoretical and empirical implications of this result.

As we have unpacked different network processes and sought to pin them down so they could be modelled, we have found that the effect of 'network structure' varies greatly depending upon the nature of a particular network process. This can be seen most extremely with the 'star' networks in which all the network ties are with one central actor. This structure is a severe impediment to mobilization in a model which assumes that actors respond to their direct information about the number of others who have acted recently: because all the actors except the 'star' know about at most one other actor's actions, they do not increase their own probabilities of action to any significant degree. By contrast, the 'star' network is the most efficient in the 'hidden organizing' model, where it is in contact with an organizer that is assumed to increase the probability of behaviour, not the total of prior actions. It would be foolish to try to decide whether 'star' networks are 'good' or 'bad' for mobilization. Instead, it must be recognized that the impact of a network structure is intimately intertwined with exactly how actors affect each others' behaviour. Verbal theorists have talked vaguely for years about information flows and influence, but it is only when you actually try to pin these ideas down to formal representations that you realize how deeply the exact specification of what those relationships are influences not only the gross levels of outcomes, but the ways in which other factors affect outcomes.

We have shown how several different kinds of network effects can be modelled, and why they are important. Our model of information flow focused on the assumption that actors increase their probability of acting as a function of the number of others they know about who have previously acted, an assumption that leads to a gradual rise in everyone's rate of action. In this model, as information diffuses so does action, and we showed that different network structures affect the pace with which this occurs.

Consistent with our other research, we also devoted attention to modelling the effects of news coverage. This is particularly important because most often the *data* we have about protest comes from newspapers. We first show that even if the newspapers are completely unbiased samplers of protests, simple random fluctuations in news coverage produce apparent cycles that are not present in the underlying protest distribution. But, of course, newspapers are not unbiased samplers. We know that they respond to the size of protest and that they are subject to issue attention cycles that may be independent of protest. Both of these patterns produce additional distortions in the protest cycles in newspapers as compared to the underlying 'real' protest cycle. But, additionally, news coverage itself affects protest and changes the protest cycle. Methodologically, this helps protest researchers, because if news coverage increases protest, it brings the 'real' protest cycle more into line with news coverage of protest. However, if the causal effect of news coverage on protest is not recognized, researchers can draw quite erroneous conclusions about the effect of protest on policy debates. More detailed studies of the interplay between protest and news coverage must be the subjects of other analyses.

Influence models assume that people's opinions change in the direction of those with whom they are in frequent contact. This assumption generates a long-term tendency for a population who has direct or indirect ties to each other to move toward one common opinion, while wholly distinct cliques move toward separate average opinions. We showed how network structures affect these processes. If networks are cliqued, these models provide some way of understanding the relationship between in-group and out-group ties in opinion formation. We also showed how this approach could be readily modified to make the network ties themselves fluid and changing, in response to contacts from others.

The approach we offered for studying influence immediately points to a large number of possible extensions. Our simple models employed only symmetric influence ties, and an obvious extension would be to see how asymmetric influence affects these results. Empirically, populations obviously do not seem to be tending toward a single common opinion, and empirically it is clear that contact between persons of different opinions can generate polarization of opinions rather than convergence. Thus, even though averaging rules like the ones we used are the most common in formal models of influence, they do not seem to generate results that fit empirical patterns. We suspect that the most promising avenue to pursue is a model that says actors will either polarize or converge when they encounter each other, with the probability of doing polarization versus convergence being a function of the distance of their opinions from each other.

Our model of 'hidden organizing' is not necessarily very elegant, but it calls attention to an important empirical phenomenon that cannot be neglected in the analysis of empirically observable protest waves. Protest data are much more spiked than standard diffusion models can accommodate. These spikes violate all the assumptions that undergird standard statistical regression models, as well. Too many scholars have been willing to run models without confronting the implications of these spikes. Yet every social movements researcher knows that 'hidden' organizing (i.e. organizing that is not reported in observable data sources) occurs. This is one example of how important it is to think about what we already know about movement processes as we seek to develop formal theory that speaks to empirical data, and as we seek to do quantitative analyses of empirical data that are soundly grounded in a theoretical understanding of the underlying processes that give rise to observable data.

Apart from providing an explanation for data spikes, our work on joint action points to the need for conceptual clarity about actors and units of analysis. Separate individuals come together to form groups, and once they are in groups, those groups act with a high level of unity. Thus protest cannot be modelled as if independent individuals are conducting it. But, of course, the groups themselves also may temporarily act together with some unity, and models of independent action of groups will not correctly describe observable data, either. We need to fit the model to the type of action. The black riots of the 1960s had relatively little coordination between communities and relatively little organization within communities, while new social movement protests have a great deal of preplanning and coordination associated with them. We should expect to see different kinds of empirical patterns arising from these different kinds of actions.

We need a middle ground between the statistical analysis of data and the development of pure formal theory. In this project, we are in dialogue with empirical data, seeking to determine the kinds of processes that could produce the patterns we can observe. As we have repeatedly stressed, the discipline of turning theory into equations reveals the ambiguity and imprecision of many past discussions of network effects, and forces us to think more seriously and deeply about just how we think things work.

NOTES

1. Stella is identical to IThink, published by the same firm for business applications, except for the examples included in the manual. The models from this paper are too complex to be printed in this chapter, but are posted on the first author's website, along with links to a free downloadable save-disabled version of the Stella programme which can be used to read and interact with the models. The home page is www.ssc.wisc.edu/~oliver. Follow links to protest research and thence to the modelling projects. A more specific URL is not provided as it is likely to change over time as the web page is updated, but the home page URL will remain the same as long as Pamela Oliver is a professor at the University of Wisconsin. Note: answer 'no' to the question of whether you wish to reestablish links, as the links will not work properly when the files are moved from their original locations, and the save-disabled demo may not have the linking option enabled.
2. However, it does not generate standard mathematical equations for some of the complex modelling constructs available in the programme, such as 'conveyors' and 'ovens,' which are useful for calculating lag effects and moving averages, nor do its equations convey arrays in standard mathematical notation.
3. This algorithm for changing the probability of action as a function of past actions is

$$p_t = p_{t-1}(1 + w_2(r_{t-1} - r_{t-2})/n),$$

where w_2 is a weighting coefficient on the lag term. If the level of action is constant, the difference is zero and $p_t = p_{t-1}$. Otherwise, the probability increases or decreases proportionately to the change in the number of actions expressed as a proportion of the number of actors. This model is very sensitive to the weighting coefficient and exhibits a tipping point: below a critical value, increases cancel out decreases, and the overall probability oscillates around its starting value, but at the critical value, the positive effect of a rising number of actions can trigger a cascade leading to unanimous action. This is a fascinating model for a feedback process, but its very complexity makes it unsuitable for simple demonstrations of network effects.

4. We might also modify this model to make it an 'adaptive learning' model (Macy 1990, 1993; Macy and Flache 1995) by specifying that actors' response to others' actions depends on whether they themselves have acted or not in the previous round. Exploring adaptive learning is also beyond the scope of this paper. We can say, however, that in our very preliminary explorations of a random-action model where the only feedback is from other actors' actions, adaptive learning appears to have no effect in relatively large groups, because the random effects cancel each other out.

9

Movement in Context: Thick Networks and Japanese Environmental Protest

Jeffrey Broadbent

NETWORKS AND SOCIAL MOVEMENTS IN SOCIETAL CONTEXT

Social movement theory has been oscillating between the Scylla and Charybdis of theoretical polarity—the effect of resource and opportunity distributions upon rational actors, on the one hand, and of subjective orientations constituting 'culture,' on the other. This chapter stresses the effect of a third factor, social relations, such as networks and roles, as a bridge between the two, and as a key to comparative research. To study the interaction of these factors, I have developed a typology of elemental factors that affect social movements and their outcomes. This typology guides the analysis of factors affecting the outcomes of environmental protest in eight communities in a southern Japanese prefecture.

The Scylla of social movement theory stresses individual rationality calculated within a 'material opportunity structure (MOS)', defined by the distribution of coercive power and instrumental, largely material resources (resource mobilization theory, political opportunity structure theory: Paige 1975; McCarthy and Zald 1977; Tilly 1978; Skocpol 1979; Goldstone 1980; Oliver 1980; Hechter 1983; Tarrow 1994: 65). The Charybdis focuses on subjective factors such as identity, meaning, schema, morality, propriety, frames, emotion, and aesthetics. This family of theory partakes both of cultural structures and cultural agency (Marx 1980; Eyerman and Jamieson 1991; Gamson 1992: 70; Melucci 1995: 42; Shefner 1995: 596; Snow and Oliver 1995: 583; Jasper 1997).

The middle way between these shoals focuses on the *social* aspect of power and movements, a social fabric of varying 'density.' In static formal terms, the social fabric consists of roles and networks, but these terms represent a very dynamic reality. 'Networks' indicate relationships (of many sorts) between 'nodes' (individuals, organizations, states or other units).[1] 'Roles' represent the location and operation of nodes within the overall dynamic network pattern (central, peripheral, broker, and others) (Heiss 1990). Over time, both become expected behaviour—normative and institutionalized. For instance, a teacher is a central sender of information within a learning network, while a student is a more peripheral receiver of information.

Bringing concepts of material opportunity structure and of culture into conjoint usage has proven hard for movement theorists. Trying to bring in a third general factor, social networks and roles, might therefore seem foolhardy. My fieldwork research on protest movements in Japan, though, forcibly directed my attention to their thick social fabric, the network and role context. In thick social fabric, as opposed to thin, daily life operates through a dense web of particular ties. These ties occupy more of their daily time and penetrate their roles and their selves more deeply. Community and neighbourhood life revolves more around other residents. In Japan, these thick networks have a vertical structure, more controlled by elders and elites (Nakane 1970). In the thick context, networks and roles penetrate the self more deeply (Markus and Kitayama 1994). The opinions of others, bearing the sanction of shame, weigh more heavily upon behaviour than in thin societies (where it may be outweighed by guilt and by coercive reinforcement). In a word, thick societies are more 'relational' (Emirbayer 1997).

Furthermore, in struggling to interpret the findings of my fieldwork, I have come to the conclusion that the social context provides the crucial bridge across the epistemological chasm that currently divides material and cultural approaches. Social networks and roles represent the dynamic aspect of the factors of power. They transmit resources, threats and opportunities, as well as public culture, and a set of norms that may differ from the private cultures held by individuals. They require rethinking of our static organizational ideas of movement, state, and other 'entities' (Melucci 1995). Roles, in this dynamic concept, can similarly affect the manifestations of culture and resources. Accordingly, including the social context more explicitly in our conceptual toolkit will help our task, especially as movement studies move increasingly outside the Euro-American location.

Not that the social aspect has been entirely neglected. While we need not concede the autonomy of the normative, the recognition that contentious politics takes place within a 'universe of binding norms' bears upon the social (Coser 1974: 124). As this book well documents, the study of the effects of social networks upon movements has been growing rapidly, and so has the theoretical importance of network analysis (see in particular Diani's Introduction). To facilitate this growth, though, and avoid the chasm of reductionism that already separates material and cultural schools; we need to see networks within a broader framework of factors. We need to analytically distinguish networks and roles from material and cultural aspects, so as to be better able to study their interaction. We need to be able to grasp the causal configurations of all three. The widening extent of social movement studies beyond the Euro-American cradle demands this theoretical expansion as well.

If we squarely recognize the importance of the social and relational behaviour, how movements and members 'break roles' and reorganize their behaviour assumes central importance. The breaking process is highly conditioned by the

density of the social network context. In a thin social context, individual ideological or moral conviction may be the strongest motivator of recruitment, while networks facilitate. But in thick social context, networks may motivate a much
greater range of action. The mobilization of existing social blocs has been recognized in social movement research: established networks may allow leaders to
mobilize large groups of actors without convincing each member of the virtues of
the cause (Klandermans 1984; Morris 1984; Marwell *et al.* 1988; McAdam *et al.*
1988: 714). But the dynamics of bloc mobilization vary from thin to thick social
fabrics and have been insufficiently explored in comparative perspective.

Crucial to the use of network and role concepts in social movement studies is
rethinking them within a broader theoretical framework, as the concept of networks and roles need not be restricted to the analysis of individual recruitment but
can be extended into all aspects of movement trajectory and contention. I am not
suggesting that networks and roles carry the primary causal weight. Assuming
that would cast us back into the chasm of reductionism. Networks and roles
remain but one aspect of the total complex of relevant factors. Rather, the task is
to discern how networks and roles interact with material and cultural factors.

To carry out this task, we need to expand our conceptual toolkit. We need a
better typology of factors. The factors in social movement theories, such as
resources, opportunity structures, frames and networks, are rooted in distinct
pots—social science paradigms. Here I label them as the material, social and cultural paradigms. Each social science paradigm grows from an exclusive set of
axioms or basic assumptions about human behaviour. The tendency to accept a
single paradigm explains the epistemological chasm between theoretical schools
(as it does between religious sects). Accordingly, the only way to grasp the interaction of social, material and cultural factors is to shatter the pots and combine
their shards into new explanatory mosaics.[2] Such iconoclasm runs contrary to scientific calls for consistency and parsimony. But tidy intellectual universes not only
create chasms, they make scholars hesitant to peer into the messiness below.
The only way to bridge the chasm is to define it away—place the insights of the
various paradigms within a single, encompassing framework. Each paradigm—
material, social and cultural—posits a distinct central principle that has both
structure and agency. Structure refers to a 'higher order patterning' that defines
the behaviour of actors (Jepperson 1991: 144; Giddens 1979: 26; 1981: 47–8;
1983). Agency refers to the capacity to break that patterning and act in new ways
(Emirbayer and Mische 1998).

The material paradigm defines structure as a distribution of positive and negative
sanctions, produced by market and/or coercive forces, inducing rational actor
response. The social paradigm defines structure as 'institutionalization,' a dominant set of roles and relationships that have force due to either their taken-
for-grantedness, or their reinforcement by normative approval from others.[3] The
cultural paradigm defines structure as a dominant pattern of subjective motivation,
an ideology, belief, moral code, intuition, cognitive schema or emotional script.

Each paradigm crafts agency from its own materials. For instance, to use protest movement examples, material agency would involve, say, inventing the sit down strike or working to rule as a form of protest. Social agency would involve breaking norms or changing the terms of symbolic exchange, for instance, scandalous behaviour like throwing potato salad at your poetry audience (Allan Ginsberg), or unfurling antipollution banners from smokestacks (Greenpeace). In cultural agency, for instance, actors would adopt a new moral code or resuscitate a buried one, as when the Ghost Dance tried to stop settler incursion through the revival of traditional religion. Or they would adopt a new belief, such as accepting global warming as a serious threat to human society.

When we let these paradigms interact, exciting possibilities emerge. How different structures align, or contradict each other, affects the 'plasticity' of the structural context, providing different opportunities for agency.[4] Material, social and cultural structures may tug at each other in ways to help the exercise of agency and the reconstruction of practice. For instance, workers may feel economically compelled to accept a work regime, but at the same time, in an act of cultural agency, develop ideologies criticizing it—*die gedanken sind frei!* In a social movement organization, members' informal social networks, not formal organizational role hierarchies, may provide the real channels of cooperation. Cultural orientations that undercut a social role (a contradiction between two structures, one cultural and one social) may augment the role occupant's capacity for agency, to act upon and change the role. For example, a teacher who totally identified with the existing school role would hesitate to introduce innovative teaching techniques, unless suggested and approved of by the proper organizational superior. But a 'critical' (or from the structural point of view, 'alienated') teacher might be more likely to introduce new techniques. Or, as Sewell notes, an actor could bring a way of thinking learned in one social context into a different context, causing change (Sewell 1992).

The preceding discussion indicates two main dimensions of difference among the shards of paradigms, what in short can be called the *malleability* and the *tangibility* of societal formations.[5] *Malleability* refers to the structure—plastic—agency dimension along which a societal formation, in this case the bond of conjoint action, can vary. *Tangibility* refers to the material—social—cultural dimension of variation in societal formations, in bonds of conjoint action. These two dimensions sum up the points of the preceding discussion.

The *malleability* dimension inserts the term 'plastic' between the familiar agency-structure duality. This term recognizes that agency and structure exist and change within and through a social medium—collectively created relational roles. Most social action manifests neither as pure structure nor pure agency, but as a kind of plastic, a 'goo' (White 1992). This goo allows limited degrees of agency and change. Agency takes place in goo. It changes a set of behaviours, not just one. From there its effects spread out to the more general structure.

The *tangibility* dimension ranges across the material, social, and cultural qualities of a societal formation. It refers to what units (either agentic actors or structural 'puppets') share that binds them into a (conflictual or cooperative) relationship. As noted above, material refers to physical sanctions, bearing upon the body, such as coercion and economic inducement that are exchanged between actors. 'I will beat you if you do not get to work by 6 a.m.' is one relational way to produce a work role. Social refers to mutually interactive practices, roles, networks and norms that actors perform and use through habit or mutual convenience. 'My co-workers and I always punch the clock before 9 a.m.' Cultural refers to internalized motivations that drive actors 'from within'. A deeply-held value of 'early to bed, early to rise …' gets people to work on time also.

If we let tangibility and malleability form the axes of a table, the resulting framework and nine cells help make sense out of the scattered confusion of paradigm shards (Fig. 9.1). Rearranging the shards according to their tangibility and malleability orders them. It makes them more available, when we want to craft new, subtly shaded pointillist mosaics representing societal formations. In effect, Fig. 9.1 represents a 'periodic table' of the elements of societal formations and processes. Its categories represent the 'elemental' relational qualities of formations, derived from the root axioms of the theoretical paradigms. To put it more formally, Table 9.1 represents the results of a conceptual (not statistical) 'factor

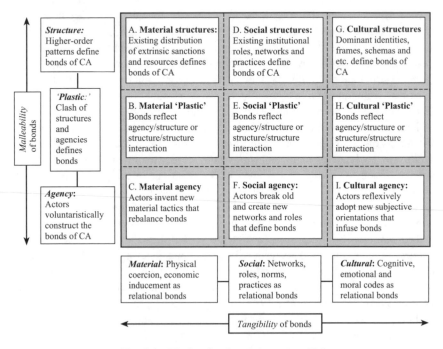

FIG. 9.1. *The bonds of conjoint action (CA)*

analysis' of the axioms of social scientific theory. The axioms 'loaded heavily' on two main dimensions, malleability and tangibility. The framework converts these axioms to elements, potential components of the socio-cultural formations and processes that need to be verified empirically. Unlike atoms, however (though more like electrons), each of these elements has only an approximate reality, because they exist in fuzzy synergy with other elements. Fuzzy synergy means that causal factors affect each other's very nature (Ragin 1987; Kosko 1993). Accordingly, elements cannot be reduced to 'variables'. While virtually posited, they must be studied *in situ*.

This is a very general framework of use to all endeavours in the social sciences, both as a heuristic sorting device and as an analytical tool. For the purposes of social movement analysis, I have specified the application of each elemental cell to the 'bonds of conjoint action'. By conjoint action I mean an influence relationship between two participants in contentious politics that affects the outcomes. The two participants in each dyad can be persons, groups, organizations, crowds, publics, states, and other collectivities. The dyads can be linked together in an interaction sequence, or can happen in isolation or distinct chains, as long as they affect outcomes. These bonds are 'the interaction mechanisms by which individual and sociocultural levels are brought together' (Gamson 1992: 71). Because this approach includes variation in both structural and tangible qualities, I call it Integrative Structurational Analysis (ISA).[6] Since the bonds can reflect structural as well as agentic conditions, the approach does not reduce to 'methodological individualism,' or more properly, 'relational dyadism'. Rather, interparticipant bonds can *embody* and hence *reflect* both malleability and tangibility. In this paper, I use the ISA approach to analyse social movements.

The interparticipant bond can be materially, socially, and/or culturally mediated. Social networks, based on mutual recognition (particularism), are but one type of bond. Others may consist more of material transfers or cultural interaction. The ISA framework helps us recognize the diverse, as well as mixed, sometimes ambiguous and contradictory, qualities of these bonds.

All bonds, including socially-mediated ones such as social networks, vary in structuring autonomy from low to high. In a low-structuring capacity, they are instrumental, the tool of actor agency. In a medium-structuring level, they define ways of doing things. At a high structuring level, they define both practices and internalized schemas. Viewing this range for social relations, agentic social networks are the wilful product of human intention, to be maintained or dropped as suits individual purposes. Medium structuring, plastic, networks 'embed' the actors in established practices, whether they like it or not (Granovetter 1985). And highly structuring networks define the actors and their motivations (Emirbayer 1997).

A social fabric or formation, the object of our study, may be a simple grey wool, or a complexly patterned and coloured design. The component threads, the different bond modalities, may be identified in the framework's nine elemental cells. The variegated mixture of material, social, and cultural elements within a formation defines its 'ontology' or essential substance. I hypothesize, therefore, that processes within a given ontology must move through it strategically, that is, with cognizance of its particular composition, or loose momentum. The specific tactics of a successful social movement, accordingly, must be largely contingent upon the ontology of its context. Success depends in part upon knowing and adroitly leveraging that context.

Identifying the ontological composition, the mixture of modalities comprising a societal formation, is not easy. At any level of societal formation, the component elements present themselves as a living *amalgam*—a merged 'compound' within selves, relationships and larger patterns. The existing amalgam may seem natural to its participants. The social researcher, though, to understand the mechanics, flow and process of the research target, must identify its ontological components, its elements, just as must a chemist working on a physical substance.

Since it can encompass so many components, this 'ontological contingency' approach helps us understand movement and political dynamics across the full range of societies. For our current purposes, the framework plainly identifies the 'plastic' row and the 'social' column, which have not received adequate attention in social movement theory. The centre of their convergence, 'social plastic,' brings to our attention a very salient question: how do network roles affect change of material and cultural factors?

Social plastic manifests as very different network properties in thick versus thin social contexts, with broad consequences. Under dense social network conditions, other types of factors, such as resources, opportunity structures and frames manifest in particular ways. They take on different ontological qualities and affect movements differently. That is, the boundaries of the elements are 'fuzzy' and change depending upon context.[7] Understanding their complex interaction processes, their conjunctures, leads us toward deciphering the causal configurations specific to the ontological formation under study.

Japan, to take the case in point, in contrast to the USA, has often been described as a socially 'thick' place. Institutionalized networks, norms and roles carry much heavier weight there, compared to the USA, for instance. Conversely, subjective motivations, such as ideology, material rationality or morality, have less connection to social action in Japan (Nakane 1970; Lebra 1976; Dale 1986; Lipset 1994; Markus and Kitayama 1994; Eisenstadt 1996). Accordingly, networks have a highly structural, normative, actor-defining quality in Japan. The ontological contingency approach would lead us to expect that both protest movements and the established power structures in Japan would operate much more through structural social network and role modalities, than in the USA. For a social movement to be successful in Japan, it would have to adroitly leverage that social context to its advantage. Thus its tactics would differ greatly from those typical of movement in the USA or many European societies.

DATA AND METHODS

The analysis in this chapter came from a larger study of Japanese environmental politics (Broadbent 1998). As part of this project, I used fieldwork methods to study and compare the responses of eight small communities to industrial pollution or its threat. All communities were located in the prefecture of Oita, on the southern island of Kyushu (Fig. 9.2). Six of the communities generated environmental protest movements, one (Ozai) showed signs of resistance but did not

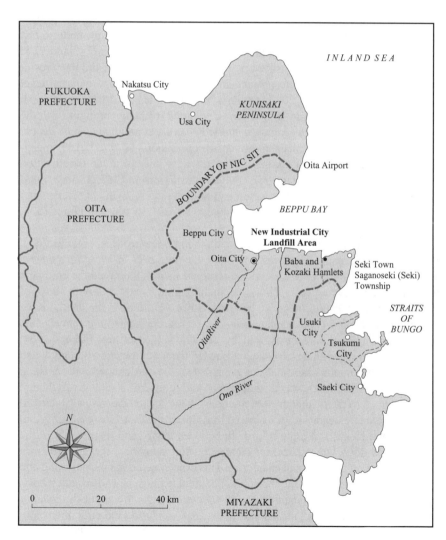

FIG. 9.2. *Oita prefecture with sites of environmental conflict*

generate a movement, and one community produced a counter-movement. The initial period of fieldwork lasted from 1978 to 1981. During this time I lived with my family in one of the communities (Ozai), and conducted intensive interviews there and at two others (Kozaki and Baba). In the other five communities, I mainly interviewed movement leaders. I returned subsequently for follow up interviews in Oita Prefecture and a few other communities. Further details of my approach can be found in my book (Broadbent 1998).

In the field, I gathered information in a variety of ways: participant observation, in-depth interviewing, survey data, archival data, and published sources such as newspaper archives. Participation in numerous gatherings related to the prefecture's environmental and political issues provided observational grounding. But the bulk of my work went into interviews with leaders, joiners and bystanders of the political establishment, businesses, unions, movements, and ordinary residents. Eventually, for the entire project (including prefectural and national level research), I conducted over 500 interviews, ranging in length from 10 min to 5 h (Broadbent 1998). Open-ended interviews, recorded manually, brought forth the best information about these highly contested issues and political events. People spoke of their own experiences and of their observations of others. The 'meanings' the respondents gave to issues and events were integral to the mobilization processes (Geertz 1973; Agar 1983; Pollner and Emerson 1983; Thorne 1983; Giddens 1994). Participant observation and in-depth interviewing are well suited to the study of complex, 'messy,' relational systems (Lincoln and Guba 1985; Mann 1986: 4; Ragin 1987: 23).

Upon return to the USA, I cross-indexed the interview records, organizational publications, newspaper clippings, and other data into over 800 response *themes* derived inductively from the data. These response themes identified the emergent important qualitative aspects of the case, including the bonds and motivations of various instances of (influential) conjoint action. Following the methods of grounded theory and ethnography, these categories represented the 'emic'—the specific motivational categories held by the actors (Glaser and Strauss 1967; Berry 1990). Along with developing a grounded theory of the case, though, I also wanted to see how the case (and the grounded theory) articulated with existing (Western and Japanese) social movement and political sociological theory. Accordingly, I tried to 'match' the emergent themes with theoretically derived 'etic' theoretical categories. In essence, I produced the elements of Fig. 9.1 in order to get a closer and more minute fit between theory and reality. Where the emic themes do not match extant elemental etic categories, the emic themes appear as their own theoretical categories. This procedure brings the emic and etic into better dialogue, improving the emic's potential to inject new ideas into theory.

This procedure is consonant with post-modern uncertainty about the validity of all received categories (Vidich and Lyman 2000). Fitting the emic themes to etic categories helps the 'dialogue of ideas and evidence' (Ragin 1987: 164). It uses a footbridge (elements and relational information), not a highway bridge (broad theories and institutional generalizations), to cross the epistemological chasm (between cultural and material theories, as well as between emic and etic concepts). The researcher examines relationships to see how actors construct power and make events happen. The aggregated qualities of power relationships produce emic themes. These themes may or may not fit into etic categories. This approach retains sensitivity to the differentiated qualities of the emic reality.[8]

Table 9.1 presents the emic relationships under each etic category. The emic categories, closely tied to the motivational social and cultural categories of the actors, comprise a grounded theory of the events. As can be observed in Table 9.1, the etic categories translate the emic information into a set of data categories derived from extant theories. This translation permits a synthetic theoretical representation of the emic reality.[9]

In other words, this procedure avoids the perennial problem of reductionism (aka 'parsimony') posed by the deductive use of a paradigmatic theory, without throwing away the insights of the theory. It allows the researcher to bring ethnographic fieldwork conclusions into easier dialogue data with theoretical propositions formed in a different milieu—in this case 'the West'. As such, emic/etic adjudication is a necessary complement of the paradigmatic reorganization advocated above.

Having collected and categorized information on all eight communities and their movements, the task became one of comparing them to arrive at generalizations. Both the method of comparison and the scope of generalization became issues.

In Qualitative Comparative Analysis, one inspects the presence or absence of causal factors across a medium-N number of cases (3 to 40). Ragin derives these causal factors from theory, and looks for their presence and their causal configurations within cases (Ragin 1987). However, I take his move toward case-sensitivity a step further, and use both deductively-derived factors and inductively-derived themes, as noted above. This brings the analysis closer to the causal configurations within each case. This study focuses on the causal configurations leading to full movement success.

Comparing communities within the same area controlled several potential sources of variation. The eight communities, like many communities throughout Japan in the 1960s and 1970s, all suffered existing or threatened harm from severe environmental pollution. They also operated under the same political institutions, regime and government, and enjoyed similar general levels of economic development. Outcomes are of course affected by movement goals and the response of political authorities to them (Gamson 1990). The movements had roughly similar reformist goals—to reduce or eliminate the effects of pollution upon community health. They operated under similar prefectural and national political and economic conditions.

Despite these similarities, though, the eight communities differed greatly in their movement mobilization and outcomes. Gamson notes two basic types of

TABLE 9.1. *Environmental movements in eight Japanese communities: affecting factors*

Factor	Community							
	Saeki city	Usuki city	Kozaki Hamlet	Seki Town	Misa-Iejima	Nakatsu city	Ozai area	Baba Hamlet
A. Material opportunity structures: The distribution of extrinsic resources (harms/benefits) affect movements								
1. New pollution harm income		•		•			•	
2. New pollution harm health	•	•	•	•		•	•	•
3. Existing pollution had harmed livelihood/ health	•			•	•		•	•
4. Profit from pollution		•		•	•		•	•
5. Permissive national POS	•	•	•	•	•	•	•	•
6. New material resources	•	•	•	•	•	•	•	•
B. Material 'plastic:' Contradictory material opportunity structures affect movements								
1. Clashing material groups			•	•	•	•	•	•
C. Material agency: Local actors invent and pursue new material goals								
D. Social opportunity structures: Existing social institutions, networks, practices channel movement outcomes								
1. Kinship hierarchy							•	•
2. Union boss hierarchy								•
E. Social 'plastic:' Contradictory social structures affect movements								
1. Competing kin hierarchies	•	•	•	•	•			•
2. Competing boss machines	•	•	•	•				
3. Competing parts within local government	•		•					•
4. Clash of gender roles	N/A	•	•		N/A	N/A	N/A	
5. Rising new middle class	•		•					•
6. Clashing trust networks	•	•	•	•	•	N/A		•
F. Social agency: Local actors break with role and norm expectations, create autonomous change								
1. Breakaway bosses	•	•	•	•				

TABLE 9.1. (*Contd.*)

G. Cultural opportunity structures: Dominant moralities, identities, schema channel mobilization

1. Deference to village leader	•		•				•
2. Deference to outside elites							•

H. Cultural 'plastic:' Contradictory popular cultural structures affect movements

1. Community tradition	•	•	•		•	•	• •
2. Local village god (*ujigami*)	N/A	N/A	•		N/A		
3. Community as 'self'	•		•		•	N/A	
4. Community-service ethic	•		•		•		
5. Environmentalist aesthetic			•		•	•	
6. Prior anti-authority values	N/A	N/A	•	•	•	•	•
7. New frame – pollution bad	•	•	•	•	•		•
8. End deferential attitudes							

I. Cultural agency: Some local actors reflexively make new cultural codes (identities, etc.) and act on them

1. New awareness of threat	•	•	•	•	•	•	• •
2. New collective identity							
3. Leader activist morality	•	•	•		•	•	

Outcomes

1. Make informal SMO	•	•	•	•	•	•	•
2. Long-term survival of SMO	•	•	•				•
3. Attainment of a major goal	•	•	•	•			
4. Change public opinion		•	•	•		•	

• = Strong effect.
N/A = Not available (missing data).
Note: Text specifies which actors are affected by the factor.

success for movements: new advantages (goal attainment) and acceptance (survival as an organization and entry into regularized politics) (Gamson 1990: 29). Other studies use different success criteria (Kriesi *et al.* 1995). This study recognizes four types of movement success: setting up a formal protest (or counter-movement) organization, survival of that organization beyond the first few years, attainment of a major policy goal, and having a major impact on public opinion. Of the eight communities, seven produced a social movement organization (including one counter-movement). Only three communities produced movements that attained all four goals.

Given that all the cases were situated within the same southern Japanese prefecture, I could not expect valid universal or even Japan-wide generalizations about protest movements. At best, in a statistical sense, I could only generalize to my eight cases. But to the extent that the results support other existing research and theory, they attain greater general plausibility.

CONDUCIVE CONFIGURATIONS

The 1960s was a time of rapid industrial growth in Japan (Uchino 1983). Most government and business elites were concerned with growth and were willing to sacrifice environmental quality to achieve it. At first the general populace too was mesmerized by the vision of jobs and the higher standard of living that growth would bring. By the mid- to late-1960s, the wave of industrialization had begun to engulf the shores of Oita Prefecture, even though it was far from the urban centres. As it had in other places throughout Japan, the new industries used minimal pollution controls and spewed smoke and waste into the surrounding air, water, and soil. Starting in the mid-1960s, industrial development sparked off sporadic eruptions of protest from communities particularly hard hit by pollution. This swelled to a national wave of pollution protest in the early 1970s (Broadbent 1998).

Oita Prefecture exemplified the social changes of this era. Oita Prefecture lies on the southern Japanese island of Kyushu, surrounding Beppu Bay at the end of the Inland Sea. In the late 1950s, eager to lift the prefecture out of rural poverty and provide good local jobs for youth, the governor of Oita Prefecture embarked on an ambitious industrialization programme. This programme placed the tall, candy-striped smokestacks of heavy industry along the shore. It brought some jobs and prosperity, but by the late 1960s, also produced severe air and water pollution in some communities. Along the coast of Oita, other communities also experienced environmental assaults from industry. Together, these communities (names in italics below) comprise the eight cases studied in this paper.

In the town of *Nakatsu*, a movement protested against government plans to build a large power plant on their shores. Further south, on the shore of Beppu Bay, the city of Oita constructed extensive landfills and an oil, petrochemical and steel refining complex (one of a number of New Industrial Cities built in Japan in the 1960s). The fishing hamlets of *Misa and Iejima*, walled from the sea by the complex, protested, but to little avail. When, in 1970, the prefectural government decided to extend the industrial complex down the coast, protest mobilization in the *Ozai* neighbourhood did not manifest strongly. Down the coast a few kilometres, though, protest appeared and stayed very strong in *Kozaki* hamlet. The fishing folk in Saganoseki (*Seki*) Town, a little further down the coast, also fielded a strong protest movement. *Baba* hamlet, though, produced a counter-movement against the Kozaki and Seki movements. Further south, *Usuki* City produced a strong movement against plans to build a cement factory on a landfill in the Usuki Bay. *Saeki* City produced a strong movement against the polluting plywood and pulp factories. Their stories are related in detail elsewhere (Broadbent 1998). First I compared important factors/themes across the cases, and then looked at their configurations and dynamics within cases, especially the three cases where protest movements were most successful.

Table 9.1 summarizes the findings sorted, in rows A through I, by the nine elemental categories of Fig. 9.1. The nine major headings represent the nine cells of the framework in Fig. 9.1. These nine headings represent 'etic' elemental categories derived from paradigmatic theories and my additions. The categories provide nine baskets, into which the various schools of social movement theory may be placed. In usage here, each category is specified in terms of its implications for the bonds of conjoint action.

Under each elemental category, A through I, are listed both etic (deductive) factors and emic (inductive) themes (the numbered headings) that bore upon outcomes in one or more community. The etic categories come from general social movement theory. The emic themes arise out of examination and classification of the fieldwork information. Where an etic factor properly described and 'predicted' an emic theme, the heading took the etic term. Where an emic theme did not mate with an etic factor, it received its own mention. As a result, the table represents a mixed etic/emic model.

The table summarizes my empirical findings on the combination of categories, factors and themes that brought about movement outcomes in each of the eight Japanese communities. In this table, both etic and emic categories express modes of bonds of conjoint action. A dot (in a cell) indicates the factor had a strong effect upon the social movement, and hence upon its success or failure, in that community.

Each dot also represents converting a community 'story' (narrative about the movement and its context) into a (categorical) 'variable'. This is only 'qualitative coding,' similar to qualitative comparative analysis (Ragin 1987). But still, extracting 'dots' from the story suffers the problems of all variables: cutting reality into discrete pieces and inadequately representing interactive dynamics (Ragin and Becker 1992; Yin 1994). Within a given story or case, 'variables' are not really discrete (Ragin 2000). They melt into each other. The act of extraction artificially cuts them out of the narrative fabric. The fabric can never be reconstructed from the variables alone. Dots may help initial comparison, therefore, but ultimately we have to understand the holistic pattern or configuration of each case. In other words, for each case, we have to explain the specific articulation between factors, themes, and outcomes.

I will first compare the pattern (Table 9.1) of dots *across* the rows, and then the pattern of dots *down* the columns. That is, I will compare individual causal factors across the eight communities. Then I will look at the pattern (configuration) of factors within each single community. Since we are interested in successful outcomes for movements, the main focus will be on the three successful cases. In any given case, a causal configuration, produced by the conjuncture of multiple factors, brings about an outcome. Even within this small group of eight cases, the three successful cases need not exhibit the same pattern. Alternative causal configurations can produce the same outcomes (Ragin 1987: 166–7).

First of all, the eight communities differed in their outcomes (bottom of Table 9.1). We note four movement outcomes: emergence as an (informal or formal) organization, long-term (years) survival as an organization, attainment of a major goal, and effecting change in (local) public opinion. Only three communities produced movements successful in all four categories: Saeki City, Usuki City and Kozaki Village. All the other five communities ranged from zero to two outcome categories. Accordingly, we can look for differences in causal factors across the rows between the communities. But we also have to understand the configurational pattern among the factors/themes 'down the row' within a single community. In other words, the 'variables' do not make sense without the 'story'. The interactions are too subtle to be captured by variables, even by 'variable interactions'. Both views are useful in distinguishing the three 'success' cases from the five 'failure' cases.

Material structural factors and themes, clustered under heading A (1 to 5), include those advanced by resource mobilization, political opportunity structure (both noted above), and sudden objective harm theories (Walsh and Warland 1983). All eight communities faced some degree of existing or threatened material harm (to health and/or income and profit) from pollution. The level of the threat differed somewhat, as did each community's history of pollution, as noted in Table 9.1. Pollution was, or posed, a severe threat in six communities (Kozaki, Saeki, Usuki, Baba, Seki and Misa-Iejima). The other two, Ozai and Nakatsu, faced milder, but still damaging, threats. This data indicates that actual or threatened severe pollution harm was a necessary factor to successful mobilization, but not a sufficient factor.

All the villages existed under the same national and prefectural political opportunity structure (POS). Post Second World War democracy supplied basic freedoms, restrained coercive repression, and forced politicians to pay greater attention to public demands. The ruling party (the Liberal Democratic Party) had been losing support and seats, so it had become more sensitive to new issues. Opposition parties, mainly the Socialist and the Communist parties and their unions, often bitter rivals, both rushed to support the protest movements. The Communist party provided dedicated lawyers, and several communities (Usuki, Kozaki) used them to file suit against the proposed polluting projects. Compared to earlier times, this POS placed few formal barriers in the way of local community protest movements. In this sense, it was a necessary condition. But because all the communities enjoyed the same formal freedoms, but not all mobilized successful protest, the POS obviously was not a sufficient condition.

In the same way, all the communities enjoyed roughly similar levels of material resources and facilities, as well as similar forms of internal social organization. Over the postwar decades until the 1970s, farmers had prospered, workers incomes had risen, commerce had expanded. People were more educated. Only in Usuki did wealthy business elites put their considerable resources behind the protest movement, to notable effect. In the other communities, the movements were entirely composed of teachers, professionals, workers, housewives, farmers, and other ordinary community members. They used their own money and time to support the movement. Accordingly, while the overall postwar rise in ordinary peoples' resources may have helped protest mobilization, resource availability cannot explain the variation among communities in movement success.

Accordingly, none of the three material structural factors can explain the variation among the eight cases in successful movement outcomes. In material plastic, competing local groups pursuing opposed material goals supported growth or environmental protection. This situation appeared in a number of the communities. Under the stress, some communities split asunder into bitterly divided factions. But material plastic was not associated with movement success outcomes. Material agency, in the sense of actors inventing new material goals, did not play an important role here. The findings indicate that the material factors/themes (A–C) may have played a necessary role, but were not in themselves sufficient, to produce full movement success. Other factors, either interacting with material ones, or on their own, were also necessary and perhaps sufficient.

Social structures (D), such as kinship hierarchies, did not determine outcomes in a fixed structural way. All the communities had fairly strong traditional vertical Japanese social network patterns through work, family, kinship, neighbourhood, gender, and local political organization. Vertical ties of obedience and obligation permeated all these arenas. Horizontal, voluntary ties such as 'friendships' (outside the vertical ties or community-created groups) were relatively scarce, compared to the West. Male elders controlled families, neighbourhood, and local government organizations. Prewar landlord families, though stripped of their land, still retained high prestige and status in communities. Local political bosses, working for conservative progrowth politicians, had over the years assiduously curried favour with the patriarchal leaders of these vertical social institutions and networks. They formed a vertical structure of social control that stretched from local residents through local bosses and politicians up to prefectural and national conservative political and governmental leaders (Fig. 9.3). This conservative vertical structure penetrated into the community through the political party, government, and big

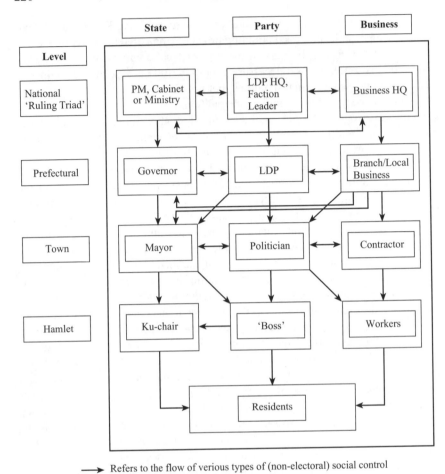

—→ Refers to the flow of verious types of (non-electoral) social control

FIG. 9.3. *The triple control machine from nation to hamlet*

business (Broadbent 1998: ch. 6). They incorporated most local 'voluntary' organizations, such as the fire department, women's clubs, youth groups, and festival committees. By themselves, conservative pressures through these vertical organizational ties could have nullified any attempts at protest mobilization. However, as Table 9.1 indicates, except for two cases, they did not have this effect.

Clashing social structures, as noted under 'social plastic' (E), disrupted the dominance of the vertical social structures. These clashes often involved the breakaway of social blocs from the dominant social structures. The dots indicate where this bloc break-away occurred. Break-away produced competing factions—pro-environment versus pro-growth—within kinship hierarchies, boss-led political machines, gender roles, and community government. Oppressed women and the new middle class have been theorized as sites of protest generation. But in the West, mobilization is mostly based on individuals, who redefine their traditional roles and then join protest movements, often encouraged by friendship networks (McAdam 1986). In the Oita cases, very little of this social agency occurred. Rather, the occasional protest leader was able to mobilize traditional blocs along local structural fault lines. The protest leader was able to do so by virtue of occupying a traditional leadership role, not a charismatic one based on proclaiming new values and roles. In this respect, leadership in these community movements differs from leadership expected by Western theory. In other words, once a traditional boss broke from his bosses in favour of resistance, he was able to carry much of his subordinate networks 'automatically' (structurally) into the protest movement. In all three successful cases, a traditional boss exercised this act of social agency (F), breaking with an old role in the vertical hierarchy of social control, and reflexively creating a new role as leader of an autonomous local group. Given the 'ontological' qualities of the Japanese formation, this act was crucial to the movement success.

Deep tradition imbued these communities, but the existing cultural structures (G) did not directly determine mobilization and outcomes. Yet, as variation among the communities clearly demonstrates, the use of culture—cultural plastic and cultural agency—sometimes crucially shunted the course of mobilization and outcomes. Villages in this area of Japan had histories of up to a thousand years. This historical depth gave residents a profound sense of identification with their community as a unit, and with kinship, landlord, and other ties within it. They deeply valued the *chi'en* ('karmic' ties based on geographical closeness) and *ketsu'en* (karmic ties based on consanguineity) among their community members. Often, only two or three surnames accounted for most of the residents. Residents from traditional families often felt their community to be a 'cooperative group brought together by fate' (*unmei kyodotai*). Traditionally, each village had a village god (*ujigami*) and a number of other local gods. In Japanese folk religion (often called Shinto) these local gods are unique to each village. They have little loyalty to central gods. Hence, the *ujigami* symbolized the village unity. The government had compounded villages into larger administrative units, but the old identities remained.

Of late, the concept of culture has been usefully problematized in social movement theory. Theorists see culture as a 'toolkit' that actors select from and use according to their needs (Swidler 1986, 1995). They see collective identity as 'constructed' through the process of movement engagement (Melucci 1995). They see the need to create and import new ways of evaluating events—'frames'—that will spur activism (Snow and Benford 1992). Each in their own way, all these theories grow from recognizing the plastic and agentic aspects of culture; that people are culture *users*. They downplay the prior (structural) emphasis of theory that people are the products of culture.

In these eight communities, the clash of contradictory subcultures and the importation of new values accompanied mobilization (H). Politicians had proclaimed the unalloyed benefits of industrial growth. But local residents, suffering directly from or threatened by the material harms of industrial pollution and the social disruption of its accompanying urbanization, increasingly doubted these assertions. Local activists, often youth or high school teachers, gave them information they trusted, due to the personal connection, about the negatives of growth: lack of personal economic benefits, health harm from pollution, and the impending disruption of community. This new 'growth harm frame' spread through local kinship and neighbourhood personal networks, providing cognitive justification to resistance. However, this new frame alone did not provide the strong or crucial impetus to mobilization implied by frame theorists (Snow and Benford 1992). I found that an oppositional subculture already existed among many village people, one that profoundly distrusted all conservative elites—bureaucrats, politicians, and business leaders alike. Accordingly, the emotional impetus to resistance was already there. The new cognitive information gave it a pragmatic target—government growth plans.

But this new frame, even energized by submerged resentment, would not in itself have been sufficient for protest mobilization—as its universal presence across all eight cases in Table 9.1 indicates. By then, everyone knew pollution was bad for you. No one liked it; many hated and resented it. But on the level of 'typical personality'—a structural facet of culture—Japanese people had not been trained to act upon personal convictions. Nor had they much experience in making personal friendships. Rather, all their lives, they had been trained to 'go along'. Relationships with institutionally-defined significant others (relatives, neighbours, and teachers) penetrated their motivations and identities more deeply than typical of Western personalities (Markus and Kitayama 1994). They were in that sense, very 'other-directed' (Riesman 1950). Therefore, most people did not feel empowered to stand up and proclaim bold resistance on their own. They waited for 'meaningful' leadership, from within their kin and neighbourhood relationships.

In Japan's vertical society, overt resistance was a daring step. It contravened the norm of going along. Moreover, though violent repression was rare, resistance had possible harmful consequences, both materially and in terms of social prestige. The social control machine controlled important material resources, but also tried to monopolize high status. In a society of 'other-directed' personalities, as noted above, high status members controlled a great deal of collective motivational affect. As noted earlier, bosses running the local political 'machine' worked through kin and neighbourhood networks. Local 'bosses' were people of some status within the community. They solidified their power in part by assiduously currying personal favour—presenting generous contributions at funerals and weddings, holding sake parties to build camaraderie, distributing small bribes at election time, finding jobs and even marriage partners for your children. For a politician of some local prestige, such as the mayor, to pay attention to an ordinary resident gave them a real status boost. The other services flowed through local personal networks as well. As a result, either requested by the boss or just out of concern for their loss of these services, locals would personally urge their activist relatives to desist from movement participation. This network pressure posed a formidable barrier to mobilization in village context.

It makes sense then, within this kind of ontological formation, that one crucial theme for successful movements should be the 'breakaway boss'. The three fully successful communities, plus one failed community, exhibited this quality. A breakaway boss broke free from his (as it was) status within the conservative social control machine to 'lead his flock' (my metaphor) into activist resistance.

However, while having a breakaway boss was a necessary condition for a successful movement (within my cases), it was not a sufficient condition. One case, Seki, had a breakaway boss but not a fully successful outcome. The same three successful cases, plus a different community, also exhibited the theme of 'leader activist morality'. These rare leaders, 'morally activist bosses,' were not total cultural innovators. They drew on certain existing moralities—professional ethics, student radicalism, and Buddhist naturalism—that others also shared. But they gave these moral codes top priority, enabling them to resist the blandishments of the establishment. In this sense, they exercised cultural agency (I).

This analysis indicates that successful protest movements in rural Japan required a leader of 'boss' status who would be willing to pull his bloc out of compliance with the vertical social control machine, and who also had the internal moral fibre to resist the enticements and threats that would surely come from 'the machine'. These two factors distinguish the successful movement communities from the failures.

DISCUSSION AND CONCLUSIONS

The preceding analysis showed how different elements, factors and themes combined to produce movement mobilization and outcomes. The role of social networks within a 'thick' societal context emerged as especially important. Using the formal logics of two methods, Integrative Structural Analysis (ISA) and Qualitative Comparative Analysis (QCA), the analysis extracted themes, factors and elements from 'messy' emic realities. It was then possible to synthesize these elements, to discern the fuzzy causal configurations that produced the observed movement outcomes.

Certain configurations of factors and themes turned out to be more important than others. Material structural factors such as political opportunities, resources and inducements from pollution provided the underlying geography of the movements. In all communities, a number of residents felt a rational interest in avoiding physical harm (from pollution). In many of the communities, a group with material interests in continuing industrial growth also appeared (introducing plasticity). In other words, material factors established mobilization potential for both sides, pro and con. In this regard, the Japanese cases resemble those in the USA

and Europe (Dunlap and Mertig 1992; Szasz 1994). But these 'objective' conditions and interests existed in all or most of the communities, so they do not
distinguish successful from failed movement communities. To understand outcomes, we have to look at the interaction between rational, material interests and
the social and cultural conditions in each community, which channelled them in
different ways.

Social and cultural structures also resembled each other closely in all these
communities, sited as they were in a relatively traditional, southern Japanese prefecture. Traditional Japanese village kinship and neighbourhood networks, with
deep historical roots and led by elder males, still animated community social
organization. Community governing bodies usually resembled a council of family
patriarchs. Social organizations such as youth and women's groups were an age or
gender typed tradition, not a 'voluntary' group. All these organizations were
closely tied to resident political 'bosses' who helped them with patronage while
building political loyalties to their conservative politician leaders. The inclusiveness of the community networks enhanced both internal solidarity and also suspi-
cion of outsiders, even those from neighbouring villages. The traditional village
formed what Nakane considers the basic social form of all Japanese social organization: vertical, personal networks oriented to the group (Nakane 1970). This
produces a *substantive localism* of community.

Japanese dominant culture articulates with this form of social organization to
accentuate its substantive localism. Shinto teaches an earthy pantheism, while
Buddhism conveys a selfless, non-conceptual existentialism. Neither supports the
idealistic and monotheistic orientations of Western religion and philosophy.
Whereas Descartes could present the essence of Western philosophy as 'I think,
therefore I am,' the Japanese Buddhist philosopher's response could be expressed
as 'Non-thinking, therefore no self' (Suzuki 1989). Centuries of state condition-
ing directed this ethic toward submissiveness to an 'organic' 'family state' (*kokka*)
until recently under a divine patriarchal Emperor. Through this confluence,
despite new currents of change, the contemporary Japanese adult self remains
much more open to profound social influence from others, including those in a
superior status. It is less individuated than the 'modal Western self' (Hofsteed
1984; Markus and Kitayama 1994). The resulting psychocultural structure supports the substantive localism of social relations. On the whole, then, ideologies
and moralities impel one less into taking personal stances than in the West. Rather,
the Japanese situation makes self-evident the wisdom of the popular adage, 'the
nail that sticks out gets hammered down.'

As Weber says these local, social, and cultural structures acted as 'railroad
switchmen' directing the rush of material interests down different pathways
(Weber 1947). Where the proper social and cultural agency occurred, this agency
switched the on-rushing material interests onto new tracks leading toward protest
mobilization and movement success. Where it did not occur, the existing social
and cultural structures (institutions and ideologies) shunted the material interests

back onto the tracks of the patronage machine. The machine compensated fears of health harm with other sorts of material payoffs, keeping opposition to industrial growth below critical threshold levels. Mobilization either did not occur, or died out without much effect.

Cultural critique alone did not suffice to stir up strong protest. New frames proclaiming the dangers of pollution entered all the communities through national media and local activists. These changed the cognitive information available. But they did not establish the emotional energy of resistance—that was already there in the community subculture. It grew from village protests over the past hundreds of years, with distrust of the state and politicians still embedded within village collective oral tradition.

This existing subculture of protest meant that, contrary to the cultural school of Japanese studies noted earlier, people did not require a great deal of 'cognitive liberation' from a deferential political culture in order to join protest. Moreover, in several of the communities, the initial circle of young activists had already been even more thoroughly 'liberated' by the democratic values they learned in postwar secondary schools. Beyond this initial circle, reaching out to the older residents, the activists' information attained credibility because they were validated by trusted networks.

Still even this combination was not enough to prod dissatisfied residents to coalesce into resistance. The final necessary ingredient was a protest leader from within the community, who enjoyed high status there. The high statuses could be derived from different qualities: being from the family of a prewar landlord family (this still held prestige); being a local political boss accustomed to giving out patronage from the dominant political party (the LDP); being the owner of an important local business. Given the vertical nature of Japanese community social organization, ordinary people felt safe in following a high status leader. This leader provided the critical social and cultural 'glue' for the local movement to cohere.

From a strictly rational point of view, we could say that the high status leader guaranteed the attainment of a 'critical mass' of protestors. Several Western scholars have proposed that people will rationally withhold joining a movement until they perceive it has the necessary critical mass (Klandermans and Oegema 1987; Oliver and Marwell 1988). For the same rational reason, they also propose that dense, centralized networks will be conducive to collective action (Marwell *et al.* 1988).

This explanation, which assumes networks to be the tools of rational individuals, may work for parts of the USA or other Western societies. But in the thick social context society observed in this paper, individual rational calculation, while not absent, played a weaker role. True, the patronage from 'machine' pressures sometimes overcame individual loyalty, getting people to switch sides. But even this was a network phenomenon, associated with the transfer of status as much as material inducement. These sorts of diverse networks subjected residents to contradictory pulls (Gould 1991, 1993*a*,*b*). But it was a situation of social structural plastic, not material agency reorganization as the rationalist Western theorists would assume. Individual wills were embedded within, indeed shaped by, the relational ties of kin, neighbourhood, and work. Accordingly, a relational explanation fits better than one based on material agency.

Ironically enough, despite the lack of firm individual morality in most residents, movement leaders had to have precisely that. The 'machine' targeted its strongest patronage to leaders. Resisting that patronage often required forgoing considerable personal profit (Broadbent 1998: chs. 4–6). As noted above, the leaders derived their motivational morality from different sources. To persist as effective leaders, though, they had to perform the contradictory task of acting on internalized individual morality, but mobilizing through traditional collective status and networks.

These findings point to social networks as the central element within the ontological formations of the communities studied. Social networks channelled material and cultural factors in ways different from a more diverse and individualistic society like the USA. In the USA, everyday institutions operate much more strongly through the cultural and material agency of individuals, as its entrepreneurial capitalism and religious activism illustrate (Williams 1970). For this reason, 'cognitive liberation' may be an effective spur to individual activism in the USA (McAdam 1982), but less so in Japan. In Japan, to the contrary, people are taught NOT to act to their consciences. Moreover, informal surveillance by immediate superiors, who in turn are connected to still higher elites, is commonplace. This vertical structure exercises considerable social control over individuals. This difference explains the relative importance of new frames and new interests in mobilizing movements in the USA (Szasz 1994). In Japan, these frames and interests are much more channelled by social networks.

While studying a few communities in a southern prefecture in Japan may seem remote and inconsequential to some people, these few cases actually provide crucial insights about the shape of the wave of environmental protest in Japan, its effects upon the larger society, and the reaction of the state and elites. The patterns observed in these communities, magnified onto the national scale, contributed to the parochialism or NIMBY (Not In My Back Yard) orientations of Japanese environmental movements. It contributed to their rapid decline after the state and business solved the worst, most evident environmental problems (Broadbent 1998: ch. 3). At the same time, the observed pattern shows how the mechanism of 'soft social control,' coming from elites, truncated the growth of an autonomous local civil society. This pattern of social control was repeated at the national level, placing many barriers in the way of movements and NGOs: great difficulties to incorporate, bureaucratic control if one did finally incorporate, virtual impossibility of obtaining non-profit, tax-exempt status, lack of philanthropic support (Broadbent 1998: 289). Accordingly, the local study illuminates national events, and even national reactions to international trends.

This paper has not attempted to create another universal theory of social movements. To the contrary, the particular combination of factors observed here achieved causal efficacy due to the local ontological formation. The observed causal configuration that brought about successful movement outcomes here would not have worked, for example, in a thin network context society. Japan is not 'unique' in any way. It simply exhibits, as do all societies, a particular *combination* of elements within an ontological formation. That is the generalizable point—that a great deal depends upon the details of the ontological context. This approach differs from the usual sociological one, which has been to assert the universal validity of certain factor or combination of factors (even if that factor may account for only a small proportion of the outcomes). Rather, it is to say that mobilization must be understood as a complex, figure-ground phenomenon. Movements take shape in tension with or opposition to an existing ontological formation, and both change thereby.

This approach casts doubt on, and leaves as an empirical question, the hope for universal theories of social movements. But neither is it to conclude a priori that all social movements or societies are unique. They are all made up of different combinations of similar basic elements, which fuse into each other in ontological formations. It is possible, using the ISA framework (or some other conceptual toolkit), to analytically disentangle these compounds into their (fuzzy, approximate) elements, and synthesize them following the observed amalgams and ontologies. That alternative causal configurations can bring about the same outcomes (Ragin 1987) strengthens the need for attention to ontology. But we may find, at the end of this road, after comparing many societal cases, that certain ontologies and movement processes bear strong family resemblances.

In the (Western) concept of the political opportunity structure, elites exercise social control mainly through material (coercive and economic) threat and incentive (Tilly 1978; Tarrow 1994). Another viewpoint in Western political studies stresses the importance of legitimacy and 'ideological hegemony' in the formation of control (Lukes 1974). The case studies of Japan presented in this paper, though, indicate another kind of social control, what could be called *social hegemony*— social control exercised primarily through local vertical networks. Under conditions of social hegemony, motivation and structure are highly mediated by network relational patterns.

The concept of social hegemony via networks will probably find many 'family resemblances' outside the Western world. My rural Japanese 'communities' had histories hundreds of years long. Traditionalist, less-industrialized 'developing' societies around the world often exhibit similar thick network social fabric (*gemeinschaft*), a conducive site for social hegemony. In such contexts, as in the Japanese cases, it is likely that abstract ideologies and public frames by themselves will have relatively little appeal. Along with coercive and economic power, they may be strongly mediated by personal relationships. Accordingly, the concept provides an interesting hypothesis for research on non-Western social movements. I am not advocating that social hegemony should be the sole explanation of anything. That would make the concept into another discrete, reductionistic 'theory' of social movements and political sociology, to be set against 'competing' theories. The ISA (Integrative Structurational Analysis) approach suggests that social hegemony is just one weighted factor among many.

The concept of social hegemony could have been recognized *without* the elaborate ISA framework proposed above. By asking the researcher to consider the full range of elements possibly at work in a given case, though, and by making it easier to combine them, the ISA approach promotes theoretical reflexivity among researchers, avoids reductionism by weighting any given factor within a range of others, and helps synthesize non-Western studies into a common conceptual framework. Theoretical growth will necessarily accumulate through successive case studies.

The particular ontological 'formula' channelling the rise and outcome of collective action in any given case will contain different specific elements and weights. Together, the relevant factors form a case-specific, dynamic amalgam. The general concept is one of a figure-ground relation between movements and context, in which different ontological amalgams define a diversity of movement and change processes. As noted above, this approach implies multiple and conjunctural causal configurations, seen within a holistic grasp of each case. Depending on the circumstances, that is, different causal configurations can lead to the same outcomes. Recognizing the diversity of ontological formations and reactions in human society will help the task of cross-societal comparative research.

NOTES

1. Of course, these terms apply equally well to nonhuman networks, such as among computers.
2. A number of scholars have called for similar kinds of synthesis (McAdam *et al.* 1988: 709, 1996; Broadbent 1989; Morris 1992; Emirbayer and Goodwin 1994; Lindberg 1995: 842–3; Buechler 1997).
3. See the neo-institutional school for this definition: (Meyer and Rowan 1991; Powell and DiMaggio 1991; Jepperson 1991).
4. Lipset's idea of cross pressures on voters illustrates the importance of plasticity, though he concludes they cause voters to withdraw from participation (Lipset 1981: 211).
5. I use the word 'formation' to imply a mixture of different elemental points (or 'pixels') combined to form a picture, representing the ontology or 'chemical composition' of a societal case under study.
6. I earlier presented this approach in (Broadbent 1989, 1998).
7. This position draws on Ragin's discussion of complexity, conjunctural causation and the fuzziness of causal factors (Ragin 1987: 83, 2000: 4).
8. Each relationship can be seen as a 'dot' with all the dots comprising a picture of the societal formation. Actually each 'dot' represents a 'tiny vibrating string' of relationship within a dyad. But this is not methodological individualism, because the qualities of

each string can reflect either macro-structural forces or individual agency forces shaping the relationship. Each string may be woven of any combination of elemental 'threads' or exchanges. This operationalizes the fuzziness of 'factors' and represents the societal formation in the fashion of chaos theory, where a massive number of data points construct a result on a new level, that of overall pattern.

9. The difficulty of adjudicating between etic and emic illustrates a fundamental problem of the social sciences in collecting and categorizing data. Though data may be hard to measure in the natural sciences, with the partial exception of higher-order biology, they do not suffer the added uncertainty generated by culturally-defined subjects.

Part IV

Theories of Networks, Movements, and Collective Action

10

Why do Networks Matter? Rationalist and Structuralist Interpretations

Roger V. Gould

My goal in this chapter is two-fold. On the one hand, I aim to offer an answer to the question posed in my title, which as is evident presupposes that networks do in fact matter. In the present context I think I am entitled to beg that question, inasmuch as one of the commonly accepted stylized empirical findings in the study of social movements is that networks do in fact matter. The answer I offer, however, brings within range a second goal, which is to use that stylized fact (together with its interpretation) to adjudicate between, and in fact to synthesize, rival perspectives concerning the appropriate way to talk scientifically about social conflict and cooperation—at the intersection of which social protest can be said to lie. In other words, I wish to employ existing theories to help us make sense of empirical data, but in so doing to gauge and possibly even augment the utility of the relevant theories. I hope to persuade you that we can use theory and empirical findings about networks and protest to learn more not just about the role of social networks in protest, but also about networks in general, about protest in general, indeed about social conflict and cooperation in general. Before I can try to do this, however, I need to expand a bit on what I think theories do, or ought to do, and how they relate, or ought to relate, to evidence.

According to one common usage, the phrase 'sociological theory' refers to an ensemble of propositions that describe empirical regularities in some phenomenon understood to be social: complex organizations, social movements, religion, science, deviance, and the like. A theory of 'the family,' for instance, might tell us that the family is a universally occurring institution that assumes primary responsibility for biological reproduction, care of dependent infants, and socialization of children according to basic norms and values.

A more restrictive usage goes further and requires that at least some of the propositions account for—rather than simply characterize—the phenomenon. For instance, a sociological theory of the family (in this case, a feminist one) might state in addition that the family as just described exists and does the things it does *because* it contributes to the maintenance of patriarchy not just within families but beyond them (and, by implication, because patriarchy organizes itself in such a way as to be self-reproducing). Similarly, a sociological theory of religion in the first sense might comprise only a definition identifying the class of phenomena to which the theory is intended to apply and a set of claims that go beyond the definition, such as, 'A religion—that is, a set of beliefs and practices relating to the sacred—always categorizes things in the world in a way that mirrors the organization of the society in which it occurs.' In the more restrictive usage, the theory would also have to include statements explaining the persistence, if not the emergence, of the phenomenon (though it would necessarily include statements of the first two types as well). A theory of religion under this usage would *also* include statements of the form, 'Religion as defined in the present theory persists (or emerges) because (insert your causal account here)'. Following the Durkheimian theory with which I began, a prominent example is, 'Religion as defined in the present theory persists (or emerges) because it reinforces the bonds tying individuals to the collectivity by representing the society as a sacred being or force during moments of collective effervescence'.

Let me say, as a way of introducing the exercise in which this paper will indulge, that I strongly prefer the latter to the former usage. I do not think this preference is merely a matter of taste: it is a matter of the consequences for the accumulation of knowledge that ensue depending on which of the two we choose.[1] Accepting the first usage allows us to call any mere collection of possibly unconnected statements a 'theory' so long as they are more or less about the same phenomenon. Any newly discovered empirical regularity about the family could in principle be added to the body of theory defined in this way without obliging us to reorganize our understanding of previously observed regularities. Theory-building would consequently consist of the addition of new stylized facts, and revision would consist principally of rejecting previously accepted generalizations on the basis of new findings—but only if the new findings directly contradicted some proposition already in the theory. In short, if we think of a theory as a mere concatenation of propositions, as opposed to an interconnected system of propositions directed toward explanation, then our theories will give us relatively little guidance about what sorts of new data to collect and how these new data should be integrated with existing knowledge, other than by tossing them into the sack of currently accepted propositions. It will be very unlikely that new discoveries will simplify what we already think we know, because of the absence of a core organizing principle (like that of explanation) requiring propositions to relate to each other in a coherent way. New pieces would not help us fit the existing pieces together; they will merely add to (or subtract from) the collection.

Now, it seems to me that what we call 'theory' in the social movements area generally looks like the second of these models, although there are moments when it is hard to tell. For the most part, theory and research has been directed at answering the question of when movements emerge, and more recently, when they succeed. Answering questions about the conditions under which something occurs is, broadly speaking, equivalent to offering an explanation of its occurrence. Moreover, even when such questions are answered with talk of 'factors' leading to movement emergence, the language used typically involves interaction or at least conjuncture. Factors such as grievances, political opportunity, resources and so forth are usually not seen as additive and substitutable ingredients in producing protest, as if an additional two bushels of grievance could substitute for a missing bushel of political opportunity; rather, they are seen as jointly necessary conditions. Occasionally we do treat movement theory as if it is a laundry list: 'mobilization occurs when groups have identifiable grievances, when they have material and organizational resources, when they perceive an opportunity for success, and when …' etc. But in our better moments we demand of our theories that they say a bit more about the interrelation of these factors, their etiology, and their contingent effects. When we do that, we are using the term 'theory' in the second sense I described.

Much the same could be said for the literature on the role of social ties, or social networks, in social movement mobilization. Although early formulations did sometimes appear to see social networks as something like a poor man's movement resource—not as good as money or weapons, but useful in a pinch—recent writing on the role of networks has taken account of what is distinctive about this sort of resource. For example, many treatments mention the sorts of properties networks can have that other 'factors' cannot, like centralization or transitivity; the conditions under which social ties might hinder rather than foster protest; the differential impact they may have depending on the kind of protest; and so on. Social networks have entered social movement theory not just as a single, detached proposition, like 'protest is more likely when aggrieved groups have cohesive social networks,' but as a pretty elaborate ensemble—one might say 'network'—of related puzzles and regularities. For instance, the literature moved fairly readily from mere descriptions of organizational networks and documentation of the impact of 'ties to activists' on recruitment to studies of the relative impact of such ties on high- and low-risk activism, of the significance of network structure for patterns of mobilization, and of the different roles occupants of different structural positions could be expected to play. Such studies have usually taken account of one another, recognizing that findings from each one could legitimately constrain or illuminate interpretations of the others (see, e.g. McAdam and Paulsen 1993; Zhao 1998).

Still, it is hard to avoid noticing that the ensemble of things we have managed to say about social ties and activism, however richly interconnected internally, nevertheless stands more or less by itself in the literature on activism overall. It is not as if people working on the topic of 'cycles of protest' have incorporated the network metaphor, let alone network-analytic methods, into their research. Nor do discussions of what 'political opportunity structures' are have much to say about the implication of social connections or their lack between potential activists and people in power: these 'structures' are usually measured, not in network terms, but in terms of overt legislative, judicial, or state action—or even self-referentially, as when movement success at time t is taken as evidence that opportunity exists at time $t + 1$. Social networks constitute a topic area within the study of social movements, with questions and answers whose implications remain for the most part within the topic area.

I would like to suggest, however, that what we have begun to learn about the role of social networks in the mobilization of protest can and in fact does tell us a lot about protest more generally—but only if we stop thinking of social ties as a separate topic in the literature. To make my case, in the remainder of the paper I will discuss a collection of stylized facts—empirical regularities distilled from a range of studies—pertaining to the link between social networks and social movements, and call attention to their implications for existing theories of how and why protest happens. My point is that when we learn something about social ties and activism, we are not just more knowledgeable about social ties and activism; we are also in a position to say more about incentives, about ideology, about emotions, and a variety of other issues besides.[2] In my effort to broaden the impact of the social networks/social movements research area, I shall concentrate on two ways of framing what we know about the subject. One framework might be called 'structuralist'; the other, 'rationalist'. In the end, I will suggest a way to transcend this distinction.

SOCIAL TIES AND RECRUITMENT

One of the first and most frequently cited facts about social ties and activism is that activists are frequently drawn into movements by people they know. (Let us leave aside for now the difficulty in saying what 'knowing' someone means.) It is now commonplace to say that social connections to people who are already mobilized are what draw new people into protest movements, religious movements, and identity movements. Another way to say this, from the activist's point of view, is that social ties to people not yet mobilized are a crucial resource in movement expansion. If there are obstacles standing between sympathizing and participating, or between feeling neutral and sympathizing, a social relationship with someone who is already a participant helps to overcome them. A now substantial body of anecdotal and systematically assembled evidence sustains this proposition (Snow *et al.* 1980; McAdam 1986; Klandermans and Oegema 1987; Fernandez and McAdam 1989; Gould 1993*a,b*).

An equally robust finding, but one that is harder to state precisely, concerns a group-level version of the phenomenon. Beginning in the 1970s, a series of studies—some historical and some contemporary—in what is now called the resource mobilization perspective challenged the popular notion that radical protest occurred among groups that were atomized, disorganized, deviant, and disoriented. Although the challenge was in part motivated by the political goal of refuting the conservative image of protesters as riffraff, it was also founded on solid empirical evidence. Studies of nineteenth-century militancy, in Europe and North America in particular, documented the social background of participants in labour protest; the typical rioter, machine-breaker, and revolutionary turned out to be a socially integrated, skilled worker or small-holding cultivator with an established presence in his (or her) community, rather than a rootless proletarian with a record of delinquency (Tilly 1978; Merriman 1978; Margadant 1979; Aminzade 1981).

This generalization, while not self-evidently a matter of social networks, can easily enough be restated to reveal that it is. Social integration on the level of the individual person takes the form of durable ties to a community or its members; and the lack of such ties had been thought to be what made people available for militant movements. On the level of social aggregates, the absence of social ties meant 'atomization,' the precondition (it was commonly thought) for the destruct-ive mass movements of the mid-twentieth century (Adorno *et al.* 1950; Arendt 1951). Given the empirical research indicating that it was integrated people who were available for militancy, most writers inferred, by extension, that it was the integrated communities that were most militant.

Although the inference seems reasonable enough, it depends on the dubious assumption that group-level social integration is essentially an aggregate version of individual-level integration—in other words, that the question of whether a group is socially integrated is the same question as whether its members are integ-rated. If the two questions are the same, then evidence of the integratedness of militants is also evidence that integrated groups are more militant. In the latter half of this paper, I will use a simple model of network-based recruitment to activism to show why the conflation of the two levels is misleading. The model offers a theoretical basis for believing that integration at the group level is a mat-ter of network structure, whereas at the level of individuals it is more a matter of quantitative connectedness. The conceptual distinction helps to resolve certain ambiguities in empirical findings concerning social ties and activism, leads to a set of new predictions, and in so doing sheds light on the phenomenon of activism in general.

TWO RIVAL PERSPECTIVES

Simply observing that social ties affect mobilization is not much of a contribution. It is a bit like noticing that people who are stricken with plague have had contact with other plague victims, but failing to relate this fact to their having breathed the air into which the latter have coughed, or to connect either of these facts to a broader germ theory that accounts for both. Of course, it is possible that there is an unspoken theory that makes eminent sense of this robust finding from the lit-erature on movement recruitment and ties it to other patterns, but I do not think so. The reason is that just about every theoretical perspective has absorbed the fact of network effects on recruitment without embarrassment. And what that means is that the way we are building theory is closer to the first model of theory that I mentioned than to the second. To illustrate what I mean I will turn to the two perspectives I referred to in my title as 'rationalist' and 'structuralist.'

Rational-choice accounts and structuralist accounts of social protest (and of other phenomena, like markets) are generally seen as rivals, yet each points to research on social ties and movement participation as confirming evidence. To be more precise, each represents the accumulation of evidence concerning networks and movement participation as an example of its own success in predicting empirical patterns from theoretical principles. In itself, that might not be so bad: after all, both the Ptolemaic and the Copernican models of the universe predict that the sun should appear to circle the earth from the standpoint of someone standing on the earth. Theories can be rivals without making contradictory empirical predictions about everything. They need only disagree about at least one thing to be competitors, provided that that one thing can in principle be linked to something observable. (If that is not true—i.e. if two theories make identical predictions about every observable thing—then they are just semantic variants of the same theory.)

The trouble is that rational-choice types and structural types go further: each side claims *superiority*, rather than equality, on the basis of network effects. Here, telegraphically, is how this happens. Structuralists like to say that social behaviour occurs in the context of local patterns—let us call them 'structures'—that channel choices and preferences in certain directions rather than others. (It does not matter much to me whether you refer to such channelling as 'constraining' or as 'enabling,' or both; it is obvious that the availability of one line of action typically comes at the expense of another line of action, and conversely that the closing off of one choice frequently generates others.[3] Consequently they are sceptical off the bat toward social scientists who try to account for behaviour with reference to putatively universal human attributes, like 'rationality' or 'self-interest'. More concretely, structural types like to see social actors as embedded in specific roles, in specific institutional frameworks, and, most importantly for the present discussion, in specific social networks that people confront in the form of obligations, entitlements, expectations, and influences.

Not surprisingly, then, sociologists of a structural bent have the following to say about the role of social networks in social movement recruitment and participation. Differential recruitment with respect to preexisting ties to activists is precisely what one should expect, say structuralists, if social behaviour is influenced not only by economic position (e.g. wage-labourer vs. employer or professional), attitudes (whatever their source), and considerations of cost and benefit, but *also* by strong social attachments to others. Structuralists might agree with Marx, for instance, that the Reformation should have taken hold first among owners of capital interested in a world-view legitimating their position. And they might agree with Weber that capitalist economic activity would appeal particularly strongly to

Calvinists concerned with finding evidence of predetermined salvation in their everyday lives. But they would also expect, net of these other patterns, that people are more likely to become Calvinist if they interact primarily with other Calvinists—above all if the latter themselves interact primarily with one another. And they would expect capitalist entrepreneurs to emerge principally within social settings populated by a lot of capitalist entrepreneurs—whether or not the latter are Calvinists. Finally, they would predict high rates of conversion to Calvinism by capitalists (or ambitions to entrepreneurship among Calvinists) in just those settings where Calvinists are disproportionately likely to be capitalists, and vice versa.

Hence the claim by structuralists to have a good explanation for the impact of ties to activists on movement recruitment. Net of individual-level factors predisposing people to participate in a given movement, a social attachment to an already-mobilized person should have an observable impact on the likelihood of joining, or remaining in, the movement. (A symmetric but seldom discussed or studied prediction is that social attachments to a strong opponent of a given cause should exert a strong negative influence on participation in that cause. The existence of this possibility is one reason, as I shall argue later on, that the group-level impact of network connectivity is not just an aggregation of the individual-level impact.) The specific psychological mechanism explaining *why* people tend to do things their associates do does not need to be known: all that we need to know is that they do. Once we recognize the fact, we have an explanation not only for the network effect at the individual level but also for a set of corollary patterns at the aggregate level, such as the nonlinear character of mobilization. Because individual actions are shaped by the actions taken around them, which are likewise shaped by surrounding actions, mobilization tends to happen in large quantities or hardly at all, leading to large fluctuations over time and space, sudden upsurges and precipitous collapses, islands of intense commitment amid seas of passivity, and so on. In other words, even when the distribution of resources, grievances, and opportunities is smooth, the distribution of mobilization outcomes is discontinuous.

Importantly, this pattern, though well known, was not specifically seen as having anything to do with network effects when the importance of social ties was first documented. So, courtesy of structural thinking, a new discovery—the impact of social ties on recruitment—has helped us to make sense of an earlier discovery, even though the later discovery was not made, or reported, with the previously known pattern in mind. This is the hallmark of good sociological theory (in sense 2): new findings are incorporated in a way that productively, and occasionally surprisingly, reorganizes our understanding of older findings.

In sum, structuralists think they have triumphed over rational-choice types because they can point to strong evidence that individual cost-benefit calculations do not explain movement participation: decisions about activism are embedded in social networks, and consequently cannot be accounted for with theories that take the rational, self-interested individual as the basic unit.

For their part, rationalists are not very impressed with such criticisms. In the first place, the idea that individuals make interdependent decisions has been accessible to them in a formal way for over half a century (or two centuries, depending on how you count), in the form of game theory—the core idea of which is that to be rational, ego must take account of what alter will do, which in turn (because alter is also assumed rational) depends on what ego will do. Blanket attacks on rational-choice theory for modelling individual behaviour as if it takes place in a vacuum are therefore misplaced.[4] It might be fair to attack neoclassical economists working on price formation in these terms; but those whose subject is closer to what we work on are much more likely to employ game theoretic models, which are intrinsically about the interdependence of individual actions.

More significantly, rationalists believe that their models of collective action are perfectly consistent with the finding that movement participation is conditioned by social relationships. As most of you are surely aware, economists and their brethren have been engaged for at least twenty years in the project of explaining cooperative social behaviour as the outcome of rational, self-interested (and yet interdependent) individual decisions. Let me be precise: when the economists claim to have explained cooperation, what they mean is that they have been able to predict the emergence of apparently cooperative behaviour without assuming the slightest inclination on anyone's part to be kind to anyone else. They believe they have succeeded in 'explaining' cooperation when they have shown that universal or at least widespread cooperation is an equilibrium—that is, a situation in which no actor has an incentive to change his or her behaviour—even for rational egoists. A rational egoist is nice if and only if it is in his or her personal interest to be nice; and this is typically the case, rationalists tell us, when everyone *else* is conditionally nice in the same way. In general, when cooperative behaviour is defined as choosing a course of action that costs ego something (relative to the alternative) but benefits alter, rational selfish people will indeed be cooperative—under certain conditions.

Those conditions are by now familiar: they are a prospect of future interaction, with the same alter or others with information about ego's past behaviour, together with a sufficiently great interest in that future to outweigh the temptation to defect now. If you will continue to be nice to me tomorrow on condition that I am nice to you today, but will punish me tomorrow and thereafter if I am not nice to you today, then the prospect of future punishments will encourage me to be nice today—provided that I know I will see you again tomorrow and the next day, and provided that I care enough about all those tomorrows. (I am sure we all know someone for whom the day after tomorrow is not a major concern relative to the present. Economists would predict a lot of noncooperation from such people.) You are thinking the same thing about me, and so under these conditions it is an equilibrium for us both to be perpetually nice to each other.

The relevance to the literature on social ties and movement recruitment should be obvious. For a rational-choice type, the essence of what it is to be tied to someone is that one expects future interaction with him or her. If we see joining an activist cause as an example of cooperative behaviour, then we have a model, namely the iterated social dilemma game—that explains the impact of friendship ties on movement recruitment: people who expect future interaction with movement participants should be more likely, all else equal (in particular, holding constant sympathy with movement goals and tactics), to join. Such people, the reasoning goes, are more likely to view joining as beneficial to themselves because their 'ties' to other joiners give the latter an opportunity to reward (or punish) their decision to join (or not to join).

This prediction is typically thought to hold even if the movement itself is directed to the benefit of third parties, such as overseas factory workers, endangered animal species, or future generations: so long as the other joiners can reward me with their continued friendship (conditional on my joining), the repeated game framework is thought to sustain an equilibrium in which cooperation—in this case, contribution to the cause—is distinct from the reward for cooperation (see, e.g. Lichbach 1998). More typically, models of rational cooperation—as in the iterated Prisoner's Dilemma game—treat A's cooperation at time $t + 1$ as B's reward for having cooperated at time t (Kreps *et al.* 1982; Axelrod 1984; Taylor 1987; Kreps 1990; Bendor and Swistak 1997). This symmetry between cooperation and its reward is a crucial ingredient in the elegance of rational-choice models of cooperation. What makes cooperation possible in this framework is that being nice to people who are nice is precisely what makes people nice to you.

So we now have a problem. Two different theoretical perspectives that present themselves as incompatible claim to have accounted for a widely accepted empirical fact, and both consequently claim to be strengthened by that achievement. (The logic here is a straightforward application of Bayes's rule: if a theory makes a specific prediction, then the confirmation of the prediction increases our confidence in the theory. An important exception to this rule is if the observation in question was the starting point for the theory. Only new predictions can strengthen our confidence in a theory—hence the vacuousness of 'explaining' the effect of sleeping pills by saying they possess the soporific tendency.) But since *both* perspectives claim to have accounted for the finding, neither can legitimately claim to have earned enhanced credibility relative to the other. How can we resolve this disagreement?

In trying to break the tie, let us leave aside the standard sociologists' reaction to economists' reductionism, which is to say that it strips away so much of social life that it cannot possibly be the right approach. Stripping away details is exactly what rat-choice modellers want to achieve: their goal is to explain as much of the world as possible with as little as possible, not to offer rich explanations of rich realities. So granting victory to the structuralists on the ground of greater richness amounts to stacking the deck against the more parsimonious rationalist story.

On the other side, let us not prematurely grant victory to the rational choice framework on the ground that it is more 'rigorous' and 'parsimonious'. It is true that game-theoretic models of cooperation are more parsimonious (i.e. as I just noted, precisely what sociologists often hold against them), and also that their presentation tends to be rigorous in the sense of including formal proofs, rather than verbal defences, of propositions. Yet rigor and parsimony in the presentation of theory have typically come at the expense of disciplined confrontations between theory and evidence. The canonical form for rationalist theories of cooperation involves an anecdote or presentation of a conventionally accepted fact (e.g. people tip servers at highway eateries), followed by a formal demonstration that the behaviour in question is an equilibrium in some model (see, e.g. Becker 1976; Axelrod 1980; Akerlof 1984; Frank 1990). The empirical exercise familiar to sociologists, in which a theoretical prediction is rendered operational and then tested systematically against evidence gathered in the real world, is quite rare.[5]

I think it is more important to concentrate on substantive issues rather than the formal ones of richness versus parsimony or theory versus evidence. Note, first, that the scope conditions for the applicability of the rational cooperation story are narrower than its advocates typically allow, and second, that the apparently simple mapping of 'prospects of future interaction' onto 'friendship' is not in fact so simple. I have already alluded to the first issue. What rationalist thinking in the repeated game framework has reliably demonstrated is that cooperation is sustainable in principle even if everyone is selfish *in the particular case where cooperation and its reward are symmetrical*. We can predict cooperation (and thus, if cooperation is observed, gain confidence in the capacity of the rationalist perspective to account for behaviour) when cooperative behaviour is interchangeable with reward behaviour. The famous case of German and British soldiers engaging in a tacit agreement to bombard each other with artillery fire only during daylight is a perfect example: 'cooperating' consisted of not shelling the other side after sundown, and 'punishing' the other side for shelling after sundown consisted of shelling the other side after sundown. We can say the same for norms of civility—norms governing, for instance, greeting colleagues in the hall, smiling when smiled at, and reciprocating gifts and invitations. In all of these examples, the way I know I am being punished is that the other person withholds the gesture I myself withheld; and I know I am being rewarded when the other person returns the favour I have bestowed.

We cannot say the same for the kinds of movement participation I just mentioned, namely those in which the benefits of participation accrue to people or to creatures who themselves could not possibly return the favour—or any other favour, for that matter. Even in those cases in which beneficiaries—such as death-row inmates who benefit from letter-writing campaigns calling for a stay of execution—can offer something in return, such as expressions of gratitude or public praise, it is not obvious that the repeated-game framework offers an explanation of what is happening. This is not to say that people who represent death-row inmates for free, spike trees in old-growth forests, or pilot their boats into waters designated for nuclear tests do not receive something (such as gratitude, approval from peers, attention from the press, or an inner sense of doing good, or a salary) in return for their actions.

But they do not receive anything like the benefits they offer, except in the most abstract sense of 'benefit'. And, to my knowledge, no one has empirically tested the robustness of the prediction of stable cooperation under repeated interaction to variations in the kind of cooperation people can offer. In particular, I am not aware of any demonstrations that mutual approval by peers for repeatedly helping the whales is a more stable or robust equilibrium than mutual approval by peers for repeatedly *not* helping the whales. So long as selfish people with prospects for future interaction can all coordinate on what sort of action merits approval, whether it is harmful or helpful to some third party who is not in a position to sanction their behaviour, it seems *a priori* that they should be no more likely to harm or help that third party unless the intrinsic costs of one action exceed those of the other. And since helping is typically more costly than harming, it is not self-evident that models of rational cooperation can easily be extended to such cases—no matter how important social approval might be.

Another scope-condition problem has to do with the temporal ordering of contributions to a cause. You may have noticed that I slid rhetorically from recruitment of new activists by old ones to mutual reinforcement of cooperative behaviour without registering the asymmetry between the two scenarios. In the former, there is a distinct ordering of contributions: activists, who have already contributed something, convince their nonactivist associates to begin contributing. In the latter, there is no such asymmetry of roles: everyone is simultaneously a past and future contributor and sanctioner of noncontributors. The story of network ties and recruitment has a beginning: there are early actors and late ones. The rational cooperation story does not: it never tells us how people can move from a situation of general noncooperation to one of general cooperation. Instead, the repeated games framework nearly always assumes that actors are cooperative at the outset—'nice,' in the IPD framework, which means that conditional cooperators begin by cooperating with others, and only defect if another actor has defected against them.

Yet any good theory of mobilization must tell us how it gets started, not just how it keeps going once begun. If what we are interested in explaining is the durability of cooperative behaviour, demonstrating that cooperation is a stable equilibrium under broad conditions is largely sufficient. But activist mobilization is by definition an episodic phenomenon, a departure from routine. Assuming that the default is cooperation in mobilizing activism, therefore, begs more than half of the question. Again, rational-choice types exaggerate the contribution they have made in 'explaining' collective action by disregarding the difference between accounting for its persistence and accounting for its emergence.

The second issue I mentioned is the matter of equating 'social ties' with 'likelihood of future interaction'. Here it seems to me that the problem may be even more vexing. In a nutshell, it is this. Let us imagine that, as your friend, I ask you to make some kind of contribution to a cause in which I am active. Let us further imagine that you do so. Is it reasonable to model my request and your compliance as a matter of cooperation by you motivated by a credible threat of sanctioning on my part? Doing so means that, implicitly, when I asked you to contribute, I was threatening to stop being your friend if you were to refuse; and that when you complied, you did so principally because you did not wish to lose my friendship, if even for a short 'punishment phase'. You took my threat seriously (say the rat-choice folks) because you knew that it would be rational for me to sanction you with withdrawal of my friendship were you to refuse to cooperate. The value to you of my friendship was sufficiently great that it outweighed your preference for not contributing, and you were confident that *I* valued your contribution sufficiently to be willing to sacrifice our friendship to get it.

But wait just a minute. If you are my friend, would not it be by definition about as painful for me to make good on my threat as it would be to you? Why should you believe that I would hurt both of us to oblige you to contribute to a cause in which you were not already active? There is no reason to expect me to be any more likely to get you to contribute by threatening to withdraw from the friendship than you would be in threatening to withdraw because I tried to make you do something you didn't wish to do. After all, I have remained friends with you so far, even though you have not been contributing to my cause; this alone makes it implausible that I value your contribution so much that your refusal will hurt me more than the loss of your friendship.

My point is that, unless they are strongly asymmetric, friendships, like marriages, are bilateral monopolies. The presumed threat of withdrawal is *not credible* unless the friendship means so little to the threatener that withdrawing it in response to noncompliance would not be costly. In any event, in light of this issue it seems difficult to swallow the easy equation of friendship with future interaction. If what makes friendship a useful resource for recruitment is the prospect of future interaction, then neighbours or casual acquaintances should be more likely targets for recruitments than friends: I can promise you greater friendship than currently obtains if I am only weakly tied to you at present, whereas the most I can offer a good friend is continued good friendship. If the only thing pushing me to recruit new activists is the benefit of increased participation, then any new members will do; and if anyone will do, then I will be most successful recruiting those within reach whom it will not hurt me to sanction. Yet the literature seems clear on the point that strong connections are a more powerful draw than weak ones (see Gould 1991; McAdam and Paulsen 1993). If future interaction and consequent threat of sanctions for noncooperation are the key elements rationalists say they are, then the central role of friendship in recruitment is an anomaly, not a confirmation.

It will help to formalize this objection, partly to make the point rigorously but also to set the terms for the formal argument I will develop in the next section. My broader aim is to show that the reasoning process characteristic of rationalist models is more compatible with what I have called 'structuralist' thinking than is normally supposed—implying, in turn, that the appearance of radically different perspectives is partly an illusion. The insights and empirical findings attributable to structuralist social scientists can be stated in terms that open-minded rationalists might accept, and the reductionist modelling practiced by rationalists can be shown to sustain predictions with which open-minded structuralists could be comfortable.

Assume, then, that two friends—let us call them Matthew and Nicole—are considering some sort of activism that both agree would be politically worthwhile but both see as costly. To give the theoretical scenario a bit of concreteness, imagine the activism would involve campaigning against capital punishment. Let us suppose that the value to each of them of participating jointly (say in terms of the gratification they would experience of knowing that they might have delayed an execution or made eventual abolition more likely) may be greater, less than, or equal to twice the value to each of one person participating: there can be synergy, diminishing returns, or merely an additive effect. In other words, imagine that the total value of any possible outcome to Matthew, V_m, is given by the following:

$$V_m = (s - c)m + (s + jm)n,$$

where V is the net payoff of acting alone, s is the benefit of one person's contribution, c is the cost (in time, effort, and so forth) of contributing to the cause, and $m, n \in \{0, 1\}$ are indicators reflecting whether Matthew and Nicole, respectively, make contributions. The parameter j, finally, represents the additional benefit of acting together. Assume that s and c are greater than or equal to 0, reflecting the assumption that contribution has beneficial effects but effort is unpleasant; and that j can take any value greater than $-2s$. (This assumption captures the possibility that joint contribution could yield either more or less than the sum of individual contributions, but could not by hypothesis be worse, net of costs, than no contribution.)

Symmetrically, let the total value to Nicole be

$$V_n = (s - c)n + (s + jn)m.$$

So, if neither contributes, $V_m = V_n = 0$; if Matthew contributes and Nicole does not, $V_m = (s - c)$ and $V_n = s$; if Nicole contributes and Matthew does not, the two payoffs are reversed; and if both contribute, then $V_m = V_n = 2s + j - c$.

If $s > c$, then there is some value of j sufficiently large that each can ignore what the other chooses to do because $s - c > 0$ and $2s + j - c > s$. Regardless of what Nicole does, Matthew prefers to contribute, and the same holds for Nicole. The outcome {Contribute, Contribute} is thus the optimal equilibrium for sufficiently large s and j.

But if $s + j < c$ (which is true whenever $s < c$, or if $s > c$ and j is sufficiently negative), each cares about what the other will choose. Let us assume that $s < c$, implying that neither will contribute if certain that the other will not.[6] If Nicole is not going to contribute, Matthew will receive 0 if he does nothing and $s - c$ (which is less than 0) if he contributes; he will therefore prefer to do nothing. If Nicole is going to contribute, Matthew will receive s if he does nothing and $2s + j - c$ if he contributes. So if $s + j > c$, implying $2s + j - c > s$, both Matthew and Nicole will expect the other to contribute, and so both will do so. (This is an example of a coordination game: both {Contribute, Contribute} and {Do Nothing, Do Nothing} are equilibria, but both prefer the former to the latter, and, because both know this, both will choose the preferred strategy.)

If, on the other hand, $s + j < c$, then each will see that it is preferable to do nothing while the other contributes (because $2s + j - c = s + (s + j) - c$, so $s > 2s + j - c$). Because each expects the other not to contribute, neither will contribute and both will receive 0. In short, in the appropriate range for the parameters s, j, and c, Matthew and Nicole find themselves in the standard Prisoner's Dilemma situation: whenever $0 < 2s + j - c < s$, neither Matthew nor Nicole will contribute even though, given that $2s + j - c > 0$, both would have preferred the situation in which both contributed.[7]

That is all quite conventional: it is well known that, in a one-shot situation, the unique equilibrium is mutual defection from the cooperative outcome {Contribute, Contribute}. It is also well known that, with repeated interaction of indefinite duration, and with individuals who care sufficiently about future payoffs, mutual cooperation is an equilibrium—*provided people start out cooperating* (in this case, contributing) and retaliate when others defect. But, to my knowledge, there has been minimal investigation within the game-theoretic tradition of how cooperation can emerge when there is none to begin with—other than to assume random attempts at cooperation in simulation studies (Macy 1991, 1993) or to assume the existence of zealots who will contribute no matter what (Oliver 1980; Oliver and Marwell 1993). Nor has there been any investigation of what role actual social relationships—as opposed to thinner sorts of connection, like 'contact' or 'expectations of future interaction'—might play in the process. I now turn to these linked issues, and show that iterated play does not by itself imply that strong friendships matter, and then modify the modelling framework to show how they might.

FRIENDSHIP, FUTURE INTERACTION, AND COOPERATION

Imagine Matthew and Nicole find themselves in the unfortunate circumstance that despite their mutual preference to both be activists, neither has done anything so far nor has an incentive to do anything now: because becoming an activist is costlier than the benefit of doing so, and because j is sufficiently low that $2s + j - c < s$, each (in effect) keeps waiting for the other to join the movement.

Now suppose that Nicole, thinking ahead, realizes that both would be better off (either directly or in some general sense of making the world a better place) if they could convince each other to join the antideath-penalty movement; but Nicole is unwilling to bear the cost of doing so all by herself. There are a lot of reasons why even a civic-minded person in this situation would resent bearing the costs of civic-mindedness alone; one that I have proposed is that people resist contributing by themselves because it makes them feel as if they are being exploited (Gould 1993*a,b*) by sympathizers who do nothing.

Nicole proposes becoming activists together, on the ground that if neither does anything than the status quo will persist, and the world will be a worse place. In a world populated by the people cooperative game theory assumes, it would be enough for Nicole to propose this and for Matthew to say yes. But this is insufficient in the noncooperative world, because Matthew would say yes, and the next morning would wake up and realize that he would be better off going back on the promise than giving up his morning to go to the demonstration at the Capitol building. Knowing this, Nicole would not go either, confirming Matthew's choice. From the standpoint of noncooperative game theory, the cooperative game theorist's answer, which is also the answer offered by many sociologists (e.g. Fireman and Gamson 1980) assumes the problem away: people solve the Prisoner's Dilemma simply by recognizing that they would all be better off by solving it. (Notice the connection between this reasoning and the functionalist assumption that institutions fulfil societal needs. How ironic that the proponents of this argument in the sociology of social movements have also been among the fiercest opponents of functionalism!)

In the noncooperative framework, Nicole must offer an inducement to Matthew to help her get them out of their mutually reinforcing routine of not joining the activist cause. (Remember, the shadow of the future works as a way to sustain cooperation when everyone starts out cooperating, but does not by itself push people out of the suboptimal state of mutual defection.) And that is where 'friendship' seems to come in, at least in the informal rendering of the game-theoretic account of activism. Let us suppose that, alongside whatever benefits or costs the two friends might expect to incur as a result of becoming activists or remaining nonactivists, they also expect a future stream of benefits from spending time together. That, presumably, is one of the things people mean by friendship, and more importantly the most relevant fact about friendship from the point of view of any rational-choice model. Friends have shared memories, mutual affection, social ties in common, and a range of other things that give people reasons to remain friends—and consequently reasons to be concerned when a friend makes future interaction conditional on some new action.

Assume, then that Nicole informs Matthew that (a) she wants both of them to join the antideath-penalty movement, and (b) that she will withhold future interaction if he does not comply. Let us not worry too much about whether Matthew will be so angered by this heavy-handed tactic that he would not care. After all, we have been assuming that both of them think activism would be a worthwhile change in their lives, so Matthew should not be too offended by the fact that Nicole is twisting his arm in this way. Formally, Nicole has promised to change the payoff structure for Matthew so that the cost of joining is offset by the threatened loss of friendship, valued at f, if he refuses to join. The scenario now involves decision-making over time, so that payoffs are accrued in each time period and decisions are made in terms of the present value of future benefits and costs.

Formally, then,

$$V_{\mathrm{m}} = \sum_{t=0}^{\infty} [((s-c)m+(s+jm)n)\cdot\lambda^t] - \sum_{t=0}^{\infty} f(1-m)n\cdot\lambda^t \quad (0\leqslant\lambda\leqslant 1),$$

where t indexes discrete time periods and λ reflects the rate at which Matthew discounts future benefits relative to the present. Assume, for simplicity, that joining a movement is a one-time event, so that if Matthew chooses $m=1$ in the present he is choosing that value for all future time periods. The expression reflects the fact that if Matthew declines to join today while Nicole joins (so that $m=0$ and $n=1$), he will receive the penalty f starting tomorrow. Now, if Matthew joins and Nicole joins, Matthew's benefit will be given by

$$V_{\mathrm{m}}(m, n=1) = \sum_{t=0}^{\infty} (2s-c+j)\cdot\lambda^t,$$

while if Matthew declines to join while Nicole goes through with her promise to join and attendant threat to withdraw friendship,

$$V_{\mathrm{m}}(m=0, n=1) = \sum_{t=0}^{\infty} s\cdot\lambda^t \sum_{t=1}^{\infty} f\cdot\lambda^t.$$

It is obvious that, for sufficiently large f and λ, Matthew will prefer to join even though, as before, $s > 2s - c + j$. In other words, if the friendship is valuable enough and if Matthew values the future sufficiently so that the costs of today's activism and future activism are outweighed by the future loss of friendship resulting from not joining, Matthew will join—if he expects Nicole to do so as well.

On the other hand, if neither joins the movement, Nicole will not withdraw her friendship and Matthew's payoff is again 0 (recall that retaining the friendship is the baseline, with $-f$ describing the *loss* of the value of the friendship). Finally, if Matthew joins and Nicole somehow does not,

$$V_{\mathrm{m}}(m=1, n=0) = \sum_{t=0}^{\infty} (s-c)\cdot\lambda^t.$$

Assuming, again that $s < c$, it is straightforward that Matthew prefers doing nothing than joining if Nicole is going to choose to do nothing. The question, then, is whether Nicole will join. Now, by hypothesis, Nicole values the friendship as well. Assuming that the value she places on the relationship is equal to the value Matthew places on it, and that she discounts the future at the same rate, Nicole's expected benefit is given by

$$V_{\mathrm{n}} = \sum_{t=0}^{\infty} [((s-c)n+(s+jn)m)]\cdot\lambda^t - \sum_{t=1}^{\infty} f(1-m)n\cdot\lambda^t,$$

which is identical to Matthew's payoff except that the loss of friendship is conditional on her joining and his not joining. Nicole then faces the following set of possible outcomes:

$$V_n(m, n = 1) = \sum_{t=0}^{\infty} (2s - c + j) \cdot \lambda^t,$$

$$V_n(m = 0, n = 1) = \sum_{t=0}^{\infty} (s - c)\lambda^t - \sum_{t=1}^{\infty} f\lambda^t,$$

$$V_n(m = 1, n = 0) = \sum_{t=0}^{\infty} s\lambda^t,$$

$$V_n(m, n = 0) = 0.$$

Sadly, Nicole sees that if Matthew declines to join ($m = 0$), she will be even unhappier joining than if she had not made the threat in the first place. Given $s < c$, her payoff from choosing $n = 1$ would already be less than zero given $m = 0$, and she would furthermore forfeit f in all future time periods if she were to cut off their friendship in fulfilment of the threat. Conditional on Matthew not joining, Nicole will therefore again prefer to stay out of the movement. On the other hand, if Matthew is going to join, Nicole would once more prefer not to do so, and so receive s rather than $2s - c + j$ in the current period and the discounted sum s in the future as well, since it will continue to exceed $2s - c + j$ in all future periods. Seeing this outcome, Matthew will expect Nicole not to join the movement, and will conclude that he has no reason to join either. In formal terms, even though the outcome {Contribute, Contribute} is a Nash equilibrium in this game, it is not a subgame-perfect equilibrium—that is, it is not robust against defections.

Observe that it would not help to assume that Matthew values the friendship more than Nicole does (i.e. to assume an asymmetric friendship), so long as Nicole puts some positive value on it. If cutting off interaction in retaliation of Matthew's refusal to join is at all hurtful to Nicole, she will prefer not to join if he does not, and also prefer not to join if he does. The threat is not credible if the threatened punishment would harm the punisher along with the target of punishment. And since it is in the nature of friendship that it hurts to hurt one's friends, we must conclude that this model does not offer a basis on which to expect that friendship ties will draw people into activism.

One could imagine that each could threaten to penalize the other for not joining, making their payoffs symmetrical. This scenario *could* sustain mutual contribution, but it amounts to a meta-game in which Matthew and Nicole coordinate their strategies so as to achieve the desired cooperative equilibrium. In other words, imagining that they can jointly settle on a solution to their social dilemma is the same as imagining that they can cooperate in resolving the underlying dilemma. Perhaps they can, but then the problem is assumed out of existence, not just for friends but for anybody—leaving no way to derive the prediction that friendship ties matter in recruitment to activism. One might resolve this problem by assuming that friendship *just is* a matter of resolving such social dilemmas, making friendship a relevant factor in situations of this kind; but it is not clear what further predictions would ensue from this assumption, leaving us in the realm of tautology.

The analysis to this point has suggested that a unilateral threat to withdraw friendship is not, at least in this formalization, a good way for Nicole to convince Matthew to join an activist cause with her, or for Matthew to convince Nicole. The implication is that it is not as easy as many have supposed for models in the repeated-game framework to account for the role of friendship ties in activism. We can posit that would-be activists adopt the inverse strategy: promising a reward in return for cooperation, rather than a penalty for noncooperation. But this strategy is, if anything, even easier for nonfriends to adopt than for close friends: if Matthew knows that Nicole will *become* his friend if they both join the movement, and if Nicole knows that Matthew will join if he knows this, then (assuming it is not costly to become friends, or to intensify an extant friendship) the model can sustain an equilibrium involving mutual joining even for people who are not yet friends. It is not hard to show that if a reward strategy of this sort is available to friends and will sustain mutual contribution, under a broad range of conditions it is also available to acquaintances; moreover, if we assume that striking up a new friendship is less difficult *or* more enjoyable than intensifying an existing one, then we should expect *more* recruitment through weak friendships than through strong ones—the contrary, as I noted earlier, of what is empirically observed.

SKETCH OF AN ALTERNATIVE

I propose that, rather than posit some property of friendship that in itself affects the likelihood of mutual recruitment to activism, we think of *activism* as having the property that it changes the value of *friendship*. This notion does not come entirely from a theoretical left field: many empirical studies have documented the transformative impact of recruitment to activist causes, both in the sense that activists' sense of themselves changes and in the sense that their relationships to others are transformed (Evans 1980; Ginsburg 1986; Melucci 1989; McAdam 1993*a*,*b*). Moreover, as I will show, it has testable implications beyond the one that makes its invocation useful, namely the differential impact of friendship relative to weaker social relationships. In particular, it draws attention to the relevance of networks of social ties, not just of dyadic ties.

A very general fact about activism—and one that implies that it will differ systematically from other kinds of recruitment—is that it represents a flight from egoism: the very thing that makes it rare, namely that it is tempting to let others make sacrifices while reaping the material or symbolic benefits of their actions, intensifies the experience of being among the few who make such sacrifices. It is not surprising, then, that people who make these sacrifices come to see themselves and each other in a different light. Just as friendships formed in combat are more intense than those forged in everyday life (and for similar reasons), friendships cultivated in an activist context are endowed with special significance. Durkheim was absolutely on the mark: actions taken by or on behalf of the collectivity are experienced as sacred.

Suppose, then, to give this lofty insight a mundane form, Nicole sees that her friendship with Matthew will mean more to her if both join the campaign to end the death penalty than if either declines to join. This is not a matter of a 'reward' she will bestow, as in the previous section, but rather a fact about what it will feel like to be friends in an activist rather than nonactivist situation. Let us describe the enhanced value of the friendship with the parameter $\delta: \delta > 1$, so that f represents the current value of the relationship and $f\delta$ the value of the transformed relationship. Suppose, furthermore, that the friendship will *decline* in value to Nicole and to Matthew if either becomes an activist without the other: in other words, the personal transformation involved in joining an activist cause both increases the value of friendships within the movement and diminishes the value of friendships across the movement boundary. Let us assume that the value declines to zero in this situation; this is a strong assumption, but it simplifies the model without changing the basic result. The strongest assumption, by far, is the following: if one of them joins the movement but the other does not, the former will in the future replace the lost relationship with a new friendship, worth $f\delta$ as well, but only after k time periods. So as not to stack the deck too heavily in favour of activism, let us assume that the nonjoiner will also establish a new friendship, but with value f, after l time periods. Varying k relative to l is one way to reflect the differential density of interaction inside and outside activist communities; it is reasonable to assume, for most types of activism, that $l > k$.

Nicole's benefit across the four possible outcomes is now described by the following function:

$$V_n = \sum_{t=0}^{\infty} [((s-c)n + (s+jn)m) \cdot \lambda^t] + \sum_{t=1}^{\infty} (f\delta)n)n\lambda^t$$
$$- \sum_{t=1}^{k}(f\delta)(1-m)n\lambda^t - \sum_{t=1}^{l} f(1-n)m\lambda^t.$$

while Matthew's is given by

$$V_m = \sum_{t=0}^{\infty} [((s-c)m + (s+jm)n) \cdot \lambda^t] + \sum_{t=1}^{\infty} (f\delta)m\lambda^t$$
$$- \sum_{t=1}^{k}(f\delta)(1-n)m\lambda^t - \sum_{t=1}^{l} f(1-m)n\lambda^t.$$

Focusing on Nicole's benefit function, the first term is the same as before; the last three terms reflect, respectively, the increase in the value of friendship when $n = 1$, the loss of this enhanced friendship for k periods if Nicole joins and Matthew does not, and the loss of (conventional) friendship for l periods if Nicole does not join but Matthew does. In other words, if Nicole becomes an activist she will have a more valuable friendship than she currently has with Matthew, but the benefit will be delayed if he does not join the movement with her. If he becomes an activist but she does not ($m = 1$ and $n = 0$), she will lose the value of their current friendship f until she finds a new friend. Finally, if $m = n = 0$, all three of these terms equal zero, reflecting continuation of the baseline relationship. So Nicole's payoff from the four possible outcomes is as follows:

$$V_n (m, n = 1) = \sum_{t=0}^{\infty} (2s - c + j) \cdot \lambda^t \sum_{t=1}^{\infty} f \delta \lambda^t,$$

$$V_n (m = 0, n = 1) = \sum_{t=0}^{\infty} (s - c) \lambda^t - \sum_{t=k+1}^{\infty} (f\delta) \lambda^t,$$

$$V_n (m = 1, n = 0) = \sum_{t=0}^{\infty} s \lambda^t - \sum_{t=1}^{l} f \lambda^t,$$

$$V_n (m, n = 0) = 0.$$

Matthew's returns from the various outcomes are, in this scenario, symmetrical to these. Now, if Nicole assumes that Matthew plans to join, then she too will choose to join if and only if

$$(s - c + j + f\delta) \cdot (1 + \lambda + \lambda^2 \cdots + \lambda^{\infty}) + f \cdot (\lambda + \lambda^2 + \cdots + \lambda^l) > 0,$$

or

$$\frac{s - c + j + f\delta}{1 - \lambda} + f \cdot (\lambda + \lambda^2 + \cdots + \lambda^l) > 0.$$

It is clear that this condition must hold for sufficiently large f, δ, and l. That is, if the friendship is strong enough, the enhancement due to joining great enough, and the waiting time to a new friendship sufficiently long, then Nicole will prefer joining over losing the friendship with Matthew.

If, on the other hand, Nicole expects Matthew not to join, she will nevertheless join the movement provided that

$$\frac{s - c}{1 - \lambda} + f\delta \cdot (\lambda^{k+1} + \lambda^{k+2} + \cdots + \lambda^{\infty}) > 0,$$

which is satisfied, again, for sufficiently large f and δ, and for sufficiently small k. In other words, Nicole will not be discouraged by the prospect of Matthew's refusal to join so long as the value of the friendship and its enhancement within the activist context are above some threshold, and provided that Nicole can expect to establish a new tie with someone inside the movement at some point sufficiently close to the present. It is these last two conditions that make the threat of cutting off a friendship credible: if Matthew knows that Nicole will establish new and valuable social relationships in the movement he is declining to join, then he knows she will become an activist even if she does not expect him to follow. Joining the movement is therefore, under the specified conditions, the dominant strategy for Nicole, and likewise for Matthew—but only if their friendship is valuable enough to them, and the prospects for enhancing its value promising enough.

We thus have the prediction that both friends will become activists, motivated not only by the benefit of joint contribution to the cause they value (which we established above is not sufficient to induce activism), but also by the benefit of enhancing a social relationship that is already valuable to both.

The assumption that activist friendships can be more valuable than nonactivist friendships, together with the assumption that converts to activism are cut off from prior friendships, has been shown to make recruitment through friendship ties an equilibrium in the repeated game framework. Consequently, it is clear that an adaptation of the standard two-person Prisoner's Dilemma can account for the empirical regularity of friendship-based recruitment. Furthermore, the adapted model yielded the prediction that stronger friendships are more likely to undergird such recruitment than weak friendships—another documented regularity. But these are not surprising theoretical results: I proposed the adaptation specifically for this purpose. To make this more than a 'curve-fitting' exercise, in which features are added to a model until it matches the available data, I need to show that the model generates further predictions that are either testable or independently known to hold true.

This turns out not to be difficult. Notice, first, that the threshold at which friendship strength (or enhanced friendship worth) makes activism a preferred strategy for, say, Nicole conditional on Matthew's joining is lowered by an increase in s, by a decrease in c, or a less negative value for j. This result can be interpreted to imply that movements facing lower chances of success, higher costs of participation, or sharply diminishing returns to contribution depend on stronger friendship ties in recruitment; movements for which success is likely (or, equivalently, benefits substantial), costs of joining are low, and later contributions are about as valuable as early ones can rely just as well on more tenuous friendships.

In addition, if the waiting time k is assumed to be related to the amount of face-to-face contact in the activist context, we have the further prediction that recruitment through friendship ties will occur disproportionally in intensely face-to-face movements (including, to look beyond the activist context for a moment, religious sects). This proposition follows from the fact that the potential joiner's threat to renounce a nonactivist friendship is more credible for small k, that is, when the waiting time before new activist friendships can be forged is brief. This is an untested prediction, so far as I am aware—but for that reason is evidence that the model I propose offers nontrivial theoretical content.

More importantly, this proposition and its inverse, involving the nonactivist waiting time l, can be seen as the kernels of specifically structural hypotheses. As with the parameter k, l can be interpreted as a reflection of the social network context of nonactivists. The easier it is for Matthew to maintain or forge friendships outside the antideath-penalty cause, reflected in a lower value for l, the less unsettling Nicole's commitment to join it appears to him, and consequently the less likely it is that her joining will draw him in as well. Although I have examined only the two-person situation, it is not hard to see that in the case of multiple actors, the network structure surrounding Nicole and Matthew is enormously consequential in a closely related way. If many of Matthew's associates are also tied to Nicole—a situation of high transitivity—then he should expect a longer wait in finding other social connections, as some of these associates (including, as a consequence, Matthew himself) will be following Nicole into activism. On the other hand, in situations of intransitivity, Matthew can expect many associates to be available for friendship outside the movement boundary, inasmuch as these associates will not be influenced by Nicole's decision, one way or the other. Again, this proposition has not been explored, to my knowledge; but the very possibility of its derivation casts light on the theoretical difference between mere connectedness on the individual level and network structure at the aggregate level.

CONCLUSIONS

Explaining the fact that social relationships are conduits for activism has proved difficult in the austere theoretical realm of rational cooperation among egoists. I have tried to show that existing models in the repeated-game framework, though often linked rhetorically to the 'networks and activism' literature, do not easily yield predictions consistent with the core findings in that literature. In the face of this difficulty, I have suggested that activism be seen as more than just rational cooperation disciplined by the prospect of future interaction. In particular, I propose that a centrally relevant fact about activism is that the selflessness it appears to express alters the value of social relationships among activists. To friends hovering on the brink of joining an activist cause, this promised shift in value represents a positive inducement; and the prospect that new contacts will readily provide replacements for friends left at the brink furnishes a negative one.

If we accept that friends like to think of themselves as similar in important ways, and that participation in a social movement represents for most activists a core element of their sense of self, then we will find it easier to accept these assumptions about how friendships are shaped by activism—and, by implication, to see why the situation I have been considering would favour recruitment through friendship ties. Your refusal to join a movement in which I have become active is not just a refusal to help the whales, or the sweatshop labourers in Malaysia, or death row inmates, or your townspeople. It is also a refusal to become what I have become: an activist with a deep commitment to a particular cause that leads me to make personal sacrifices. If this is indeed how activists see things, then it is clear why the implicit withdrawal of friendship is a credible threat: if you decline to join, then I will genuinely feel distanced from you. It will hurt me less to spurn your friendship than was the case before our commitments diverged—and it will hurt me less than it will hurt you, because I am likely to find new contacts whose commitments and actions make them viable candidates to substitute for the friendships I have renounced.

This reasoning leads to the following conclusion, which I at least find ironic. Rationalist models of cooperation offer an elegant way to talk about and account for cooperative behaviour in a range of situations, and writers in the rationalist tradition have suggested that this range encompasses the situation of movement participation and recruitment. But thinking through this application has made it apparent that the empirical regularity models of rational cooperation supposedly explained is not in fact readily derivable from the repeated-game framework. In this framework, friendships should be less likely to serve as conduits for recruitment than other, weaker social connections; yet the available empirical evidence shows that the contrary holds. It is only by exploring the deeper character of activism and its connection to the type of social tie we call friendship that it becomes possible to talk convincingly about the credibility of sanctions in the recruitment of friends. I find this ironic because the rationalist calculus works, in this instance, only through the operation of a social process that is much more familiar to structuralists than to rationalists. At the same time, it is the formalism of rational-choice thinking that made it possible to recognize the particular significance of friendship, as distinct from social connections more broadly, in this context.

In addressing this puzzle, I do not think I have solved the previous one, which is how to account for the temporal ordering of activism. Even if we can understand on what basis the current cadre of activists can cajole themselves, or perhaps the next group, into participating, we still have no account of the first movers. If people are converted or recruited by others to whom they are tied, who recruited the first recruiters? At any movement's early stages, the commitment of the first generation of activists should be no match for the pull of their social ties in the opposite direction. I suspect there is a role here for inspiration of a kind not easily incorporated either into rationalist arguments or structuralist ones. Martin Luther, Mohandas Gandhi, Lucy Stone, Ho Chi Minh, Nat Turner, Jeanne D'Arc—these are not people who got involved because someone they knew persuaded them to do so (unless we count inner voices, which in some of these cases surely did play a part). But the important lesson, in any event, is that by taking prediction and empirical testing seriously I have been able to go beyond the stalemate of two theories simultaneously claiming credit for having made sense of a significant observed regularity.

I have been more pointed in my criticisms of the rationalist approach than in my comments about structuralist arguments; and it is true that I invoked structuralist arguments to resolve problems I identified in the rational-choice account. But it would be better to see this as a backhanded compliment to the rationalists: their arguments can be criticized so pointedly because their theories can be shown to make strong predictions. If game theorists are wrong more often than structuralists, it is at least partly because they are willing to make predictions specific enough to be wrong. Writers of the structuralist variety (and I accuse myself in saying this) are much more likely to make general-sounding statements with fuzzy truth-conditions, or to make precise statements only *after* peeking at the empirical results. Neither tactic is scientifically defensible, even if it does make it more difficult to prove one wrong.

NOTES

1. There are of course other common usages of the word 'theory'. One amounts to 'conceptual framework,' which simply means a set of related terms and concepts for describing phenomena of interest, without any propositions that could in principle turn out to be false. Another could be glossed as 'hypothesis,' as in, 'I have a theory that my car will overheat if I run the engine at 5000 rpms.' Finally, there are 'theories' that I prefer to call 'proposed causal explanations,' such as the 'spatial mismatch theory' explaining rising wage inequality in the USA in terms of the inability of low-skilled workers to travel to or live near places where they might find employment. Logically, this sort of 'theory' is analogous to the kind of explanatory theory I have been discussing; it nonetheless differs significantly because it is dedicated to explaining a particular phenomenon in a circumscribed time and place. It is not a 'theory of wage inequality,' let alone 'a theory of social stratification'. It is a theory—or, as I would say, a proposed explanation—of why wage inequality has risen in the USA since 1980. What makes it theoretical is the fact that not everyone accepts it—a colloquialism we need not accept.

2. I do not mean to give the impression that there is something special about social networks that makes broader inferences of this kind possible. Much the same can be said about 'framing' and activism, about 'grievances' and activism, and the like—and occasionally is. What I am saying is that the tendency to see 'networks and movements' as a separate research area has permitted us to miss the opportunity to link findings in this area to broader theoretical issues.

3. For example, the classification of some category of object—say, companionship—as 'not for sale' surely constrains individual choice about how much time to spend with various people, but simultaneously makes possible the forging of a kind of attachment that we describe with terms like 'friendship,' 'affection,' or 'love'. In the absence of the decommodification of social interaction, it would be very difficult to be friends with someone in the sense we currently give that term. See Silver (1991); Hirschman (1993). If I were prone to anatomical analogies, I would refer to this complementarity of constraint and enabling as an 'epiglottal' social mechanism.

4. In any event, the issue of whether individualism is the only appropriate ontological stance for social science should not be decided through metatheoretical debate. It should be decided by asking (1) whether individualistic approaches account for the data they define as relevant more successfully than other approaches; and (2) whether there are no *other* sorts of data that *other* kinds of approaches can account for more successfully than individualistic approaches. If either question can be answered negatively, then methodological individualism (rationalist or not) is only one of several viable approaches. *A priori* arguments for or against individualism are more common, but they amount to little more than judgments of personal taste.

5. Empirical research in the form of experiments designed to test theoretically derived hypotheses is emerging in the form of behavioural economics. There will always,

however, be social scientists who prefer evidence gathered in naturally occurring social contexts, especially when the ideas under investigation have to do with the operation of institutions rather than the nature of the individual psyche.

6. In the situation in which $s > c$ but j is sufficiently negative that $s + j < c$, Matthew and Nicole find themselves in a version of 'Chicken,' which some have also interpreted as the Volunteer's Dilemma: each would prefer to contribute if the other will not, and each would prefer not to contribute if the other does. I do not treat this scenario here for the sake of space. Two things to notice about this situation are (1) the only equilibrium involving mutual cooperation is in 'mixed' strategies, which is to say an equilibrium in which both Matthew and Nicole contribute with probability $p < 1$; and (2) it is unlikely to apply well to the situation of friendship-based recruitment, inasmuch as it seems implausible that Matthew could recruit Nicole, or vice versa, by saying 'I might join, so you should too.'

7. Obviously, for sufficiently large c doing nothing will always be preferable for both, regardless of what the other person does—just as for sufficiently small c both will always contribute. These two scenarios are irrelevant for the present discussion because Matthew and Nicole's decisions are independent.

11

Cross-talk in Movements: Reconceiving the Culture-Network Link

Ann Mische

Relations in networks are about what people do in interaction. In social movement networks, people do more than simply exchange resources, transmit ideas, or develop identities, activities that many recent accounts of movement networks have described. Since most participants belong to a variety of social networks at once, they engage in myriad, complex negotiations among the multiple dimensions of their ongoing involvements, which are often embedded in overlapping network formations. These negotiations affect a wide range of relational processes, from recruitment and outreach to political coordination, dispute, and alliance-building. These relation-building activities in turn draw upon cultural practices of talk and communication within and across different kinds of movement settings.

There is a growing consensus—already verging on the taken-for-granted—that both networks and culture *matter* for social movement dynamics and outcomes. However, our understanding of the link between these is still relatively undeveloped. Most recent work exploring this link has stayed within a narrow, restricted understanding that focuses primarily on movement cohesion and solidarity-building, neglecting the wider range of relational processes that influence the growth, effectiveness, and influence of social movements. This limited approach is, I argue, the result of an inadequate understanding that tends to see both networks and culture in static and substantialist terms. What we need is a more dynamic conception in which social networks are seen not merely as locations for, or conduits of, cultural formations, but rather as *composed of* culturally constituted processes of communicative interaction. This means that we should shift our attention away from cultural forms such as 'identities' or 'frames,' toward the study of how these forms are shaped, deployed, and reformulated in conversation, as this unfolds

I would like to thank Nina Bandelj, Mario Diani, David Gibson, Mustafa Emirbayer, John Levi Martin, Doug McAdam, Paul McLean, Francesca Polletta, Ziggy Rivken-Fish, Mimi Sheller, Sidney Tarrow, Charles Tilly, Harrison White, Elisabeth Wood, King-to Yeung, Viviana Zelizer and the participants at the Loch Lomond conference on Social Movements and Networks and the Workshop on Contentious Politics at Columbia University for their helpful comments and suggestions on this paper.

across social movement forums over the course of movement development. Communication is a dynamic, fluid, interactive, and yet socially structured phenomenon that composes relationships both within and across the multiple network formations that give form and life to social movements.

While a series of recent studies has explored the communicative dimension of social movements, few of these researchers have yet incorporated formal network analysis into their work. And conversely, network analysts have been notoriously slow to unpack the cultural dimension of the 'ties' they study or the processes by which these are generated, sustained, and transformed over time (Emirbayer and Goodwin 1994; Mische and White 1998). I argue that by reconceiving networks as multiple, cross-cutting sets of relations sustained by conversational dynamics within social settings, we gain important analytical leverage for understanding relation formation in social movements. This understanding highlights the multi-layered, contingent, and yet still patterned nature of relations within and across movements. By focusing on *mechanisms of relation formation in conversational settings*, this approach helps us to bridge the divide between formal network techniques and interpretive approaches to communicative interaction.

Moreover, such an approach can also provide insight into questions of interest to social movement analysts that neither network techniques nor cultural analysis, taken alone, are able to give. While network analysis can map different relational structures associated with episodes of mobilization, and cultural analysis can document the claims and categories upon which mobilization draws, what is lacking in either case is a way to understand the mechanisms by which network structures and cultural forms interact and change over time in response to contentious interaction. These changes, in turn, go on to influence the success or failure of important mobilizing processes such as recruitment, outreach, coordination, and alliance formation. Using examples from my research on Brazilian youth organizations, I describe a core set of conversational mechanisms that are highly contingent on (and constitutive of) crosscutting network relations: identity qualifying, temporal cuing, generality shifting and multiple targeting. I discuss the ways in which these mechanisms are constrained by different kinds of relational contexts, as well as the ways in which they contribute to network building and mobilizing processes in social movements. Finally, I suggest some challenges this revised understanding of the link between culture and networks poses for future empirical research.

NETWORKS, CULTURE, AND SOCIAL MOVEMENTS

By this time, it is commonplace to argue that political participation depends heavily on the existence of social networks. Studies of social movements, civic culture, and democratic processes have heralded the central importance of networks, both as conduits of information and resources, and as qualitative supports for the social and cultural ties essential to community-building, solidarity, and/or collective action. Recent empirical studies have described the role of informal and organizational networks in the development of civic 'virtues' and democratic practices (Putnam 1993, 1995; Somers 1993, 1994), as well as in the recruitment and mobilization of social movements, the development of collective identities, and the transmission of ideological and tactical innovations (Snow *et al.* 1980; McAdam 1986, 1988*a,b*; Gould 1991, 1993*a,b*, 1995; Friedman and McAdam 1992; McAdam and Paulsen 1993; Meyer and Whittier 1994; Mueller 1994; Tilly 1995*a,b*; Diani 1995, 1997). Moreover, the language of networks (and 'networking') has long been part of the working vocabulary of social actors themselves, used both instrumentally as a means to political ends, as well as normatively, as a political value in itself, often in opposition to more traditional (i.e. centralized and hierarchical) organizational models.

Yet with this analytic and normative excitement about the role of networks in political processes, we also encounter a notable clouding of the question of what precisely networks represent, and what sorts of cultural processes take place across them. There are two important shortcomings to current approaches to the relationship between networks and culture in the social movement literature: (1) they provide an overly cohesive view of the cultural effects of network relations; and (2) they do not pay enough attention to processes of communication *across* (rather than just within) different kinds of movement networks.

Many recent studies have treated networks as privileged sites for the production of social cohesion and collective identity in social movements. Dense movement networks are commonly seen as fostering solidarity, trust, community, political inclusion, identity-formation, and other (by implication) valuable social outcomes. The roots of this approach can be found in Melucci's (1989) description of the construction of collective identities in the 'submerged networks' of everyday life, in which new, experimental worldviews and social relationships are developed by small groups in response to emergent tensions. While recent work on identity and networks has adopted a more structuralist formulation, the major focus of this work has remained on feelings of solidarity and group belongingness built around 'valued identities,' the construction of which becomes in itself one of the 'ends' of participation in movements (capable of overcoming, among other things, the free rider problem of rational action theory (Friedman and McAdam 1992)). In this view, the principal value of social networks is that they provide densely relational sites for face-to-face interaction in which collective identities are formed.

While dense interpersonal ties are certainly essential at certain moments in the construction of movement solidarity, this argument is problematic on several accounts. On a substantive level, it tends to focus on the positive social potential of network ties, stressing social cohesion and neglecting the role of networks in relations of power, influence, or political dispute.[1] It also tends to direct attention to the density of relations within movement networks, rather than the overlap or mutual influence across multiple types of ties. Recently, social movement theorists have begun to pay attention to the fact that people belong to multiple networks, and therefore have multiple possibilities for collective identity formation. Studies by Roger Gould (1991, 1993*a,b*, 1995) and Doug McAdam (1988*a,b*, 1996) show how preexisting solidarities—including friendship or neighbourhood ties and organizational affiliations—are critical to recruitment and mobilization (see also Fernandez and McAdam 1989). Most of this work, however, has remained anchored in the cohesion framework. While some exploratory attention has been given to possible conflicts between different kinds of ties (McAdam and Paulsen 1993; Passy 2001*a,b* and in this book), the main thrust of such work is to show how diverse network affiliations reinforce each other in the construction of new collective identities and movement communities, primarily through direct interpersonal contact.

However, there are important aspects of social movement mobilization and influence that cannot be accounted for simply in terms of social connectedness. For example, how do small, tight-knit groups of activists succeed (or fail) in multiplying their influence beyond their own ranks? How do new ideas enter into movement communities and challenge them to reevaluate projects and practices? What gives certain leaders or organizations greater opportunities for mediation or control of relations between groups? How does network structure influence internal disputes in movements as well as external alliance-formation (and how do these processes in turn reflect back upon networks)? At certain times in the life of a movement, 'bridges' (or the lack of them) may be more important than dense, close knit ties (Granovetter 1973; Burt 1992); moreover, important problems (as well as opportunities) are posed by the overlap between multiple types of ties and affiliations, and the diverse projects and practices actors bring with them into cross-network interactions.

A step toward addressing these questions can be seen in the recent work that views networks not just as sites for the production of movement solidarity, but also as conduits for the transmission of identities, repertoires, and frames across different kinds of movements. Meyer and Whittier (1994) describe 'spillover' effects between feminist and peace movements, arguing that these are influenced by four mechanisms of transmission: organizational coalitions, overlapping movement communities, shared personnel, and changes in political opportunity structures. This suggests the important role of both bridging relations (brokerage, alliance-making) and overlapping organizational memberships in facilitating communication and influence across movements. However, they do not detail the structural dynamics of this influence, depicting relations between the two movements mostly in incremental terms. Additional problems emerge when we move beyond simply looking at 'influence' or 'diffusion' across movements, and attempt to specify the dynamics of intersecting movement relations.

The multiple ties and memberships often noted among activists are not merely sites for the production and transmission of resources, identities, and frames.

They also pose important challenges (as well as opportunities) in day-to-day communication within and across movements. Activists belonging to multiple networks and organizational sectors must negotiate the different identities, projects, and styles of participation associated with their various involvements. Overlapping memberships may support processes of interest to social movement analysts, such as recruitment, coordination, and alliance formation. They may encourage innovative repertoires and new hybrid forms of political participation. But they may also lead to tensions or disputes, when actors' diverse identities and commitments interfere with each other and impede mobilization or coalition building. We need to examine the communicative mechanisms by which actors steer their way among their various affiliations (and associated identities and projects) as they construct alliances, coordinate activities, and battle over vision and strategy.

COMMUNICATIVE PRACTICES IN MOVEMENT SETTINGS

To address these questions, it is not enough to simply 'fill in' network approaches with the analysis of cultural forms such as identities, repertoires, or framing processes. The deeper problem with both the production site and transmission belt approaches described above is that they are on shaky ontological grounds when we look at the actual processes by which relations and meanings are generated and transformed. In both perspectives, cultural forms such as identities and frames flow through (or are generated by) previously structured networks, leaving primary causal force with the structural properties of the relational system. The networks take on a substantial, reified quality, removed from the actual dynamics of interaction. And culture in turn becomes reified into a 'package' whose content becomes an autonomous thing that resides in or travels across equally static and autonomous network formations.

Certainly it is possible to study formal network morphology as abstracted from the content of 'ties' or the processes by which they are generated (Cohen 1989). And it is equally possible to study cultural forms according to the formal properties of language and discourse, as recent work in the sociology of culture has demonstrated (Alexander and Smith 1993; Spillman 1995; Kane 1997). The formal logics of social relations and cultural structures do not map straightforwardly onto each other, but have a degree of relative autonomy that can be studied independently (Alexander 1988; Emirbayer 1997). Yet without conflating social networks and cultural forms, it is possible to direct our inquiry at the logic of connection between them. To do this, we need to shift the angle of vision away from networks or culture per se, toward an analysis of how these come together in interaction. In other words, we should not see networks merely as sites for or conduits of cultural forms, but rather we should look at how both of these are generated in social practices, that is, by the dynamics of communicative interaction.

Communication in social movements does not only involve language; it also involves talk. As Gary Fine points out, '[m]ovement actors are awash in talk'

(Fine 1995: 142); activists talk about the problems with the existing society as well as the nature and shape of the alternative society that they believe they are working for; they debate issues of tactic and strategy; they trade war stories and gossip about fellow activists; they plan events, negotiate logistics, and distribute responsibilities. Recently Charles Tilly (1998) has echoed this observation by describing social movements (and contentious politics more generally) as composed of on-going 'conversations' among movement actors, between movements and challengers, between activists and their publics. Tilly stresses that such conversations are based on 'incessant improvisations' and yet constrained by the previous history of relations of actors; they involve contingent manoeuvres and shifting deployment of these relations in ways that go on to reshape these relations themselves. 'Conversation in general shapes social life by altering individual and collective understandings, by creating and transforming social ties, by generating cultural materials that are then available for subsequent social interchange, and by establishing, obliterating, or shifting commitments on the part of participants' (Tilly 1998: 10).[2]

It is through these conversations that what we commonly describe as 'network ties'—for example, friendship, assistance, exchange of ideas, resources, or support—are co-constructed and take on meaning and weight within the practical operations as well as the legitimizing lore of social movements. While a few recent studies have highlighted this conversational, talk-centred dimension of social movements (Gamson *et al.* 1982; Klandermans 1988, 1992; Johnston 1991, 1995; Gamson 1992*a,b*, 1995), only rarely have these been situated within the concrete, relational settings of social movement forums (although see Fine 1995; Polletta 1998). The recent focus on collective action frames (Snow *et al.* 1986; Snow and Benford 1988, 1992; Ellingson 1995; Babb 1996) moves in this direction by examining how activists construct different kinds of interpretive links between preexisting and movement-based schemas of thought and action. As originally formulated by Snow *et al.* (1986), the framing perspective draws on Goffman's theory of how joint definitions of the situations are constructed by actors co-engaged in conversations. Unfortunately, much of the conversational thrust of Goffman's concept has been lost in subsequent analyses that tend to see collective action frames in primarily cognitive, content-laden terms.[3]

However, there are a few recent studies that focus explicitly on the communicative dimension of culture in movements. For example, Marc Steinberg (1998, 1999*a,b*) advocates a dialogic approach to discourse in social movements, arguing that the recent literature on collective action frames tends to depict these as stable meaning systems that can be unproblematically transmitted between speakers and targets. Drawing upon Bahktin's theory of 'speech genres,' Steinberg draws attention to the multivocality of discourse and its embeddedness in wider fields of on-going communication. Likewise, Paul McLean (1998) stresses the fluid and multidimensional character of political communication by returning to Goffman's early conception of 'keying' practices, in which actors signal which of many possible frames (or definitions of the situation) is being invoked in a given instance. McLean argues that such practices have a network dimension, in that what are often being 'keyed' are specific relations between actors—that is, friendship ties, patron–client relations, relations of deference, familiarity, or respect. Other researchers have argued that we need to look beyond the content of discourse in order to examine the specific social and institutional *settings* in which conversation is produced. Both Nina Eliasoph (1996, 1998) and Paul Lichterman (1995*a,b*, 1996, 1999) have shown how the expression of identity, commitment, and public concern varies systematically according to the particular group settings in which conversation takes place. This is due to shifts in what Goffman calls conversational *footings*, defined as shared assumptions about 'what talk itself is for in a situation' (Eliasoph 1996: 268).

What these authors have in common is an insistence that the effects of culture on collective action (and vice versa) are not simply a matter of language or discourse as such, but rather of the interactive context in which discourse is enacted. We can sum up the theoretical implications of their arguments in the following four points: (1) communication involves a jointly constructed definition of the situation, whether this is understood as a discursive genre, a conversational footing, or a style of relation-building; (2) because there are multiple possible ways any situation can be construed, meanings are inherently multivocal, unstable, and ambiguous in interpretation (although this ambiguity can increase or decrease in different contexts of interaction); (3) one of the tasks of discourse is the construction of social relations, which are themselves shifting and multilayered; and (4) potential meanings and relations can be activated or deactivated, made visible or invisible, by individuals and groups within the constraints of social settings.

While such an approach is inherently relational, most of these authors do not employ formal network analysis in their work. However, they do provide important clues as to how this might be done. Relations are constructed through discourse, which cues not only the type but also the terms and scope of those relationships— what kind of rights and obligations they entail, how they relate to other sorts of relations the actors may be embedded in. While network analysts have traditionally left the cultural content of 'types of ties' as a sort of black box encasing the ones and zeros of their data matrices, recently some of them have begun to draw attention to the discursive nature of network ties.[4] Recently, Harrison White and his colleagues (White 1992, 1995; Mische and White 1998) have argued that bundles of narratives and discursive signals define *network domains*, that is, specialized fields of interactions characterized by clusters of relations and associated sets of stories. Such network domains have a temporal as well as a relational dimension, structured not only by identities, but also by *narratives* (Somers 1992, 1993; Polletta 1998) about where actors are coming from and where they are going to. Actors are continually switching back and forth across network domains (and associated social settings) in their day-to-day lives.

For social movement activists, this means not only moving among the multiple organizations and institutional spheres to which they belong, but also among the (often overlapping) roles and relations that these imply (e.g. organizer, strategizer, cheerleader, advisor, recruiter, negotiator, not to mention student, family member, drinking buddy, and romantic partner). In social settings, such relations may be foregrounded or backgrounded, put into 'play' or strategically suppressed, according to the logic and demands of the local context. This relational play happens discursively, through signals or cues by which some relations (and accompanying narratives) are 'keyed' and/or 'articulated' (linked together) in different ways. By tracking such signalling mechanisms as they occur *in conversation*, we can observe processes of relation formation, maintenance, and transformation—that is, of the generation and reconfiguration of networks—as well their effects on the life of the movement.

FROM MAPPING TO MECHANISMS: LINKING NETWORKS AND CULTURE

If these approaches give us a new conceptualization of the link between networks and culture, we are still faced with the challenge of locating these phenomena— and charting their conditions and effects—in empirical social process. Here we find a strong tension between mathematical mapping techniques and ethnographic or textual analysis, since each involves a necessary reduction of the other. Whereas formal mapping techniques and related network-analytic routines allow researchers to see overall structural patterns that surpass the viewpoint of any given actor (or 'node' in a network), they lose the multi-textured, contingent, and often ambiguous 'give and take' of actual interaction. On the other hand, more qualitative methodologies can help to preserve the richness of local context, but ignore the global topography. I want to argue not only for the complementarity of these approaches, but also for the development of new techniques that make possible their integration. The goal of this integration is not to uncover static structures governed by general laws that apply to all cases, but rather to find a set of general communicative mechanisms that organize action across a variety of different movement contexts.

To move from the primarily descriptive techniques of formal network analysis to a focus on mechanisms in social interaction requires that we view the topographical maps produced by formal techniques as the result of many local, contingent, and intersecting relational processes. Here I build upon recent discussions of mechanisms in sociological theory (Elster 1989; Stinchcombe 1991; Hedström and Swedberg 1998) as well as recent attempts by social movement theorists to expand the understanding of mechanisms beyond the framework of methodological individualism (Tilly 2001; McAdam *et al.* 2001). The latter define mechanisms as 'a delimited class of events that alter relations among specified sets of elements in identical or closely similar ways over a variety of situations' (McAdam *et al.* 2001: 17). The point of this focus on mechanisms is to allow for mid-range generalizations about regularized patterns of interaction that allow for contingency and contextual specificity at both local and larger-scale levels.[5]

Mapping Multiple Relations

Formal network analysis can point toward mechanisms by showing us how different kinds of relationships (with their accompanying discursive processes) concatenate in systematic ways, both reflecting and influencing the dynamics of communicative interaction. There are a variety of network techniques that allow us to analyse the intercalation of multiple types of ties, most notably blockmodelling techniques (White *et al.* 1976) that locate 'equivalence classes' among actors tied to third parties, as well as role algebras (Boorman and White 1976; Pattison 1993), which allow us to study links (or 'entailments') between multiple sets of relations. When applied straightforwardly to ties between actors or groups (e.g. kinship, friendship, advice, and resource exchange), such methods can be used in conjunction with cultural analysis to look for correspondences or associations between network structures and discursive forms. For example, Peter Bearman (1993) uses blockmodelling techniques to show how the changing structure of kinship and patron/client relations created the 'structural prerequisites' for the emergence of abstract religious rhetorics, which went on to influence elite participation in the English Civil War.

We can also take an approach that more directly highlights the conversational dimension of social ties. For example, if one hypothesizes that political alliance-building across groups is facilitated by informal friendship relations as well as political discussion among leaders (see e.g. Diani 1995), one could look at the intercalation of say, four types of ties among movement leaders from different organizations, all of which imply a certain kind of communication: 'discuss politics with,' 'plan events with,' 'negotiate alliances with,' and 'drink beer with'. These might sort out into different leadership blocks for which these types of communication intercalate in similar ways, thus mapping the communicative role structure among movement leaders across a multi-organizational field. One could then see whether these blocks can be characterized by categorical attributes—such as group membership, leadership rank, class position, or other identity markers—as well as by different ways of talking politics.

Such an approach could allow us to locate structural patterns that point toward the conversational dynamics associated with different clusters of ties, hence leading us from mapping to mechanisms. For example, we might test the hypothesis that top leaders share more cross-group political discussion and/or beer-drinking ties than lower level activists, suggesting a mechanism by which informal conversation among leaders smoothes over the negotiation of intergroup relations.

Or we might examine the hypothesis that there is more flexible, multivalent talk (as opposed to rigidly ideological discourse) when friendship ties mediate political negotiation, suggesting a mechanism by which friendship has a 'loosening' or flexibilizing' effect on political discourse.

Exploring Complex Conjunctures

While these extensions of network techniques are based on a conversational understanding of political culture, they remain blind to one element that scholars like Eliasoph and Lichterman have noted is extremely important to political communication: its location in social settings. Settings can be defined analytically in a number of ways: as the organizational context in which talk happens, as the group of individuals who are present, as the kind of activity they are engaged in, as the physical location of that activity, or as a particular episode or event. Usually, these different components of social settings are associated in regularized ways. So an alternative analytical strategy is to explore how different *conjunctures* of setting-defining elements—individuals, groups, activities, and events—are associated with particular kinds of talk and ties.

There are a variety of ways to do this mathematically, many of which build on the insight of Ronald Breiger (1974) into the duality of the affiliation relationship. In its most well known formulation, this approach exploits the Simmelian observation that relations between individuals are determined by the groups they belonged to, and conversely, that relations between groups are determined by the individual members they have in common. A number of notable studies have applied these procedures to the analysis of recruitment, mobilization, and alliance-making across multi-organizational fields, including Rosenthal *et al.* (1985), Fernandez and McAdam (1988), Bearman and Everett (1993), Diani (1995 and in this volume) and Osa (2001 and in this volume).

We can incorporate a communicative dimension by extending this analysis to include not only persons and groups, but also discourse, practices, and social movement events. One way to do this is through an algebraic technique known as Galois (or 'concept') lattices (Freeman and White 1993; Wille 1996). Galois lattices are ideal for exploring what I am calling conjunctural associations because they display the dual relationships between elements in a two-mode data matrix in a simultaneous graphical form. Lattices map relations of inclusion and intersection between associated subsets of two (or more) sets of elements. Each node on a lattice can be treated as a particular conjuncture of elements, ordered in relation to other possible conjunctures in a given associative field. This is a very flexible exploratory technique that can be extended to many kinds of cultural and historical analysis, as recent works by Mohr and Duquenne (1997) and Schweizer (1993, 1996) has shown.

In my research on the 1992 Brazilian impeachment movement (Mische 1998), I use lattices to examine conjunctures of activists, organizations, and/or their projects as these come together *at public events*. I explore how events serve as settings for cross-group communication and mediation, which in turn contribute to the convergence of cross-sectoral coalitions. In a recent extension of this work (Mische and Pattison 2000), Philippa Pattison and I use a tripartite version of lattice analysis to map changes in the presence of organizations and/or their projects at events during different stages in Brazil's impeachment movement. In the early stage, organizations tended to meet in sectorally segmented settings in which opposition was linked to the particularistic projects of labour, student, or professional organizations. As the movement converged, groups came together in increasingly broader combinations, leading to what we call the *interanimation* (to borrow a term from Bakhtin) of the discourse in play at movement events. In the final stage, the discourse simplified considerably, reflecting a *suppression* of public discourse as a broad coalition of radical, moderate, and elite actors restricted their discussion to a narrow cluster of projects related to citizenship and public ethics. In this way, the lattice mapping techniques allowed us to locate two general socio-cultural mechanisms—interanimation and suppression—by which coalitions are negotiated among other otherwise contentious sets of movement actors.

CROSS-TALK IN ACTION: EXPLORING THE BRAZILIAN CASE

One possible objection to the mathematical techniques described above is that they only show the changing topography of discursive relations across groups, not the actual dynamics of communication within social settings. Another way of examining the network implications of talk in movements is through a more micro-level analysis of conversational mechanisms as they play out within and across particular movement contexts. Again, such analysis can combine interpretive techniques, using ethnographic and textual data, with more quantifiable analyses of patterns of conversational exchange. Here I will provide a few brief exploratory examples of communicative mechanisms from my ethnographic research on Brazilian youth activism in the 1990s, in order to suggest directions for more systematic research.

In my research, I encountered a context in which diverse organizational and interpersonal networks were superimposed in a highly complex and interwoven set of social movement communities.[6] Most of the Brazilian activists I studied belonged to more than one organization at once: nearly all of the student activists also belonged to political parties and/or factions; many had previous or continuing experience in church, community, or professional organizations; many of them had also accumulated multiple positions in internal coordinating bodies nested within these distinct movement sectors. Young people often knew each other from several of these forums; they may have had different relative positions in each. Moreover, the organizations themselves had complex relationships ranging from exchange of resources or advice to ideological formation or coparticipation in alliances and events. The different relationships implied by these multiple affiliations influenced each other in complex ways, requiring a holistic approach to the study of relation-building that is attentive to how multiple dimensions of relations are activated and deactivated through a variety of conversational mechanisms.

The four conversational mechanisms that I describe below all represent means by which actors jockey over the multiple dimensions of their memberships, identities, and projects in order to build relations with other actors. In that sense, these culturally constituted network-building mechanisms help to explain how ties are constructed and sustained—whether those ties are with new recruits, with fellow group members, or with external allies or opponents. While these can be considered 'strategies' or 'practices' (or what Goffman (1959) calls 'techniques') from the point of view of the individual actors,[7] they can be seen as 'mechanisms' from the perspective of explanatory theory-building: they consist of regularized local processes that recur across many different kind of contexts and which contribute to higher-level relational process: for example, in this case, social movement recruitment, coordination, and coalition-building.

The first two represent what I call 'compartmentalizing' mechanisms, since they represent attempts by actors to discursively segment elements of their multiple identities and projects as a way of building ties with other actors. The second two represent what I call 'conflation' mechanisms, since they depend upon the discursive fusion of diverse dimensions of projects and identities in order to heighten the multivocality of discourse, again as a way of constructing relations with other actors.[8] All four mechanisms indicate that solidarity-building is not the only cultural dimension of movement networks; rather, actors use conversational mechanisms both to build ties with other actors and to jockey for their own (and their groups') positions in an often conflictual and competitive multi-organizational field.

Identity Qualifying

One way that network affiliations are signalled discursively is through 'identity qualifiers'—cues as to which aspect of an actor's multiple identities and involvements are active 'right now,' in a particular set of utterances. McAdam and Paulsen (1993) refer to such cues as 'aligning statements' by which actors associate themselves with particular reference groups. When people belong to multiple groups, they frequently need to switch back and forth between different identities that might be 'in play' within a movement context. My interviewees would often herald what they were saying with the phrase 'as' (in Portuguese, *como*), as in, 'as a representative of the students' or 'as a member of the Worker's Party' or 'as a youth pastoral coordinator'. A given conversation might contain several such switches, as the activists felt it necessary to discursively compartmentalize their identities in order to indicate which of their various organizational hats they were wearing at that moment. We can see this mechanism at work in the following quote from the president of the National Student Union (UNE), who was also a militant in the Communist Party:

I want to make clear that this is a personal position. *As president of UNE*, I represent the interests of Brazilian students, and I have broader positions. UNE does not defend socialism, nor the armed revolution. *I am a socialist by conviction*, but at the congress of UNE, I was against the inclusion of the socialist banner in the programme. (Lindberg Farias, *Folha de São Paulo* 8/31/92, italics added)

This statement illustrates the discursive juggling act many youth leaders performed as they articulated the projects of the multiple organizations to which they belonged. Although dominated by leftist leaders, the National Student Union was trying to build ties to more mainstream students by supporting educational reform and defence of students' interests, not a communist revolution. As a Communist Party member, the UNE president was clearly engaged in projects that surpassed the 'intermediary' goals of the student union (including a fierce dispute for control of that organization with other partisan youth). And yet *while preserving his identity as a communist* (and therefore his ties to his copartisans), he was able to compartmentalize that identity and say, in effect, 'for these purposes (representing *students*), being a communist does not matter.' Note, however, the qualifier that he considered his convictions 'as a socialist' to be more 'personal' than his positions as president of UNE, and therefore on a different discursive footing. This raises the question of whether his audience will decide *not* to set aside consideration of his communist convictions, causing his attempt at relation-building to break down. When successful, these types of identity qualifiers allow actors to strategically segment different dimensions of their multiple involvements while still maintaining them in play, in this case contributing both to external recruitment and outreach as well as to internal cohesion and interpartisan disputes.

Temporal Cuing

A second way in which actors construct relations discursively is through what I call 'temporal cuing,' that is, keying into a particular temporal dimension of the 'projective narratives'[9] of a potential interactive partner. Relation formation involves cuing into the temporal scaffolding of other individuals and groups, since relations are ostensibly formed to 'do something' together in the foreseeable future, whether that means engaging in ideological debate, forming an alliance, or planning a joint campaign. Here the focus shifts from identity markers (which define boundaries of inclusion and exclusion) to narrative construction, that is, the temporal formatting of the stories actors tell each other about their histories, purposes, and capacity to intervene. The temporal dimensions of political relations are signalled discursively through a variety of discursive markers, including temporal 'deictics' (contextualizing references such as verb tense and temporal adverbs (Levinson 1983; Hanks 1992)); narrative genre (e.g. utopian elegy vs. practical strategizing); and more mechanical processes involving calendars and timetables.

As groups build ties with other actors, they use such markers to signal which aspects of evolving projects are relevant to the interaction at hand. This may involve the temporal compartmentalization of different dimensions of a group's projective narratives; for example, actors may connect with potential alliance-partners on the short-term dimension of their projects while strongly disagreeing with them on the long-term, or vice versa. In Brazil, this sort of temporal cuing was evident in the facility the Communist Party youth had in negotiating alliances with their ideological enemies, the Social Democrats, by keying into flexible, short-term narratives of democratic reform, while provisionally compartmentaliz-ing these from their longer-term revolutionary projects. This was in marked con-trast to the Workers' Party youth, whose long-term vision of socialism was in crisis while their shorter-term narratives were paralysed by internal dispute, decreasing narrative flexibility and making them rigidly purist as interaction part-ners. By failing to engage in effective temporal cuing practices, the Worker's Party consistently lost out to their Communist rivals in disputes over student movement alliances and leadership, despite their broader ideological appeal. Here we see that it is not merely ideological content that determines group affinities, but more importantly, it is *the manner in which each group constructs political time* that has a critical influence on its capacity to form communicative ties with other groups.

Generality Shifting

A third communicative mechanism that is important for relation formation is what I call 'generality shifting,' in which speakers slide up or down levels of abstraction in regards to the generality or inclusiveness of identity categories. While the previ-ous two mechanisms worked by compartmentalizing different dimensions of actors' identities and projects, this one works by conflating broad and narrow inter-pretations of discursive categories and building on their ambiguity. Actors learn to play off of the multivalence of such categories as they attempt to build alliances and generate public support. An example is the narrative play surrounding the cat-egories of 'student' and 'civic' during the 1992 Brazilian impeachment movement. When activists claimed that the *students* were at the forefront of the *civic* coalition to impeach the president, there was intentional ambiguity in the reference. The cat-egory of 'student' could refer to the hundreds of thousands of (mostly nonactivist) high school and college students who hit the streets, or it could refer to the more restricted sub-field of the organized student movement and its associated projects and disputes. The coupling of the broader and narrower definitions of the 'student' identity allowed student leaders riding the crest of the movement to claim credit for the youth mobilization on behalf of student organizations. Likewise, 'civic' could refer to the loose array of sectorally differentiated organizations (community, professional, labour, and business, as well as 'student'), each with their own competing projects and demands, or it could be given a more restricted definition, referring to a provisional coalition on issues related to the 'common good'.

These distinctions are not simply a matter of definition for the analyst; rather, the manner by which the actors themselves slide between narrower and broader self-designations is a critical component of coalition formation. This dual dynamic—of the general and the particular, the civic and the sectoral—works to build relations in a public arena, while also maintaining particularistic identities in a sort of eager latency. By encasing discourse within a ritualized mantle of generality that still lets competing projects peek out from time to time, actors establish a collective footing that allows for joint action while preserving the possibility of a narrower, self-interested spin (e.g. when reported to one's home base, or in subsequent discussions with the media). Such publics create new possibilities for coordination and coalition-building among contending actors, while also threatening to break down into the 'merely' particular projects and identities of which they are composed. By using categorical ambiguity to create a provisional unity in heterogeneous movement settings, generality shifting can contribute to processes of mobilization and alliance formation in a multi-organizational field.

Multiple Targeting

We can locate a fourth mechanism for discursive tie construction: 'multiple targeting,' in which speakers aim their talk at many different audiences at once. Like generality shifting, this mechanism builds directly on the multivocality of discourse by conflating different possible discursive meanings; it exploits the fact that it is not always possible to segment one's audiences and thus the same words will often be interpreted from multiple points of view. This can be considered the inverse of the 'robust action' described by Padgett and Ansell (1993), in which central actors maintain strategic ambiguity by segmenting their multiple networks. Social movement activists are often faced with situations in which segmentation breaks down—often purposefully so, when they attempt to construct broad-based alliances or when they invite people with different degrees of involvement to movement-building events. Leaders are usually aware that their words will be heard differently by new recruits than by battle-worn faction leaders, representatives of the media or emissaries of allied groups (not to mention the occasional academic researcher). The ability to infuse one's discourse with multilayered cues is an important leadership skill on which the success of coordination and alliance-building may often rest.

I often witnessed such dynamics in my ethnographic work, as sub-groups spun off in different combinations and then came back to state positions to the wider plenary. An example is a national meeting of the youth of the Workers' Party, which was called to coordinate strategies for an upcoming national student conference. Most of the youth belonged to disputing internal factions as well as state or regional youth commissions; many also had additional affiliations in specialized student associations; gay rights, feminist, or black groups; or urban or agrarian popular movements. That meant that the youth were charged with *hearing* the discourse expressed at the meeting on multiple levels, just as speakers were charged with targeting it to multiple audiences. High-level leaders summoned each other into segmented huddles, after which they would return to the floor to signal the results of the negotiation through new discursive positionings. These needed to be carefully gauged with the appropriate degree of ambiguity to satisfy both their own faction members and those in competing factions—as well as high-level party leaders and outside observers—all without scaring off the unaligned. This of course was a tricky task that often threatened to break down, raising interesting questions about the conditions under which strategic ambiguity fosters consensus-building and when it dissolves into dispute or polarization, thus influencing emerging network structures within the movement.

The methods by which we can 'capture' these kinds of mechanisms empirically vary considerably. Ethnographic research seems to be the key for observing many of the mechanisms described above, which could be noted in observed speech during meetings or informal exchanges, as well as in interviews with activists. However, it would also be possible to systematize such observations, either through observational coding (using audio tapes, video tapes, or real time coding sheets) or through the use of content analysis techniques, which could locate discursive signals such as aligning statements, temporal markers, or sliding categories. Many of these mechanisms also appear in written texts, such as organizational documents, speeches or letters, which would make the analysis of discursive relation formation possible for historical researchers as well (for an innovative example, see McLean 1998). These data could then be crossed with network data on different kinds of ties or affiliations, or on the relational composition of social settings, in order to locate the network conditions under which these mechanisms come into play. Where this approach differs from standard content analysis techniques is that we are not just interested in discursive content, but rather the 'play' of discourse in interaction, its role in the construction of relations, its sense of footing, its appropriateness to a setting, its intended audiences and temporal structure.

EMBEDDING MECHANISMS: BUILDING RELATIONS IN MOVEMENTS

One challenge of this approach will be to combine this sort of setting-based observation of conversational dynamics with the formal mapping techniques described earlier, that is, to find a way of relating a bird's eye view of structure with a close analysis of action on the ground. Both network topography and setting-based dynamics matter for social movement processes; they can be understood as different analytical moments of the same phenomena. While topographical mapping techniques locate particular settings (and their different analytical components) within larger structural contexts, the study of conversational dynamics shows us how these play out amidst the contingent interplay of real social interaction.

The kinds of mechanisms sketched above provide a bridge between these, offering a middle level of generalizability that taps into both formal and interpretive methodologies.

There are two directions of influence between conversational mechanisms and formal relational structures that interest us here. One is the way that embeddedness in relational contexts facilitates or constrains the use of different kinds of mechanisms, while the other is the way in which these mechanisms 'loop back' to affect the formal topography of relational contexts. Here I can offer a few exploratory hypotheses as to how these two kinds of influence might affect relation-building processes of interest to social movement analysts, such as recruitment, outreach, and alliance-building.

Mechanisms in Context

All four conversational mechanisms described above would appear on the surface to imply a high degree of strategic mobility. Actors deploy these mechanisms in the attempt to build relations with other actors, whether through the compartmentalization of different aspects of their identities and narratives, or by conflating these identities and narratives through the strategic use of ambiguity. But actors are not free to conflate and compartmentalize in any way they want; rather their capacity to do so is limited by their location in different kinds of relational contexts, including institutions, networks, and settings of interaction.

One important constraining factor may come from the *institutional logics* (Friedland and Alford 1991; Powell 1991) of the overlapping organizations with which an actor is affiliated. Some organizational identities (and/or their accompanying projects) may be more easily segmented and/or conflated than others, due at least in part to their characteristic cultural forms or 'logics' of interaction. For example, in the Brazilian case, political party membership could be readily combined with some forms of participation—such as student, labour, or popular movements—but less easily combined with others, such as religious, professional, business or other 'civic' organizations. This was due in part to the highly instrumental, competitive logic of the political parties, as well as their strongly combative narratives, which clashed in various ways with the practices and narratives of the more moderate, nonpartisan groups. This leads to a number of interesting hypotheses. Political party members who also belong to groups with strong nonpartisan logics might be compelled to make frequent use of compartmentalizing mechanisms, in order to reassure their audiences that their partisan hat (and its accompanying competitive logic) has been provisionally suppressed. On the other hand, when speaking to more hardcore student or labour audiences (in which almost everyone belongs to political parties), activists might feel less compelled to segment their partisan identities and be more likely to use conflation mechanisms such as generality shifting and multiple targeting, in which student and partisan narratives could be ambiguously intertwined. These hypotheses suggest ways in which the institutional logics of intersecting organizations may affect the kinds of mechanisms used by actors to manoeuvre among them.

A second source of constraint may come from the structure of *overlapping organizational networks*. Since not all movement contexts contain as high a degree of organizational overlap as in the Brazilian case, it is important to examine how the degree and range of overlap influences the manner and frequency with which these mechanisms are used. Even in the Brazilian case, there was considerable variation in the distribution of affiliations. Some activists (such as many top leaders) belonged to a wide array of organizations, often reaching across different institutional sectors (e.g. partisan, student, religious, and/or professional). Others only belonged to one or two, limiting manoeuvrability across networks and their ability to employ the mechanisms described above. One possibility is that activists at the intersection of many overlapping organizational networks (or alternatively, leaders of organizations that are highly central in the multi-organizational field) may develop greater adeptness at using compartmentalizing and/or conflation mechanisms in order to manage their multiple relationships, in contrast to less embedded or more marginalized actors, whose discourse may be comparatively univocal as a result. An alternative possibility is that it may in fact be marginalized groups attempting to construct bridges to more central, mainstream actors who are more likely to employ these mechanisms, in their attempt to submerge or obfuscate the more objectionable dimensions of their identities and projects (see McLean 1998).

A third possible constraint on the use of these mechanisms comes from the logic and composition of the *interaction setting* itself. Certain settings require different genres of conversation; it makes a difference if one is talking at a protest rally, a church meeting, a backroom planning session, a private rendezvous or a public bar. In addition, we need to pay attention to the identities and affiliations of interaction partners: do they belong to one's own group, to opposing groups, or to target groups such as the media or potential allies? How homogeneous or heterogeneous is the audience? Here we have to keep in mind that it is not just networks or memberships that matter, but also how these relations are represented, activated, or suppressed in social settings. One hypothesis might be that leaders facing more complex, relationally heterogeneous ('cross-group') audiences would use more conflation mechanisms—either playing off of the nested levels of generality of seemingly inclusive categories, or infusing discourse with ambiguous statements that could be interpreted differently by various audiences. In contrast, those speaking to simpler 'in-group' audiences might use less ambiguous, more univalent discourse, while those speaking to 'out-group' audiences might be more likely to employ compartmentalizing mechanisms in order to mediate differences.

From Mechanisms to Networks

If the above examples represent possible ways in which relational contexts influence the use and effectiveness of conversational mechanisms, we still need to examine the other side of the coin: how such mechanisms affect network structures, and how these formal patterns in turn go on to influence the course and impact of social movements. Here I provide a few suggestions as to how we might build upon the mechanisms described here in order to theorize about some of the broader relational processes of interest to social movement analysts.

Recruitment and outreach: One of the things activists do through the compartmentalizing and conflation mechanisms described above is to reach out to people outside of their own movement organizations, whether for purposes of recruitment or fund-raising, or simply to improve relations with the public and/or the media. They do that knowing that many potential recruits, donors, or sympathizers are not likely to agree with *all* the dimensions of their identities and projects. To do this, they have to signal which of these are most worthy of their audiences' attention and support, even if this means sidelining important aspects of their own self-understanding. Or alternatively, it means becoming skilled at exploiting the ambiguity and multivalence of broad categories, so that outsiders see their own concerns reflected in the discourse of a movement, even if the activists themselves have a different interpretation. The ability of activists to use the mechanisms described here could therefore have an important effect on a movement's ability to gain supporters, thus influencing its success or failure.

These processes might affect the network structures of social movements in different ways. One hypothesis is that movement actors who fail to successfully compartmentalize potentially objectionable aspects of their identities and projects (e.g. the fact that most student movement members belong to partisan factions, or that they are working to overthrow the system) will reinforce their marginality, leading to the creation of dense activist ghettos, isolated from mainstream networks. On the other hand, those who too completely adapt to the discourse of outside targets will lose their internal adherents and become absorbed by mainstream networks, thus losing any independent leverage and becoming drained of challenging power. In contrast, actors skilled in using the compartmentalizing mechanisms of identity qualifying and/or temporal cuing might be more likely to appeal to outsiders without losing their distinctive identity and vision. In network terms, compartmentalization may allow actors to become effective *network bridgers* between radical enclaves and mainstream networks, thus having greater success not only in movement growth but also in internal longevity and (perhaps!) the ability to challenge existing power structures.

Alliances and coalitions: While political opportunity structures and imminent threats or dangers may provide conditions for coalitions (Staggenborg 1986), those alliances must be talked out and built up discursively. The discussion above suggests that there may be certain types of talk across organizations (and certain types of settings in which that talk plays out) that make some attempts at alliance building more likely to succeed than others. Leaders must know when to jockey for inclusion of their particularistic projects in a coalition, and when to suppress these and focus on more consensual issues. Likewise, they must know how to make strategic use of broad, multivalent umbrella-type categories (like citizenship, nationalism, democracy, socialism, brotherhood, or community), even though they know that their coalition-partners may have very different interpretations of what these terms mean, as well as of the intermediary steps by which they should be pursued over time. These sorts of coalition-building processes are mediated by the discursive mechanisms described above, although the conditions underlying when they work and when they fail is a compelling theoretical and empirical question.

One possible network implication is that actors who are adept at using the strategic ambiguity involved in conflation mechanisms might become central actors in alliance networks, since these mechanisms enhance their ability to simultaneously maintain relationships with many heterogeneous actors at once. By playing on categorical ambiguity or the multivalence of discourse, conflation allows actors to make their words do distinct work with many different kinds of audiences, thus enhancing their *network centrality*, along with their leadership, influence, and control in the multi-organizational field (Diani in this book). They may also be more effective at using this kind of ambiguity to build broad-based coalitions, contributing to the construction of a provisional unity among heterogeneous or conflicting actors (i.e. so-called 'strange-bedfellow coalitions'). On the other hand, actors who remain wedded to particularistic categories or demand strict interpretations of their collective project (thus denying the ambiguity that makes them useful) might find themselves marginalized or excluded from alliance networks or broad-based coalitions, which might (positively or negatively) affect the overall success of the mobilization.

FURTHER CHALLENGES

The conversational mechanisms described here contribute to processes of relation-formation that may be critical to the breadth, effectiveness and impact of a movement. In this way they build networks, conceived dynamically as sets of jointly constructed relations (and associated narratives) held in play over an extended period of time. These relations can be studied from a bird's eye perspective using formal techniques that abstract from local context, or they can be studied by searching for on-the-ground mechanisms that play out amidst local contingencies. I have argued that these two approaches can be complementary—that formal mapping can point toward local mechanisms, while the study of mechanisms can suggest formal patterns at a more global level.

Yet to marshal this combination of mapping and mechanisms into substantive theory-building, there are difficult challenges that researchers face. One challenge is the problem of *scope conditions*: certainly not all of the mechanisms described above work equally well in all circumstances. The frequency and/or effectiveness of these mechanisms in contributing to recruitment, outreach, or alliance-building might vary according to different kinds of political opportunity structures, stages in a protest cycle, ideological positions, or forms of movement organization. Some sorts of relations, identities or projects might be more (or less) susceptible to compartmentalization or conflation; certain hats may not come 'off' as easily as others, and some meanings may defy ambiguous interpretations. Thus the broader social, political, and cultural conditions under which these mechanisms contribute to the life of a movement represent an important area for future theory and research.

Another important challenge is the question of *measurement*. While the research proposed here stresses contingency and context, it still makes a claim to move beyond thick description to find patterns in complexity in the search for (at least partially) generalizable mechanisms. To that end, ethnographic or textual analysis must often be complemented by data reduction techniques of various kinds. Observational and textual coding schemes can be used either in conjunction with qualitative data analysis programs or with formal analytical procedures such as network and lattice analysis, or alternatively with other sorts of relational scaling techniques such as MDS or correspondence analysis. Methods for sequential analysis such as time series or optimal matching (Abbott and Hrycak 1990) might help to capture the temporal dynamics of these processes; these might be used together with more interpretive forms of narrative analysis to clarify the temporal structure of collective projects (for a good overview of the use of formal techniques in cultural analysis, see Mohr (1998)). None of these techniques relieve the researcher of her hermeneutic responsibilities; interpretation is involved at all stages of research, from observation and data collection to coding strategies, selection of analytic techniques and discussion of results. These techniques are merely heuristic tools that allow us to move beyond the specificity of the case (and the perspectives of the individual participants) toward an expansion of the analytical toolkit of social movement theory.

The approach outlined here moves significantly beyond current treatments of the relationship between culture and networks in that it sees networks not as channels or conduits for cultural forms, but rather as themselves constituted by cultural processes of talk and interaction. Network relations are co-constructed through ground-level conversational mechanisms, which concatenate into more or less firmly constituted 'structures' that go on to influence social movement in systematic ways. Recognition of the co-constituting character of networks and culture can help to move us toward a deeper understanding of the dynamic, contingent, and multilayered character of social movements and of social processes more generally.

NOTES

1. This focus on cohesion is surprising, given the strong attention to power and conflict within resource mobilization and political process approaches, as well as attention in the social networks literature to how networks shape relations of power and exclusion, influence and

control (see Knoke 1990*a,b*). Perhaps because culture has been left out of the picture for so long, now that it is 'coming back in' to social movement theory it is seen primarily in terms of community, solidarity, etc., rather than recognized for its crucial role in the larger process of contention.

2. Note that Tilly uses 'conversation' in a broadly metaphoric sense, to refer not only to 'talk' or even to face-to-face interaction, but rather to communicative process more generally. He does this to distinguish his relational ontology from others focusing on instrumental reasoning or on inner psychic processes. While I largely focus in this paper on conversational processes that take place within the context of talk in movements, it is important to keep in mind that not all communication is reducible to face-to-face conversation, and that most of the conversational mechanisms that I describe have analogues in relational processes occurring outside of the realm of face-to-face interaction. The specification of these analogues awaits future study.

3. Recently, the analysis of collective action frames has come under a variety of criticisms from scholars within and outside of the framing literature: that frame analysis is prone to reification and pays inadequate attention to agency and emotion (Benford 1997); that it is overly ideational (McAdam 1996); that it is overly instrumentalist and strategic in conception (Zald 1996; Goodwin and Jasper 1999); that it retains a dichotomous understanding of culture and structure (Polletta 1996, 1999*a,b*); and that it is inattentive to the dialectical relationship between discourse and event (Ellingson 1995).

4. Recent attempts to bridge the culture-network divide include Erickson (1988, 1996); Brint (1992); Carley (1992, 1993); Bearman (1993); Emirbayer and Goodwin (1994); Mohr (1994); Anheier *et al.* (1995); Gould (1995); Mische (1996, 1998); Ansell (1997); Emirbayer (1997); Mohr and Duquenne (1997); Franzosi (1998, 1999); McLean (1998); Martin (1999); Wiley and Martin (1999); Mische and Pattison (2000).

5. As McAdam *et al.* (2001: 21) argue, 'Big structures and sequences never repeat themselves, but result from differing combinations and sequences of mechanisms with very general scope.' Elster echoes this focus on contingency and uncertainty when he states 'mechanisms are *frequently occurring and easily recognizable causal patterns that are triggered under unknown conditions or with indeterminate consequences. They allow us to explain but not to predict*' (Elster 1998: 45, italics in original).

6. During my fieldwork in Brazil (1993–7), I conducted participant observation with eight different youth organizations, including student, religious, pre-professional, anti-discrimination and business organizations. I also accompanied the youth branches of several political parties, including the Worker's Party (PT), the Communist Party of Brazil (PCdoB), and the Brazilian Social Democratic Party (PSDB). In addition to observations at meetings and events, I collected taped interviews with over 70 activists as well as 350 questionnaires with information on organizational trajectories, time management strategies, social networks, and personal and collective projects.

7. Whether these are conscious strategies or taken-for-granted practices is an empirical question and most likely can be understood as a matter of degree. Certainly some of the mechanisms described here are deployed by actors as premeditated tactics, while others are imposed by the cultural logic or 'scripts' of a particular relational setting, or by the emergent definition of the situation co-constructed in interaction.

8. These conflation and compartmentalization mechanisms are similar to the cognitive mechanisms that Zeruabavel (1993) describes as 'lumping' and 'splitting,' or what Harrison White might call 'coupling and decoupling'. What distinguishes these from

purely cognitive mechanisms is that these mechanisms are employed by actors within the play of social interaction, in the interest of relation-formation, bringing them out of the head (or the text) and into the situational dynamics of interaction.

9. This discussion of projective narratives builds upon earlier work (Mische 1998; Emirbayer and Mische 1998) on how actors' projections about the future influence their actions, including their ability to coordinate those actions with others. Projects can be defined as '*evolving, imaginatively constructed configurations of desired social possibility, accompanied by an implicit or explicit theorization of personal and/or collective capacity to act to achieve that possibility*' (Mische 1998: 46–7). Here I am interested in collective projects as expressed in the public narratives of organizations, which help to embed those organizations in space and time (Somers 1992).

12

Beyond Structural Analysis: Toward a More Dynamic Understanding of Social Movements

Doug McAdam

It is common today to decry the 'structural bias' in social movement research. For instance, in their critical survey of political process theory, Goodwin and Jasper (1999: 27) argue that 'there has ... also been a strong structural bias ... in the way political opportunities are understood and in the selection of cases for study. Even those factors adduced to correct some of the problems of the political opportunity structure approach—such as "mobilizing structures" and "cultural framing"—are subject to the same structural distortions.' As will become clear from this chapter, I have considerable sympathy with this general line of critique. But before offering a qualified endorsement of the cultural turn in social movement studies, I want to provide a brief sociology of knowledge account of how structure came to be privileged in the field *and* tout the very real scholarly gains that followed from this emphasis. For to say that contemporary movement theory is overly structural is to miss the essential contributions that 25 years of structurally oriented research have made to our understanding of nonroutine, or contentious, politics.

FROM PSYCHOLOGY TO STRUCTURE

My first exposure to the academic study of social movements came in 1971 when, much to my surprise, the professor in my Abnormal Psychology class devoted several weeks to a discussion of the topic. I say 'surprise' because, as an active participant in the antiwar movement, it certainly came as news to me that my involvement in the struggle owed to a mix of personal pathology and social disorganization. But, reflecting the dominant theories of the day, those were the twin factors emphasized in the course.

At a macro, sociological level, social disorganization was seen as the immediate precipitant of movement emergence. Movements were held to arise when rapid social change (e.g. industrialization and urbanization) occasioned a generalized breakdown of social order (Turner and Killian 1957; Kornhauser 1959; Lang and

Lang 1961; Smelser 1962). Movements, in this view, were groping, if ineffective, collective efforts to restore social order and the sense of normative certainty disrupted by change. As such they owed more to psychological, than political or economic, motivations.

But even in the face of generalized social disorder, everyone was not equally 'at risk' of being drawn into the movement activity. Supplementing the macro relationship between social disorganization and movement emergence were a host of micro 'theories' arguing for a link between this or that set of individual and/or personality factors and movement participation (Adorno *et al.* 1950; Hoffer 1951; Kornhauser 1959; Feuer 1969; Klapp 1969; Rothman and Lichter 1978). Though differing in their specifics, social marginality or isolation was a general theme in most of these accounts. So various social or psychological 'deficits' were held to dispose individuals toward movement participation, even if social disorganization furnished the general impetus to collective action.

Both the macro emphasis on social disorganization and the micro stress on isolation and marginality accorded well with the then-dominant pluralist model of America politics (Truman 1953; Dahl 1961, 1967; Polsby 1963). Pluralists viewed the USA as a broad, open, and at least minimally responsive political system, featuring bargaining and negotiation by a wide array of groups who shared relatively equally in power. The presence of social movements could be seen as inconsistent with the theory, *unless* those movements are seen, not as instrumental political efforts, but as therapeutic vehicles through which needy people cope with the ill effects of social and personal disorganization. And so a tidy scholarly division of labour emerged: with pluralists explaining the workings of institutional politics and social movements, in Gamson's (1990: 133) felicitous phrase, left to 'the social psychologist whose intellectual tools prepare him to better understand the irrational'.

The turbulence of the 1960s simultaneously undermined scholarly faith in pluralism and made the apolitical view of social movements increasingly untenable. If American politics was less an open arena than an entrenched 'power structure,' then one hardly needed psychologists to understand the impulse to protest. Movements were simply politics by other means; rational efforts to generate leverage by groups (e.g. minorities and women) normally denied access to institutional channels. Working from these assumptions, a new generation of more structurally oriented movement analysts began to formulate very different theoretical accounts of movements *and* to produce consistent empirical results quite at odds with traditional expectations. This was true at both the group and individual level. While movements often did emerge against a backdrop of rapid change and generalized instability, it was rarely the most disorganized segments of society who were in the forefront of these struggles. On the contrary, analysts of contention began to amass impressive evidence attesting to the catalytic role of established groups or networks—'mobilizing structures' as they would come to be dubbed (McAdam *et al.* 1996)—in the origin of movements. Studies of insurgency in nineteenth-century

Europe showed that collective action tended to develop within stable neighbour-hood and work contexts (Tilly *et al.* 1975; Merriman 1978; Margadant 1979; Aminzade 1981). The civil rights movement was shown to have emerged within the central institutions of the southern black community (Morris 1984; McAdam 1999). The antiwar movement developed on northern college campuses, with resi-dential colleges experiencing higher rates of participation than commuter cam-puses (Orum 1972). The two wings of the U.S. women's movement developed out of the State Commissions on the Status of Women (Freeman 1973) and established networks of women who had been active in the southern civil rights movement (Evans 1980). The list of studies could be multiplied many times over without altering the central point: structural stability, not disorder, appears to facilitate movement emergence.

At the micro level, similar findings began to proliferate. Though isolation and social marginality had long been assumed to be predictors of individual activism, numerous studies showed that people with structural ties to movements were far more likely to be drawn into the struggle than were their more isolated counter-parts (Bolton 1972; Snow *et al.* 1980; Walsh and Warland 1983; Rosenthal *et al.* 1985; Broadbent 1986; McAdam 1986; Briet *et al.* 1987; Klandermans and Oegema 1987; Fernandez and McAdam 1988; Gould 1993*a,b*, 1995; McAdam and Paulsen 1993; Opp and Gern 1993; Diani 1995).

For all their real or presumed narrowness, these exclusively structural studies have shaped the field in important and generally salutary ways. Let me highlight what I see as the two most important contributions to come from this structural research programme. First, it had the effect of overturning the traditional psychological con-ception of social movements and reorienting the field to the study of organizations, networks, power, and politics. This has meant that political sociologists, political sci-entists, organizational scholars, and network researchers have tended to dominate the study of social movements. And while this approach to the field comes with its own set of blinders—some of which I hope to explore here—I am quite willing to betray my bias and say for the record that it is far more accurate and analytically use-ful to regard movements fundamentally as organized political phenomena rather than as spontaneous expressions of personal and social disorganization.

The second great contribution of the structural research programme is that it has been, well, ... a *research* programme. That is, maybe even more important than the fundamental theoretical changes noted above, was the *methodological* shift which accompanied it. While proponents of the older collective behaviour school had primarily engaged in a form of armchair theorizing, the newer genera-tion of movement scholars shared a general commitment to systematic empirical research. As much as anything, it was this commitment that stimulated the phe-nomenal growth of the field over the past two decades and established the consist-ent empirical findings touched on above.

These findings have been reproduced in so many discrete studies that they can now be regarded as empirical regularities in the emergent mobilization of a movement. The establishment of these 'facts' underscores the very real contributions of the structural research programme to the study of social movements. That said, the fact that we know very little about the dynamic *processes* and *mechanisms* that account for these regularities, points up the limits of the structural programme and suggests that we may, at least for the study of movement origins, have reached the limits of the programme's usefulness.

BEYOND STRUCTURAL VARIABLES: SEARCHING FOR EXPLANATORY *MECHANISMS*

Motivated by the same general conclusions regarding the contributions and limits of the structural research programme, McAdam *et al.* (2001) call, in their recent book, for a move away from static structural models to a search for the dynamic *mechanisms* (and concatenated *processes*) that shape 'contentious politics'. By mechanisms, the authors mean 'a delimited class of events that alter relations among specified elements in identical or closely similar ways over a variety of situations' (2001: 11). I will offer some clarifying examples of such mechanisms later in the chapter. For now, I merely want to underscore the important methodological implication that follows from the approach urged by the authors. Rather than seeking to confirm the aforementioned structural regularities for yet another discrete movement, scholars should invest instead in methods designed to identify and better understand the interactive dynamics that account for the consistent structural findings. So, for example, if movements tend to develop within established social settings, what are the specific *mechanisms* that typically serve to transform a church, a college dorm, a neighbourhood, etc., into a site of emergent collective action? Similarly, if certain network variables predict movement participation, what interactive dynamics help account for the relationship?

To begin to answer these questions, movement researchers will need to supplement the traditional macro and micro staples of movement analysis—case studies or event research in the case of the former and survey research in connection with the latter—with a more serious investment in ethnography and other methods designed to shed empirical light on the *meso-level* dynamics that shape and sustain collective action over time. I will have a bit more to say on the issue of methods at the close of the chapter. Here I am more interested in highlighting the important conceptual point implicit in this methodological injunction. I remain:

convinced that the real action in social movements takes place at some level intermediate between the macro and micro. It is there in the existing associational groups or networks of the aggrieved community that the first groping steps toward collective action are taken ... Most of our research has missed this level of analysis. We have focused the lion's share of our research energies on the before and after of collective action. The "before" research has focused on the macro and micro [structural] factors that make movements and individual activism more likely. The "after" side of the research equation is composed of the few studies that focus on the outcomes of collective action. But we haven't devoted a lot of attention to the *ongoing accomplishment of collective action*. How do ... [structural] propensities get translated into specific mobilization attempts? What are the actual dynamics by which movement activists reach decisions regarding goals and tactics? How concretely do SMOs seek to recruit new members? To answer these question, what is needed is more systematic qualitative fieldwork into the dynamics of collective action at the intermediate meso level. (McAdam *et al.* 1988; emphasis in original)

This plea to substitute qualitative fieldwork for more traditional quantitative methods of movement analysis would appear to reverse what most researchers see as the conventional sequence of methodological strategies. That is, one often thinks of qualitative research as an exploratory strategy designed to yield formal hypotheses that can be tested using the techniques of quantitative research. A cursory review of methods textbooks confirms that, to the extent that qualitative and quantitative techniques are linked at all, it is in the aforementioned sequence (Nachimas and Nachimas 1976). But the two can be deployed in reverse order as well. Quantitative analysis can be used, as in the study of social movements, to uncover certain recurrent empirical relationships, that can then be interrogated more fully using systematic qualitative methods. It is this somewhat unconventional reversal of the relationship between qualitative and quantitative approaches that I am advocating here.

ILLUSTRATING THE PROGRAM: THREE EXEMPLARS

I want to use the balance of the chapter to illustrate the approach being advocated. Drawing wherever possible on the other contributions to this volume, I want to take three established structural 'facts' associated with the origins of contention and speculate a bit about the dynamic mechanisms that may account for the recurrence of these findings in a host of empirical studies of movement emergence. At present, simple structural explanations are typically advanced to account for all three facts.

- *Fact #1:* recruits to a movement tend to know others who are already involved.
  Account: by providing prospective recruits with a mix of information and solidary incentives, prior social ties encourage entrance into the movement.
- *Fact #2:* most social movements develop within established social settings.
  Account: established social settings provide insurgents with the various resources (e.g. recognized leaders, communication channels, networks of trust, etc.) needed to launch and sustain collective action.
- *Fact #3:* emerging movements tend to spread along established lines of interaction.
  Account: information, rendered credible by prior contact with the innovator, mediates the spread of a movement.

In my view, these structural accounts are, at best, incomplete explanations of the facts, masking, in all cases, the play of far more interesting and contingent mechanisms, which combine structural and cultural elements. I take up each fact in turn.

Prior Social Ties as a Basis of Movement Recruitment

As Gould notes in his chapter for this volume, 'one of the first and most frequently cited facts about social ties and activism is that activists are frequently drawn into a movement by people they know' (p. 236). But, as he goes on to say, 'simply observing that social ties affect mobilization is not much of a contribution. It is a bit like noticing that people who are stricken with plague have had contact with other plague victims' (p. 237). To their credit, network analysts have not simply hypothesized these affects; as noted above and reviewed by Passy in her chapter, these analysts have also produced a great deal of empirical work attesting to the relationship. 'We are now aware that social ties are important for collective action, but we still need to theorize … the actual role of networks' (Passy, p. 22). Without specifying the mechanisms that account for the affect, movement researchers are guilty of assaying a structurally determinist explanation of movement recruitment. We are left with the unfortunate impression that individuals who are embedded in movement networks are virtually compelled to get involved by virtue of knowing others who are already active. There are a host of good reasons why we should reject this simple structural imperative, but here I will limit myself to three.

First, the above account skirts the important question of origins. That is, to say that people join movements because they know others who are involved, ignores the obvious point that on the eve of a movement, there are no salient others already involved to pull ego into activism. Second, the structural account fails to acknowledge conceptually or address empirically the fact that potential recruits invariably possess a multitude of 'prior social ties' that are likely to expose them to conflicting behavioural pressures. Here we confront the hoary problem of sampling on the dependent variable. Overwhelmingly, the studies of movement recruitment start by surveying activists after their entrance into the movement. But showing that these activists were linked to the movement by some prior social tie does not prove the causal potency of that tie. No doubt there are also many non-activists with ties to someone in the movement who did not participate, perhaps because salient others outside the movement put pressure on them to remain uninvolved.

The final key lacuna of the structural account of movement recruitment is the one mentioned above and which Gould and Passy take as the starting point for their exemplary chapters: proponents of the structural account have generally failed to sketch a distinctive model to explain the observed effects. The structuralists are not alone in this. For all the importance they attach to social construction and human agency, many culturalists advance an implicit view of the individual that is curiously determinant in its own right. Individuals act, not on the basis of structural/network influences, but the impact of disembodied culture. But in both cases, the effect is similar: the potential for individual autonomy and choice is largely denied, replaced by a conception of the individual as acted upon, rather than acting.

For their part, rational choice theorists have articulated a model (with multiple variants) of entrance into collective action. And while I think it implies a truncated view of individual motivation and action, I nonetheless take seriously the need for such a model and for the identification of dynamic mechanisms and processes that bridge the micro, meso, and macro dimensions of movements. I do not pretend to deliver a complete model of this sort here. But, in keeping with the efforts of Passy and especially Gould, I think we can move in this direction. I begin by making a single foundational point: in my view a viable model of individual action must take account of the fundamentally social/relational nature of human existence. This is not to embrace the oversocialized conception of the individual that I see informing the work of most structuralists and some culturalists. Consistent with the rationalists, I too stress the potential for individual autonomy and choice. Where I part company with the rationalists is in the central importance I attach to one powerful motivator of human action. I think most individuals act routinely to safeguard and sustain the central sources of meaning and identity in their lives. As a practical matter, this means frequently prizing solidary incentives over all others and, in particular, conforming to the behavioural dictates of those whose approval and emotional sustenance are most central to our lives and salient identities.

How might this foundational tenet translate into a specific account of movement recruitment? In 1993, I coauthored an article with Ronnelle Paulsen in which we offered a sequential account of the onset of individual activism. We argued (p. 647) that:

the ultimate decision to participate in a movement would depend on four ... [mechanisms]: (1) the occurrence of a specific recruiting attempt, (2) the successful linkage of movement and [salient] identity, (3) support for that linkage from persons who normally serve to sustain the identity in question, and (4) the absence of strong opposition from others on whom other salient identities depend.

Echoing the central theme of this chapter, we then closed the article with the following plea (p. 663):

the most important implication of this research is as much social psychological as structural. Network analysts of movement recruitment have been overly concerned with assessing the structure of the subject's relationship to the movement without paying sufficient attention to the social psychological processes that mediate the link between structure and activism ... [P]rior ties would appear to encourage activism only when they (a) reinforce the potential recruit's strong identification with a particular identity and (b) help to establish a strong linkage between that identity and the movement in question. When these processes of *identity amplification* and *identity/movement linkage* take place, activism is likely to follow ... Movement analysts, then, need to be as attuned to the [cultural] *content* of network processes as to the *structures* themselves.

Though we did not use the term *mechanism* in the article, we clearly had the underlying concept in mind when we identified *identity amplification* and *identity/ movement linkage* as key 'processes' in movement recruitment. Translated more fully into the language of this chapter, we were attempting, in the earlier article, to sketch a dynamic recruitment *process* composed of four component *mechanisms*. Figure 12.1 presents the *process* schematically.

The process sketched in Fig. 12.1, and the empirical results reported in the 1993 article, accord nicely with the central themes and conclusions of the work by Passy and Gould in this volume. In closing this section, it is worth highlighting the various points of convergence between the three chapters. In her effort to better specify the structural account of recruitment, Passy ascribes three crucial *functions* to network ties. These she terms the *structural-connection, socialization,* and *decision-shaping functions*. These three functions bear a striking similarity to three of the four mechanisms identified in Fig. 12.1. Passy's *structural-connection* function is essentially the same as the *recruitment attempt* in Fig. 12.1. That is, prior ties can connect a potential activist through a concrete recruitment attempt. What Paulsen and I termed *identity-movement linkage*, Passy calls the *socialization function* of networks. Finally, Passy's *decision-shaping function* is more or less synonymous with the *positive influence* mechanism shown in Fig. 12.1. The important point for Paulsen and me was that although these various mechanisms could occur independently, the likelihood of successful recruitment was dramatically increased when they occurred sequentially through the efforts of a single, highly salient prior tie. So if, for example, a very close friend asked you to take part in a demonstration *(recruitment attempt),* and worked both to create a plausible link between the action and an identity she/he knew you prized *(identity-movement linkage)* and to

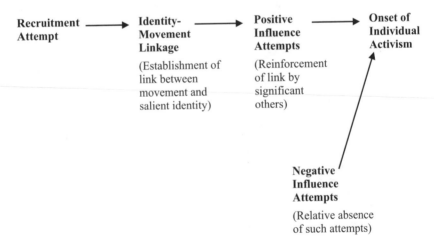

FIG. 12.1. *The process of individual recruitment*

argue for the correctness of the action in general terms *(positive influence attempt)*, I think it is very likely that you would take part, especially if you encountered little or no opposition to the action from salient others.

This hypothetical example is very close to the one that Gould models toward the end of his chapter. The unique, and I think entirely justified, supposition that Gould builds into this model is that a recruitment attempt by a prior tie works, not because of any threatened loss of sociability for nonparticipation (which is what rationalists argue) but because shared involvement comes to be viewed as a way of enhancing the existing relationship. But this, as Gould notes, will only work if the two individuals in question are very close friends. Indeed, the model predicts that the closer, more affectively salient the tie, the more likely the recruitment effort will succeed. This is entirely consistent with what Paulsen and I argue in the earlier article. To the extent that a single, highly *salient* (read: Gould's 'strong') tie orchestrates the three mechanisms identified in Fig. 12.1, the successful recruitment of the target into activism is very likely.

Established Social Settings as the Locus of Movement Emergence

As noted previously, it has become part of the received wisdom of movement theory that episodes of contention almost always develop within established social settings (for a summary of this literature, see McCarthy 1996). Besides the classic studies that helped establish the fact (Freeman 1973; Tilly *et al.* 1975; Margadant 1979; Evans 1980; Aminzade 1981; Morris 1984; McAdam 1999), a host of more recent works have served to confirm it. In his work on the 1989 Chinese student movement, Zhao (1998, 2001) shows how the dense ecological concentration of college campuses in Beijing served as the locus of initial mobilization. Glenn (2001), among others, documents the role that a network of independent theatre companies played in the origins of the Civic Forum movement in Czechoslovakia. In some earlier work, Osa (1997) highlights the central structural importance of the Catholic Church to the dissident movement in Poland. In her chapter for this volume, Osa expands on the earlier work by showing how the growth of opposition networks in Poland, predict both movement emergence and the peak periods of protest activity within a cycle of contention.

Consistent with these studies, proponents of the political process model have long emphasized the role of established organizations or associational networks in the onset of contention. Absent any such 'mobilizing structure,' incipient movements were thought to lack the capacity to act even if afforded the opportunity to do so. As straightforward and seemingly self-evident as this proposition would appear to be, it must be remembered that, when first voiced, it contradicted the emphasis on social breakdown and disorganization so central to the collective behaviour tradition. Since this particular debate was joined, it seems clear that the weight of empirical evidence favours the organizational camp over the breakdown school. All well and good. But, as with the notion of 'prior tie,' the 'mobilizing structure' concept has too often been treated as an objective structural facilitator of protest, rather than a contested site of interaction that can give rise to opposite lines of action. The point is, existing groups or networks (as well as prior ties) are as apt to constrain as to facilitate protest. Bottom line: it is not prior ties or group structures that enable protest, but rather the interactive conversations that occur there and succeed in creating shared meanings and identities that legitimate emergent collective action.

The point can be made more concretely by revisiting one of the classic cases that helped confirm the critical importance of established groups in the origins of contention. Movement scholars have thoroughly documented the central role played by the black church in helping to launch the civil rights movement (Oberschall 1973; Morris 1984; McAdam 1999). But while the movement's debt to the black church is widely acknowledged, the standard narrative account of the origins of the civil rights struggle obscures an organizational and *cultural* accomplishment of enormous importance. Until the rise of the movement, it was common for social observers—black no less than white—to depict the black church as a generally conservative institution with a decided emphasis, not on the 'social gospel in action,' but rather on the realization of rewards in the afterlife (Johnson 1941; Mays and Nicholson 1969; Marx 1971). Nor did the inherent conservatism of the institution entirely disappear as a result of the civil rights movement. As Charles Payne's (1996) magnificent book on the movement in Mississippi makes clear, the conservative nature of local black clergy remained an obstacle to local organizing even during the movement's heyday.

Given this more complicated portrait of the black church, the importance and highly contingent nature of initial mobilization attempts should be clear. To turn even some black congregations into vehicles of collective protest, early movement leaders had to engage in a lot of creative cultural/organizational work, by which the aims of the church and its animating collective identity were redefined to accord with the goals of the emerging struggle. This is a collaborative *cultural* project that has far more to do with social construction and redefinition than with the kind of objective inventory of organizational resources suggested by the current *structural* account of movement origins. Prior organization and all the resources in the world matter little if their use is not governed by shared meanings and identities legitimating contention.

This discussion brings us, inevitably, back to the limits of the structural research project. By starting from the accomplished fact of collective action, and then working back in time to note that movements tend to arise in established social settings, structural analysts exaggerated the link between organization and action. By, once again, selecting on the dependent variable—emergent collective action—they could detect the exceptional cases where existing groups birthed movements, but not the far more numerous examples of such groups constraining action. Moreover their methods—principally case study and event research—were essentially those of the outsider, making it impossible for them to observe the

FIG. 12.2. *The process of 'emergent mobilization'*

interactive dynamics that shaped the exceptional cases. The 'insider' approach embodied in qualitative fieldwork would redress this problem.

But what concrete social mechanisms should movement ethnographers attend to in such settings? Even if one embraces the rigorously inductive ideal of 'grounded theory' (Glaser and Strauss 1967), it is probably impossible (and undesirable in my view) to enter the field without some sensitizing hunches concerning what one is going to find. Adapted from previous work (McAdam 1999; McAdam *et al.* 2001), Fig. 12.2 represents a provisional attempt to do that for the *process* by which an existing social group *mobilizes* for contentious action. I see three *mechanisms* as key to this process.

1. Attribution of threat or opportunity. The routine monitoring and interpretation of events and environmental conditions is the foundation for all group life, routine as well as contentious. Accordingly, for me, the initial catalyst for insurgent mobilization comes in the form of an emergent group-level account of some new threat to, or opportunity for, the realization of group interests. That said, for all their importance, these crucial interpretive dynamics are largely absent from the traditional structural account of movement emergence. As Goodwin and Jasper (1999) note, rather than emphasize the culturally constructed nature of perceived opportunities (or threats), movement theorists have characterized the environmental impetus to action as owing to the objective features of a particular 'political opportunity *structure*'. But,

rather than look upon "opportunities and threats" as objective structural factors, we see them as subject to attribution [and emergent construction]. No opportunity, however objectively open, will invite mobilization unless it is (a) visible to potential challengers and (b) perceived to be an opportunity. The same holds true for threats, an underemphasized corollary of the model ... Attribution of opportunity or threat is an activating mechanism responsible in part for the mobilization of previously inert populations. (McAdam *et al.* 2001: 43)

2. Social appropriation. An emerging group-level account of threat or opportunity is hardly sufficient to ensure a movement, however. For collective attributions of threat or opportunity to key emergent action the interpreters must command sufficient resources and numbers to provide a social/organizational base for mobilization. When this is the case, the ideational challenge inherent in fashioning an account of the threat/opportunity gets joined to a more narrowly organizational one. As a prerequisite for action, would-be insurgents must either create an organizational vehicle and its supporting collective identity or, more likely, *appropriate*

an existing organization and the routine collective identity on which it rests. In short, the collective account of threat or opportunity must become the animating frame for an organizationally able collective.

In my view, Gould's two person model of recruitment has implications for collective mobilization as well. Basically, he is describing a process of interpersonal appropriation in the service of a movement. That is, the recruiter is seeking to appropriate the solidaristic bonds of trust and affect she/he shares with the friend on behalf of the movement. But there is a group level analogue to this dyadic process. In a close-knit group situation, an established (or emergent) leader or organizer can also call on the existing loyalties of group members in an effort to leverage action. Indeed, in his chapter on local environmental movements in Japan, Broadbent offers a clear example of this kind of leader based appropriation and its crucial importance to the broader process of mobilization. Broadbent (p. 222–23) explains:

In Japan's vertical society, overt resistance was a daring step. It contravened the norm of going along. Moreover, though violent repression was rare, resistance had possible harmful consequences, both materially and in terms of social prestige. In a society of "other-directed" personalities … high status members controlled a great deal of collective motivational affect. As noted earlier, bosses running the local political "machine" worked through kin and neighbourhood networks … They solidified their power in part by assiduously currying personal favour—presenting generous contributions at funerals and weddings, holding sake parties to build camaraderie, distributing small bribes at election time, finding jobs and even marriage partners for your children … [O]ther services flowed through personal networks as well. As a result, either requested by the boss or just out of concern for their loss of services, locals would personally urge their activist relatives to desist from movement participation. This network pressure posed a formidable barrier to mobilization in village context. It makes sense then … that one crucial theme for successful movements should be the "breakaway boss." The three fully successful communities, plus one failed community, exhibited this quality. A breakaway boss broke free from his … status within the conservative social control machine to "lead his flock" … into activist resistance.

Or, to phrase it in my terms, drawing on the considerable moral and interpersonal capital each had mobilized during his tenure as boss, these leaders were able to successfully *appropriate* the structures they commanded on behalf of a local movement. In stressing the importance of local leaders in the mobilization of local activism, Broadbent suggests that Japan may be distinctive in this regard. In such a traditional, 'other regarding,' society, leaders may play more of a role in the appropriation and mobilization of local social structures than in Western countries. Perhaps, but it is worth noting that in his chapter on the rise of the Nazi movement in Germany, Helmut Anheier, offers fascinating empirical evidence of much the same leader-based appropriation process described by Broadbent. Even if further comparative study of movement origins confirms Broadbent's surmise, the role of local leaders in the appropriation of existing social groups or networks is very likely to remain a key mobilizing mechanism across a wide variety of contentious episodes.

3. Innovative action. The final component mechanism of the mobilization process is *innovative contentious action*, defined simply as action that, by its contentious nature, departs from previous collective routines and signals to other parties a fundamental change in the action orientation of, and relationship to, the group in question. Such action is extremely likely to develop when shared perceptions of threat or opportunity come, through appropriation, to serve as the motivating frame of an established group. But it is important to underscore that such action is a contingent accomplishment in its own right. Even should a group view its situation as newly threatening or opportune, it may refrain from innovative action for strategic reasons. For that reason, innovative action is identified as a third contingent mechanism shaping mobilization.

The Spread of a Movement Along Existing Lines of Interaction

The vast majority of contentious episodes never spread beyond the local settings in which they first develop. But in the case of major movements, at least some degree of *scale shift* takes place (McAdam *et al.* 2001: ch. 10). By the *process* of *scale shift*, we mean 'a change in the number and level of coordinated contentious action leading to broader contention involving a wider range of actors and bridging their claims and identities' (McAdam *et al.* 2001: 331). The process of scale shift, or movement spread, has not received the same level of attention as either *emergent mobilization* or *movement recruitment*. But, as with these other two processes, the work that has been done on the spread of contention tends, once more, to reproduce the structural bias inherent in the field (Jackson *et al.* 1960; Pinard 1971; McAdam and Rucht 1993; Strang and Meyer 1993; Soule 1997; McAdam 1999). The general tendency has been to interpret the spread of contention on the basis of traditional diffusion theory, which holds that innovations or new cultural items diffuse along established lines of social interaction (Rogers 1983). But as Oliver and Meyer make abundantly clear in their contribution to this volume, the spread of contention is a very complicated phenomenon that almost certainly does not conform to a single unvarying pattern.

The effort to model the spread of contention as but a specialized instance of diffusion once again truncates our understanding of the phenomenon in question. To say that most such instances benefit from prior ties between innovators and adopters tells us no more about the contingent dynamics of scale shift than the previous two structural 'facts' tell us about the processes of recruitment and mobilization, respectively. It is reasonable to assume that many, if not most, instances of strictly local contention involve groups whose members are also linked to others beyond their local context. So why do so many cases of local contention fail to spread elsewhere? As with *mobilization* and *recruitment*, certain structural conditions may be necessary, but hardly sufficient, to insure the process in question. As before, the question becomes: what contingent social-cultural mechanisms mediate movement spread? This is essentially the same question that Oliver and

Myer take up in their chapter. Their innovative approach involves 'struggling with what empirical data patterns actually look like, and trying to model the underlying processes that could be giving rise to these patterns' (p. 199). I take a different tack, identifying, as before, a set of linked mechanisms that would seem to condition the likelihood of scale shift. I see scale shift as a robust process consisting of two distinct pathways, though the two can, and frequently do, co-occur in a given movement. This process is shown in Fig. 12.3.

Before taking up each mechanism in turn, let me first describe the process in general terms. Localized collective action spawns broader contention when information concerning the initial action reaches a geographically or institutionally distant group (through either *diffusion* or *brokerage*) which, on the basis of this information, defines itself as sufficiently similar to the initial insurgents (*attribution of similarity*) as to motivate *emulation*, leading ultimately to *coordinated action* between the two sites.

I am using the term diffusion here in a somewhat specialized way to refer only to the transfer of information along established lines of interaction, while brokerage entails information transfers that depend on the linking of two or more previously unconnected social sites. (In his interesting empirical contribution to the volume, Diani explores some of the empirical correlates of brokerage in the

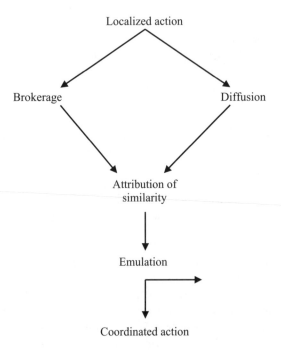

FIG. 12.3. *The process of 'scale shift' or 'movement spread'*

Milanese environmental movement.) I make this distinction to call attention to a significant difference in the nature and likely impact of scale shift depending on whether diffusion or brokerage tends to predominate as the mediating mechanism. Movements that spread primarily through diffusion will almost always remain narrower in their geographic and/or institutional locus than contention that spreads through brokerage. Why? Because such movements will not be able to transcend the typically segmented lines of interaction which characterize social/political life.

While diffusion and brokerage represent different pathways to scale-shift, both work through the two additional mechanisms shown in Fig. 12.3. The first of these, *attribution of similarity*, I define as the identification of actors in different sites as being sufficiently similar as to justify common action. This mechanism is one that some scholars of diffusion have stressed as mediating between information and adoptive action (Strang and Meyer 1993; McAdam and Rucht 1993). The idea is simple enough. Information alone will not lead someone to adopt a new idea, cultural object, or behavioural practice. Adoption, in turn, depends on at least minimal identification between innovator and adopter.

What factors make such identification more likely? It results, first, from the deliberate attempts of agents of diffusion/brokerage to frame the claims and identities of influence targets as sufficiently similar to their own as to justify coordinated action. We see such deliberate influence attempts all the time in contentious politics: the brokering of a clerical–monarchist–regionalist coalition against Paris in the Vendée revolt in France (Tilly 1964); the appropriation of existing ministerial networks to forge a regional alliance of movement leaders in the early days of the civil rights struggle (McAdam 1999); the Free Men–Free Soil–Fremont electoral campaign of 1856 by the Republicans in antebellum America (McAdam *et al.* 2001). Movement entrepreneurs who wish to increase their appeal to either previously connected or disparate groups work constantly to draw parallels between the group they represent and the targets of their influence attempts. Indeed, Snow and Benford (1988, 1992) have termed this process 'frame bridging,' and highlighted its importance in the unfolding of a protest cycle.

However, attribution of similarity need not be so purposive or strategic a process. A second factor encouraging identification among different actors is Strang and Meyer's (1993) concept of 'institutional equivalence'. The authors highlight the tendency of policymakers within particular institutional domains (e.g. urban planning) to identify with their counterparts in other countries, thus facilitating the spread of policy innovations, in the absence of purposive influence attempts by the innovators. In the history of contentious politics we see institutional equivalence encouraging scale shift in the channelling effect of mass production on industrial action; workers in mass production units with similar relations to management have historically found it much easier to join their struggles to others in similar situations than, say, to handicraft workers in isolated workshops.

The second and final mechanism mediating scale shift is *emulation*, defined here simply as collective action modelled on the actions of others. While straightforward

as a mechanism, its inclusion in Fig. 12.3 underscores a point made earlier in connection with the discussion of emergent mobilization. Awareness of a prior action,
even when accompanied by strong identification with the actor, does not necessarily guarantee emulative action on the part of the observing group. We can well
imagine groups learning of and strongly identifying with a contentious action by
another group and yet refraining from action out of fear or a sensible desire to
monitor the reaction of authorities before deciding whether to act themselves. The
point is, emulative action is a contingent outcome in its own right and therefore
properly modelled as a mechanism distinct from diffusion/brokerage and attribution of similarity.

Although diffusion and brokerage often combine in major movements, there
are significant differences in the character and likely impact of scale shift depending on which of the two predominates as the mediating mechanism. Contention
that spreads primarily through diffusion may be dramatic and consequential in its
effects, but because it never transcends existing lines of interaction, it will almost
always remain narrower in its reach and impact than contention that spreads
substantially through brokerage.

By the same line of reasoning, diffusion is far more likely to be the mediating
mechanism of movement spread than brokerage: more likely because actors who
are connected through lines of interaction are already more likely to attribute similarity to themselves; and also because diffusion requires a much lower investment
in time and entrepreneurial energy than brokerage. It follows that, brokerage,
though less common than diffusion, is likely to be far more consequential in its
effects. To the extent that brokered ties succeed in encouraging previously disconnected groups to identify with one another, contention can quickly spread beyond
narrow geographic, institutional, and/or categorical boundaries and produce
new identities that are more durable than the incidents that gave rise to them. To
take but a single well-known case of this, by brokering a set of ties between the
southern civil rights movement and northern white college campuses, the 1964
Freedom Summer project set in motion a significant 'revolution beyond race'
by encouraging many seemingly disparate groups (e.g. white college students,
women, chicanos, gays and lesbians, etc.) to identify with and draw action implications from African-Americans (McAdam 1988a,b, 1995).

CONCLUSIONS

The structural research programme on social movements has produced several
consistent empirical findings. However, the meaning of these findings and, more
importantly, the actual social processes that account for them remain opaque.
What, for example, does it mean to say that movements develop within established
social settings when most such settings appear to constrain rather than facilitate
mobilization? Not much, unless we can identify the intervening *mechanisms* that

condition these divergent outcomes. That is what I have tried to do here for three important *processes—individual recruitment, emergent mobilization*, and *scale shift*—that figure prominently in the movement literature. In doing so, it should be clear that I am not so much abandoning the structural approach to the study of contention as seeking to supplement it with the insights and methods from more culturally (and rationally) oriented movement scholars. After all, networks are centrally implicated in all three of the processes discussed above. But instead of focusing on the formal network component of each, I have chosen instead to speculate a bit about the interactive dynamics that may animate these network based processes.

Needless to say, these three processes hardly exhaust the movement dynamics one might be interested in mapping in the more dynamic, mechanistic terms discussed here. Indeed, the chapter that perhaps most fully realizes the programmatic aims I have tried to articulate, is Anne Mische's work on 'cross-talk in movements'. The process of interest for Mische is none of the three discussed here, but rather the neglected phenomenon of *movement coalition formation and maintenance*. Given that most successful movements necessarily involve some degree of coalition formation, Mische's focus is germane to a host of critical movement issues, including the all important topic of movement outcomes. To account for variation in her process, Mische identifies and discusses in great detail, a host of promising *conversational mechanisms* that would seem to have important implications for a number of other movement processes, including those touched on in this chapter.

In bringing her impressive chapter to a close, Mische takes up an issue that is highly germane to the realization of the ambitious research programme called for here. I refer to the all important issue of systematic method. As she (p. 278) puts it:

Another important challenge is the question of *measurement*. While the research proposed here stresses contingency and context, it still makes a claim to move beyond thick description to find pattern in complexity in the search for ... generalizable mechanisms. To that end, ethnographic or textual analysis must often be complemented by data reduction techniques of various kinds.

While space constraints prevent a full exploration of methodological possibilities, I want, at the very least, to heartily second Mische's call for a more ambitious and strategic mix of qualitative and quantitative research strategies in the study of social movements and contention. And what might some of these approaches be? Besides the obvious need for thick ethnographic descriptions of movement processes, a range of other options are open to us, if we are willing to set aside the narrow methodological divisions that currently characterize the social sciences. Modelling of either the formal sort employed by Gould in his article, or the more inductive, data driven approach used to good effect by Oliver and Meyer, can be valuable tools in this effort. So central is conversation to the cultural mechanisms discussed here, that we would be remiss to ignore the methodological riches inherent in the various forms of conversational and discourse analysis. Finally, the experimental method could be harnessed to this effort as well. Besides small group studies in the lab, we could also take a page from Gamson's seemingly end-less book of methodological tricks and try to simulate contention through natural-istic experiments of the sort that he and his colleagues devised in *Encounters with Unjust Authority* (1982).

These few suggestions hardly exhaust the topic, nor do they begin to convey the daunting methodological challenges that await anyone who would seek to take up the research programme advocated here. Challenges aside, what I feel confident about is that when joined with the theoretical pluralism embraced here, this more catholic approach to research methods promises to move us well beyond the essen-tially static and descriptive structural facts that currently pass for theory in the study of social movements and contention. This volume is dedicated to that end.

13

Networks and Social Movements:
A Research Programme

Mario Diani

In this book we have charted the contribution of network perspectives to the study of social movements and collective action at different levels. We have illustrated how networks affect individual contributions to collective action in both democratic (Passy) and non-democratic (Anheier) organizations; how patterns of interorganizational linkages reflect different styles of collective action and affect the circulation of resources both within movement milieux and between movement organizations and the political system (Osa, Diani, Ansell); and how network concepts and techniques may be used to generate a more nuanced account of key elements of the relationship between movements and the broader political process, such as the role of elites (Broadbent), the configuration of alliance and conflict structures in a political system (Tilly and Wood), and the clustering of episodes of collective action in broader cycles (Oliver and Myers). We have also highlighted the differences in the logics of different theoretical perspectives (Gould, Mische).

Achieving greater clarification regarding the use of a polysemic concept like network, and mapping recent developments in several areas of inquiry, might not be a negligible achievement in its own right. My question here is whether it would not be possible and desirable to go one step further, and attempt to integrate into a specific research programme what many might still regard as a fairly heterogeneous set of intellectual questions and procedures. In the previous chapter, Doug McAdam has presented his proposal for an expansion along interpretive lines of the structural programme, which he largely identifies with network accounts of individual recruitment and participation. More specifically, he has called for a greater recognition of the role of cultural forms and discourses in constructing social relations and constituting the mechanisms through which networks operate. In doing so, not only has he effectively integrated many of our chapters, but he has also provided a possible bridge between research on social movements and broader controversies in social science.

McAdam's chapter may also be read as an invitation to social movement researchers to go beyond the empirically defined boundaries of their specific field of inquiry and engage in the search for more general mechanisms which can illuminate not only the traits and developments of specific social movements, but a much broader range of 'dynamics of contention', from revolution to democratization (McAdam *et al.* 2001; Tilly 2001). The tendency to embed social movement analysis in broader social science frameworks is certainly not new, even though it has taken different forms in North America, where the dialogue with organization theory has been most intense (Zald and McCarthy 1987), and in Europe, with the analysis of movements overlapping at times with the analysis of macrostructural change (Habermas 1981; Offe 1985), cognitive praxis (Eyerman and Jamison 1991), or identity dynamics in information society (Melucci 1996).

There is nothing wrong, and a lot to commend, in these orientations. They may act as an antidote to disciplinary parochialism; they may also facilitate the spread of important research findings beyond the professional subgroups who happen to have a direct empirical interest in certain specific phenomena. At the same time, however, as a direct consequence of the greater integration between social movement studies and other fields, the question arises 'What is peculiar to the contribution of social movement research—in this particular case, of network approaches to social movements?' Social movement researchers may have paid more attention than other scholars to certain themes: for example, the relationship between networks and individual participation has been more frequently explored by them than by students of political parties. But this is not in itself very revealing. The real question is whether there is a distinctive theoretical contribution.

On one level, this may look like an empty question: there are innumerable areas in which scholars conventionally identified as 'social movement researchers' have contributed to the understanding of broader social processes, from collective action dynamics (Oliver and Marwell 2001) to identity formation (Melucci 1996), from the mobilization of social resources (McCarthy and Zald 1977) to changes in forms of public action (Tilly 1978, 1995a–d). However, most of these contributions would still be entirely meaningful if their authors did not speak of 'movements' at all. The concept of social movement has always had uncertain status among American scholars, who have preferred terms like protest, collective action, and so on. In Europe, even people who emphasized the analytical nature of the concept of 'social movement' (e.g. Melucci 1995, 1996) suggested dropping it owing to its too strong association with industrial society, and only stuck to it for lack of better alternatives. In this chapter I take a different approach. I argue that focusing on the concept of social movement—in particular, treating movements as networks—enables us to identify a specific social dynamic, which differentiates social movements from cognate processes. This can both facilitate crossfertilization with other intellectual fields and emphasize the distinctiveness of social movement research.

DEFINING MOVEMENTS

Few would deny that social networks are an important component of social movements. But do we really need to go so far as to assign the concept of social network a central position in our theoretical and empirical work? A few years ago, a systematic comparison of definitions of 'social movements' by scholars from different intellectual traditions led me to identify in a view of movements as networks a potential terrain for convergence and paradigmatic integration in the field. More specifically, I defined social movements as networks 'of informal interactions, between a plurality of individuals, groups or associations, engaged in a political or cultural conflict, on the basis of a shared collective identity' (Diani 1992: 13).[1]

Approaching movements as networks enables us to capture their peculiarity vis-à-vis cognate forms of collective action and contentious politics better than current dominant paradigms. Social movements are distinctive neither because of their adoption of radical forms of action, nor because of their interest in new issues or their predilection for loose organizational forms (Diani 2000*b*). They are distinctive because they consist of formally independent actors who are embedded in specific local contexts (where 'local' is meant in either a territorial or a social sense), bear specific identities, values, and orientations, and pursue specific goals and objectives, but who are at the same time linked through various forms of concrete cooperation and/or mutual recognition in a bond which extends beyond any specific protest action, campaign, etc. We get closer to a social movement dynamic the more there is a coupling of informal networks, collective identity, and conflict; the more, in other words, the following conditions are simultaneously satisfied:

1. actors are engaged in a social conflict, that is, they promote initiatives meant to damage other social actors who are either denying them access to social resources (however defined) they feel entitled to, or trying to take away from them resources over which they currently exert control;
2. actors share a collective identity while maintaining their own as individual activists and/or members of specific organizations. They identify each other as part of a collective effort, which goes beyond specific initiatives, organizations, and events. It is mutual recognition that defines the boundaries of a movement, which are by consequence inherently unstable. Identity is built on the basis of interpretations or narratives which link together in a meaningful way events, actors, and initiatives which could also make perfect sense (but a different one) if looked at independently or embedded in other types of representation;
3. actors (individuals and/or organizations) exchange practical and symbolic resources through informal networks, that is, through coordination mechanisms, which are not subject to formal regulation and where the terms of the exchange and the distribution of duties and entitlements are entirely

dependent on the actors' agreement. Accordingly, the ever present attempts to shape strategic decisions by specific organizations are subject to unstructured and unpatterned negotiations.

Focusing on definitions of social movements does not aim at identifying a discrete set of empirical phenomena, even less at placing them in a specific cell of a broader typology; rather, it is a way to identify the basic traits of a distinct social process, which we can then use along with other models to analyse specific episodes of contention (see Table 13.1). Our task then becomes to find out to what extent we have, within any particular and concrete instance of contention, a social movement dynamic in progress, rather than other forms of collective action, and how the different dynamics interact. That is when the discriminant capacity of the concept is tested. To illustrate this point, let us look at the complex of events, organizations, activities, and like-minded individuals conventionally labelled as the 'environmental movement'.

First, the presence of conflict differentiates social movements from 'non-conflictual movements', that is, forms of collective action conducted by networks of actors who share solidarity and an interpretation linking specific acts in a longer time perspective, but who do not identify any specific social actor as an opponent. We might come across instances of sustained collective action on environmental problems that imply broader identities yet do not imply any conflict. A model of environmental action as a collective effort aiming entirely at the solution of practical cases of pollution through voluntary work, or the transformation of environmental consciousness through education, would match this profile. In that case, the identity would connect people, organizations, events, and initiatives in a meaningful, longer-term collective project, transcending the boundaries of any specific organization or campaign, but there would be no space for conflictual dynamics.

Second, the informal nature of the networks differentiates movements from 'organizations', that is, coordinated forms of interaction with some established membership criteria and some patterned mechanisms of internal regulation. We shall often come across instances in which environmental action is mainly conducted within the boundaries of specific organizations, which are the main source

TABLE 13.1. *Social movements and cognate collective dynamics*

	Informal networks	Collective identity	Conflict
Social movements	0	0	0
Non-conflictual movements	0	0	
Political organizations/sects		0	0
Coalitions	0		0

of participants' identities, whereas the loyalty to the 'movement' as a whole is far weaker, and so are opportunities for individuals to play any role unless their participation is mediated by specific organizations. In this case we would have not a 'social movement dynamic' in progress, but the mobilization of a set of specific organizations trying to acquire full ownership of an issue. In the most extreme case, we might have one single organization taking full control of the issue—as the Bolshevik party and the Nazi party to a large extent managed to do in their respective cases.

Third, the presence of an identity, which transcends the boundaries of any specific event, and also enables actors to connect different episodes of collective action, sets social movements apart from coalitions. Accordingly, we might find that the expression 'environmental movement' denotes little more than a set of largely independent events and activities, each reflecting a specific conflict, and each supported by a specific coalition, but with few links across events and coalitions. In a coalition dynamic, the absence of collective identity would prevent the establishment of connections between activities located at different points in time and space, and the local networks would not concatenate in broader systems of solidarities and mutual obligations.

Finally, we might also come across a 'social movement dynamic' proper. In that case, individuals and organizations, engaged in innumerable initiatives to protect the environment against its socially identifiable 'enemies', would share a broad identity and would be able to link their specific actions into a broader narrative and into a broader collective 'we', while renouncing their own peculiarity. Events which could otherwise be the result of ad hoc coalitions and expressions of NIMBY orientations would then acquire a new meaning and be perceived as part of a larger, and longer-term, collective effort.

In this perspective, the role of networks is radically different from that of facilitators of individual recruitment and participation, which has been traditionally assigned to them. Rather than preconditions and resources for (individual or group) action, networks become the analytical tool, which enables us to capture the dualistic nature of action. Looking at network configurations is an opportunity to address explicitly and empirically the issue of the duality between action and structure (Emirbayer and Goodwin 1994; Emirbayer and Mische 1998; Mische and Pattison 2000; Mohr 2000; Livesay 2002). Social ties discourage certain courses of action and facilitate others, which in turn affects how actors attribute meaning to their social linkages, thus (re)creating rules and arrangements perceived as relatively stable and 'structural'. Through cultural production and multiple involvements, people create webs of ties that enable them to further act collectively and shape their future behaviour. The origin of network ties becomes a major focus of investigation (McPherson *et al.* 2001; Kenis and Knoke 2002).

More specifically, networks and the attached systems of mutual obligation correspond to a form of social organization with more than passing commonalities with the network organizations explored by organizational theories: independence of the single components, horizontal integration, flexibility in goals and strategies, multiple levels of interaction with the possibility of communitarian elements (Podolny and Page 1998; Gulati and Gargiulo 1999; Pichierri 1999). Of course, there are also some obvious differences, as those who have strongly associated network organizations with instrumental and/or circumscribed goals (Pichierri 1999) would be quick to point out. However, while the relevance of the subcultural—eventually counter-cultural—dimension is once again variable, many profit-oriented network organizations also rely on identities and solidarities generated by the community (e.g. industrial districts in Italy: Trigilia 1986). Those versions of the network organization theory most influenced by neo-institutionalism (Powell 1990; Hall and Taylor 1996; Pierson 2000) are best equipped to capture the interplay between the instrumental dimension of exchanges and the flow of mutual recognition and obligations, which make this form of organization feasible.

The network perspective has at the same time some significant advantages over established theories, and the potential to engage in a fruitful dialogue with them. In relation to resource mobilization theory, viewing movements as networks allows us to get over the tendency to treat movements as organizations of a peculiar type, and therefore to address the issue of the relationship between movements, parties, and interest groups from a different perspective. Admittedly, the distinction between movements and social movement organizations (SMOs) is very clear in the programmatic formulations of the resource mobilization perspective (McCarthy and Zald 1977). Likewise, attention has been paid to inter-organizational relations among SMOs, with a special focus on the interplay of competition and cooperation in a specific movement industry. However, all in all it is safe to claim that resource mobilization theory mainly focuses on (social movement) organizations, rather than on the linkages between them, and the processes of meaning construction which may—or may not—render them part of a broader collective effort. But if movements are organizations, then inevitably misleading questions about whether specific organizations should be approached as movement organizations or interest groups arise, and dialogue across professional boundaries—as well as attempts to grasp the peculiarity of concrete processes—becomes difficult (Leech 2001). If we maintain our focus on single organizations, there is indeed no ground to claim that the Worldwide Fund for Nature is an SMO rather than a public interest group, or Earth First! a social movement rather than a radical grassroots organization. Identifying them as one or the other depends ultimately on the socially constructed professional identities of the researchers (on environmental organizations compare, e.g., Rucht 1989 and Jordan and Maloney 1997).

If, alternatively, we regard movements as non-hierarchical network forms of organization with boundaries defined by collective identity—that is, by actors' mutual recognition as members of the movement linked by a distinctive culture and solidarity—then the questions introduced earlier take on a different meaning. The issue will no longer be whether a specific organization is a SMO or an interest group, or whether a 'movement' has become an interest group, but how and if different actors, both individuals and organizations, with varying degrees of formal structure, relate to each other. We have social movement processes in motion, the more we observe sustained interactions between different political organizations, which go beyond a single-issue campaign to draw on, and reproduce, distinctive collective identities. If, on the contrary, the very same organizations act mainly on their own, and are the main focus for their activists' loyalties, to the detriment of broader movement identities, then we have political dynamics that are closest to the classic models of interest politics (Diani 2001). In these terms, 'social movement organization' is defined not in terms of attributes, but in terms of relations: SMOs are all those groups who identify themselves, and are identified by others, as part of the same movement, and exchange on that basis.

In relation to new social movements theory, scholars traditionally associated with this approach, such as Touraine or Melucci,[2] have contributed substantially (more through their analysis of identity dynamics than through that of identity in information society) to the understanding of key aspects of the social process I associate with social movements—namely, the creation and maintenance of a specific conflictual network. Melucci's analysis of the internal complexity of collective actors who are usually portrayed—and portray themselves—as homogeneous and coherent is of particular relevance here, as it provides us with the intellectual tools to identify the complex negotiations which take place between different actors in the emergence and reproduction of a movement identity. While this is a fundamental insight, Melucci's (1996: 113–17) strong association of network forms of organization with new movements—as opposed to the more bureaucratic forms of 'old' movements—is problematic. The main analytical gain from the network perspective is that the existence of a (new) movement is no longer tied to the existence of distinct (new) conflictual stakes, and no specific correspondence is expected between the two. A network form may be a useful analytical tool to apply to both 'old' and 'new' movements; likewise, conflicts on issues of knowledge control, and opposing technicians and experts to bureaucrats and technocrats, may not necessarily result in extensive network forms of organization but instead be carried on by formal organizations acting as experts' interest groups (e.g. Hoffman 1989).

In relation to political process theories, a network perspective can counteract their tendencies to identify movements with strings of protest events (Kriesi *et al.* 1995). There is of course widespread recognition of the problems attached to treating movements as aggregates of actors/events and ignoring identity dynamics and interactions within such aggregates (e.g. Tarrow 1998*b*: 57–8). Still, when it comes to research practice the tendency to treat movements as aggregates persists. A network view of movements places the attention more squarely on the connectivity between events, both in terms of meaning attribution and in terms of chains of actors (connected by events) and events (connected by actors). Accordingly, events falling within the same broad category may or may not turn out to be related to a specific movement, depending not only on the definitions of the conflict adopted by mobilized actors, but also on the continuity guaranteed by individual activists and organizations.

MAPPING MOVEMENT NETWORKS

It would be unfair to claim that attention to the interdependence between actions, identity, and networks is unique to the perspective presented in this chapter. Within this book, most chapters focus on the dynamic nature of networks, even though authors might not share the focus on the concept of social movement. Where this perspective is different, however, is in the centrality assigned to the idea of network as the basis for a theory of social movements.[3] In order to build such a theory, an important task is to define parameters to identify the structure of movement networks, and then elaborate appropriate theoretical models to explain certain network patterns and/or certain actors' incumbency of specific positions. To this purpose I refer to two important dimensions of networks, namely, the opposition between decentralized and hierarchical structures, and segmented and reticulated structures (Gerlach and Hine 1970; see also Philips 1991; Knoke 1990a: ch. 5).

The concept of network centralization allows us to differentiate between the informality of social movement networks and the frequently related, if misplaced, assumption of the absence of asymmetries and differences within those networks. An informal network may indeed range from being totally decentralized to totally centralized. Although the extent to which differences in centralization correspond to differences in influence and possibly power remains to be seen, organizations most central in movement networks have been found to play a greater role in external exchanges to powerful actors, which suggest something about their potential leadership (as Diani's and Ansell's chapters in this book illustrate). At the very minimum, differences in centrality testify to a tendency of flows of exchanges and communication to concentrate towards specific actors, and thus to affect how a movement operates and builds its identity.

The level of network segmentation reflects the extent to which communication between actors is prevented by some kind of barrier. In formal terms, we may characterize it as the average number of intermediate steps, necessary to reach any one node in the network from any other node.[4] In substantive terms, this concept reflects the distance that separates members of a network (in our case, of a movement) on a number of possible grounds. Criteria for segmentation may vary, depending on the ties we are looking at: it might be ideological segmentation, where the relational distance increases with the difference in ideological stances between actors; or issue distance, if the decisive factor is represented by differences in the levels of interest in specific issues.

By combining these two dimensions we obtain four types of network structure (see Figs 13.1–13.4). In the illustrations that follow, all actors will be assumed to recognize each other as parts of the same movement, and focus will be on real exchanges. However, one could apply the same logic to the analysis of mutual recognitions of identity. It is important to acknowledge the distinction between identity networks and concrete ones. While identity reflects in both '[agents'] mental models and in their patterns of interaction with others' (Carley 1999: 16; see also Howard 1994), networks of mutual recognition do not necessarily overlap with the networks which result from alliance-building, information exchanges, shared resources and multiple memberships. It is admittedly sensible to assume that the feelings of identity tend to be stronger among actors who collaborate on a regular basis than among those who relate occasionally, or hardly ever. However, one has also to recognize the difference between 'real' exchanges—which may not necessarily imply identity, as in instrumental, ad hoc coalitions—and actors' interpretation of their social space in terms of who is perceived as close/similar/part of the same collectivity, and who is not. 'Who identifies whom and is identified by whom as part of a movement' is an interesting question in itself (Melucci 1984, 1996), which may lead to the identification of several network forms, regardless of whether actors actually interact with each other.

Movement Cliques

A clique (better: a 1-clique) is a decentralized, reticulate network, where all nodes are adjacent to each other (Scott 1992: 117; see Fig. 13.1). This type of structure is conventionally associated with a redundancy of ties, which in turn suggests a pattern of linkages with a strong expressive dimension, and a high investment in the building and maintenance of the network. There is also a very high level of mutual engagement among nodes in the network, which results in high reticulation and null segmentation. The clique is also a decentralized network, in which there is no opportunity for any actor to control exchanges among network members. To be sustained over time, this pattern of relations requires a strong equalitarian culture. The number of ties that actors are engaged in also suggests that involvement in this specific network is likely to reduce their opportunities to engage in external relationships (obviously allowing for substantial differences in the resources controlled by specific actors, and thus in their network-building capacity). A clique configuration may result from strong ideological and/or cultural affinities between network members with a strong emotional involvement. It may also originate, however, from other more practical factors such as the strong interest in a specific issue or set of issues.

Social movements, which emerge in parallel with the development of a major protest cycle, and subcultural and counter-cultural movements in general, are the most likely to display a relational pattern, which at least for some time approximates this model. In the first case, the mounting of a fundamental challenge to established institutions might facilitate the spread of strong equalitarian and

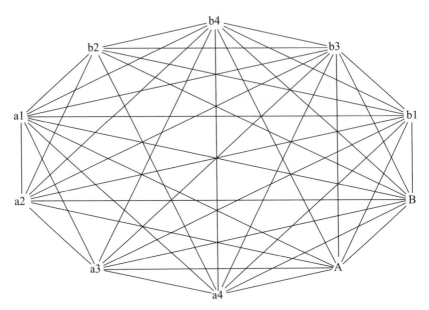

FIG. 13.1. *Clique structure*

participatory identities, which cross the boundaries of any specific organization and reject any principle of hierarchy, even informal (one example being the student movement of the late 1960s in Italy: Passerini 1988). In the second case, the distinctiveness of the cultural model adopted by the movement facilitates—and requires—horizontal patterns of interaction between movement actors. Accounts of movements with a strong identity like the gay and lesbian ones also suggest a similar profile (Taylor and Whittier 1992). It has to be said, however, that the very level of investment required to sustain this model reduces the chances to find examples of it in movement networks with a large population, while it may be more possible to find it within sections of them. For example, in his study of the Greek environmental movement Botetzagias (2000) found a strong clique consisting of the large majority of the most important environmental organizations in the country, but with very sparse ties involving other less prominent organizations.

Policephalous Movements

Figure 13.2 illustrates a centralized, segmented structure. By comparison to other structural patterns, this network is at least partially segmented, as the distance between some of the actors is relatively long. The presence of horizontal linkages between semi-peripheral actors suggests the persistence of efforts to engage

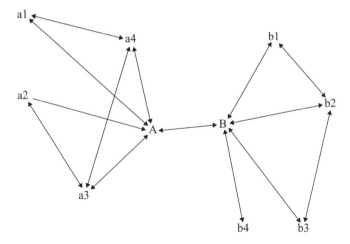

FIG. 13.2. *Policephalous structure*

actively in collective action without delegating important tasks to a few centrally positioned actors. Nonetheless, the network is also relatively centralized, as some actors (A and B) are involved in more links than the others and are therefore in the best position to control relational flows within the network. This may in turn result in greater influence for them.

An example of a policephalous structure comes from the Australian women's movement (Sawer and Groves 1994). The difference between the organizations created after the Second World War and those, which emerged during the second wave of women's mobilization in the 1970s was reflected in the structure of the movement network. It consisted of two components, which were both strongly connected internally, but had little ties between them. The two organizations at the core of those sectors (NCW-National Council of Women for the cluster grouping more established organizations, and WEL-Women's Electoral Lobby for the more recently developed sector) did not have direct ties to each other (Sawer and Groves 1994: 451). In this case, in contrast to the Milanese environmental movement analysed by Diani (Chapter 5 in this book), centrality and brokerage roles did not overlap. Another example of the tension between centralization and relatively dense peripheral cliques may be found in the transformation of the Italian movements in the early 1970s. While the student movement at its very origins was originally largely a network of independent or semi-independent local action committees, approximating clique structures of relations, it was gradually controlled by political organizations with a broader political scope and a more distinct ideological profile. Organizations like Lotta Continua or Avanguardia Operaia developed special linkages to cultural associations (e.g. Circoli Ottobre, related to Lotta Continua), student action groups at high school or university level, groups of radical trade unionists (e.g. CUB, related to Avanguardia Operaia), etc. (Lumley 1990). While the extent of formal association of these groups with the main new left organizations varied considerably, they also maintained a signifi-cant degree of interaction among themselves and with other movement organiza-tions in specific localities or on specific issues. This generated a policephalous structure, which displayed at the same time a certain amount of centralization, but considerable levels of density.

Centralized, Nonsegmented Networks (Wheel/star Structures)

A wheel-shaped network (Fig. 13.3) combines high centralization with low seg-mentation. There is one central position coordinating exchanges across the network and acting as a linking point between peripheral components that are not directly related to each other. Incumbents of that position are likely to exert con-siderable influence over the network in terms of the pooling and redistribution of resources. The lack of horizontal exchanges at the periphery, and the relatively low number of ties activated suggest a comparatively low level of investment in the building of the network as a whole. Network members are likely either to be involved in a considerable amount of exchanges with actors outside the movement boundaries, or to conduct most of their projects on their own.

   This is a network characterized by an instrumental pattern of linkages, with most actors investing the minimal resources in linkage-building. Ties to a central actor are sufficient to secure easy access to the rest of the network through a minimal number of intermediate steps. While peripheral positions are unlikely to exert any substantial influence over the network as a whole, the low level of investment in

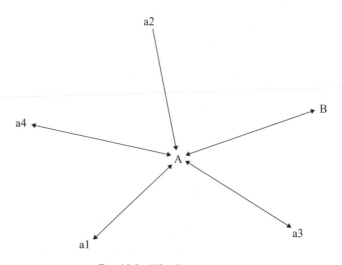

Fɪɢ. 13.3. *Wheel/star structure*

linkage-building suggests that this may not be among their incumbents' priorities. At the same time, the very existence of a coordinating node, which controls all exchanges, ensures a relatively low segmentation of the network: peripheral nodes may not feel overtly committed to network building, yet feel close enough to share a common partner to which network coordination is somehow delegated.

Examples of wheel structure include those movements, which combine a fairly high degree of inclusiveness with a low propensity to expand the scope of collective action beyond the actors' specific interests and the most obvious central political goals as articulated by the movement core actors at any given point in time. Environmental movements often match this profile. Italian environmentalism in the 1980s (Diani 1995, and this book) and British environmentalism in the previous decade (Lowe and Goyder 1983) presented a pattern of relationships where a group of core—and strongly interconnected—organizations acted as a bridge between a number of local actors, who acted mostly on an independent basis. The same actors had, however, frequent contacts and exchanges with actors who did not share in an environmental identity but were still prepared to collaborate on specific issues.[5] Another example comes from the women's movement in Canada in the late 1980s–early 1990s. Although 29 out of 33 major national organizations were connected to each other, the overall amount of exchanges was fairly low, and they were mostly filtered by one central organization, the Canadian National Action Committee—NAC (Philips 1991).

Segmented, Decentralized Networks

This model (Fig. 13.4) reflects a largely atomistic style of action within the network. It is indeed difficult even to think of a network in this case, as actors largely operate either on their own, or developing small collaborations on specific issues. They are either unable or unwilling to develop more extended and encompassing linkages. They focus on their specific and restricted areas of concern, and reject attempts by prospective leaders to coordinate their action into broader overarching projects.

This highly segmented and decentralized structure is unlikely to fit the concrete experience of any specific social movement. However, it is important to refer to it here as it captures the formal properties of a system of interaction, which reflects the absence of social movement dynamics. Interestingly, it can accommodate substantively very different types of collective action. On the one hand, the model fits a style of pluralistic politics, in which specific actors tend to maximize their own outcomes without paying any attention to the broader moral constraints/obligations such as those attached to large-scale collective identities. This is a situation in which movement identities are at their lowest vis-à-vis organizational identities, and in which loyalties go to the latter rather than the former. In such a model, specific organizations operate as (public/private) interest groups, community organizations, and even political parties in several political arenas. They may

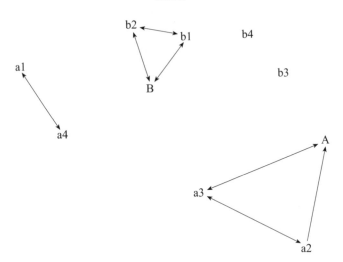

FIG. 13.4. *Segmented, decentralized network*

well get involved in multiple coalitions, but without developing long-term identifications to any of them. Greenpeace is a proper example: it may be involved in coalitions with other environmental organizations, however (a) it gives priority to the organization's identity over the movement's; (b) it denies relevance to the collaborative activities in which it is involved (at least in the UK: Rootes 2002; data about Italy—Diani and Forno 2002—suggest a more alliance-oriented attitude). On the other hand, this formal model captures the relationships—better, the lack of relationships—between actors which are distinctly radical in their challenges to political and/or cultural institutions, yet do so by emphasizing their organizational, rather than movement identities. For example, religious sects—or sectarian revolutionary parties—come to operate along these lines when they abstain from cooperation with similar actors following a combination of quest for ideological purity and attempts to discredit potential competitors for the same pool of constituents. Despite substantial differences in content, both examples reflect a weakening of the process that I refer to as 'social movements', in favour of processes that assign greater space to organizations as sources of agency and identity. Among our contributors, Osa most clearly identifies this model: while there were only a few ties between organizations in the 1960s, in the absence of sustained mobilizations and a proper movement dynamic, the number of connected organizations and the extent of their integration grew dramatically in the momentous years between 1976 and 1981.

A RESEARCH PROGRAMME IN SOCIAL MOVEMENT NETWORK ANALYSIS

How to translate these abstract models into a specific research agenda? My proposal rests on four key concepts: multilevel analysis, multiplexity of linkages, time, and homophily. Below, I illustrate how established social movement perspectives may contribute to its implementation.

Multilevel Analysis

For obvious practical reasons, most analysis of social movements focus either on individual participants, or on organizations, protest events, etc. It is very difficult to integrate all these different components into a unitary framework. Yet this is precisely what we have to do if we are to grasp the complex nature of sustained collective contention and recognize the multiplicity of ties, actors, and events which make up the empirical episodes we define 'social movements'. One possible way to achieve this goal is through an expansion of Simmel's intuition on the 'duality of persons and groups' (Breiger 1988; Simmel 1955; Diani 2000*b*): while persons are linked by their shared memberships of social groups, groups are likewise connected by the members they happen to share. The identity of persons is ultimately the result of the particular intersection of their group memberships, while the position of groups depends on the multiple memberships of their members.

This idea enables us to expand considerably on the assumption that networks only consist of direct ties between homogeneous actors, and to start to build a more complicated picture. While there is no space here to elaborate on the technical aspects of this approach, based on an elementary application of matrix algebra (Namboodiri 1984; Laumann and Knoke 1987; Breiger 1988; Diani 2002), it represents a powerful yet simple analytical tool which may allow for several distinct applications. So far, recognition of the duality of persons and groups has driven attempts to map, among others, interorganizational and interpersonal ties in movement milieus (Fernandez and McAdam 1988, 1989; McAdam and Fernandez 1990), ties between organizations in Italy (Diani 1995) or Poland (Osa, Chapter 4 in this book), or ties between different movement sectors (Carroll and Ratner 1996). It could be, however, conveniently expanded to include all the events, activities, and actors, which may be meaningful to analyse in order to capture the complexity of social movements.

For example, we could look at how individuals are linked by participation in the same protest events, by patronizing the same alternative cafés or bookshops, or at least sharing in the same cultural activities, or by being exposed to the same media. We might do the same, obviously with the proper adaptations, for organizations too, and chart their involvement in protest and/or cultural events. We would then be able to identify the multiple levels of relationship, which may exist between actors engaged in collective activities. For example, treating joint participation in protest events as an indicator of a link has made it possible to identify different network patterns linking environmental organizations, with varying centralization and segmentation, in different European countries (Rootes 2002).

Of particular interest are the applications of this logic to entities other than individuals or organizations. A more sophisticated example, which integrates individuals, events, and cultural narratives ('projects'), comes from Ann Mische's work on mobilizations in contemporary Brazil (1998, and Chapter 11 in this book; Mische and Pattison 2000). Along these lines, we could look at the role of persons and/or groups in establishing connections between events, by participating in them. For an organization, getting involved in different events implies at the very minimum the recognition of some compatibility and commonality between them; for an individual it is a reflection of how that person combines interest in different issues (even allowing for the gap between perceived interest in some issues, and actual involvement: Klandermans 1988). Likewise, we could look for a structure of connections between different subcultural activities—not to mention the even more complex case in which individuals or organizations establish connections between different categories of phenomena such as protest events and subcultural events (e.g. when the same individuals both attend specific demonstrations and are part of distinctive cultural milieus).

Single and Multiple Linkages

The approach proposed here allows recognizing the multiplicity of ties linking actors in a social movement network. How to treat those linkages is, however, an open question. One possibility would be treating them in an additive way, thus distinguishing between multiple, 'strong' ties from weaker ties, based on fewer types of connections. Alternatively, one could acknowledge the heterogeneity of network linkages when this is the case, and try to account for differences between specific network structures. For example, in the Milan environmental movement the network of interorganizational relations had a more centralized, wheel structure than the network based on multiple memberships and intragroup personal friendships, and illustrating those differences was useful to highlight the opposition between a largely instrumental model of interorganizational models and a distribution of multiple memberships which was close to a clique structure and pointed at widespread inclusiveness in the definition of the identity of the movement (Diani 1995).

As usual, the choice between the two approaches is largely driven by the specific theoretical perspective. If we are mainly interested in identifying the most solid components of a movement, then looking at multiplexity in additive terms might be advisable (commitment to collective action is often supported by strong ties: della Porta 1988; Krackhardt 1992). If on the other hand we are interested in the extent to which organizations and/or individuals mobilizing on certain issues find at least some ground for exchange, then acknowledging differences in network structures might be preferable. Of course, the model can be further complicated by including in the map mutual recognition between actors as part of the same movement, to measure to what extent specific links also carry with them broader solidarities and identities (two organizations may cooperate in alliance and share some core personnel, yet still not regard themselves as part of any broader social movement: that is after all how many coalition dynamics operate).

Networks and Time

This framework also allows us to organize data with a view to diachronic analysis, the centrality of which is well documented in our book by chapters by Osa, Tilly and Wood, and Oliver and Myers. If individuals and organizations operate as links between events, then it is also possible to explore the potential continuities in issues and activities over time. Of course, one has to take into account changes in organizational identities, or in basic orientations in movement milieus, or in dominant political cultures. These and other changes prevent us from assuming exactly the same meaning for events at different points in time, even though the organizations and/or individuals involved happen to be the same. Nonetheless, this logic of analysis is worthy of attention, for its potential to map flows of people and organizations across events at different points in time, and the connections between events that these establish.

At the same time it is important to remember that in themselves, the models presented in the previous section do not imply any necessary trend. In particular, I do not suggest any reframing of the 'from movement to institution' dynamic along relational lines (e.g. in terms of 'from clique to wheel ...'). If such a reading might fit the evolution of the radical movement sector in Italy (for a formulation of this hypothesis see Diani 1992*b*), it does not universally apply. For example, in his analysis of the evolution of environmental movement networks in Spain, based on data from press reports of environmental protests, Jimenez (2002) illustrates a transformation from a wheel to a policephalous structure between 1988 and 1997, as the movement specific identity strengthened, and the aggregate of local environmental initiatives led eventually to a broader political project—if one largely conducted along conventional lines. What these models offer, then, are simply tools to try and make sense of specific network configurations, and of the specific concatenations between them.

Structural Homophily

The perspective outlined here does not displace existing paradigms of social movement analysis but rather uses them for different purposes. They may contribute to the analysis of movement networks particularly at the level of what social network scholars label 'homophily' processes (McPherson *et al.* 2001): that is to say, the identification of the actors' attributes which may facilitate the establishment of linkages between them. While the crucial element in social life may not be attributes but relations, sharing certain traits nonetheless encourages or constrains network building (e.g. Blau and Schwartz 1984). The question then becomes what traits are more salient at any point in time, and under what conditions different attributes may or may not play a major role. On this ground each of the current paradigms can offer important insights. Let us illustrate some of them with reference to the two criteria I have used to characterize different network structures, centralization, and segmentation.

Resource mobilization theories draw our attention to how the distribution of organizational resources may affect the role played by different actors in a network, in particular, whether more central actors owe their position to a greater control of resources. Although both Diani's and Ansell's chapters largely support this line of argument, this need not necessarily be the case as radical movements may well develop around groups strong on charismatic leadership but weak on organizational resources. A relational version of this approach could stress the importance of existing social ties (or social capital) between groups as predictors of network centrality (as again illustrated by Diani's chapter here). It is also important to look at competition dynamics among movement organizations as a potential source of fragmentation within networks (Zald and McCarthy 1980; Staggemborg 1986). Future explorations along these lines should be conducted in more intense dialogue with parallel developments in organization theory (Podolny and Page 1998; Gulati and Gargiulo 1999; Kenis and Knoke 2002).

Macro-sociological analyses of social movements may also offer a significant contribution to the network perspective. In particular, theories of new social movements may help us specify the different mobilization issues that movements are campaigning on, and to relate them to network properties. For example, Diani (1995) found that organizations with a different level of interest in urban ecology issues also differed in their centrality within the Milanese environmental network, with conservation groups being overall more peripheral. Focusing on the properties of individuals, theories of 'new politics' (Dalton 1996) may also provide useful insights, for example, by suggesting that certain positions in movement networks might be more frequently occupied by groups with a distinct class profile (whether new or old middle class, or working class). Analogous distinctions might also usefully account for fragmentation within a sector of organizations broadly dealing with very similar issues, for example, for the difficult collaboration between middle class environmentalists and 'environmental justice' campaigners in specific localities (Lichterman 1995a, 1996). Differences in the background of movement activists have also been found to be a predictor of movement fragmentation: in 1980s Milan, environmental groups with a high share of activists with a past history in the radical movements of the 1970s shared a similar structural position in the network, and so did groups with no personal connections to that political phase (Diani 1995: ch. 5).

As Mische's chapter here most powerfully argues, differences in framing and discursive strategies may also illuminate the structure of a given pattern of ties. What are the main frames held by actors playing a central role in a movement network? To what extent is the centrality of specific actors due to their mastery of framing skills, or to their being identified within a specific frame, which happens to be dominant at a given point in time? And do these frames coincide with, or differ from, those adopted by actors who operate as brokers, that is, as bridges between different milieux of collective action? As Osa's chapter suggests, networks of oppositional actors, especially at times when opportunities for mass protest are limited, may well be fragmented along lines which largely overlap with differences in fundamental ways of framing conflicts and their stakes.

Finally, the contribution of political process theorists may take two different forms. It may highlight the importance of factors which shape the structure of traditional divisions and cleavages, for example, a salient left–right cleavage is likely to influence relational patterns even in a movement which aspires to cut across it.[6] However, political process approaches may also highlight under which conditions certain differences may prove more or less effective at shaping alliances and segmentation. In particular, movements operating in a close political environment may be expected—once again all the rest being equal—to rely more on ideological incentives than movements who have a reasonable chance of being influential through inclusion in the political process. Emphasis on ideology as a mobilizing weapon and on collective identities will be likely to affect the solidity of network forms based on mutual recognition. On the one hand, it will make it difficult to reproduce the strong collective commitment necessary to support dense structures like the clique: organizational identities will tend to prevail as organizations compete to get their ideological standpoints accepted as the movement's orthodoxy. On the other hand, the growing centrality of ideological discourse will pose similar problems to structures, which also rely on mutual recognition, but with a lower degree of emotional investment like the wheel. In one case, the network will collapse because of the struggle for ideological purity, in the other case, because of latent differences in orientations between its components becoming more salient in the new context. Both transformations might lead to segmented or policephalous structures.

CONCLUSIONS

The view of movements outlined in this chapter challenges three popular, if often implicit assumptions (or, borrowing from Tilly (1984), 'pernicious postulates') of social movement research:

(1) that the study of social movements is tantamount to the study of the organizations active within them;
(2) that network forms of organization are distinctive of (new) social movements focusing on issues of identity rather than political change; and
(3) that social movements tend to coincide with the public challenges conducted against authorities and opponents on specific sets of issues.

While few would openly subscribe to such assumptions, in practical terms research is frequently inspired by them, witness the disentangling between studies of identity processes and that of organizational network dynamics, or of the latter and protest event investigations. The goal of the research programme sketched here is to facilitate the development of an integrated approach, which enables to translate awareness of the link between networks, actions, and identities in specific research activities. Its basic points are the following:

(1) recognition of the duality of network processes as a precondition to appropriate multilevel investigations;
(2) attention to the network processes connecting events, activities, and ideas, and not only to those linking individuals or organizations;
(3) recognition of the multiplicity of networks potentially linking different actors or events;
(4) attention to the time dimension in network processes;
(5) recognition of the value of current approaches to social movements in the investigation of homophily processes.

Hopefully, taking each of these elements seriously will also provide the basis for a comparative analysis of social movement networks, to complement what has been achieved so far in comparative research focusing on cycles of protest and contention (Kriesi *et al.* 1995; della Porta 1995; Rootes 2002), individual orientations and activities (Dalton 1996; Norris 2002), organizations (van der Heijden *et al.* 1992; Kriesi 1996). Admittedly, the perspective outlined in this chapter represents a peculiar, and to some extent radical way to reorganize the insights and inputs coming from the different chapters of this book. It should not be received as an accurate reflection of a collectively agreed conclusion—to the contrary, many contributors to this book would probably take issue with this line of argument. But perhaps this is not so surprising for a book devoted to social movements: after all, it is not so rare for political or intellectual innovation to originate out of maverick and over-ambitious attempts to impose some unity and coherence where there was little. This book might not be that different.

NOTES

1. This approach was influenced by Melucci's argument (for his final statement, see Melucci 1996) in favour of an analytical view of social movements as a specific type of collective action. My specific definition was mainly influenced by Tilly's (1978) concept of *catnet*, Pizzorno's (1996) view of identity, and Melucci's (1996) concept of submerged networks.
2. However, such association is not always consensual: Melucci in particular recurrently expressed his unease with the 'new social movements' label (1996).
3. By 'theory of social movements' I mean a set of propositions which explicitly address the analytical peculiarity of the concept of social movement vis-à-vis cognate concepts, and treat the concept as the building blocks of a distinctive theoretical argument.

One could also take the argument one step further and claim (as I have done elsewhere: Diani 2000*a*) that for all the richness of empirical results, the methodological break-throughs, and the increasing conceptual sophistication, we still lack a social movements theory proper. What we have nowadays are theories which, in contrast, treat 'movement' as a largely denotational term to identify phenomena which could be—and indeed frequently are—equally referred to with cognate concepts such as 'protest activity,' 'coalition,' 'sect', 'interest group', etc. (Diani 1992*a,b*). But this would be going too far in the present context.

4. Reachability, in network analysis terms (Wasserman and Faust 1994: 107).
5. In Milan in the mid-1980s, ties to nonenvironmental actors were about half of those to environmental actors (Diani 1995: 134–5).
6. I illustrate this dynamic in reference to the Italian environmental movement of the 1970s, where the persistent strength of left–right divisions played against the development of systematic alliances between political ecologists and conservationists (Diani 1995).

References

Abbott, A. and Hrycak, A. (1990). 'Measuring resemblance in sequence data: An optimal matching analysis of musicians' careers', *American Journal of Sociology*, **96**: 144–85.

Adorno, T. W., Frenkel-Brunswick, E., Levinson, D. J., and Sanford, R. N. (1950). *The Authoritarian Personality*. New York: Harper.

Ajzen, I. and Fishbein, M. (1980). *Understanding Attitudes and Predicting Social Behavior*. Englewood Cliffs: Prentice Hall.

Akerlof, G. A. (1984). *An Economic Theorist's Book of Tales: Essays that Entertain the Consequences of New Assumptions in Economic Theory*. New York: Cambridge University Press.

Alexander, J. (1988). *Action and Its Environments*. New York: Columbia University Press.

—— and Smith, P. (1993). 'The discourse of American civil society: A new proposal for cultural studies', *Theory and Society*, **22**: 151–207.

—— Giesen, B., Munch, R., and Smelser, N. J. eds. (1987). *The Macro–Micro Link*. Berkeley/Los Angeles: University of California Press.

Alwin, D. F. and Krosnick, J. A. (1991). 'The reliability of survey attitude measurement. The influence of question and respondent attributes', *Sociological Methods and Research*, **20**: 139–81.

Aminzade, R. A. (1981). *Class, Politics, and Early Industrial Capitalism: A Study of Mid-Nineteenth-Century Toulouse*. Albany, NY: State University of New York Press.

Andrews, M. (1991). *Lifetimes of Commitment*. Cambridge: Cambridge University Press.

Anheier, H. K. (2001*a*). 'Movement entrepreneurs: Single members and the German Nazi Party, 1925–30', London School of Economics, unpublished manuscript.

——(2001*b*). 'Sociology of voluntary associations,' in N. J. Smelser, P. B. Baltes, and D. L. Sills (eds.), *International Encyclopedia of the Social and Behavioral Sciences*. Oxford: Elsevier.

—— and Ohlemacher, T. (1996). 'Aktivisten, netzwerke und bewegungserfolg: Die 'Einzelmitglieder' der NSDAP 1925–30', *Kölner Zeitschrift für Soziologie und Sozial-psychologie*, **48**: 677–703.

—— and Neidhardt, F. (1998). 'The NSDAP in Munich: Membership profile and development 1925–30', *American Behavioral Scientist*, **41**: 1219–36.

—— Gerhards, J., and Romo, F. P. (1995). 'Forms of social capital and social structure in cultural fields: Examining Bourdieu's social topography', *American Journal of Sociology*, **100**: 859–903.

—— Neidhardt, F., and Vortkamp, W. (1998). 'The ups and downs of the Nazi movement: Activity cycles of the Munich NSDAP, 1925–30', *American Behavioral Scientist*, **41**: 1262–81.

Ansell, C. K. (1997). 'Symbolic networks: The realignment of the French working class, 1887–94', *American Journal of Sociology*, **103**: 359–90.

——(2001). *Schism and Solidarity in Social Movements*. Cambridge: Cambridge University Press.

Arato, A. (2000). *Civil Society, Constitution, and Legitimacy*. Boulder, CO: Rowman and Littlefield Publ., Inc.

Archer, J. E. (2000). *Social Unrest and Popular Protest in England, 1780–1840*. Cambridge: Cambridge University Press.

Arendt, H. (1951). *The Origins of Totalitarianism*. New York: Harcourt Brace.

Ascherson, N. (1982). *The Polish August: The Self-Limiting Revolution*. New York: The Viking Press.

Axelrod, R. (1984). *The Evolution of Cooperation*. New York: Basic Books.

Babb, S. (1996). ' "A true American system of finance": Frame resonance in the U.S. labor movement, 1866–86', *American Sociological Review*, **61**: 1033–52.

Baddeley, A. (1979). 'The limitations of human memory: Implications for the design of retrospective surveys,' in L. Moss and H. Goldstein (eds.), *The Recall Methods in Social Surveys*. London: University of London Institute of Education.

Balser, D. B. (1997). 'The impact of environmental factors on factionalism and schism in social movement organizations', *Social Forces*, **76**: 199–228.

Barber, B. (1984). *Strong Democracy: Participatory Politics for a New Age*. Berkeley: University of California Press.

Barkan, S. E., Cohn, S. F., and Whitbaker, W. H. (1995). 'Beyond recruitment: Predictors of differential participation in a national antihunger organization', *Sociological Forum*, **10**: 113–33.

Barker, C., Johnson, A., and Lavalette, M. eds. (2001). *Leadership in Social Movements*. Manchester: Manchester University Press.

Barkey, K. and van Rossem, R. (1997). 'Networks of contention: Villages and regional structure in the seventeenth-century Ottoman Empire', *American Journal of Sociology*, **102**: 1345–82.

Bearman, P. (1993). *Relations into Rhetorics: Local Elite Social Structure in Norfolk, England, 1540–1640*. New Brunswick, NJ: Rutgers University Press.

——and Everett, K. D. (1993). 'The structure of social protest 1961–83', *Social Networks*, **15**: 171–200.

——and Stovel, K. (2000). 'Becoming a Nazi: A model for narrative networks', *Poetics*, **27**: 69–90.

Becker, G. S. (1976). *The Economic Approach to Human Behavior*. Chicago: University of Chicago Press.

Bendix, R. (1952). 'Social stratification and political power', *American Political Science Review*, **6**: 357–72.

Bendor, J. and Swistak, P. (1997). 'The evolutionary stability of cooperation', *The American Political Science Review*, **91**: 290–307.

Benford, R. (1997). 'An insider's critique of the social movement framing perspective', *Sociological Inquiry*, **67**: 409–30.

Bernhard, M. (1993). *The Origins of Democratization in Poland*. New York: Columbia University Press.

Bernhard, M. (1996). 'Civil society after the first transition: Dilemmas of post-communist democratization in Poland and beyond', *Communist and Post-Communist Studies*, **29**: 309–30.

Berry, J. (1990). 'Imposed etics, emics, and drived etics: The conceptual and operational status in cross-cultural psychology,' in T. Headland, K. Pike, and M. Harris (eds.), *Emics and Etics: The Insider/Outsider Debate*. Newbury Park: Sage.

Bethel, N. (1969). *Gomulka: His Poland and his Communism*. London: Longmans, Green and Co. Ltd.

Blau, P. M. (1982). 'Structural sociology and network analysis. An overview,' in P. Marsden and L. Nan (eds.), *Social Structure and Network Analysis*. Beverly Hills/London: Sage.

——and Schwartz, M. (1984). *Crosscutting Social Circles*. Orlando, FL: Academic Press.

Blokland, T. (2001). 'Bricks, mortar, memories: Neighbourhood and networks in collective acts of remembering', *International Journal of Urban and Regional Research*, **25**: 268–83.

Boissevain, J. (1974). *Friends of Friends*. Oxford: Blackwell.

Bolton, C. D. (1972). 'Alienation and action: A study of peace group members', *American Journal of Sociology*, **78**: 537–61.

Bonacich, P. (1972). 'Factoring and weighting approaches to status scores and clique identification', *Journal of Mathematical Sociology*, **2**: 13–120.

——(1987). 'Power and centrality: A family of measures', *American Journal of Sociology*, **92**: 1170–82.

Bonchek, M. (1995). 'Grassroots in cyberspace: Recruiting members on the internet', paper for the Annual Meeting of the Midwest Political Science Association. Chicago.

Boorman, S. A. and White, H. C. (1976). 'Social structure from multiple networks: II. Role structures', *American Journal of Sociology*, **81**: 1384–446.

Booth, A. and Babchuk, N. (1969). 'Personal influence networks and voluntary association affiliation', *Sociological Inquiry*, **39**: 179–88.

Borgatti, S. and Everett, M. G. (1992). 'Notions of position in social network analysis', *Sociological Methodology*, **22**: 1–35.

————and Freeman, L. (1992). *UCINET IV Reference Manual*. Columbia, SC: Analytic Technologies.

——————(1998). *UCINET V Reference Manual*. Columbia, SC: Analytic Technologies.

Botetzagias, I. (2000). 'Patterns of networking and interaction for Greek ENGOs', paper for the ECPR Joint Sessions, Copenhagen, April.

Bourdieu, P. (1977). *Outline of a Theory of Practice*. Cambridge/New York: Cambridge University Press.

Brass, D. J. and Burkhardt, M. (1993). 'Potential power and power use', *Academy of Management Journal*, **36**: 441–70.

Breiger, R. L. (1974). 'The duality of persons and groups', *Social Forces*, **53**: 181–90.

——(1988). 'The duality of persons and groups', in B. Wellman and S. D. Berkowitz (eds.), *Social Structures: A Network Approach*. Cambridge: Cambridge University Press.

——(1990). 'Social control and social networks: A model from Georg Simmel', in C. Calhoun, M. W. Meyer, and R. W. Scott (eds.), *Structures of Power and Constraint*. New York: Cambridge University Press.

——(2000). 'A tool kit for practice theory', *Poetics*, **27**: 91–115.

——Boorman, S. A., and Arabie, P. (1976). 'An algorithm for clustering relational data with application to social network analysis and comparison with multidimensional scaling', *Journal of Mathematical Psychology*, **12**: 328–83.

Briet, M., Klandermans, B., and Kroon, F. (1987). 'How women become involved in the women's movement of the Netherlands', in M. F. Katzenstein and C. Mueller (eds.), *The Women's Movements of the United States and Western Europe: Consciousness, Political Opportunities, and Public Policy*. Philadelphia: Temple University Press.

Brint, S. (1992). 'Hidden meanings: Cultural content and context in Harrison White's structural sociology', *Sociological Theory*, **10**: 194–208.

Broadbent, J. (1986). 'The ties that bind: Social fabric and the mobilization of environmental movements in Japan', *International Journal of Mass Emergencies and Disasters*, **4**: 227–53.

——(1989). 'Environmental politics in Japan: An integrated structural analysis', *Sociological Forum*, **4**: 179–202.

——(1998). *Environmental Politics in Japan: Networks of Power and Protest*. Cambridge: Cambridge University Press.

Browder, G. (1972). 'Problems and potentials of the Berlin document center', *Central European History*, **5**: 362–80.

Brown, H. M. (1989). 'Organizing activity in the women's movement', in B. Klandermans (ed.), *Organizing for Change*. Greenwich, Conn.: JAI Press.

Brustein, W. (1996). *The Logic of Evil*. New Haven: Yale University Press.

Bryman, A. (2000). *Quantity and Quality in Social Research*. London: Routledge.

Brzezinski, Z. (1967). *The Soviet Bloc: Unity and Conflict*, rev. edn. Cambridge, MA: Harvard University Press.

Buechler, S. (1997). 'New social movement theories', in S. Buechler and F. K. Cylke (eds.), *Social Movements: Perspectives and Issues*. Mountain View, CA: Mayfield Publishing Co.

Burnham, W. D. (1972). 'Political immunization and political confessionalism. The United States and Weimar Germany', *Journal of Interdiscplinary History*, **3**: 1–30.

Burt, R. (1992). *Structural Holes: The Social Structure of Competition*. Cambridge: Harvard University Press.

Calhoun, C. (1989). 'Protest in Beijing: The conditions and importance of the Chinese student movement of 1989', *Partisan Review*, **56**: 563–80.

——(1998). 'Community without propinquity revisited: Communication technology and the transformation of the urban public sphere', *Sociological Inquiry*, **68**: 373–97.

Camic, C. (1980). 'Charisma: Its varieties, preconditions, and consequences', *Sociological Inquiry*, **50**: 5–23.

Cancian, F. M. and Ross, B. L. (1981). 'Mass media and the women's movement: 1900–77', *Journal of Applied Behavioral Science*, **17**: 9–26.

Carley, K. (1992). 'Extracting, representing and analyzing mental models', *Social Forces*, **70**: 601–36.

——(1993). 'Coding choices for textual analysis: A comparison of content analysis and map analysis', *Sociological Methodology*, **23**: 75–126.

——(1999). 'On the evolution of social and organizational networks', in S. Andrews and D. Knoke (eds.), *Networks in and Around Organizations. Research in the Sociology of Organizations*, Vol. 16. Stamford, CT: JAI Press.

Carroll, W. K. and Ratner, R. S. (1996). 'Master framing and cross-movement networking in contemporary social movements', *Sociological Quarterly*, **37**: 601–25.

Cattacin, S. and Passy, F. (1993). 'Der niedergang von bewegungsorgansiationen. Zur analyse von organisatorischen laufbahnen', *Kölner Zeitschrift für Soziologie und Sozialpsychologie*, **25**: 419–38.

Charlesworth, A. (1979). *Social Protest in a Rural Society*. Cambridge: Institute of British Geographers.

Chong, D. (1991). *Collective Action and the Civil Rights Movement*. Chicago: University of Chicago Press.

Chwe, M. S. Y. (1999). 'Structure and strategy in collective action', *American Journal of Sociology*, **105**: 128–56.

Coen van Rij, J. (1994). *To Join or Not to Join. An Event-history Analysis of Trade-Union Membership in the Netherlands*. Ph.D. Thesis. University of Amsterdam.

Cohen, I. J. (1989). *Structuration Theory: Anthony Giddens and the Constitution of Social Life*. New York: St. Martin's Press.

Coleman, J. S. (1990). *Foundations of Social Theory*. Cambridge, MA: Belknap.

Cook, K. S. and Whitmeyer, J. M. (1992). 'Two approaches *to* social structure: Exchange theory and network analysis', *Annual Review of Sociology*, **18**: 109–27.

—— Emerson, R., Gillmore, M., and Yamagishi, T. (1983). 'The distribution of power in exchange networks', *American Journal of Sociology*, **89**: 275–305.

Coser, L. (1974). *The Functions of Social Conflict*. Glencoe: Free Press.

Curtis, R. L. and Zurcher, L. A. Jr. (1973). 'Stable resources of protest movements: The multi-organizational field', *Social Forces*, **52**: 53–61.

Dahl, R. A. (1961). *Who Governs: Democracy and Power in an American City*. New Haven, CT: Yale University Press.

—— (1967). *Pluralist Democracy in the United States*. Chicago: Rand McNally.

Dale, P. N. (1986). *The Myth of Japanese Uniqueness*. New York: St. Martin's Press.

Dalton, R. (1994). *The Green Rainbow*. New Haven: Yale University Press.

—— (1996). *Citizen Politics in Western Democracies*. Chatham, NJ: Chatham House.

—— and Kuechler, M. eds. (1990). *Challenging the Political Order: New Social and Political Movements in Western Democracies*. Cambridge: Polity Press.

Davies, N. (1982). *God's Playground: A History of Poland*. New York: Columbia University Press.

De Boek, P. and Rosenberg, S. (1988). 'Hierarchical classes: model and data analysis', *Psychometrica*, **53**: 361–81.

de Tocqueville, A. (2000). *Democracy in America*, trans. and ed. by H. C. Mansfield and D. Winthrop. Chicago: University of Chicago Press.

della Porta, D. (1988). 'Recruitment processes in clandestine political organizations: Italian left-wing terrorism', in B. Klandermans, H. Kriesi, and S. Tarrow (eds.), *From Structure to Action*. Greenwich: JAI Press.

—— (1992) ed. *Social Movements and Violence*. Greenwich, CT: JAI Press.

—— (1995). *Social Movements, Political Violence, and the State*. Cambridge: Cambridge University Press.

—— and Diani, M. (1999). *Social Movements*. Oxford/Cambridge, MA: Blackwell.

Denzin, N. K. (1989). *Interpretive Biography*. London: Sage.

Deuterlein, E. ed. (1982). *Der Aufstieg der NSDAP in Augenzeugenberichten*. München: Deutscher Taschenbuchverlag.

Diani, M. (1992*a*). 'The concept of social movement', *Sociological Review*, **40**: 1–25.

—— (1992*b*). 'Analysing social movement networks', in M. Diani and R. Eyerman (eds.), *Studying Collective Action*. Newbury Park/London: Sage.

—— (1995). *Green Networks. A Structural Analysis of the Italian Environmental Movement*. Edinburgh: Edinburgh University Press.

—— (1996). 'Linking mobilization frames and political opportunity structures: Insights from regional populism in Italy', *American Sociological Review*, **61**(6): 1053–69.

—— (1997). 'Social movements and social capital', *Mobilization*, **2**: 129–47.

—— (2000*a*). 'The relational deficit of ideologically structured action: Comments on Mayer Zald', *Mobilization*, **5**: 17–24.

—— (2000*b*). 'Simmel to Rokkan and beyond: Elements for a network theory of (new) social movements', *European Journal of Social Theory*, **3**: 387–406.

—— (2000*c*). 'Social movement networks virtual and real', *Information, Communication and Society*, **3**: 386–401.

—— (2001). 'Social movement organizations vs. interest groups: A relational view', paper presented at the ECPR First General Conference, Canterbury, 6–8 September.

—— (2002). 'Network analysis', in B. Klandermans and S. Staggenborg (eds.), *Methods in Social Movement Research*. Minneapolis: University of Minnesota Press.

—— (forthcoming). 'Networks and participation', in H. Kriesi, D. Snow, and S. Soule (eds.), *The Blackwell Companion to Social Movements*. Oxford: Blackwell.

—— and Donati, P. R. (1984). 'L'oscuro oggetto del desiderio: Leadership e potere nelle aree del movimento', in A. Melucci (ed.), *Altri Codici*. Bologna: il Mulino.

—— and Lodi, G. (1988). 'Three in one: Currents in the Milan ecology movement', in B. Klandermans, H. Kriesi, and S. Tarrow (eds.), *From Structure to Action*. Greenwich, Conn.: JAI Press.

—— and Forno, F. (2002). 'The evolution of environmental protest in Italy 1988–97', in C. Rootes (ed.), *Environmental Protest in Western Europe*. Oxford: Oxford University Press.

DiMaggio, P. J. and Powell, W. W. (1991). 'Introduction', in W. W. Powell and P. J. DiMaggio (eds.), *The New Institutionalism in Organizational Analysis*. Chicago, IL: University of Chicago Press.

Donati, P. R. (1996). 'Building a unified movement: Resource mobilization, media work, and organizational transformation in the Italian environmentalist movement', in L. Kriesberg (ed.), *Research in Social Movements, Conflict and Change*, Vol. 19. Greenwich, Conn.: JAI Press.

Downs, A. (1972). 'Up and down with ecology—the issue attention cycle', *The Public Interest*, **28**: 38–50.

Downton, J. V. (1973). *Rebel Leadership*. New York: Free Press.

Dryzek, J. S. (1996). 'Political inclusion and the dynamics of democratization', *American Political Science Review*, **90**: 475–87.

Dunlap, R. and Mertig, A. (1992). 'The evolution of the U.S. environmental movement from 1970 to 1990: An overview', in R. Dunlap and A. Mertig (eds.), *American Environmentalism*. Philadelphia: Taylor and Francis.

Ebers, M. (1999). 'The dynamics of inter-organizational relationships', in S. Andrews and D. Knoke (eds.), *Networks in and Around Organizations. Research in the Sociology of Organizations*, Vol. 16. Stamford, CT: JAI Press.

Edwards, B., Foley, M. W., and Diani, M. eds. (2001). *Beyond Tocqueville: Social Capital, Civil Society, and Political Process in Comparative Perspective*. Hanover: University Press of New England.

Eisenstadt, S. N. (1996). *Japanese Civilization a Comparative View*. Chicago, Ill.: The University of Chicago Press.

Eliasoph, N. (1996). 'Making a fragile public: A talk-centered study of citizenship and power', *Sociological Theory*, **14**: 262–89.

—— (1998). *Avoiding Politics: How Americans Produce Apathy in Everyday Life*. Cambridge: Cambridge University Press.

Ellingson, S. (1995). 'Understanding the dialectic of discourse and collective action: Public debate and rioting in Antebellum Cincinnati', *American Journal of Sociology*, **101**: 100–44.

Elster, J. (1989). *Nuts and Bolts for the Social Sciences*. Cambridge: Cambridge University Press.

——(1998). 'A plea for mechanisms', in P. Hedstrom and R. Swedberg (eds.), *Social Mechanisms: An Analytical Approach to Social Theory*. Cambridge UK: Cambridge University Press.

Emirbayer, M. (1997). 'A manifesto for a relational sociology', *American Journal of Sociology*, **103**: 281–317.

——and Goodwin, J. (1994). 'Network analysis, culture, and the problem of agency', *American Journal of Sociology*, **99**: 1411–54.

——and Mische, A. (1998). 'What is agency?', *American Journal of Sociology*, **103**: 962–1023.

——and Sheller, M. (1999). 'Publics in history', *Theory and Society*, **28**: 145–97.

Erickson, B. (1982). 'Networks, ideologies, and belief systems', in P. Marsden and L. Nan (eds.), *Social Structure and Network Analysis*. Beverly Hills/London: Sage.

——(1988). 'The relational basis of attitudes', in B. Wellman and S. D. Berkowitz (eds.), *Social Structure: A Network Approach*. Cambridge: Cambridge University Press.

——(1996). 'Culture, class, and connections', *American Journal of Sociology*, **102**: 217–51.

Evans, S. (1980). *Personal Politics: The Roots of Women's Liberation in the Civil Rights Movement and the New Left*. New York: Vintage Books.

Eyerman, R. and Jamieson, A. (1991). *Social Movements: A Cognitive Approach*. University Park: The Pennsylvania State University Press.

Falter, J. (1991). *Hitlers Wähler*. München: H.C. Beck.

Fangen, K. (1999). 'On the margins of life: Life stories of radical nationalists', *Acta Sociologica*, **42**: 357–73.

Fantasia, R. (1988). *Cultures of Solidarity. Consciousness, Action, and Contemporary American Workers*. Berkeley CA/London: University of California Press.

Farro, A. (1991). *La Lente Verde*. Milan: Angeli.

Fernandez, R. (1991). 'Structural bases of leadership in intraorganizational networks', *Social Psychology Quarterly*, **54**: 36–53.

——and McAdam, D. (1988). 'Social networks and social movements: Multiorganizational fields and recruitment to Mississippi freedom summer', *Sociological Forum*, **3**: 357–82.

——————(1989). 'Multiorganizational fields and recruitment *to* social movements', in B. Klandermans (ed.), *Organizing for Change*. Greenwich, Conn.: JAI Press.

——and Gould, R. (1994). 'A dilemma of state power: Brokerage and influence in the national health policy domain', *American Journal of Sociology*, **99**: 1455–91.

Feuer, L. (1969). *The Conflict of Generations: The Character and Significance of Student Movements*. New York: Basic Books.

Fine, G. (1995). 'Public narration and group culture: Discerning discourse in social movements', in H. Johnston and B. Klandermans (eds.), *Social Movements and Culture*. Minneapolis: University of Minnesota Press.

Fischer, C. (1995). *The Rise of the Nazis*. Manchester: Manchester University Press.

Franzosi, R. (1998). 'Narrative as data: Linguistic and statistical tools for the quantitative study of historical events', *International Review of Social History*, **43**: 81–104.

——(1999). 'The return of the actor. Interaction networks among social actors during periods of high mobilization (Italy, 1919–22)', *Mobilization*, **4**: 131–49.

Freeman, J. (1973). 'The origins of the women's liberation movement', *American Journal of Sociology*, **78**: 792–811.

Freeman, L. C. (1979). 'Centrality in social networks. I. Conceptual clarifications', *Social Networks*, **1**: 215–39.

——and White, D. R. (1993). 'Using Galois lattices to represent network data', *Sociological Methodology*, **23**: 127–45.

Friedland, R. and Alford, R. R. (1991). 'Bringing society back in: Symbols, practices, and institutional contradictions', in W. W. Powell and P. J. DiMaggio (eds.), *The New Institutionalism in Organizational Analysis*. Chicago: University of Chicago Press.

Friedman, D. and McAdam, D. (1992). 'Collective identity and activism: Networks, choices, and the life of a social movement', in A. D. Morris and C. Mueller (eds.), *Frontiers in Social Movement Theory*. New Haven: Yale University Press.

Friszke, A. (1994). *Opozycja polityczna w PRL 1947–80* [Political Opposition in Poland]. London: Aneks.

Galaskiewicz, J. (1985). 'Interorganizational relations', *Annual Review of Sociology*, **11**: 281–304.

Gamson, W. A. (1990 [1975]). *The Strategy of Social Protest*. Belmont, CA.: Wadsworth, 2nd edn.

——(1992). 'The social psychology of collective action', in A. D. Morris and C. Mueller (eds.), *Frontiers in Social Movement Theory*. New Haven: Yale University Press.

——(1995). 'Constructing social protest', in H. Johnston and B. Klandermans (eds.), *Social Movements and Culture*. Minneapolis: University of Minnesota Press.

——Fireman, B., and Rytina, S. (1982). *Encounters with Unjust Authority*. Homewood, IL: Dorsey Press.

Gerhards, J. and Rucht, D. (1992). 'Mesomobilization: Organizing and framing in two protest campaigns in West Germany', *American Journal of Sociology*, **98**: 555–95.

Gerlach, L. and Hine, V. (1970). *People, Power, Change: Movements of Social Transformation*. Indianopolis: Bobbs-Merrill.

Giddens, A. (1981). *A Contemporary Critique of Historical Materialism*. London: Macmillan.

——(1983). *Central Problems in Social Theory: Action, Structure and Contradiction in Social Analysis*. Berkeley: University of California Press.

——(1984). *The Constitution of Society*. Berkeley: University of California Press.

Gill, J. (1983). *The Nazi-Movement in Baden, 1920–45*. Chapel Hill: University of North Carolina Press.

Ginsburg, F. (1986). *Contested Lives: The Abortion Debate in an American Community*. Berkeley: University of California Press.

Giugni, M. and Passy, F. eds. (2001). *Political Altruism?* Boulder: Rowman and Littlefield.

Glaser, B. and Strauss, A. L. (1967). *The Discovery of Grounded Theory: Strategies for Qualitative Research*. New York: Aldine Publishing Company.

Glenn, J. K., III. (2001). *Framing Democracy: Civil Society and Civic Movements in Eastern Europe*. Stanford, CA: Stanford University Press.

Goffman, E. (1959). *The Presentation of Self in Everyday Life*. New York: Anchor Books.

Goffman, E. (1974). *Frame Analysis*. New York: Harper and Row.

Goldstone, J. (1980). 'The weakness of organization: A new look at Gamson's the strategy of social protest', *American Journal of Sociology*, **85**: 1043–60.

Goodwin, J. and Jasper, J. (1999). 'Caught in a winding, snarling vine: The structural bias of political process theory', *Sociological Forum*, **14**: 27–54.

Gould, R. V. (1991). 'Multiple networks and mobilization in the Paris commune, 1871', *American Sociological Review*, **56**: 716–29.

——(1993*a*). 'Trade cohesion, class unity, and urban insurrection: Artisanal activism in the French commune', *American Journal of Sociology*, **98**: 721–54.

——(1993*b*). 'Collective action and network structure', *American Sociological Review*, **58**: 182–96.

——(1995). *Insurgent Identities: Class, Community, and Protest in Paris from 1848 to the Commune*. Chicago: University of Chicago Press.

——and Fernandez, R. (1989). 'Structures of mediation', *Sociological Methodology*, **19**: 89–126.

Gouldner, A. W. ed. (1965). *Studies in Leadership*. New York: Russell and Russell.

Granovetter, M. (1973). 'The strength of weak ties', *American Journal of Sociology*, **78**: 1360–80.

——(1985). 'Economic action and social structure: The problem of embeddedness', *American Journal of Sociology*, **91**: 481–510.

Gray, B. (1989). *Collaborating*. San Francisco: Jossey-Bass.

Gulati, R. (1995). 'Social structure and alliance formation patterns', *Administrative Science Quarterly*, **40**: 619–52.

——and Gargiulo, M. (1999). 'Where do interorganizational networks come from?' *American Journal of Sociology*, **104**: 1439–93.

Habermas, J. (1981). 'New social movements', *Telos* n.49: 33–7.

——(1989). *The Structural Transformation of the Public Sphere*. Cambridge, MA: MIT Press.

Hall, P. and Taylor, R. (1996). 'Political science and the three new institutionalisms', *Political Studies*, **44**: 936–57.

Hamilton, R. F. (1982). *Who Voted for Hitler?* Princeton: Princeton University Press.

Hampton, K. and Wellman, B. (2001). 'Long distance community in the network society', *American Behavioral Scientist*, **45**: 477–96.

Hanks, W. F. (1992). 'The indexical ground of deictic reference', in A. Duranti and C. Goodwin (eds.), *Rethinking Context: Language as an Interactive Phenomenon*. Cambridge: Cambridge University Press.

Hathaway, W. and Meyer, D. S. (1994). 'Competition and cooperation in social movement coalitions', *Berkeley Journal of Sociology*, **38**: 157–83.

Hechter, M. ed. (1983). *The Microfoundations of Macrosociology*. Philadelphia: Temple University Press.

Heckathorn, D. D. (1993). 'Collective action and group heterogeneity: Voluntary provision versus selective incentives', *American Sociological Review*, **58**: 249–68.

——(1996). 'The dynamics and dilemmas of collective action', *American Sociological Review*, **61**: 250–77.

Hedström, P. (1994). 'Contagious collectivities: On the spatial diffusion of Swedish trade unions, 1890–1940', *American Journal of Sociology*, **99**: 1157–79.

——and Swedberg, R. eds. (1998). *Social Mechanisms: An Analytical Approach to Social Theory*. Cambridge, UK: Cambridge University Press.

——Sandell, R., and Stern, C. (2000). 'Mesolevel networks and the diffusion of social movements: The case of the Swedish social democratic party', *American Journal of Sociology*, **106**: 145–72.

Heiss, J. (1990). 'Social Roles', in M. Rosenberg and R. Turner (eds.), *Social Psychology, Sociological Perspectives*. New Brunswick: Transaction Publishers.

Herzog, D. (1998). *Poisoning the Minds of the Lower Orders*. Princeton: Princeton University Press.

Hirsch, E. L. (1990). 'Sacrifice for the cause: Group processes, recruitment, and commitment in a student social movement', *American Sociological Review*, **55**: 243–54.

Hobsbawm, E. J. and Rudé, G. (1968). *Captain Swing*. New York: Norton.

Hoffer, E. (1951). *The True Believer: Thoughts on the Nature of Mass Movements*. New York: Mentor Books, the New American Library.

Hoffman, L. M. (1989). *The Politics of Knowledge. Activist Movements in Medicine and Planning*. Albany, NY: SUNY Press.

Hofsteed, G. (1984). *Culture's Consequences: International Differences in Work-Related Values*. Newbury Park: Sage Publications.

Hoover Institution Archives. Poland collections. SB III/II, 'Geneza i przebieg wypadków marcowych w (1968) r.'[Origins and course of the March (1968) events]. Hoover Institution on War, Revolution, and Peace. Stanford, California.

Howard, J. (1994). 'A social cognitive conception of social structure', *Social Psychology Quarterly*, **57**: 210–27.

Inglehart, R. (1977). *The Silent Revolution*. Princeton: Princeton University Press.

Jackson, M., Petersen, E., Bull, J., Monsen, S., and Richmond, P. (1960). 'The failure of an incipient social movement', *Pacific Sociological Review*, **3**: 35–40.

Jamison, A., Eyerman, R., and Cramer, J. (1990). *The Making of the New Environmental Consciousness*. Edinburgh: Edinburgh University Press.

Jasper, J. (1997). *The Art of Moral Protest: Culture, Biography, and Creativity in Social Movements*. Chicago: University of Chicago Press.

——and Poulsen, J. (1993). 'Fighting back: Vulnerabilities, blunders, and countermobilization by the targets in three animal campaigns', *Sociological Forum*, **8**: 639–57.

Jenson, J. (1993). 'Naming nations: Making nationalist claims in Canadian public discourse', *Canadian Review of Sociology and Anthropology*, **30**: 337–58.

Jepperson, R. (1991). 'Institutions, institutional effects and institutionalism', in W. Powell and P. DiMaggio (eds.), *The New Institutionalism in Organizational Analysis*. Chicago: University of Chicago Press.

Jimenez, M. (2002). 'Spain', in C. Rootes (ed.), *Environmental Protest in Western Europe*. Oxford: Oxford University Press.

Johnson, C. S. (1941). *Growing up in the Black Belt*. Washington D.C.: American Council of Education.

Johnston, H. (1991). *Tales of Nationalism: Catalonia, 1939–79*. New Brunswick, NJ: Rutgers University Press.

——(1995). 'A methodology for frame analysis: From discourse to cognitive schema', in H. Johnston and B. Klandermans (eds.), *Social Movements and Culture*. Minneapolis: University of Minnesota Press.

Jones, A., Hutchinson, R., van Dyke, N., and Gates, L. (2001). 'Coalition form and mobilization effectiveness in local social movements', *Sociological Spectrum*, **21**: 207–31.

Jordan, G. and Maloney, W. (1997). *The Protest Business*. Manchester: Manchester University Press.

Jowitt, K. (1992). *New World Disorder: The Leninist Extinction*. Berkeley: University of California Press.

Kane, A. (1997). 'Theorizing meaning construction in social movements: Symbolic structures and interpretation during the Irish land war, 1879–1992', *Sociological Theory*, 15: 249–76.

Karpinski, J. (1982). *Countdown: The Polish Upheavals of 1956, 1968, 1970, 1976, 1980*. New York: Karz-Cohl.

Kater, M. H. (1977). 'Quantifizierung und NS-Geschichte. Methodologische Überlegungen über Grenzen und Möglichkeiten einer EDV-Analyse der NSDAP-Sozialstruktur von 1925 bis 1945', *Geschichte und Gesellschaft*, 3: 453–84.

——(1971). 'Zur Soziographie der frühen NSDAP', *Vierteljahreshefte für Zeitgeschichte*, 19: 124–59.

——(1983). *The Nazi Party. A Social Profile of Members and Leaders*. Cambridge, MA: Harvard University Press.

——(1985). 'Generationskonflikt als Entwicklungsfaktor in der NS-Bewegung vor 1933', *Geschichte und Gesellschaft*, 11: 217–43.

Keane, J. (1988). *Democracy and Civil Society*. London: Verso.

Kenis, P. and Knoke, D. (2002). 'How organizational field networks shape interorganizational tie-formation rates', *Academy of Management Review*, 27: 275–93.

——and Schneider, V. (1991). 'Policy networks and policy analysis: Scrutinizing a new analytical toolbox', in B. Marin and R. Mayntz (eds.), *Policy Networks. Empirical Evidence and Theoretical Considerations*. Frankfurt/Boulder, CO: Campus Verlag/Westview Press.

Kielbowicz, R. B. and Scherer, C. (1986). 'The role of the press in the dynamics of social movements', *Research in Social Movements, Conflict and Change*, 9: 71–96.

Killian, L. (1984). 'Organization, Rationality, and Spontaneity in the Civil Rights Movement', *American Sociological Review*, 49: 770–83.

Kim, H. and Bearman, P. S. (1997). 'The structure and dynamics of movement participation', *American Sociological Review*, 62: 70–93.

Kitschelt, H. P. (1986). 'Political opportunity structures and political protest: Anti-nuclear movements in four democracies', *British Journal of Political Science*, 16: 57–85.

Kitts, J. (2000). 'Mobilizing in black boxes: Social networks and SMO participation', *Mobilization*, 5: 25–30.

Klandermans, B. (1984). 'Mobilization and participation. Social-psychological expansions of resource mobilization theory', *American Sociological Review*, 49: 583–600.

——(1988). 'The formation and mobilization of consensus', in B. Klandermans, H. Kriesi and S. Tarrow (eds.), *From Structure to Action*. Greenwich, Conn.: JAI Press.

——ed. (1989). *Organizing for Change*. Greenwich, Conn.: JAI Press.

——(1990). 'Linking the "Old" and "New": Movement networks in the Netherlands', in R. Dalton and M. Kuechler (eds.), *Challenging the Political Order: New Social and Political Movements in Western Democracies*. Cambridge: Polity Press.

——(1992). 'The social construction of protest and multiorganizational fields', in A. D. Morris and C. Mueller (eds.), *Frontiers in Social Movement Theory*. New Haven: Yale University Press.

——(1997). *The Social Psychology of Protest*. Oxford: Blackwell.

——(2000). 'Must we redefine social movements as ideologically structured action?', *Mobilization*, 5: 25–30.

——and Oegema, D. (1987). 'Potentials, networks, motivations and barriers: Steps toward participation in social movements', *American Sociological Review*, **52**: 519–31.

Klapp, O. (1969). *Collective Search for Identity*. New York: Holt, Rinehart, and Winston.

Knoke, D. (1990*a*). *Political Networks*. Cambridge: Cambridge University Press.

——(1990*b*). *Organizing for Collective Action*. Hawthorne, NY: Aldine de Gruyter.

——(1994). 'Networks of elite structure and decision making', in S. Wasserman and J. Galaskiewicz (eds.), *Advances in Social Network Analysis*. Thousand Oaks/London: Sage.

——and Wood, J. R. (1981). *Organized for Action: Commitment in Voluntary Organizations*. New Brunswick, NJ: Rutgers University Press.

——and Kuklinski, J. H. (1982). *Network Analysis*. Newbury Park, CA: Sage.

——and Burt, R. S. (1983). 'Prominence', in R. S. Burt and M. Minor (eds.), *Applied Network Analysis*. Beverly Hills/London: Sage.

——and Wisely, N. (1990). 'Social movements', in D. Knoke (ed.), *Political Networks*. Cambridge/New York: Cambridge University Press.

——Pappi, F. U., Broadbent, J., and Tsujinaka, Y. (1996). *Comparing Policy Networks*. New York/Cambridge: Cambridge University Press.

Koopmans, R. and Statham, P. (1999). 'Political claims analysis: Integrating protest event and political discourse approaches', *Mobilization*, **4**: 40–51.

Kornhauser, W. (1959). *The Politics of Mass Society*. Glencoe, Ill.: Free Press.

Koshar, R. (1987). 'From stammtisch to party: Nazi joiners and the contradictions of grass roots facism in Weimar Germany', *Journal of Modern History*, **59**: 1–24.

Kosko, B. (1993). *Fuzzy Thinking: The New Science of Fuzzy Logic*. New York: Hyperion.

Krackhardt, D. (1992). 'The strength of strong ties: The importance of philos in organizations', in N. Nohria and R. Eccles (eds.), *Networks and Organizations*. Cambridge, MA: Harvard University Business School Press.

——and Brass, D. J. (1994). 'Intraorganizational networks: The micro side', in S. Wasserman and J. Galaskiewicz (eds.), *Advances in Social Network Analysis*. Thousand Oaks/London: Sage.

Kreps, D. F. (1990). *Game Theory and Economic Modelling*. New York: Clarendon Press.

Kreps, D. M., Milgrom, P., Roberts, J., and Wilson, R. (1982). 'Rational cooperation in the finitely repeated prisoner's dilemma', *Journal of Economic Theory*, **27**: 245–52.

Kriesi, H. (1988). 'Local mobilization for the people's petition of the Dutch peace movement', in B. Klandermans, H. Kriesi, and S. Tarrow (eds.), *From Structure to Action*. Greenwich, Conn.: JAI Press.

——(1993). *Political Mobilization and Social Change*. Aldershot: Avebury.

——(1996). 'The organizational structure of new social movements in a political context', in D. McAdam, J. D. McCarthy, and M. N. Zald (eds.), *Comparative Perspectives On Social Movements*. Cambridge/New York: Cambridge University Press.

——Koopmans, R., Duyvendak, J. W., and Giugni, M. (1995). *New Social Movements in Western Europe*. Minneapolis: University of Minnesota Press.

Kubik, J. (1994). *The Power of Symbols Against the Symbols of Power: The Rise of Solidarity and the Fall of State Socialism in Poland*. University Park, PA: The Pennsylvania State University Press.

Lacquer, W. (1996). *Fascism*. New York: Oxford University Press.

Lang, K. and Lang, G. (1961). *Collective Dynamics*. New York: Crowell.

Laumann, E. O. and Pappi, F. (1976). *Networks of Collective Action*. New York: Academic Press.

Laumann, E. O., Pappi, F., and Knoke, D. (1987). *The Organizational State. Social Choice in National Policy Domains*. Madison, WI: University of Wisconsin Press.

——Galaskiewicz, J., and Marsden, P. V. (1978). 'Community structure as interorganizational linkages', *Annual Review of Sociology*, **4**: 455–84.

——Marsden, P. V., and Prensky, D. (1983). 'The boundary specification problem in network analysis', in R. S. Burt and M. Minor (eds.), *Applied Network Analysis*. Beverly Hills, CA: Sage Publications.

Lebra, T. S. (1976). *Japanese Patterns of Behavior*. Honolulu: University of Hawaii Press.

Leech, B. (2001). 'Social movements and interest groups: Same message, different frequencies', paper presented at the ECPR First General Conference, Canterbury, 6–8 September.

Lemieux, V. (1997). 'Reseaux et Coalitions', *L'Annee Sociologique*, **47**: 55–71.

Lepak, K. J. (1988). *Prelude to Solidarity: Poland and the Politics of the Gierek Regime*. New York: Columbia University Press.

Lepsius, R. M. (1978). 'From fragmented party democracy to government by emergency decree and national socialist takeover: Germany', in J. Linz and A. Stepan (eds.), *The Breakdown of Democratic Regimes: Europe*. Baltimore: The Johns Hopkins University Press.

Levinson, S. C. (1983). *Pragmatics*. New York: Cambridge University Press.

Lichbach, M. I. (1998). *The Rebel's Dilemma*. Ann Arbor: University of Michigan Press.

Lichterman, P. (1995a). 'Piecing together multicultural community: Cultural differences in community-building among grassroots environmentalists', *Social Problems*, **42**: 513–34.

——(1995b). 'Beyond the seesaw model: Public commitment in a culture of self-fulfillment', *Sociological Theory*, **13**: 3.

——(1996). *The Search for Political Community*. New York/Cambridge: Cambridge University Press.

——(1999). 'Talking identity in the public sphere: Broad visions and small spaces in sexual identity politics', *Theory and Society*, **28**: 101–41.

Lin, N., Ensel, W. M., and Vaughn, J. C. (1981). 'Social resources and strength of ties: Structural factors in occupational status attainment', *American Sociological Review*, **46**: 393–405.

Lindberg, S. (1995). 'Farmers' movements and cultural nationalism in India: An ambiguous relationship', *Theory and Society*, **24**: 837–68.

Linz, J. (1967). 'Cleavages and consensus in West German politics: The early fifties', in S. M. Lipset and S. Rokkan (eds.), *Party Systems and Voter Alignments*. New York: Free Press.

——(1976). 'Some notes toward a comparative study of fascism in historical perspective', in W. Laqueur (ed.), *Fascism*. Berkeley: University of California Press.

——(1978). *The Breakdown of Democratic Regimes: Crisis, Breakdown, and Re-equilibration*. Baltimore and London: The Johns Hopkins University Press.

Lipset, S. M. (1960). *Political Man*. New York: Anchor Books.

——(1981). *Political Man: The Social Bases of Politics*. Baltimore, MD.: Johns Hopkins University Press, rev. and updated edn.

——(1994). 'Binary comparison: American exceptionalism—Japanese uniqueness', in M. Dogan and A. Kazancigil (eds.), *Comparing Nations*. Oxford: Blackwell.

Lipski, J. J. (1985). *KOR: A History of the Workers' Defense Committee in Poland, 1976–81*. Berkeley: University of California Press.

Lo, C. Y. H. (1992). 'Communities of challengers in social movement theory', in A. Morris and C. Mueller (eds.), *Frontiers in Social Movement Theory*. New Haven: Yale University Press.

Lofland, J. (1996). *Social Movement Organizations*. Hawthorne, NY: Aldine de Gruyter.

Lowe, P. D. and Goyder, J. M. (1983). *Environmental Groups in Politics*. London: Allen and Unwin.

Luker, K. (1984). *Abortion and the Politics of Motherhood*. Berkeley, CA: University of California Press.

Lukes, S. (1974). *Power: A Radical View*. London: Macmillan.

Lumley, R. (1990). *States of emergency*. London: Verso.

Macy, M. W. (1990). 'Learning-theory and the logic of critical mass', *American Sociological Review*, **55**: 809–26.

——(1991). 'Chains of cooperation: Threshold effects in collective action', *American Sociological Review*, **56**: 730–47.

——(1993). 'Backward-looking social-control', *American Sociological Review*, **58**: 819–36.

——and Flache, A. (1995). 'Beyond rationality in models of choice', *Annual Review of Sociology*, **21**: 73–91.

Margadant, T. W. (1979). *French Peasants in Revolt: The Insurrection of 1851*. Princeton: Princeton University Press.

Markus, H. R. and Kitayama, S. (1994). 'The cultural construction of self and emotion: Implications for social behavior', in S. Kitayama and H. R. Markus (eds.), *Emotion and Culture: Empirical Studies of Mutual Influence*. Washington, D.C.: American Psychological Association.

Marsden, P. V. (1982). 'Brokerage behaviour in restricted exchange networks', in P. Marsden and N. Lin (eds.), *Social Structure and Network Analysis*. Beverly Hills/ London: Sage.

——(1983). 'Restricted access in networks and models of power', *American Journal of Sociology*, **88**: 686–717.

Martin, J. L. (1999). 'Entropic measures of belief system constraint', *Social Science Research*, **28**: 111–34.

Marwell, G. and Oliver, P. (1993). *The Critical Mass in Collective Action*. Cambridge: Cambridge University Press.

————and Prahl, R. (1988). 'Social networks and collective action. A theory of critical mass. III', *American Journal of Sociology*, **94**: 502–34.

Marx, G. T. ed. (1971). *Racial Conflict*. Boston: Little Brown.

——(1980). 'Conceptual problems in the field of collective behavior', in H. M. J. Blalock (ed.), *Sociological Theory and Research: A Critical Appraisal*. New York: The Free Press.

Mays, B. and Nicholson, J. W. (1969). *Negro's Church*. New York: Arno Press and the New York Times.

McAdam, D. (1982). *Political Process and the Development of Black Insurgency, 1930–70*. Chicago: University of Chicago Press.

——(1983). 'Tactical innovation and the pace of insurgency', *American Sociological Review*, **48**: 735–54.

——(1986). 'Recruitment to high risk activism: The case of freedom summer', *American Journal of Sociology*, **92**: 64–90.

McAdam, D. (1988*a*). *Freedom Summer*. New York: Oxford University Press.

—— (1988*b*). 'Micromobilization contexts and recruitment *to* activism', in B. Klandermans, H. Kriesi, and S. Tarrow (eds.), *From Structure to Action*. Greenwich, Conn.: JAI Press.

—— (1995). ' "Initiator" and "Spin-off" movements: Diffusion processes in protest cycles', in M. Traugott (ed.), *Repertoires and Cycles of Collective Action*. Durham, N. C.: Duke University Press.

—— (1996). 'The framing function of movement tactics: Strategic dramaturgy in the American civil rights movement', in D. McAdam, J. D. McCarthy, and M. N. Zald (eds.), *Comparative Perspectives on Social Movements: Political Opportunities, Mobilizing Structures, and Cultural Framings*. Cambridge: Cambridge University Press.

—— (1999). *Political Process and the Development of Black Insurgency, 1930–70*. Chicago: University of Chicago Press, 2nd edn.

—— and Fernandez, R. (1990). 'Microstructural bases of recruitment *to* social movements', in L. Kriesberg (ed.), *Research in Social Movements, Conflict and Change*, vol.12. Greenwich, Conn.: JAI Press.

—— and Paulsen, R. (1993). 'Specifying the relationship between social ties and activism', *American Journal of Sociology*, **99**: 640–67.

—— and Rucht, D. (1993). 'The cross-national diffusion of social movement ideas', *Annals of the AAPSS*, **528**: 56–74.

—— McCarthy, J. D., and Zald, M. N. (1988). 'Social movements', in N. J. Smelser (ed.), *Handbook of Sociology*. Newbury Park: Sage.

—— —— —— eds. (1996). *Opportunities, Mobilizing Structures, and Framing Processes*. Cambridge/New York: Cambridge University Press.

—— Tarrow, S., and Tilly, C. (2001). *Dynamics of Contention*. Cambridge and New York: Cambridge University Press.

McCarthy, J. D. (1996). 'Mobilizing structures: Constraints and opportunities in adopting, adapting, and inventing', in D. McAdam, J. D. McCarthy, and M. N. Zald (eds.), *Comparative Perspectives on Social Movements*. Cambridge/New York: Cambridge University Press.

—— and Zald, M. N. (1977). 'Resource mobilization and social movements: A partial theory', *American Journal of Sociology*, **82**(6): 1212–41.

—— McPhail, C., and Smith, J. (1996). 'Images of protest: Dimensions of selection bias in media coverage of Washington demonstrations, 1982 and 1991', *American Sociological Review*, **61**: 478–99.

McKay, G. (1996). *Senseless Acts of Beauty: Cultures of Resistance Since the 1960s*. London: Verso.

McLean, P. (1998). 'A frame analysis of favor seeking in the renaissance: Agency, networks, and political culture', *American Journal of Sociology*, **104**: 51–91.

McPherson, M. and Rotolo, T. (1996). 'Testing a dynamic model of social composition: Diversity and change in voluntary groups', *American Sociological Review*, **61**: 179–202.

—— Popielarz, P., and Drobnic, S. (1992). 'Social networks and organizational dynamics', *American Sociological Review*, **57**: 153–70.

—— Smith-Lovin, L., and Cook, J. M. (2001). 'Birds of a feather: Homophily in social networks', *Annual Review of Sociology*, **27**: 415–44.

Melucci, A. ed. (1984). *Altri codici*. Bologna: il Mulino.

—— (1989). *Nomads of the Present*. Philadelphia: Temple University Press.

——(1995). 'The process of collective identity', in H. Johnston and B. Klandermans (eds.), *Social Movements and Culture*. Minneapolis: University of Minnesota Press.

——(1996). *Challenging Codes*. Cambridge/New York: Cambridge University Press.

Merriman, J. M. (1978). *The Agony of the Republic: The Repression of the Left in Revolutionary France, 1848–51*. New Haven, CT: Yale University Press.

Meyer, D. S. and Whittier, N. (1994). 'Social movement spillover', *Social Problems*, **41**: 277–98.

Meyer, J. W. and Rowan, B. (1991). 'Institutionalized organizations: Formal structure as myth and ceremony', in W. Powell and P. DiMaggio (eds.), *The New Institutionalism in Organizational Analysis*. Chicago: University of Chicago.

Michels, R. (1959). *Political Parties*. New York: Dover.

Michnik, A. (1993). *The Church and the Left*, trans. and ed. by David Ost. Chicago: University of Chicago Press.

——Tischner J., and Zakowski, J. (1995). *Miedzy Panem a Plebanem* [Between the Lord and the Rectory]. Cracow: Znak.

Minkoff, D. (1997). 'Producing social capital: National social movements and civil society', *American Behavioral Scientist*, **40**: 606–19.

Mische, A. (1996). 'Projecting democracy: The construction of citizenship across youth networks in Brazil', in C. Tilly (ed.), *Citizenship, Identity, and Social History*. Cambridge: Cambridge University Press.

——(1998). *Projecting Democracy: Contexts and Dynamics of Youth Activism in the Brazilian Impeachment Movement*, Doctoral dissertation, New School for Social Research.

——and White, H. (1998). 'Between conversation and situation: Public switching dynamics across network-domains', *Social Research*, **65**: 695–724.

——and Pattison, P. (2000). 'Composing a civic arena: Publics, projects, and social settings', *Poetics*, **27**: 163–94.

Mizruchi, M. S. (1996). 'What do interlocks do?', *Annual Review of Sociology*, **22**: 271–98.

——and Schwartz, M. eds. (1987). *Intercorporate Relations*. Cambridge/New York: Cambridge University Press.

——and Galaskiewicz, J. (1994). 'Networks of interorganizational relations', in S. Wasserman and J. Galaskiewicz (eds.), *Advances in Social Network Analysis*. Thousand Oaks/London: Sage.

Mohr, J. (1994). 'Soldiers, mothers, tramps and others: Discourse roles in the 1907 New York City charity directory', *Poetics*, **22**: 327–57.

——(1998). 'Measuring meaning structures', *Annual Review of Sociology*, **24**: 345–70.

——(2000). 'Introduction: Structures, institutions, and cultural analysis', *Poetics*, **27**: 57–68.

——and Duqenne, V. (1997). 'The duality of culture and practice: Poverty relief in New York City, 1888–1917', *Theory and Society*, **26**: 305–56.

Morgan, E. S. (1988). *Inventing the People. The Rise of Popular Sovereignty in England and America*. New York: Norton.

Morris, A. D. (1984). *The Origins of the Civil Rights Movement: Black Communities Organizing for Change*. New York: The Free Press.

——(1992). 'Political consciousness and collective action', in A. D. Morris and C. Mueller (eds.), *Frontiers in Social Movement Theory*. New Haven: Yale University Press.

Mueller, C. M. (1994). 'Conflict networks and the origins of women's liberation', in E. Laraña, H. Johnston, and J. R. Gusfield (eds.), *New Social Movements: From Ideology to Identity*. Philadelphia: Temple University Press.

Mueller, C. M. (1997). 'International press coverage of East German protest events, 1989', *American Sociological Review*, **62**: 820–32.

Mueller, E. N. and Opp, K.-D. (1986). 'Rational choice and rebellious collective action', *American Political Science Review*, **80**: 471–87.

Mühlberger, D. (1991). *Hitler's Followers: Studies in the Sociology of the Nazi Movement*. London: Routledge.

——(1995). 'A "Workers Party" or a "Party Without Workers"?', in C. Fischer (ed.), *Weimar, the Working Classes and the Rise of National Socialism and the Working Classes in Weimar Germany*, pp. 47–78. Oxford: Berghahn.

Mullins, P. (1987). 'Community and urban movements', *Sociological Review*, **35**: 347–69.

Münchner, S. (1993). *München – Hauptstadt der Bewegung*. München: Klinkhardt und Biermann.

Munger, F. (1979). 'Measuring repression of popular protest by English Justices of the Peace in the industrial revolution', *Historical Methods*, **12**: 76–83.

——(1981*a*). 'Suppression of popular gatherings in England, 1800–30', *American Journal of Legal History*, **25**: 111–40.

——(1981*b*). 'Contentious gatherings in Lancashire 1750–1893', in L. A. Tilly and C. Tilly (eds.), *Class Conflict and Collective Action*. Beverly Hills: Sage.

Mushaben, J. M. (1989). 'The struggle within: Conflict, consensus and decision making among national coordinators and grass-roots organizers in the West German peace movement', in B. Klandermans (ed.), *Organizing for Change*. Greenwich, Conn.: JAI Press.

Mutti, A. (1996). 'Reti Sociali: Tra Metafore e Programmi Teorici', *Rassegna Italiana Di Sociologia*, **37**: 5–30.

Myers, D. J. (1996). 'The diffusion of collective violence', paper presented at the annual meeting of the American Sociological Association.

——(1997). 'Diffusion models for riots and other collective violence', Ph.D. Thesis, Sociology, University of Wisconsin, Madison.

——(2000*a*). 'The diffusion of collective violence: Infectiousness, susceptibility and mass media networks', *American Journal of Sociology*, **106**: 178–208.

——(2000*b*). 'Media, communication technology and protest waves', paper presented at the conference 'Social Movement Analysis: The Network Perspective.' Ross Priory, Loch Lomond, 22–24 June.

——(2001). 'Modeling social diffusion processes using event history analysis: Some conceptual issues, practical considerations and empirical patterns', paper presented to the Institute of Social and Economic Research and Policy, Columbia University, New York, NY. Available as working paper 2001–01, Department of Sociology Working Paper Series, University of Notre Dame.

——and Caniglia, B. S. (2000). 'Media bias in the coverage of racial riots: National versus local media outlets', paper presented at the annual meeting of the Midwest Sociological Society.

——and Oliver, P. E. (2000). 'The opposing forces diffusion model: The initiation and repression of collective violence', working paper presented at the University of Notre Dame.

Nachimas, D. and Nachimas, C. (1976). *Research Methods in the Social Sciences*. New York: St. Martin's Press.

Nakane, C. (1970). *Japanese Society*. Berkeley: University of California Press.

Namboodiri, K. (1984). *Matrix Algebra. An Introduction*. London/Newbury Park: Sage.

Neidhardt, F. and Rucht, D. (1993). 'Auf dem Weg in die Bewegungsgesellschaft?—Über die Stabilisierbarkeit sozialer Bewegungen', *Soziale Welt*, **44**: 305–26.

Nohria, N. and Eccles, R. G. eds. (1992). *Networks and Organizations. Structure, Form, and Action*. Boston, MA: Harvard Business School Press.

Norris, P. (2002). *Democratic Phoenix*. New York/Cambridge: Cambridge University Press.

NSDAP, (1935). *Parteistatistik. Stand vom 1. Januar 1935*. München: Der Reichsorganisationsleiter der NSDAP.

Oberschall, A. (1973). *Social Conflict and Social Movements*. Englewood Cliffs: Prentice-Hall.

——(1989). 'The 1960 sit-ins: Protest diffusion and movement take-off', *Research in Social Movements, Conflicts and Change*, **11**: 31–53.

——(1993). *Social Movements*. New Brunswick: Transaction Books.

——and Kim, H. (1996). 'Identity and action', *Mobilization*, **1**: 63–85.

Offe, C. (1985). 'New social movements: Changing boundaries of the political', *Social Research*, **52**: 817–68.

Ohlemacher, T. (1996). 'Bridging people and protest: Social relays of protest groups against low-flying military jets in West Germany', *Social Problems*, **43**: 197–218.

Oliver, P. (1980). 'Rewards and punishments as selective incentives for collective action: Theoretical investigations', *American Journal of Sociology*, **85**: 1356–75.

——(1984). 'If you don't do it, nobody else will: Active and token contributors to collective action', *American Sociological Review*, **49**: 601–10.

——(1989). 'Bringing the crowd back in', in L. Kriesberg (ed.), *Research in Social Movements, Conflict and Change*, vol. 11. Greenwich, Conn.: JAI Press.

——and Marwell, G. (1988). 'The paradox of group size in collective action: A theory of critical mass II', *American Sociological Review*, **53**: 1–8.

————(1992). 'Mobilizing technologies for collective action', in A. D. Morris and C. Mueller (eds), *Frontiers in Social Movement Theory*. New Haven: Yale University Press.

——and Myers, D. J. (1999). 'How events enter the public sphere: Conflict, location, and sponsorship in local newspaper coverage of public events', *American Journal of Sociology*, **105**: 38–87.

——and Maney, G. M. (2000). 'Political process and local newspaper coverage of protest events: From selection bias to triadic interactions', *American Journal of Sociology*, **106**: 463–505.

——and Marwell, G. (2001). 'Whatever happened *to* critical mass theory? A retrospective and assessment', *Sociological Theory*, **19**: 292–311.

——and Myers, D. J. (forthcoming). 'The coevolution of social movements.' *Mobilization*.

——Marwell, G., and Teixeira, R. A. (1985). 'A theory of the critical mass. I. Interdependence, group heterogeneity, and the production of collective action', *American Journal of Sociology*, **91**: 522–56.

——————(1988). 'The paradox of group size in collective action: A theory of the critical mass. II', *American Sociological Review*, **53**: 1–8.

Olzak, S. (1992). *The Dynamics of Ethnic Competition and Conflict*. Stanford, CA: Stanford University Press.

Opp, K.-D. (1989). *The Rationality of Political Protest*. Boulder: Westview Press.

——and Gern, C. (1993*a*). 'Dissident groups, personal networks, and spontaneous cooperation. The East German revolution of 1989', *American Sociological Review*, **58**: 659–80.

References

Orum, A. M. (1972). *Black Students in Protest*. Washington D.C.: American Sociological Association.

Osa, M. (1997). 'Creating solidarity: The religious foundations of the Polish social movement', *East European Politics and Societies*, **11**: 339–65.

——(2001). 'Mobilizing structures and cycles of protest: Post Stalinist contention in Poland, 1954–9', *Mobilization*, **6**: 211–31.

——(2003). *Solidarity and Contention: Networks of Polish Opposition*. Minneapolis: University of Minnesota Press.

——and Corduneanu-Huci, C. (2003). 'Running uphill: Political opportunities in nondemocracies', *Comparative Sociology*, **4**: 1–25.

Ost, D. (1990). *Solidarity and the Politics of Anti-politics: Opposition and Reform in Poland Since 1968*. Philadelphia: Temple University Press.

Ostrom, E. (1998). 'A behavioral approach *to* the rational choice theory of collective action', *American Political Science Review*, **92**: 1–22.

Padgett, J. F. and Ansell, C. K. (1993). 'Robust action and the rise of the Medici, 1400–34', *American Journal of Sociology*, **98**: 1259–319.

Paige, J. (1975). *Agrarian Revolution*. New York: Free Press.

Passerini, L. (1988). *Autobiografia di gruppo*. Florence: Giunti.

Passy, F. (1998). *L'action altruiste*. Genève-Paris: Droz.

——(2001*a*). 'Political altruism and the solidarity movement', in M. Giugni and F. Passy (eds.), *Political Altruism?* Boulder: Rowman and Littlefield.

——(2001*b*). 'Socializing, connecting, and the structural agency/gap. A specification of the impact of networks on participation in social movements', *Mobilization*, **6**: 173–92.

——and Giugni, M. (2000). 'Life-spheres, networks, and sustained participation in social movements. A phenomenological approach to political commitment', *Sociological Forum*, **15**: 117–44.

Pattison, P. (1993). *Algebraic Models for Social Networks*. Cambridge: Cambridge University Press.

Payne, C. (1996). *I've Got the Light of Freedom*. Berkeley: University of California Press.

Pearce, J. (1980). 'Apathy or self-interest? The volunteers' avoidance of leadership roles', *Journal of Voluntary Action Research*, **9**: 85–94.

Pelczynski, Z. A. (1980). 'The decline of Gomulka', in R. F. Leslie (ed.), *The History of Poland Since 1983*. Cambridge: Cambridge University Press.

Pfaff, S. (1996). 'Collective identity and informal groups in revolutionary mobilization: East Germany in 1989', *Social Forces*, **75**: 91–117.

Pharr, S. J. (1990). *Losing Face: Status Politics in Japan*. Berkeley: University of California Press.

Philips, S. (1991). 'Meaning and structure in social movements: Mapping the network of National Canadian Women's Organizations', *Canadian Journal of Political Science*, **24**: 755–82.

Pichierri, A. (1999). 'Organizzazioni Rete, Reti di Organizzazioni: Dal Caso Anseatico alle Organizzazioni Contemporanee', *Studi Organizzativi*, **3**: 19–42.

Pickerill, J. (2000). 'Environmentalism and the net: Pressure groups, new social movements and new ICTs', in R. Gibson and S. Ward (eds.), *Reinvigorating Government? British Politics and the Internet*. Aldershot: Ashgate.

Pickvance, C. G. (1975). 'On the study of urban social movements', *Sociological Review*, **23**: 29–49.

Pierson, P. (2000). 'Increasing returns, path dependence, and the study of politics', *American Political Science Review*, **94**: 251–67.

Pinard, M. (1968). 'Mass society and political movements: A new formulation', *American Journal of Sociology*, **73**: 682–90.

——(1971). *The Rise of a Third Party: A Study in Crisis Politics*. Englewood Cliffs, NJ: Prentice-Hall.

Piven, F. F. and Cloward, R. A. (1977). *Poor People's Movements*. New York: Vintage.

————(1992). 'Normalizing collective protest', in A. Morris and C. Mueller (eds.), *Frontiers in Social Movement Theory*. New Haven: Yale University Press.

Pizzorno, A. (1986). 'Sur la rationalité du choix démocratique', in P. Birnbaum and J. Leca (eds.), *Sur l'individualisme*. Paris: Presses de la Fondation nationale des sciences politiques.

——(1996). 'Decisioni o interazioni? La micro-decisione del cambiamento sociale', *Rassegna italiana di sociologia*, **37**: 107–32.

Plotz, J. M. (2000). *The Crowd: British Literature and Public Politics*. Berkeley: University of California Press.

Podolny, J. and Page, K. (1998). 'Network forms of organization', *Annual Review of Sociology*, **24**: 57–76.

Poggio, A. (1996). *Ambientalismo*. Milan: Bibliografica.

Polletta, F. (1996). 'Culture and its discontents: Recent theorizing in the cultural dimensions of protest', *Sociological Inquiry*, **67**: 431–50.

——(1998). '"It Was Like a Fever..." narrative and identity in social protest', *Social Problems*, **45**: 137–59.

——(1999a). '"Free Spaces" in collective action', *Theory and Society*, **28**: 1–38.

——(1999b). 'Snarls, quacks, and quarrels: Culture and structure in political process theory', *Sociological Forum*, **14**: 63–70.

Polsby, N. W. (1963). *Community Power and Political Theory*. New Haven, CT: Yale University Press.

Powell, W. (1990). 'Neither market nor hierarchy: Network forms of organization', *Research in Organizational Behavior*, **12**: 295–336.

——(1991). 'Expanding the scope of institutional analysis', in W. Powell and P. J. DiMaggio (eds.), *The New Institutionalism in Organizational Analysis*. Chicago: University of Chicago Press.

——and DiMaggio, P. (1991). 'Introduction', in W. Powell and P. J. DiMaggio (eds.), *The New Institutionalism in Organizational Analysis*. Chicago: University of Chicago Press.

Prakash, S. and Selle, P. eds. (2003). *Investigating Social Capital*. New Delhi: Sage.

Price, R. (1999). *British Society, 1680–1880*. Cambridge: Cambridge University Press.

Pridham, G. (1973). *Hitler's Rise to Power: The Nazi Movement in Bavaria*. St Albans: Hart-Davis MacGibbon.

Putnam, R. D. (1993). *Making Democracy Work: Civic Traditions in Modern Italy*. Princeton: Princeton University Press.

——(1995). 'Bowling alone, revisited', *The Responsive Community*, **5**: 18–33.

Ragin, C. (1987). *The Comparative Method*. Berkeley: University of California Press.

——(2000). *Fuzzy-Set Social Science*. Chicago: University of Chicago.

Ragin, C. and Becker, H. (1992). *What is a Case?* Cambridge: Cambridge University Press.

Raina, P. ed. (1991). *'Te Deum' Narodu Polskiego. Obchody Tysiąclecia Chrztu Polski, 1966–7* [Processions of the Millennium of Poland's Baptism, 1966–7]. Olsztyn: Warmińskie Wydawnictwo Diecezjalne.

——ed. (1994). *'Kościół w PRL. Dokumenty* [The Church in the People's Republic of Poland. Documents.]', 2 vols. Poznań: Wyd. w Drodze.

——(1995). *'Kardynał Wyszyński. Orędzie Biskupów a Reakcja Władz* [Cardinal Wyszyński, the Bishops' Letter and the Reaction of the Authorities]'. Warsaw: Wyd. Książka Polska.

Ray, K., Savage, M., Tampubolon, G., Longhurst, B., Tomlison, M., and Warde, A. (2001). 'An exclusive political field? Membership patterns and networks in social movement organizations', paper presented at the Social Movements Stream, European Sociological Association Conference, 26 August–1 September, Helsinki.

Rheinghold, H. (1993). *The Virtual Community*. New York: Harper and Row.

Riesman, D. (1950). *The Lonely Crowd*. New Haven: Yale University Press.

Rochon, T. and Meyer, D. S. eds. (1997). *Coalitions and Political Movements*. Boulder, CO: Lynne Rienner.

Rogers, E. M. (1983). *Diffusion of Innovations*. New York: The Free Press, 3rd edn.

Rootes, C. ed. (2002). *Environmental Protest in Western Europe*. Oxford: Oxford University Press.

Rose, R. (2001). 'When government fails: Social capital in an anti-modern russia', in B. Edwards, M. Foley, and M. Diani (eds.), *Beyond Tocqueville*. Hanover, NH: University Press of New England.

Rosenthal, N., Fingrutd, M., Ethier, M., Karant, R., and McDonald, D. (1985). 'Social movements and network analysis', *American Journal of Sociology*, **90**: 1022–54.

——McDonald, D., Ethier, M., Fingrutd, M., and Karant, R. (1997). 'Structural tensions in the nineteenth century women's movement', *Mobilization*, **2**: 21–46.

Rothman, F. D. and Oliver, P. E. (1999). 'From local to global: The anti-dam movement in Southern Brazil, 1979–92', *Mobilization*, **4**: 41–57.

Rothman, S. and Lichter, S. R. (1978). 'The case of the student left', *Social Research*, **45**: 535–609.

Rovelli, C. (1988). 'I Modelli Organizzativi delle Associazioni Ambientaliste', in R. Biorcio and G. Lodi (eds.), *La Sfida Verde*. Padua: Liviana.

Rucht, D. (1989). 'Environmental movement organizations in West Germany and France', in B. Klandermans (ed.), *Organizing for Change*. Greenwich, Conn.: JAI Press.

——(1996). 'The impact of national contexts on social movement structures: A cross-movement and cross-national comparison', in D. McAdam, J. D. McCarthy, and M. N. Zald (eds.), *Comparative Perspectives on Social Movements: Political Opportunities, Mobilizing Structures, and Cultural Framings*. Cambridge: Cambridge University Press.

Rudé, G. F. E. (1964). *The Crowd in History; a Study of Popular Disturbances in France and England, 1730–1848*. New York: Wiley.

Rudlof, W. (1992). 'Notjahre – Stadtpolitik in Krieg, Inflation und Weltwirtschaftskrise 1914 bis 1933', in R. Bauer (ed.), *Geschichte der Stadt München*, pp. 336–68. München: Beck.

Sandel, M. (1996). *Democracy's Discontent: America in Search of a Public Philosophy*. Cambridge, MA: Belknap Press.

Sandell, R. (1999). 'Organizational life aboard the moving bandwagons: A network analysis of dropouts from a Swedish temperance organization, 1896–1937', *Acta Sociologica*, **42**: 3–15.

Sandler, T. (1992). *Collective Action*. Ann Arbor: University of Michigan Press.

Savage, M. (1996). 'Space, networks, and class formation', in N. Kirk (ed.), *Social Class and Marxism*. London: Scolar Press.

Sawer, M. and Groves, A. (1994). ' "The Women's Lobby": Networks, coalition building and the women of middle Australia', *Australian Journal of Political Science*, **29**: 435–59.

Schäfer, W. (1957). *NSDAP. Entwicklung und Struktur der Staatspartei des Dritten Reiches*. Hannover: Norddeutsche Verlagsanstalt.

Schmitt-Beck, R. (1989). 'Organizational interlocks between new social movements and traditional elites', *European Journal of Political Research*, **17**: 583–98.

——(1990). 'Die Bedeutung der Massenmedien für soziale Bewegungen', *Kölner Zeitschrift für Soziologie und Sozialpsychologie*, **42**: 642–62.

Schou, A. (1997). 'Elite identification in collective protest movements', *Mobilization*, **2**: 71–86.

Schutz, A. (1967). *Collected Papers*. The Hague: Martinus Nijhoff.

Schweitzer, R. A. (1979). 'A study of contentious gatherings in early nineteenth century Great Britain', *Historical Methods*, **12**: 123–7.

—— and Simmons, S. C. (1981). 'Interactive, direct-entry approaches to contentious gathering event files', *Social Science History*, **5**: 317–42.

Schweizer, T. (1993). 'The dual ordering of actors and possessions', *Current Anthropology*, **34**: 469–83.

——(1996). 'Actor and event orderings across time: Lattice representation and boolean analysis of the political disputes in Chen village, China', *Social Networks*, **18**: 247–66.

Scott, J. (2000). *Social Network Analysis*. London: Sage, 2nd edn.

——(1997). *Corporate Business and Capitalist Classes*. Oxford: Oxford University Press.

Seligman, A. (1992). *The Idea of Civil Society*. New York: Free Press.

Seton-Watson, H. (1950). *The East European Revolution*. London: Methuen and Co.

Sewell, W. J. Jr. (1992). 'A theory of structure: Duality, agency, and transformation', *American Journal of Sociology*, **98**: 1–29.

Shefner, J. (1995). 'Moving in the wrong direction in social movement theory', *Theory and Society*, **24**: 595–612.

Sheller, M. (2000). 'From social networks to social flows: Re-thinking the movement in social movements', paper for the Conference 'Social movement analysis: The network perspective.' Ross Priory, Loch Lomond, 22–4 June.

Shibutani, T. (1966). *Improvised News: A Sociological Study of Rumor*. Indianapolis: Bobbs-Merrill.

Sik, E. and Wellman, B. (1999). 'Network capital in capitalist, communist, and postcommunist countries', in Barry Wellman (ed.), *Networks in the Global Village*. Boulder, CO: Westview Press.

Simmel, G. ([1908] 1955). 'The web of group affiliations', in *Conflict and the Web of Group Affiliations*, trans. by R. Bendix. New York: Free Press.

Singer, B. D. (1968). 'Mass media and communication process in the Detroit riot of 1967', *Public Opinion Quarterly*, **34**: 236–45.

Skocpol, T. (1979). *States and Social Revolutions*. New York: Cambridge University Press.

Smelser, N. J. (1962). *Theory of Collective Behavior*. New York: Free Press.

Snow, D. A. and Benford, R. D. (1988). 'Ideology, frame resonance, and movement participation', in B. Klandermans, H. Kriesi, and S. Tarrow (eds.), *From Structure to Action*. Greenwich: JAI Press.

Snow, D. A. and Benford, R. D. (1992). 'Master frames and cycles of protest', in A. D. Morris and C. Mueller (eds.), *Frontiers in Social Movement Theory*. New Haven: Yale University Press.

——and Oliver, P. (1995). 'Social movements and collective behavior, social psychological dimensions and considerations', in K. Cook, G. Fine, and J. House (eds.), *Sociological Perspectives on Social Psychology*. Boston: Allyn and Bacon.

——Burke Rochford, E. A. Jr., Worden, S. K., and Bernford, R. D. (1986). 'Frame alignment processes, micromobilization, and movement participation', *American Sociological Review,* **51**: 464–81.

——Zurcher, L. A., and Ekland-Olson, S. (1980). 'Social networks and social movements: A microstructural approach to differential recruitment', *American Sociological Review*, **45**: 787–801.

Snyder, D. and Kelly, W. R. (1977). 'Conflict intensity, media sensitivity and the validity of newspaper data', *American Sociological Review*, **42**: 105–23.

Somers, M. (1992). 'Narrativity, narrative identity, and social action: Rethinking English working-class formation', *Social Science History*, **16**: 591–630.

——(1993). 'Citizenship and the place of the public sphere: Law, community, and political culture in the transition to democracy', *American Sociological Review*, **58**: 587–620.

Soule, S. A. (1997). 'The student divestment movement in the United States and tactical diffusion: The Shantytown protest', *Social Forces*, **75**: 855–82.

Spillman, L. (1995). 'Culture, social structures, and discursive fields', *Current Perspectives in Social Theory*, **15**: 129–54.

Staggenborg, S. (1986). 'Coalition work in the pro-choice movement', *Social Problems*, **33**: 623–41.

——(1988). 'The consequences of professionalization and formalization in the pro-choice movement', *American Sociological Review*, **53**: 585–606.

Statistisches Reichsamt. (1927). 'Berufszählung' *Statistik des Deutschen Reiches 1925*. Band 402.II. Berlin: Verlag von Reimar Hobbing.

Stehle, H. (1965). *The Independent Satellite: Society and Politics in Poland Since 1945*. New York: Frederick A. Praeger.

Steinberg, M. W. (1998). 'Tilting the frame: Considerations on collective action framing from a discursive turn', *Theory* and *Society*, **27**: 845–72.

——(1999a). 'The talk and back talk of collective action: A dialogic analysis of repertoires of discourse among nineteenth-century English cotton spinners', *American Journal of Sociology*, **105**: 736–80.

——(1999b). *Fighting Words: Working-class Formation, Collective action, and Discourse in Early Nineteenth-century England*. Ithaca, N.Y.: Cornell University Press.

Steinfeld, R. J. (2001). *Coercion, Contract, and Free Labor in the Nineteenth Century*. Cambridge: Cambridge University Press.

Sternwell, Z. (1994). *The Birth of Fascist Ideology*. Princeton: Princeton University Press.

Stinchcombe, A. (1968). *Constructing Social Theories*. Chicago/London: University of Chicago Press.

——(1991). 'The conditions of fruitfulness of theorizing about mechanisms in social science', *Philosophy of the Social Sciences*, **21**: 367–88.

Stolle, D. (1998). 'Bowling alone, bowling together: Group characteristics, membership and social capital', *Political Psychology*, **19**: 497–525.

Strang, D. and Meyer, J. W. (1993). 'Institutional conditions for diffusion', *Theory and Society*, 47: 242–43.

Strangleman, T. (2001). 'Networks, place and identities in post-industrial mining communities', *International Journal of Urban and Regional Research*, 25: 253–67.

Suzuki, D. (1989). *Essays in Zen Buddhism*. New York: Grove Atlantic.

Swidler, A. (1986). 'Culture in action: Symbols and strategies', *American Sociological Review*, 51: 273–86.

——(1995). 'Cultural power and social movements', in H. Johnston and B. Klandermans (eds.), *Social Movements and Culture*. Minneapolis: University of Minnesota Press.

Szajkowski, B. (1983). *Next to God ... Poland: Politics and Religion in Contemporary Poland*. New York: St. Martin's Press.

Szasz, T. (1994). *Ecopopulism*. Minneapolis: University of Minnesota Press.

Szulc, T. (1995). *Pope John Paul II, the Biography*. New York: Pocket Books.

Tarrow, S. (1989). *Democracy and Disorder*. Oxford: Clarendon Press.

——(1992). 'Mentalities, political cultures, and collective action frames: Constructing meaning through action', in A. D. Morris and C. Mueller (eds.), *Frontiers of Social Movement Theory*. New Haven, CT: Yale University Press.

——(1994). *Power in Movement*. Cambridge: Cambridge University Press.

——(1998*a*). 'Studying contentious politics: From event-full history to cycles of collective action', in D. Rucht, R. Koopmans, and F. Neidhardt (eds.), *Acts of Dissent*. Berlin: Sigma.

——(1998*b*). *Power in Movement*. Cambridge: Cambridge University Press, 2nd edn.

Taylor, M. (1987). *The Possibility of Cooperation*. New York: Cambridge.

Taylor, V. and Whittier, N. (1992). 'Collective identity in social movement communities: Lesbian feminist mobilization', in A. Morris and C. Mueller (eds.), *Frontiers in Social Movement Theory*. New Haven: Yale University Press.

————(1995). 'Analytical approaches to social movement culture: The culture of the women's movement', in H. Johnston and B. Klandermans (eds.), *Social Movements and Culture*. Minneapolis/London: University of Minnesota Press/UCL Press.

Thornton, P. (1999). 'The sociology of social entrepreneurship', *Annual Review of Sociology*, 25: 19–46.

Tilly, C. (1964). *The Vendée*. Cambridge: Harvard University Press.

——(1978). *From Mobilization to Revolution*. Reading, MA: Addison/Wesley.

——(1984). *Big Structures, Large Processes, Huge Comparisons*. New York: Russell Sage Foundation.

——(1994). 'Social movements as historically specific clusters of political performances', *Berkeley Journal of Sociology*, 38: 1–30.

——(1995*a*). 'Citizenship, identity and social history', in C. Tilly (ed.), *Citizenship, Identity and Social History*. Cambridge: Cambridge University Press.

——(1995*b*). 'Political identities.' CSSC Working Paper Series 212. New School for Social Research.

——(1995*c*). *Popular Contention in Great Britain, 1758–1834*. Cambridge, Mass.: Harvard University Press.

——(1995*d*). 'To explain political processes', *American Journal of Sociology*, 100: 1594–610.

——(1997). 'Parliamentarization of popular contention in Great Britain, 1758–1834', *Theory and Society*, 26: 245–73.

Tilly, C. (1998). 'Contentious conversations', unpublished paper, Columbia University.

——(1998*a*). 'Political identities', in M. P. Hanagan, L. Page Moch, and W. te Brake (eds.), *Challenging Authority. The Historical Study of Contentious Politics*. Minneapolis: University of Minnesota Press.

——(1998*b*). 'Social movements and (all sorts of) other political interactions—local, national and international—including identities', *Theory and Society*, **27**: 453–80.

——(2001). 'Mechanisms in political processes', *Annual Review of Political Science*, **4**: 21–41.

——(2002). *Stories, Identities, and Political Change*. Lanham, MD: Rowman and Littlefield.

——and Schweitzer, R. A. (1982). 'How London and its conflicts changed shape, 1758–1834', *Historical Methods*, **15**: 67–77.

——Tilly, L., and Tilly, R. (1975). *The Rebellious Century, 1830–1930*. Cambridge, Mass.: Harvard University Press.

Tindall, D. (2000). 'Personal networks, identification, and movement participation over time', paper presented for the conference 'Social movement analysis: The network perspective.' Ross Priory, Loch Lomond, 22–4 June.

Touraine, A. (1981). *The Voice and the Eye*. Cambridge: Cambridge University Press.

Trigilia, C. (1986). *Grandi Partiti e Piccole Imprese. Comunisti e Democristiani nelle Regioni a Economia Diffusa*. Bologna: il Mulino.

Truman, D. (1953). *The Governmental Process*. New York: Knopf.

Turner, R. and Killian, L. (1957). *Collective Behavior*. Englewood Cliffs, N. J.: Prentice-Hall.

Udy, S. (1962). 'Administrative rationality, social setting and organizational development', *American Journal of Sociology*, **68**: 299–308.

Uzzi, B. (1996). 'The sources and consequences of embeddedness for the economic performance of organizations: The network effect', *American Sociological Review*, **61**: 674–98.

van der Aalst P. and Walgrave, S. (2001). 'Globo-protesters: Virtual or real?', paper presented at the Social Movements Stream, European Sociological Association Conference, 26 August–1 September, Helsinki.

van der Heijden, H.-A., Koopmans, R., and Giugni, M. (1992). 'The West European environmental movement', in L. Kriesberg (ed.), *Research in Social Movements, Conflict and Change, Supplement 2*. Greenwich, Conn.: JAI Press.

van Deth, J. (2000). 'Interesting but irrelevant: Social capital and the saliency of politics in Western Europe', *European Journal of Political Research*, **37**: 115–47.

Van Dyke, N. (1998). 'Hotbeds of activism: Locations of student protest', *Social Problems*, **45**: 205–20.

Van Mechelen, I., de Boek, P., and Rosenberg, S. (1999). 'Indclass: A three-way hierarchical classes model', *Pychometrica*, **64**: 9–24.

Vidich, A. and Lyman, S. (2000). 'Qualitative methods: Their history in sociology and anthropology', in N. Denzin and Y. Lincoln (eds.), *Handbook of Qualitative Research*. Thousand Oaks, CA: Sage Publications, Inc., 2nd edn.

Vlasto, A. P. (1970). *The Entry of the Slavs into Christendom*. Cambridge: Cambridge University Press.

Wałęsa, L. (1987). *A Way of Hope*. New York: Henry Holt and Co.

Walker, J. L. Jr. (1997). *Mobilizing Interest Groups in America: Patrons, Professions* and *Social Movements*. Ann Arbor: University of Michigan.

Walsh, E. J. and Warland, R. H. (1983). 'Social movement involvement in the wake of a nuclear accident: Activists and free riders in the TMI Area', *American Sociological Review*, **48**: 764–80.

Wasserman, S. and Faust, K. (1994). *Social Network Analysis*. Cambridge/New York: Cambridge University Press.

Weber, M. (1947). *The Theory of Social and Economic Organization*, trans. and ed. by T. Parsons. New York: Oxford University Press.

Wellman, B. (1988). 'Structural analysis: From method and metaphor to theory and substance', in B. Wellman and S. D. Berkowitz (eds.), *Social Structures: A Network Approach*. Cambridge: Cambridge University Press.

—— and Berkowitz, S. D. eds. (1988). *Social Structure: A Network Approach*. Cambridge: Cambridge University Press.

—— Haase, A., Witte, J., and Hampton, K. (2001). 'Does the Internet increase, decrease, or supplement social capital?', *American Behavioral Scientist*, **45**: 436–55.

White, H. (1988). 'Varieties in markets', in B. Wellman and S. D. Berkowitz (eds.), *Social Structures: A Network Approach*. Cambridge: Cambridge University Press.

—— (1992). *Identity and Control*. Princeton: Princeton University Press.

—— (1995). 'Network switchings and bayesian forks: Reconstructing the social and behavioral sciences', *Social Research*, **62**: 1035–63.

—— (2002). *Markets From Networks*. Princeton: Princeton University Press.

—— Boorman, S., and Breiger, R. (1976). 'Social structure from multiple networks: I. Blockmodels of roles and positions', *American Journal of Sociology*, **81**: 730–99.

White, M. (1992). *The Japanese Overseas: Can They Go Home Again?* Princeton, NJ: Princeton University Press.

Whittier, N. (1995). *Feminist Generations: The Persistence of the Radical Women's Movement*. Philadelphia: Temple University Press.

Wiley, J. A. and Martin, J. L. (1999). 'Algebraic representations of beliefs and attitudes: Partial order models for item responses', *Sociological Methodology*, **29**: 113–46.

Wille, R. (1996). 'Introduction to formal concept analysis', Technische Hochschule Dormstadt, Fachbereich Mathemetatik, Preprint-Nr. 1878.

Williams, B. A. and Matheny, A. R. (1995). *Democracy, Dialogue, and Environmental Disputes: The Contested Languages of Social Regulation*. New Haven: Yale University Press.

Williams, R. M. Jr. (1970). *American Society: A Sociological Interpretation*. New York: Alfred A. Knopf.

Wilson, J. (2000). 'Volunteering', *Annual Review of Sociology*, **26**: 215–40.

Yin, R. K. (1994). *Case Study Research: Design and Methods*. Thousand Oaks: Sage Publications.

Zablocki, B. (1980). *Alienation and Charisma*. New York: Free Press.

Zachary, W. W. (1977). 'An information flow model for fusion and fission in small groups', *Journal of Anthropological Research*, **13**: 452–73.

Zald, M. N. (1996). 'Culture, ideology, and strategic framing', in D. McAdam, J. D. McCarthy, and M. N. Zald (eds.), *Comparative Perspectives on Social Movements: Political Opportunities, Mobilizing Structures, and Cultural Framings*. Cambridge: Cambridge University Press.

—— (2000). 'Ideologically structured action: An enlarged agenda for social movement research', *Mobilization*, **5**: 1–16.

Zald, M. N. and McCarthy, J. D. (1980). 'Social movement industries: Competition and cooperation among movement organizations', in L. Kriesberg (ed.), *Research in Social Movements, Conflict, and Change*. Greenwich, CT: JAI Press.

————(1987). *Social Movements in An Organizational Society*, New Brunswick, Transaction.

Zerubavel, E. (1993). *The Fine Line: Making Distinctions in Everyday Life*. Chicago: University of Chicago Press.

Zhao, D. (1998). 'Ecologies of social movements: Student mobilization during the 1989 prodemocracy movement in Beijing', *American Journal of Sociology*, **103**: 1493–529.

——(2001). *Power of Tiananmen*. Chicago: University of Chicago Press.

Zofka, Z. (1986). 'Between Bauernbund and national socialism. The political reorientation of the peasants in the final phase of the Weimar Republic', in T. Childers (ed.), *The Formation of the Nazi Constituency*. London/Sydney: Croom Helm.

Index

influence (*Continued*)
    122, 151, 155, 175, 176–82, 185–9,
    191–5, 198–202, 209, 224, 238,
    257–60, 265, 270, 273–4, 276–9,
    287–8, 294, 305, 308–9, 317
information flows, 183–91
interest groups, 2, 3, 6, 53, 54, 107, 125, 304,
    305, 311
interorganizational exchanges, 3, 6, 14, 67–9,
    83, 102, 105, 110, 112, 121–4, 130,
    304, 314

leadership, 105–6, 272, 276
left-right cleavage, 119–20
left-wing organizations, 85–6, 97, 99, 101,
    114, 117
local government, 110, 113, 115, 220

meaning attribution, 5, 12, 305
mechanisms, 4, 18, 22–7, 174–6, 199–202,
    268–77, 286–96
media, 8, 10, 77–8, 85–6, 106, 110, 113, 115,
    177, 183–6
memberships, overlapping, 64–6, 262
meso-level approaches, 4, 284–5, 287
middle classes and movement participation,
    62–4
multilevel analysis, 312
multiple linkages, 69–70, 266–7, 313–4

neo-institutionalism, 4, 304
national politics, emergence of, 166–72
network patterns, 88–90, 96–9, 306–12
new social movements, 9, 31, 44–5, 124–5,
    196, 202,
new social social movements theory, 9, 305,
    316, 318–20

outcomes, 25, 200, 205, 210, 214, 218–20,
    222–5, 228–9, 239, 249–52, 258–60,
    285, 296–7, 311

Parliament (Britain), 148–70
participation, 3, 6–9, 12, 21–30, 33–6, 40–3,
    51, 300
party formation, 51–8
political institutions and public agencies,
    ties to, 106, 110, 113, 115,128–35
political opportunities, 15–16, 53, 119–20,
    210, 214, 218, 227, 305
political process theory, 15, 77, 82, 278, 282,
    289, 305, 317
positional analysis, 65–7, 70, 130, 133–7,
    139–40, 143, 145, 204–5

power, 6, 50, 77–9, 86, 90–4, 101, 106, 112,
    116, 153–5, 167–73, 181, 204–5, 210,
    213, 216, 222, 227, 235, 260, 276–8,
    282–3, 292, 306
protest events, 84–5, 92, 152–60
psychological approaches to collective action,
    281–84

qualitative approaches to social networks, 28,
    41, 214, 224

rational models of collective action, 11, 16,
    25, 94, 121–4, 205, 211, 238–41,
    243–4, 247, 255–6, 287, 314
reachability, 319
recruitment, 2, 4, 7–9, 16, 17, 22, 27,
    33–5, 38, 42–4, 53, 66, 131, 148, 179,
    186, 206, 235–7, 242–3, 248–9,
    252–61, 266–9, 273–6, 286–9, 291–2,
    296–8, 303
relations, types of, 7, 10, 17, 258, 264
resource mobilization theory, 52–3, 82, 108,
    204, 218, 238, 278, 304–5
right-wing movements, 50, 52, 69, 71, 72

simulation models, 174–99, 297
social capital, 3, 15, 118–19, 316
social movement organizations, 2–3, 6,
    10–11, 23–8, 30, 33–5, 41, 44,
    107–14, 116–23, 125–8, 179, 193,
    276, 285, 299, 304, 310, 316
social movements, definitions, 3–4, 301–6,
    318
social organization, network forms of, 4, 7,
    125–7, 175, 220, 225–6, 303–4
social relay, 193
socialization 23, 31–5, 41, 45
solidarity, 79, 80, 92–6, 98–102
social theory and social networks, 3, 233–56,
    265–8
spatial dimension and social networks, 58–62
structural equivalence, 127, 130, 132, 134,
    135, 139, 144–5
structure and agency, 2, 4, 23, 26, 204–10,
    265–8
subculture, 7, 9, 14, 15, 18, 126–7, 142, 223,
    226

time, social networks and, 42, 162–72,
    176–83, 315

women's movements, 309, 311
working class action, 11, 84, 91, 93, 95, 96,
    162, 271, 272